THE NEW CHOSEN PEOPLE:
IMMIGRANTS IN THE UNITED STATES

A Census Monograph Series

WITHDRAWN

THE NEW CHOSEN PEOPLE: IMMIGRANTS IN THE UNITED STATES

Guillermina Jasso

Mark R. Rosenzweig

for the
National Committee for Research
on the 1980 Census

RUSSELL SAGE FOUNDATION / NEW YORK

AKF 2192-2/3
M-817 M

The Russell Sage Foundation

The Russell Sage Foundation, one of the oldest of America's general purpose foundations, was established in 1907 by Mrs. Margaret Olivia Sage for "the improvement of social and living conditions in the United States." The Foundation seeks to fulfill the mandate by fostering the development and dissemination of knowledge about the political, social, and economic problems of America. It conducts research in the social sciences and public policy and publishes books and pamphlets that derive from the research.

The Board of Trustees is responsible for oversight and the general policies of the Foundation, while administrative direction of the program and staff is vested in the President, assisted by the officers and staff. The President bears final responsibility for the decision to publish a manuscript as a Russell Sage Foundation book. In reaching a judgment on the competence, accuracy, and objectivity of each study, the President is advised by the staff and selected expert readers. The conclusions and interpretations in Russell Sage Foundation publications are those of the authors and not of the Foundation, its Trustees, or its staff. Publication by the Foundation, therefore, does not imply endorsement of the contents of the study.

Library of Congress Cataloging-in-Publication Data

Jasso, Guillermina.
  The new chosen people: immigrants in the United States /
Guillermina Jasso and Mark R. Rosenzweig.
      p.   cm. — (The Population of the United States in the 1980s)
  Includes bibliographical references and index.
  ISBN 0-87154-404-0
  1. Immigrants—United   States.   2. United   States—Emigration   and   immigration.
3. United States—Emigration and immigration—Government policy. I. Rosenzweig, Mark
Richard, 1947–   II. Title. III. Series.
JV6455.5.J37   1990   90-38766
304.8′73—dc20

The paper used in this publication meets the minimum requirements of American National Standard for Information Sciences—Permanence of Paper for Printed Library Materials, ANSI Z39.48-1984.

Cover and text design: HUGUETTE FRANCO

10 9 8 7 6 5 4 3 2 1

The National Committee for Research on the 1980 Census

The committee is sponsored by the Social Science Research Council, the Russell Sage Foundation, and the Alfred P. Sloan Foundation, in collaboration with the U.S. Bureau of the Census. The opinions, findings, and conclusions or recommendations expressed in the monographs supported by the committee are those of the author(s) and do not necessarily reflect the views of the committee or its sponsors.

Foreword

The New Chosen People is one of an ambitious series of volumes aimed at converting the vast statistical yield of the 1980 census into authoritative analyses of major changes and trends in American life. This series, "The Population of the United States in the 1980s," represents an important episode in social science research and revives a long tradition of independent census analysis. First in 1930, and then again in 1950 and 1960, teams of social scientists worked with the U.S. Bureau of the Census to investigate significant social, economic, and demographic developments revealed by the decennial censuses. These census projects produced three landmark series of studies, providing a firm foundation and setting a high standard for our present undertaking.

There is, in fact, more than a theoretical continuity between those earlier census projects and the present one. Like those previous efforts, this new census project has benefited from close cooperation between the Census Bureau and a distinguished, interdisciplinary group of scholars. Like the 1950 and 1960 research projects, research on the 1980 census was initiated by the Social Science Research Council and the Russell Sage Foundation. In deciding once again to promote a coordinated program of census analysis, Russell Sage and the Council were mindful not only of the severe budgetary restrictions imposed on the Census Bureau's own publishing and dissemination activities in the 1980s, but also of the extraordinary changes that have occurred in so many dimensions of American life over the past two decades.

The studies constituting "The Population of the United States in the 1980s" were planned, commissioned, and monitored by the National Committee for Research on the 1980 Census, a special committee appointed by the Social Science Research Council and sponsored by the Council, the Russell Sage Foundation, and the Alfred P. Sloan Foundation, with the collaboration of the U.S. Bureau of the Census. This committee includes leading social scientists from a broad range of fields—demography, economics, education, geography, history, political science, sociology, and statistics. It has been the committee's task to select the main topics for research, obtain highly qualified specialists to carry out that research, and provide the structure necessary to facilitate coordination among researchers and with the Census Bureau.

The topics treated in this series span virtually all the major features of American society—ethnic groups (blacks, Hispanics, foreign-born); spatial dimensions (migration, neighborhoods, housing, regional and metropolitan growth and decline); and status groups (income levels, families and households, women). Authors were encouraged to draw not only on the 1980 census but also on previous censuses and on subsequent national data. Each individual research project was assigned a special advisory panel made up of one committee member, one member nominated by the Census Bureau, one nominated by the National Science Foundation, and one or two other experts. These advisory panels were responsible for project liaison and review and for recommendations to the National Committee regarding the readiness of each manuscript for publication. With the final approval of the chairman of the National Committee, each report was released to the Russell Sage Foundation for publication and distribution.

The debts of gratitude incurred by a project of such scope and organizational complexity are necessarily large and numerous. The committee must thank, first, its sponsors—the Social Science Research Council, the Russell Sage Foundation, and the Alfred P. Sloan Foundation. The long-range vision and day-to-day persistence of these organizations and individuals sustained this research program over many years. The active and willing cooperation of the Bureau of the Census was clearly invaluable at all stages of this project, and the extra commitment of time and effort made by Bureau economist James R. Wetzel must be singled out for special recognition. A special tribute is also due to David L. Sills of the Social Science Research Council, staff member of the committee, whose organizational, administrative, and diplomatic skills kept this complicated project running smoothly.

The committee also wishes to thank those organizations that contributed additional funding to the 1980 census report—the Ford Foundation and its deputy vice president, Louis Winnick, the National Science Foundation, the National Institute on Aging, and the National Institute of Child Health and Human Development. Their support of the research program in general and of several particular studies is gratefully acknowledged.

The ultimate goal of the National Committee and its sponsors has been to produce a definitive, accurate, and comprehensive picture of the U.S.

population in the 1980s, a picture that would be primarily descriptive but also enriched by a historical perspective and a sense of the challenges for the future inherent in the trends of today. We hope our readers will agree that the present volume takes a significant step toward achieving that goal.

CHARLES F. WESTOFF

Chairman and Executive Director
National Committee for Research
on the 1980 Census

For GSL and JJR, AP, AR, RB, and HR

Acknowledgments

The production of this book would not have been possible without the help of many people and institutions. The Social Science Research Council provided substantial financial support. Supplementary moneys were also provided by the Rockefeller Foundation and by the Bush Fellowship Program of the University of Minnesota. Frank D. Bean and the staff of the Population Research Center at the University of Texas kindly provided us with extracts from the 1980 Census Public Use Samples. Christine A. Davidson, Roger Kramer, Lisa S. Roney, Margaret Sullivan, and Robert Warren of the U.S. Immigration and Naturalization Service aided us in our analysis and interpretation of INS data. Eric M. Larson, U.S. General Accounting Office, and Seton Stapleton, U.S. Department of State, provided helpful information about visa backlog data. Emmanuel Skoufias, now at Pennsylvania State University, helped with the merging of INS immigration and naturalization records and in the management of the Census Public Use Sample tape extracts.

The accuracy and clarity of our book was improved significantly as a consequence of the close readings of selected chapters by Charles F. Westoff, Princeton University, John M. Goering, U.S. Department of Housing and Urban Development, and Linda W. Gordon, U.S. Department of Health and Human Services. The transformation of the original manuscript into a finished book was performed with efficiency and grace by Priscilla Lewis, Lisa Nachtigall, Charlotte Shelby, Dorrie Ackerman, and other members of the editorial staff of the Russell Sage Foundation. We are grateful to all of these readers of our manuscript in its various stages and to our colleagues at the University of Iowa, the University of Minnesota, the U.S. Immigration and Naturalization Service, and the U.S. Select Commission on Immigration and Refugee Policy for helpful discussions about the many substantive issues relevant to immigration to the United States.

Contents

List of Tables

List of Figures

List of Forms

INTRODUCTION

Overview: Who Are the Foreign-Born?

THE ABSORPTION of persons born outside the United States into full participation in U.S. society represents one of the enduring hallmarks of the United States as a country. Stories of immigrant success, for example, are used to illustrate the openness of opportunities in the United States that are derived from principles of political and economic freedom. But the foreign-born are also at times seen as competitors for scarce resources who may alter the cherished traditions and ways of life of native-born U.S. citizens—despite the relatively small proportion of foreign-born in the total U.S. population, never higher since 1900 than 14.7 percent (1910) and falling to as low as 4.7 percent in 1970 (see Figure I.1).

Because the criteria by which immigrants are admitted—are "chosen"—embody some of the fundamental values of a society and because of the dual view of immigrants as symbols of ideals and hopes and as threats to economic and social well-being, immigration policy provokes sharp debate, and, as we shall see, U.S. immigration laws have undergone many changes and reforms over the last century.

In this book our analysis of the foreign-born population of the United States—how it has changed over time and why—is based principally on U.S. Census data describing this population in the twentieth century sup-

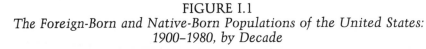

FIGURE I.1
The Foreign-Born and Native-Born Populations of the United States:
1900–1980, by Decade

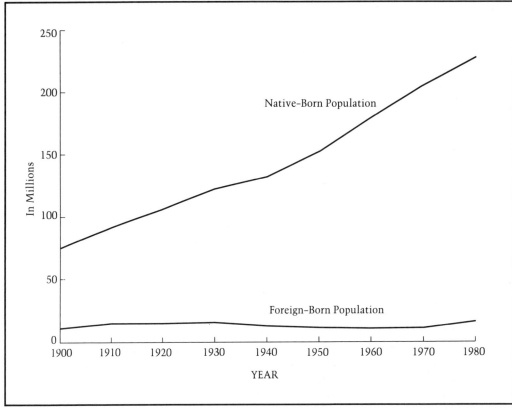

plemented with data from administrative records pertaining to legal immigrants. In contrast to the growth and composition of the U.S. native-born population, which depends on processes of births and deaths, on fertility and marital decisions, the foreign-born population is primarily shaped by the criteria for immigration defined by law and by choices made by persons outside the United States, by native-born persons, and by the resident U.S. foreign-born. Thus, an understanding of the behavior of the foreign-born population requires an examination of the process of migration into (and out of) the United States. This book is thus as much about immigrant behavior as it is about the foreign-born.

The U.S. foreign-born population consists of people who were "chosen" in a very different way than the native-born. The foreign-born are people who chose to come to the United States and who choose to remain, consistent with the constraints set by immigration laws, which themselves reflect the choices of the U.S. resident population. While parents choose (unilaterally) to have *a* child, with imperfect knowledge about its character- istics once born, and with no participation by that child in the decision, most immigrants are chosen, from the host country's perspective, on the basis of their known characteristics—their skills or, principally, their kin- ship relationship to U.S. residents—and immigrants choose whether or not to become permanent members of the U.S. population, given the opportu- nity to do so. To understand these chosen people, it is thus necessary to understand the determinants of this selection process, as well as who makes the choices.

This is a particularly appropriate time to examine closely the U.S. foreign-born population. As Figure I.2 shows, the foreign-born population in 1980—14.1 million—is the largest it has been since 1930, when, at 14.2 million, it was the largest it has ever been in U.S. history. As Figure I.3 shows, the share of the foreign-born population in the total U.S. population in 1980, at just over 6 percent, is the highest it has been since 1950, when it was nearly 7 percent; and, as Figure I.4 shows, the increase in the size of the foreign-born population between 1970 and 1980, by 4.46 million persons, is the largest decadal increase in the twentieth century—indeed, the largest increase since 1850. Moreover, the growth in the foreign-born population accounted for 19.1 percent of the total increase in the U.S. population as a whole between 1970 and 1980, the highest share since the 1900–1910 decade, when the proportion was 19.9 percent.

Figure I.4 also shows that the total number of immigrants who came to the United States between 1970 and 1980 was exceeded by the total num- ber of immigrants who came in both the 1901–1910 and 1911–1920 dec- ades. The discrepancy between the number of immigrants who arrive and the change in the size of the foreign-born population arises for two princi- pal reasons. First, not all immigrants remain in the United States; the change in the size of the foreign-born population is the net of immigration (inflows) and emigration (outflows). Figure I.4 suggests the possibility that emigration has been substantial: between 1930 and 1970 the foreign-born population actually declined while immigration never ceased. (We examine emigration trends intensively in Chapter 3.)

Second, the counts of immigrants in Figure I.3 are counts of a particu- lar type of migrant: those foreign-born who were legally admitted to perma- nent residence in the United States. The foreign-born population defined in the U.S. Census, from which population figures are derived, however, con- sists of all persons born abroad (except those born to American parents) regardless of their legal status; immigrants in the legal sense are a subset of the foreign-born. These legal distinctions are important because legal status circumscribes the choices that the foreign-born may make while resident in

FIGURE I.2
Total Foreign-Born Population in Census Years: 1900–1980

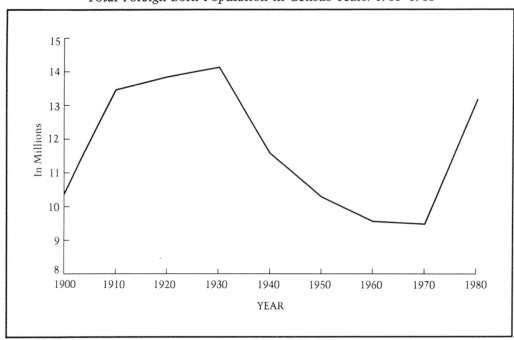

the United States. Indeed, immigration to the United States is a process shaped importantly by legal restrictions. It is thus necessary to be precise about terms.

Immigrants, Non-Immigrants, and Illegal Immigrants

Persons included in the U.S. foreign-born population and who are not U.S. citizens may be immigrants, non-immigrants, or "illegal" immigrants. The technical definition of an "immigrant," consistent with current U.S. law, is as follows:[1] an alien (i.e., a person who is not a citizen or national of the United States)[2] who is granted the privilege of residing *permanently* in

---

[1]The basic codification of U.S. laws on immigration and nationality is contained in Title 8, "Aliens and Nationality," of the U.S. Code of Federal Regulations. For a useful introduction to U.S. immigration and nationality law, see U.S. Congressional Research Service (1988).

[2]Under U.S. law, all citizens of the United States are nationals of the United States, but nationals are not necessarily citizens. Non-citizen nationals may include residents of the Outlying Territories of the United States; for example, at the dissolution of the Trust Territory of

FIGURE I.3
The Foreign-Born Population:
Percentage of U.S. Total Population, by Decade, 1900–1980

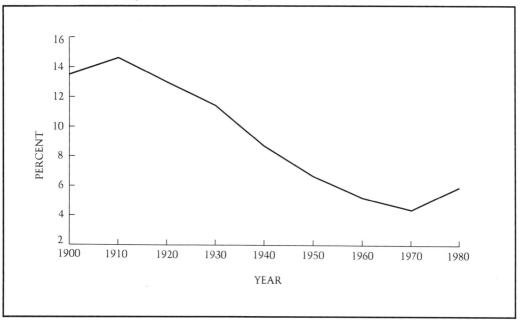

the United States. Such a person, also known as a "permanent resident alien," enjoys many of the rights of citizenship excepting, principally, the right to vote, to hold certain public offices, and to engage in certain occupations and activities reserved for citizens. Thus, not all persons who migrate to the United States are technically immigrants. Moreover, immigrant status can be conferred to persons already resident in the United States.

Among the members of the foreign-born population who are counted in the census but who are not immigrants are persons who reside in the United States as legal "non-immigrants," that is, aliens admitted to the United States for a temporary period and for a specific purpose. The non-immigrant visa categories vary greatly in the restrictions they impose on length of stay and on paid employment. The categories which permit employment, for example, place restrictions on the number of hours of work per week, on the duration of employment, and on the freedom to change employer or to change occupation. Thus, legal non-immigrants may include individuals who have visas permitting long-term employment with a

the Pacific, effective 3 November 1986, when the Northern Mariana Islands became a Commonwealth associated with the United States, U.S. citizenship was granted to its residents.

5

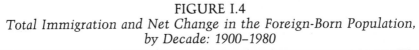

FIGURE I.4

*Total Immigration and Net Change in the Foreign-Born Population,
by Decade: 1900–1980*

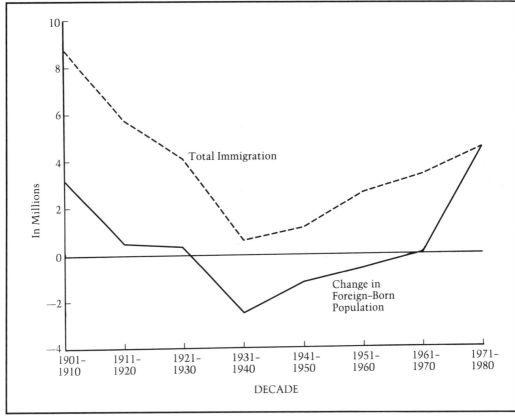

specific employer, such as an international organization (the International Monetary Fund, the World Bank) or a foreign firm; students, whose visas place restrictions on the amount and timing of paid employment; and tourists, whose stay in the United States is of limited duration and who may not work for pay.

Another group of foreign-born residents who are neither immigrants, naturalized citizens, nor legal non-immigrants are those who have no explicit legal status under immigration law. Such persons have been given many names—"illegal immigrants," "illegal aliens," "deportable aliens," or "undocumented aliens." Such individuals may have entered the United States illegally, without entitlements to do so, or may have, after entering legally as non-immigrants for a temporary visit, violated the terms of their entry visa—for example, by staying longer than allowed or by accepting unauthorized employment.

The existence of a subpopulation residing in the United States under conditions which render them deportable is a manifestation of the scarcity of immigrant visas. As noted above, the immigrant selection process has two components: (1) a *self-selection* component, covering the decision by foreign-born persons to seek immigration to the United States,[3] and (2) an *eligibility-conferring* component. The latter incorporates both decisions by the U.S. government to permit the immigration of some persons and not others and decisions by U.S. citizens and residents to participate in the eligibility-conferring process as sponsors of prospective immigrants. Each of these two components may be thought of as generating a population, the first of *aspiring immigrants* and the second of *persons eligible to become immigrants.* Chapter 1 will focus on these components, considering the determinants of the decision to seek immigration and the series of laws that express U.S. decisions concerning the admission of immigrants.

The two populations—of aspiring immigrants and of eligible immigrants—may differ in size and in characteristics, and it is the intersection of the two populations that in turn generates *eligible visa applicants*, individuals who both seek to immigrate to the United States and are eligible for a permanent-resident visa. A large number of eligible visa applicants have to wait many years to receive a visa, however, depending on the match between their characteristics and the rules of visa allocation. For example, while over 500,000 persons per year have been admitted to permanent residence in the United States from 1980 through 1988, as of January 1989 the number of eligible visa applicants waiting for a visa was over 2.3 million.

Thus, illegal aliens may include both aspiring immigrants who are not eligible for an immigrant visa and eligible visa applicants who are not willing to remain in the visa queue but who may eventually receive a visa, if their illegal status is not discovered in the interim. In contrast, legal non-immigrants may include both persons in the visa queue and eligible persons not in the queue, since many non-immigrants have no wish to become U.S. immigrants.

In order to fully understand the immigration process and the behavior of the U.S. foreign-born, information on each of the populations involved would be useful. Available data, however, provide information principally on two populations—legal immigrants and the U.S. resident foreign-born. Little is known about either the size or characteristics of the non-resident, foreign-born populations of persons either wanting to immigrate or eligible

---

[3]The self-selection component is often discussed under the rubric of "demand for immigration."

to immigrate. The response to recent legislation providing U.S. visas on a first-come–first-served or on a lottery basis suggests that the number of noneligible visa aspirants may be quite large. In January 1987 1.4 million applications were received for 10,000 new visas made available in Fiscal Years (FYs) 1987 and 1988 to citizens of 36 countries as part of the 1986 Immigration Reform and Control Act.[4] And in March 1989 over 3 million persons entered a lottery established by Congress, for 20,000 visas to be allocated in FYs 1990 and 1991 to citizens of 162 countries.

Census population counts of foreign-born U.S. residents, while recording country of birth and acquisition of U.S. citizenship through naturalization, do not distinguish among the non-naturalized by their legal status. Yet in 1980 over one half of the U.S. foreign-born were not U.S. citizens; and because legal status restricts behavior, principally in the labor market, the absence of such information makes it difficult to fully understand the behavior of the foreign-born and the consequences of changes in U.S. immigration laws. In Chapter 7, we explore the consequences of legal status for economic mobility based on administrative records of the Immigration and Naturalization Service (INS) describing legal immigrants. For the most part, however, we will not be able to distinguish among the foreign-born by legal status with respect to a wide variety of topics, as our principal data source, the U.S. Census of Population, does not provide visa information.

How large are the various foreign-born subpopulations in the United States? Accurate information is available on the number of persons who acquire an immigrant visa in a given year. And for a limited time, from 1950 to 1980, all permanent resident aliens were required by law to report their addresses to the INS each year, data we exploit in Chapter 3 to estimate the emigration of immigrants. With respect to (legal) non-immigrants, it is difficult to know how many persons become non-immigrants in a given year because data systems record events (i.e., entries into the United States), not persons. Non-immigrant admissions, excluding temporary visitors for business and pleasure and aliens in transit, have been averaging close to 1 million per year in recent years (1984–1988). This overstates the number of new legal non-immigrants because of multiple entries. Because non-immigrant departures are incompletely recorded there is thus little information on the population of legal non-immigrants.

The question of the size of the illegal-migrant population has received considerable attention. As is widely recognized, however, the very nature of a clandestine existence precludes enumeration of or proper random sampling from this population. In the absence of direct data, researchers have proposed and implemented a number of indirect-estimation methods, using

---

[4]It is widely believed that the number of applications exceeded the number of applicants because individuals submitted multiple applications.

a wide variety of sources, including census and Current Population Survey (CPS) data, legal-immigration data, foreign-country emigration surveys, vital statistics, and data on apprehended illegal aliens. In the past decade, there have been two major assessments of research on illegal aliens. Siegel, Passel, and Robinson (1980), in a comprehensive research review prepared for the U.S. Select Commission on Immigration and Refugee Policy, concluded that the number of illegal aliens residing in the United States in any given year in the late 1970s was in the range of 3.5 million to 6 million.[5] Hill (1985b), in an assessment prepared for the National Academy of Sciences Panel on Immigration Statistics, concluded that the range in 1980 was probably 1.5 million to 3.5 million illegal aliens (11 to 25 percent of the total foreign-born population) and that there is no evidence of an increase in the size of the illegal alien population in the late 1970s and early 1980s.[6] More recently, Woodrow, Passel, and Warren (1987), using data from the CPS, estimated that the size of the undocumented population was 3,158,000 as of June 1986; the estimated Mexican component was 2,196,000.[7] Passel and Woodrow (1987) estimated that the average net annual increment to the illegal population was, in the years 1979–1983, in the range of 100,000 to 300,000; of course, the average gross annual increment would be greater.

Recent legislation makes it possible to assess these estimates of the size of the illegal-alien population and suggests that they may overestimate the magnitude of the illegal population or, at least, the *permanence* of such a population. The Immigration Reform and Control Act of 1986 (IRCA) enabled (1) the legalization of illegal immigrants who had lived in the Unit-

---

[5]Siegel et al. (1980, p. 19) write: "The total number of illegal residents in the United States for some recent year, such as 1978, is almost certainly below 6.0 million, and may be substantially less, possibly only 3.5 to 5.0 million. The existing estimates of illegal residents based on empirical studies simply do not support the claim that there are very many millions (i.e., over 6 million) of unlawful residents in the United States. . . . The available evidence indicates that the size of the Mexican population living illegally in the United States is smaller than popular estimates suggest. The Mexican component of the illegally resident population is almost certainly less than 3.0 million, and may be substantially less, possibly only 1.5 to 2.5 million." The studies reviewed included Lancaster and Scheuren (1978), Heer (1979), early reports of the Mexican-government CENIET survey, and the authors' own unpublished work.

[6]Hill (1985b, p. 243) writes: "[E]ven the commonly quoted range of 3–6 million illegals may be too high. . . . Though no range can be soundly defended, a population of 1.5 to 3.5 million illegal aliens in 1980 appears reasonably consistent with most of the studies. . . . There is no empirical basis at present for the widespread belief that the illegal alien population has increased sharply in the late 1970's and early 1980's." The studies reviewed included, in addition to those reviewed by Siegel et al. (1980), the more recent work of Garcia y Griego (1980) and of Bean, King, and Passel (1983), as well as work subsequently published by Warren and Passel (1987).

[7]See also Passel and Woodrow (1987) and Woodrow (1988). Note that the estimated Mexican component incorporates an increment of 610,000, as part of an adjustment for misreporting of nativity. This adjustment is discussed in the appendix to this chapter.

ed States since 1972[8] and (2) the conditional legalization of two groups, those who had lived in the United States since 1982 and certain aliens who had performed agricultural work in the United States. During FYs 1987 and 1988, a total of only 48,059 persons became permanent resident aliens under the 1972 registry provision. This is a small proportion of the entry-year-specific estimates that had been produced. For example, Passel and Woodrow (1987, p. 1316) estimated that the size of the illegal-alien population aged 14 and over who had entered between 1960 and 1969 (and including Mexicans who entered before 1960) was 522,000 as of the 1980 census and 419,000 as of the June 1983 CPS; Woodrow (1988) estimated the number of illegal aliens who had entered before 1970 (and including Mexicans who entered before 1960) at 265,000 as of the June 1986 CPS. Of course, many resident illegal aliens eligible for legalization may have chosen not to take advantage of the program. If the Woodrow estimate is accurate, however, the program participation rate would have to have been less than one-fifth.

Passel and Woodrow (1987, pp. 1321–22) also have concluded that "the undocumented population resident as of January 1, 1982, is likely to have been in the range of 2.5 to 4 million" but that, by the time of the legalization program, the eligible number would be smaller since "many . . . would undoubtedly have died, emigrated, or otherwise be ineligible to legalize their status." As of May 1989, the actual number of applications received from persons claiming to be residing illegally in the United States since 1982 was 1,768,089, and from the agricultural-worker group 1,301,804. To the extent that death is unlikely to be a major factor reducing the size of the illegal population (e.g., if illegal aliens are relatively young, as widely believed), the overestimates of the size of this population are due to errors in the estimates of the initial population, very high rates of return migration in the illegal alien population, or great reluctance among the eligible population to participate in the program. We discuss the characteristics of illegal aliens in the context of the economy in Chapter 7.

Persons from abroad but resident in the United States differ from each other and from the native-born not only in their legal status but also with respect to the country they arrive from or were born in and the number of years they have been in the United States. Moreover, the foreign-born residing in the United States in 1980 who entered the United States in different years also faced very different immigration rules, as there have been three major pieces of legislation substantially altering immigration laws between 1950 and 1980. Thus, many of the foreign-born were "chosen" in distinct-

---

[8]The United States, through Section 249 of the Immigration and Nationality Act, permits admission to permanent resident alien status for illegal aliens who have lived in the United States for a long period of time; IRCA changed the requisite date of inception of U.S. residence from 30 June 1948 to 1 January 1972.

ly different ways. Such heterogeneity in the rules of entry must be taken into account in studying the foreign-born population. Fortunately, information on year at entry and country of birth are provided in the census data.

The Organization of this Volume

The focus of this study is on the foreign-born population resident in the United States in the last two decades, 1960–1980. It is useful, however, to compare this group with the foreign-born population in 1900 and 1910, when immigration was at its highest levels in this century, and with the native-born population in both time periods. We thus also examine these groups. We focus on topics of particular pertinence to the foreign-born population, such as their emigration, naturalization, language, and the role of immigration laws in determining the number and type of immigrants. In addition, we compare the characteristics and behaviors of the foreign-born, such as their earnings, participation in the labor market, schooling, and fertility, with those of the native-born. Because the foreign-born represent the survivors of a complex migration choice process, involving the changing selection criteria embodied in U.S. immigration laws and the choices of individuals residing both in the United States and abroad, we emphasize the important role of immigration "selectivity" in shaping the characteristics and behavior of the foreign-born population.

There are two topics related to immigration on which we will focus less attention. We will not engage in comprehensive comparisons among groups of the foreign-born defined by their origin country. Readers interested in knowing how Poles in Chicago compare with Peruvians in Los Angeles or the number of South Koreans residing in New York City in 1960 compared with 1980 will not find such information here. We will, however, attempt to explain salient differences across groups of persons coming from different countries as they relate to the important determinants of immigration. For example, we will examine why female immigrants from West Germany since World War II have substantially outnumbered male immigrants from that country (for example, in FY 1988, 75 percent of the West German immigrants aged 20 and over were women), why naturalization rates have been substantially higher among immigrants from the Eastern Hemisphere than among those from the Western Hemisphere and why this discrepancy will probably decrease in the future, why Spanish-speaking immigrants tend to locate in southwestern states, and why immigrants from high-income countries located far from the United States have higher earnings than do other immigrants.

We will also not make a quantitative assessment of the economic impact of immigration—the consequences of the immigration of the foreign-born for the earnings, employment (or unemployment), and welfare of the native-born. We will, however discuss some of the channels by which immigration influences the economic status of various groups and examine the location and roles of the foreign-born in the economy, their economic progress relative to the native-born, and their aggregate impact on the U.S. welfare system. A complete evaluation of the economic consequences of immigration is beyond the scope of this book for two reasons. First, the foreign-born population is only a small proportion of the total work force (6.7 percent in 1980). Isolating the effects of immigration from the effects of other factors that influence employment and earnings would be difficult without fully analyzing these other factors (e.g., the increased labor force participation of women, foreign trade, unionization, foreign investment). Moreover, any significant impact of immigrants, legal or nonlegal, on the labor market is concentrated in few areas and sectors, as we show in Chapter 7. Census data do not provide the kind of detail required to study these localized effects. And a rigorous analysis of the economic effects of undocumented aliens using census data would be difficult indeed, although we are able to make some inferences about the characteristics of one component of the illegal population. Second, and perhaps most important, a complete and credible evaluation of the full economic effects of immigration requires, at the very least, the development of a framework for understanding all of the forces shaping wages and employment, of which immigration plays only one part—a task clearly beyond the scope of this book. Moreover, it must be stressed that the economic effects of immigration are not confined to their impact on employment and wages: immigrants influence the prices and availability of items consumed and affect the returns to capital investments, both human and financial.[9] In Chapter 7 we discuss some of the difficulties of identifying the labor market impact of immigrants.

We organize our study as follows. We follow this thematic introduction with a brief discussion of our data sources and their limitations. We begin in Chapter 1 with a consideration of the selection of immigrants from the point of view of U.S. policy. We provide a brief review of changes in immigration laws and a description of the basic immigration "rules" in operation since 1965. We also set out the basic behavioral framework describing the choices of migrants and potential migrants that we use to guide our analysis in subsequent chapters, and we examine changes in the educational attainment of the foreign-born population between 1960 and 1980 as

---

[9]The difficulties of studying the economic impact of immigrants have not deterred social scientists from addressing this topic. The Department of Labor (1989) released a major summary of the findings on the impact of immigration on earnings and employment based on over 200 studies. This report, discussed in more detail in Chapter 7, does not attempt to discuss the effects of immigration on prices or rates of return to capital.

manifestations of the selectivity associated with the interactions between immigration law and the decisions of the foreign-born.

Chapter 2 is concerned with the process by which immigrants become U.S. citizens. We examine in particular how changes in immigration laws and origin-country conditions influence the propensities of immigrants to naturalize and whether such laws can account for the marked differences across country-of-origin groups in naturalization rates. Chapter 3 describes the emigration of the U.S. foreign-born from the United States and its determinants: how emigration has changed over time, differs across country-of-origin groups, and affects the changes in the observed characteristics of an immigrant entry cohort over time. Naturalization and emigration are the polar extremes of immigration, one signifying the ultimate absorption of immigrants into the body of U.S. citizens and the other the choice of immigrants not to "take root." Chapters 4 through 6 focus on the implications of the "family" provisions of U.S. immigration law. In Chapter 4 we look at "marital migration": the receipt of an immigrant visa through marriage to a U.S. citizen, currently the class of admission accounting for the largest number of immigrant visas, and the marital behavior of the foreign-born. Marriage is examined both in terms of its role in assimilation, through intermarriage, and as a route to U.S. immigration. Implications of changes in U.S. immigration laws for the sex-ratio of immigrants, for divorce rates among the foreign-born, and for the number of "mixed" marriages involving U.S. citizens and the foreign-born are also discussed. Chapter 5 considers the part of immigration that involves the reunification of family members—parents, children, and siblings—and the implications of the family reunification provisions of immigration law for the composition of households in the foreign-born population. Chapter 6 investigates how the family provisions of immigration law, which theoretically could lead to an explosive growth in the number of foreign-born persons *entitled* to a U.S. visa, actually influence the size and composition of the flow of immigrants and examines the characteristics of the U.S. citizen sponsors of immigrant spouses and parents.

In Chapter 7 we consider the roles of the foreign-born (legal and illegal) in the U.S. economy and the impact of immigration on the well-being of the native-born as workers, consumers, and investors. We examine in particular the question of whether the earnings of a typical immigrant catch up to or overtake those of a native-born citizen as length of residence in the United States increases. We also examine and compare income inequality, participation in welfare programs, propensities to own homes, be self-employed, and participate in the labor market across the native- and foreign-born populations, across different immigrant entry cohorts, and across time periods for particular entry cohorts. This chapter also considers how differences in legal status influence earnings growth and whether the differences in the characteristics of the countries of origin of the foreign-born can explain the observed differences in their earnings in the United States.

Chapter 8 examines the English-language ability and locational choices of the foreign-born. Comparisons are made between the German-speaking foreign-born in 1900 and the Spanish-speaking foreign-born in 1980, the largest common foreign-language groups in their respective time periods. The economic returns to English-language ability in both groups are assessed, as is the influence of country characteristics and time in the United States on the propensity to learn English. We also consider how parents' inability to speak English affects their children's English-language ability and whether this relationship has changed significantly since the beginning of the twentieth century.

In Chapter 9 we look at the two major refugee groups among the foreign-born who have entered the United States since 1960—Cubans and the Indochinese—persons chosen under very different criteria than those used for other groups. We consider their choice of location and their occupational and skill distributions and, within each group, examine whether there are discernible differences across entry cohorts.

In Chapter 10 we look at how the foreign-born invest in their children. We consider both the fertility and schooling investment behavior of the foreign-born compared with the native-born and how origin-country conditions are reflected in their choices. The average educational and earnings levels of the foreign-born, of native-born first-generation adult children of the foreign-born, and of the native-born with native-born parents are also compared, in 1900, 1910, 1960, and 1970. In the final chapter of the book, we briefly assess U.S. immigration policies, in particular the 1965–1980 immigration reforms, in the light of our findings and trends in immigration from 1978 to 1988.

Data Sources

The data base for studying the U.S. foreign-born population has a number of widely recognized deficiencies. Indeed, the National Academy of Sciences study (Levine et al. 1985) of immigration statistics gave its report the subtitle, *A Story of Neglect.* For example, no information on emigration has been collected since 1957; and the annual registration of aliens, which produced estimates of the number and location of currently resident non-naturalized immigrants, was discontinued after 1980. Most important, there has never been a data set of sufficient size to permit distinctions across groups—defined by year of entry, age, or country of origin—that follows *individual* immigrants over time. Thus, it is very difficult to obtain information on how a typical immigrant fares in the United States after he or she arrives or whether the process of immigrant "assimilation" has changed historically. Stories of individual immigrant successes or failures must rely on individual case histories, which, however colorful, may or may not be representative or typical of the foreign-born.

The data situation is not hopeless. The availability of U.S. Census Public Use Samples for adjacent census years—1900, 1910, and 1960, 1970, 1980—containing machine-readable information on the individuals in probability (representative) samples of all U.S. residents inclusive of the U.S. foreign-born categorized by date of entry allows us to come close to having a true longitudinal data set, with some important differences, as we describe below. Moreover, we have assembled a new data set, based on a probability sample of the administrative records from the INS, with information on those foreign-born who became immigrants (permanent resident aliens) in 1971 matched with their individual naturalization records in all of the years after their "entry" up to 1981. Thus, we can look at a subset of these immigrants—those who naturalized—at two points in time: at immigration and at naturalization.

As described below and elaborated in subsequent chapters, both of these microdata sources have serious shortcomings. Accordingly, it is often difficult to obtain a clear answer to many of the important questions concerning immigration. Often the findings are highly dependent on the assumptions under which they are obtained, some of them rather heroic. Knowledge about U.S. immigration is substantially constrained by data problems, and thus it is important to discuss the characteristics of the available data sets before proceeding to use them to investigate some of the issues concerning the U.S. foreign-born.

U.S. Decennial Censuses

Table I.1 summarizes the migration-related information collected in each of the censuses whose microdata samples we shall examine. Two important features of these data sets are (1) their ample size, facilitating examination of population groups whose size is relatively small; and (2) the information they provide on date of entry for the foreign-born, either location of residence five years prior to the census date (1960), time-period of entry (1970, 1980), or exact year of immigration (1900, 1910). Such information makes it possible to compare "recent entrants"—those foreign-born persons who came to the United States less than five years prior to the census survey—across two adjacent census years at the beginning of the century and across the three most recent adjacent censuses and to observe the *change* in the characteristics of three cohorts of recent entrants across a ten-year period.

TABLE I.1

Migration-Relevant Information on Foreign-Born Persons,
Recorded in Public Use Samples of the U.S. Decennial Censuses of Population: 1900, 1910, 1960–1980

Datum/Census	1900	1910	1960 (2.5%)	1970 (5%)	1970 (15%)	1980
Country of Birth	Yes	Yes	Yes	Yes	Yes	Yes
Father's and Mother's Country of Birth	Yes	Yes	Father only, if both FB[a]	No	Father only, if both FB[a]	No
Year of Entry	Yes	Yes	No	Yes[b]	No	Yes[b]
Resided Abroad Five Years Ago	No	No	Yes	No	Yes	Yes
Naturalization	Men only	Men only	No	Yes	No	Yes
Literacy	Yes	Yes	No	No	No	No
Mother Tongue	No	Yes	Yes	No	Yes	No
Ability to Speak English	Yes (binary)	Yes (binary)	No	No	No	Yes[c] (ordinal)
Other Language Currently Used at Home	No	Yes, if English not spoken	No	No	No	Yes

[a]FB denotes foreign-born.
[b]Year of entry was coded in categories as follows:
1970: 1965–1970; five-year categories, 1945–1964; ten-year categories, 1915–1944; open-ended category, before 1915.
1980: 1975–1980; five-year categories, 1960–1974; ten-year category, 1950–1959; open-ended category, before 1950.
[c]This question is asked only if the person speaks a language other than English at home.

With data from adjacent censuses, we can compare how new entrants, selected under different immigration rules, differ initially and how they fare in their immigrant "careers." The three recent-entrant cohorts that can be observed across a ten-year period are (1) those foreign-born persons who in both 1900 and 1910 report year of immigration between 1895 and 1900, (2) those foreign-born persons who in 1960 report having lived abroad five years earlier and who in 1970 report year of entry between 1955 and 1959, and (3) those foreign-born persons who in 1970 report year of entry between 1965 and 1970 and who in 1980 report year of entry between 1965 and 1969. All three of these recent-entrant cohorts are observed at the same durations, at on average 2.5 and 12.5 years after entry. Note that these three recent-entrant cohorts ("vintage" 1895–1900, 1955–1959, and 1965–1969) provide the only opportunity to observe and contrast the behavior, across a ten-year period, of equal-duration cohorts of new immigrants *who entered in different historical periods.*[10]

Unfortunately, the inferences about the migration process that can be drawn from census data are severely limited because of three serious shortcomings: (1) the lack of information on characteristics particularly relevant to the study of migration in the post-1921 restriction era, (2) the cross-sectional nature of the census data, and (3) the lack of firm knowledge concerning the rate and stability of coverage.

The decennial censuses do not contain information on the precise legal status (viz., legal immigrant, legal non-immigrant, illegal alien) of the foreign-born. In the years before quantitative restrictions were imposed, it could safely be assumed that anyone admitted to the United States could remain in the United States permanently; distinctions based on alienage applied uniformly to all of the non-naturalized; the residency requirement for naturalization was reckoned from the date of admission. Moreover, in those days there were fewer visitors and tourists than there are today. Accordingly, the census questions obtained sufficient information to study migration behavior (subject, as will be seen, to problems of coverage and of the cross-sectional character of the data).

In the era of quantitative immigration restrictions and massive travel, the foreign-born in the United States are no longer homogeneous with respect to legal status. Absent information on legal status, it is impossible to distinguish among immigrants (legal permanent resident aliens and those among them who have become naturalized citizens) and "visitors" of a

---

[10]As well, the 1955–1959 and 1965–1969 recent-entrant cohorts provide the sole opportunity to compare, across a ten-year period, equal-duration cohorts of persons who entered in different *post–World War II* historical periods. The other two cohorts which can be observed in the 1970 and 1980 censuses—the 1950–1959 and the 1960–1964 entry cohorts—have equal-duration counterparts which can be observed in the 1900 and 1910 censuses—the 1880–1889 and 1890–1994 entry cohorts, respectively.

wide variety, including non-immigrants and illegal or deportable aliens, as we have noted.

Census data have several shortcomings that hamper the inferences that may be drawn. Because of the lack of information on legal status, it is not possible to use census data to measure the probabilities that immigrants will become U.S. citizens. For example, if the same proportion of immigrants from each of two countries naturalize, but the countries differ greatly in the number of their nationals who are non-immigrants in the United States, then their naturalization rates, if calculated from census data, will erroneously appear to differ greatly.

Legal status may also be related to the behaviors commonly assumed to indicate assimilation and adjustment. For example, direct participation in the U.S. labor market—what is usually meant by experience in the United States—is differentially accessible to the foreign-born. While permanent resident aliens may move about freely, maneuver for job-skills acquisition and for employment, those non-immigrants who have work authorization may be tied to one employer as a condition of their visa. If labor mobility is an important component of earnings growth, then to the extent that there is an unmeasured change in the proportion of the foreign-born who are (legal) immigrants among those foreign-born who entered in the same year, inferences about the earnings returns to the "experience" of immigrants may be seriously biased. (Inaccuracies with respect to information on nativity and year of immigration in census data also result from the absence of questions on legal status. These are discussed in the appendix to this introduction.)

A second principal shortcoming of census data is that they provide a picture of a mobile population at one point in time; they are "cross-sectional." Their limitations in social science research are well known: studies based on cross-sectional data cannot reveal the patterns of dynamic processes and cannot disentangle age, period, and cohort effects. Thus, when one cross-sectional data set is used to study immigrant behavior, it is impossible to distinguish between the effects of experience in the United States and the effects of factors associated with the immigrant's "vintage"—that is, with conditions in both the origin country and the United States at the time of entry (including the rules for the selection of immigrants in effect at the time of admission to permanent resident status). For example, in studies of the earnings of immigrants based on cross-sectional data, it is impossible to distinguish between two potential facts: (1) that immigrants improve their earnings as their time in the United States increases and (2) that each successive entry cohort of immigrants has possessed lower earnings potential (possibly as a consequence of the law for the selection of immigrants).

Cross-sectional data have an additional weakness when used to study migration processes. The respondents enumerated in the decennial censuses represent the *survivors* of entry cohorts, cohorts which may be selectively and differentially trimmed by *emigration* decisions. For example, if immigrants who subsequently emigrate from the United States are nonrandomly self-selected and if the selection mechanisms operate differentially across entry cohort and/or country of origin—if, to illustrate, the low achievers from the 1955 entry cohort leave while the high achievers from the 1965 entry cohort leave—then the true assimilation effect of an immigrant who remains in the United States cannot be identified.

Emigration also affects inferences about immigrant assimilation based on the tracking of the progress of an aggregate cohort across successive cross-sectional censuses. Because of *selective* emigration, the life-course mobility of any individual will be confounded with shifts over time in the mixture of different subsets of the foreign-born in the individual's entry cohort. For example, if the high earners in a cohort emigrate, it may appear that the cohort has made no progress when in fact the survivors (initially low earners) have substantially increased their earnings.

The validity of inferences concerning changes over time both within and between cohorts of foreign-born persons also hinges on the degree to which there have been changes in the coverage of these populations by the census. Experts believe that the 1960 census had a net undercount of 2.7 percent and the 1970 census a net undercount of approximately 2.2 percent.[11] Although a wide range of estimates of the coverage in the 1980 census have been published (see, e.g., Citro and Cohen 1985), there does not yet appear to be a consensus. Currently preferred estimates are in the range of 0.5 to 1.4 percent (Citro and Cohen 1985, pp. 148, 177), suggesting substantial improvement in net coverage.

Unfortunately, net coverage may not be the most appropriate measure of coverage, as it is possible that the two components of coverage error—omissions and erroneous inclusions—may change differentially.[12] Moreover, relative coverage may differ by nativity and/or legal status.[13] At this time, it would be prudent to interpret cautiously results based on compari-

---

[11]These estimates of net undercount for the 1960 and 1970 censuses were obtained by Siegel (1974) and Passel et al. (1982), respectively, and are currently regarded as the preferred estimates (Bailar 1985; Citro and Cohen 1985).

[12]For example, it is possible that the 1980 census had a net undercount of zero because of omissions and erroneous inclusions exactly offsetting each other (see Bailar 1985).

[13]Work undertaken by Passel, Cowan, and Wolter (1983) and Passel and Robinson (1984) suggests undercoverage of 1 percent in the 1980 census for all legal residents (regardless of nativity). Warren and Passel (1987) estimate that approximately 2 million deportable aliens were counted in the 1980 census. Although coverage cannot be estimated without an independent count, Warren and Passel (1987, p. 391) argue that the set of available information (e.g., agreement of school enrollment figures and census data on children; the fact that very few housing units were missed) suggests that "coverage of undocumented aliens must have been relatively high."

sons made *across* decennial censuses, noting the possible operation of coverage change as well as true behavioral change.

INS Administrative Records: The 1971 Immigrant Cohort

Precise information on persons granted permanent resident alien status and on those among them who subsequently naturalize is collected by the INS. Selected cross-tabulations are published in their *Annual Report* and *Statistical Yearbook*.[14]

In addition to this published information, we make use of a 1-in-100 microdata sample from the cohort of persons admitted to permanent resident alien status during FY 1971 (the period between 1 July 1970 and 30 June 1971), matched to the naturalization records from July 1971 to February 1981 (both dates inclusive). The FY 1971 immigrant cohort numbered 370,478; the random sample numbered 3,758.[15] This data set thus includes information from the INS new-immigrant record (G-188) for all persons in the sample and information from the INS naturalization record (G-173) for that subset who had naturalized by the end of February 1981.[16]

The principal advantage of the INS 1971 cohort sample is that it provides information enabling the assessment of the assimilation of one important group of the foreign-born: legal immigrants. Moreover, as a consequence of knowing legal status, the *duration* in that legal status is precisely known. It is thus possible to study the determinants of naturalization rates, since normally eligibility to naturalize depends on both legal status and length of residence. It is also possible—though, as will be seen below, with less ease—to study the effects of duration in the United States on employment status and occupation.

The information obtained from the new-immigrant record and the naturalization record includes (1) personal characteristics, including age, sex, marital status, state of residence (or intended residence for persons entering to become permanent residents), occupation; (2) origin-country information, including country of birth, country of last permanent residence, country of chargeability (for numerically limited visas), country of former nationality (for those who naturalize); and (3) statutory classifications, including the provision of law under which the person became an immigrant, the provision of law under which the person was admitted for

---

[14]The *Annual Report* published data for many of the series of interest from 1943 through 1977 and the *Statistical Yearbook* has published data since 1978. Both have included several historical time series. Additional historical time series are collected in U.S. Bureau of the Census (1975).

[15]The random sample was obtained by applying a sampling factor of .01.

[16]We shall also analyze longitudinal information on the 1975 and 1978 entry cohorts of Indochinese refugees. Discussion of those data is postponed to Chapter 9.

non-immigrant temporary residence prior to immigration (if the person was adjusting from non-immigrant to immigrant while in the United States), and the category of law under which the person became naturalized, as well as all the relevant dates—of admission to permanent residence, of admission to the prior non-immigrant residence (if an adjustment of status), and of naturalization.

The INS cohort data thus provide considerable detail on the circumstances of a given person's becoming an immigrant and acquiring U.S. citizenship. It is possible to distinguish important features of a foreign-born person's migration-relevant biography. Examples of such biographies are (1) a person who entered the United States as a non-immigrant with a foreign-student visa in 1968, who married a U.S. citizen, becoming an immigrant as the spouse of a U.S. citizen in 1971, and who naturalized in 1978, reporting marital status as divorced; (2) a person from Cuba who was paroled into the United States in 1968, who became a permanent resident in 1971, and who naturalized in 1976.

The INS cohort sample data have two important shortcomings. First, important information relevant to the assimilation process is missing: information on earnings, education, family and household structure, and language.[17] In addition, information on occupation obtained from the new immigrant file is problematic, at least for persons who are (1) entering to become permanent residents (as opposed to persons adjusting status in the United States) and (2) entering without labor certification. These problems are addressed in Chapter 7. Second, although the data provide longitudinal information on naturalization for the entire cohort sample, they provide information at two points in time concerning other characteristics only for the subset who naturalize. Thus, information on occupation, marital status, and state of residence is longitudinal only for a self-selected portion of the sample.

Data Describing Countries of Origin

A central theme of our analysis of the foreign-born is that changes in the world external to the United States—for example, in transportation costs, in relative economic growth rates, or in the geographical location of political regimes—will influence the size and composition of the U.S. foreign-born population. Accordingly, we supplement both the census and INS data with information on the social, economic, political, and informa-

---

[17]Moreover, these data refer to individuals and do not permit reconstruction of families. For example, in the existing new-immigrant files it is impossible to link the record of a person admitted as the spouse of a third-preference immigrant with the record of the corresponding third-preference principal.

tional environment in the individual's country of origin. This information permits an assessment of the effects of origin-country characteristics on decisions to immigrate and decisions by immigrants to remain in the United States. These data, listed in Table I.2, include (1) socioeconomic characteristics, including Gross National Product (GNP) per capita, average annual inflation rate, adult literacy rate, type of economy (centrally planned or open), and population size; and (2) characteristics of the country's bilateral relation with the United States, including whether or not English is one of the country's official and/or principal languages,[18] whether or not the United States broadcasts to that country in one of its native languages, whether or not the country hosts a U.S. military base, distance to the United States, the number of persons from that country residing in the United States, the number of naturalized citizens from that country, and the quality of reception in the United States of that country's shortwave radio broadcasts.[19]

The information on origin-country characteristics is quite limited. Country-specific data on the variables listed above are mostly absent prior to 1960 and are missing as of 1980 for a substantial number of countries,

TABLE I.2
Migration-Relevant Characteristics of the Country of Origin

A. Socioeconomic Characteristics
   Gross national product (GNP) per capita
   Average annual inflation rate
   Adult literacy rate
   Type of economy
   Population size

B. Characteristics of the Country's Bilateral Relation with the United States
   Distance to the United States
   English an official or dominant language
   Hosts U.S. military installations
   VOA broadcasts in native language
   Compatriots resident in U.S.
   Compatriots citizens of U.S.
   Quality of reception in U.S. of country's shortwave broadcasts

SOURCES: World Bank, *World Tables;* United Nations, *Demographic Yearbook;* U.S. Department of State, *Atlas of U.S. Foreign Relations; World Radio TV Handbook;* U.S. Census of Population; *Encyclopaedia Britannica.*

[18]Not all countries have an official language. If English is the dominant native language of such a country, it was classified with the English-language group.

[19]These data are obtained from the United Nations, *Demographic Yearbook* (various years); World Bank, *World Tables* (1984); *World Radio TV Handbook* (various years); U.S. Department of State, *Atlas of United States Foreign Relations* (1983); and U.S. Census (various years); supplemented by information from the *Encyclopaedia Britannica.*

including some important immigrant-sending countries. Moreover, a deeper analysis of the influence of origin-country conditions in determining who comes to the United States and who stays would require more refined information, including data on the distribution of incomes, on the returns to schooling by schooling level, on family structure and family size, on wage rates by sex and age, and so on. Such data are not available for a sufficiently large number (or a random sample) of countries to permit a reliable analysis of their influence.[20] Our analyses, incorporating the available origin-country information, indicate that at least some of the variables listed in Table I.2 do predict in a systematic way immigrant behavior in the United States and suggest that as the quality and coverage of such cross-national data improve, our understanding of immigration and the behavior of the foreign-born in the United States will also be enhanced.

Moreover, while the census data, the INS cohort data, and the data describing the characteristics of immigrant-sending countries have many shortcomings, by combining them we believe that we can obtain a comprehensive and useful understanding of both the process of immigration and of the evolution of the foreign-born population of the United States in recent decades. To do so, however, also requires an understanding of the changes in and characteristics of U.S. immigration laws as well as a framework with which to study the U.S. foreign-born. It is these elements of our analysis that we turn to in Chapter 1.

Appendix: Ambiguities in Census Data

This appendix discusses ambiguities associated with the questions pertaining to nativity, year of immigration, and naturalization in the 1980 census questionnaire.

The 1980 census measures nativity (for all persons in sampled households) by asking, in question 11:

In what State or foreign country was this person born?

followed by the instruction:

Print the State where this person's mother was living when this person was born. Do not give the location of the hospital unless the mother's home and the hospital were in the same State.

[20]Some consequences of choosing a nonrandom sample of origin countries on the basis of data availability for making accurate inferences about U.S. immigration are examined in Jasso and Rosenzweig (1990).

Thus, there potentially exists a set of individuals who were in fact born in the United States, whose mothers had homes in other countries, who now live in the United States, and who appear in the census as foreign-born but who are U.S. citizens by birth. This set probably consists mostly of persons whose parental homes were in Canadian and Mexican areas close to the U.S. borders, but may include as well persons from many other countries whose parents traveled to renowned medical centers for childbirth.

The wording of question 11 could result in (1) the underestimation of the size of the native-born population and (2) the introduction of error into the measurement of citizenship and naturalization.[21]

With respect to the measurement of citizenship and naturalization, question 11 acts as a "screen" for question 12.a, which asks:

> If this person was born in a foreign country, is (he/she) a naturalized citizen of the United States?

The permissible responses are:

> (1) Yes, a naturalized citizen; (2) No, not a citizen; or (3) Born abroad of American parents.

Thus a person from the subgroup described above who truthfully answered question 11 has a problem with question 12. Since the condition for question 12 is not satisfied (i.e., he/she was not born in a foreign country), question 12 may be skipped altogether. On the other hand, since question 11 shows the name of a foreign country, the person may check the response category "Yes, a naturalized citizen" as being logically closest to the truth. Neither alternative is satisfactory to the researcher. If question 12 is skipped, there results a strange refusal on the naturalization item. If question 12 is not skipped, there results an overestimate of naturalizations, relative to the true naturalizations recorded by the INS.[22]

---

[21]The U.S. Bureau of the Census has removed this source of ambiguity from the questionnaire used in the 1990 census enumeration. The 1990 questionnaire eliminates the instruction, "Print the State where this person's mother was living when this person was born. Do not give the location of the hospital unless the mother's home and the hospital were in the same State," retaining only the question of the individual's place of birth.

[22]How do individuals in this difficult situation respond to the questions? Warren and Passel (1987, pp. 377–378) estimate that 215,000 persons who reported U.S. nativity were in fact born in Mexico and that 375,000 Mexico-born persons incorrectly reported themselves naturalized citizens. Warren and Passel reason (1) that the 1980 population of U.S.-born Mexican-origin persons should equal the "survived" 1970 population and (2) that the number of naturalized foreign-born persons should equal the number of INS-recorded naturalizations. However, if persons born in the United States to residents of Mexico subsequently move to the United States, then, given the wording of the 1980 census questions, an alternative interpretation of the responses is as follows: 590,000 persons born in the United States to Mexican-resident parents moved to the United States in the decade of the 1970s; when faced with the 1980 census questions, 36 percent answered question 11 with their place of birth rather than

Information on year of immigration is derived from the responses to question 12.b:

When did this person come to the United States to stay?

This question cannot be interpreted unambiguously. For example, legal non-immigrants might reason that they have never come to the United States "to stay" and leave it blank. Or they might reason that the requested date refers to the year they came to do what they are doing now, or perhaps the year they first came for an extended period. The situation is not much better for legal immigrants. For those whose lives conform to the question's implicit stereotype, the year of immigration is indeed the year they entered the United States with an immigrant visa. But since many immigrants enter the United States as visitors (e.g., as students) and only subsequently become eligible for and obtain an immigrant visa, such persons might reason that the requested year is the year they came as a visitor. Accurate information on year of admission to a particular legal status is important for at least two reasons: (1) years as an immigrant determines eligibility to naturalize; and (2) years in a particular legal status determines the length of experience of particular kinds, such as experience in job search in the United States.

Moreover, another group of persons of interest to the student of migration processes is lost in these data. This is the group consisting of persons born in the United States to foreign parents living in the United States (e.g., parents who are students or exchange visitors or even permanent resident aliens), who return to their parents' native country at varying ages and are raised there, and who as adults decide to exercise their U.S. citizenship and move to the United States. These persons disappear into the native-born segment of the population, given that the question on year of immigration (question 12.b), "When did this person come to the United States to stay?" is asked only of persons born in a foreign country (as defined in question 11). This group of persons would appear to constitute an ideal "control" group in studies of migration behavior, for, especially if they left the United States in infancy, they would share all of the traits associated with an immigrant's self-selection and all of the characteristics associated with the environment in the "origin country" while at the same time being absolved of the necessity to compete for a visa by dint of kin or skills, as well as of the bars to U.S. employment in certain occupations reserved for citizens.[23]

---

their mother's residence and thus did not have to answer question 12.a on citizenship, while 64 percent answered question 11 with their mother's residence rather than their place of birth and then chose the naturalization response to question 12.a as the closest to the truth.

[23]This means that the "native-born" segment of the census-enumerated population is also heterogeneous with respect to experience in the United States.

1

HOW THE CHOSEN ARE CHOSEN

THE SUBSTANTIAL changes in world conditions over the past several decades and the no less substantial shifts in the criteria used by the United States for the selection of immigrants are likely to have had a profound influence on the characteristics of newly entering cohorts of immigrants. Such "cohort effects" would manifest themselves in two ways: differences in the initial, at-entry, characteristics of immigrants and differences in the extent and pace of their progress in the United States. To understand the historical patterns of immigration and the experience of different immigrant groups it is thus necessary to understand immigration policies and conditions in the United States and the world as they have evolved over time.

A comprehensive examination of all of the factors determining the worldwide "demand" for immigration is beyond the scope of this book. A fundamental feature of the contemporary U.S. immigration experience, however, is that the number of people who would like to immigrate to the United States exceeds the number that current law permits. Immigration laws thus substantially determine who and how many immigrate to the United States.

In this chapter we examine the role of U.S. immigrant selection policy in influencing the size and composition of U.S. immigration, as well as the effects of immigration on those policies. We first review briefly the history of U.S. immigration legislation with particular attention to the historical changes in the criteria used by the United States to choose who may immigrate. We then describe in some detail the selection criteria embodied in current U.S. immigration law; that is, U.S. immigration law as of early 1990.

In the second part of this chapter, we describe the framework we will use to guide our analysis, in subsequent chapters, of the specific behaviors and characteristics of the U.S. foreign-born. In this second part we are concerned with how immigrants select themselves and how their behavior and choices are in turn influenced by the selection criteria of U.S. immigration law. To illustrate the interactions between world conditions, U.S. immigration policies, and the self-selection processes characterizing immigration, we examine and compare the skill (literacy and schooling) levels of immigrant entry cohorts across historical periods and across different countries and areas of origin.

A Brief History of U.S. Immigration Law

Determining How Many and From Where: Exclusions, Ceilings, and Quotas

The history of U.S. immigration law is predominantly characterized by increased attempts to control who can enter and reside permanently in the United States, in large part in response to rapid shifts in the size and composition of immigrant flows. In the first century of the United States as a country, there were no numerical limits on the number of persons entering or staying in the United States, and any foreign-born person was free to choose the United States as his/her residence. This period ended in 1875 with the first Immigration Act, which, among other exclusions, barred prostitutes and convicts, and which was followed by a succession of new laws that placed restrictions on who could reside in the United States based on their place of birth and their personal characteristics, inclusive of their occupation. Such qualitative restrictions determining who could *not* enter were then supplemented with both explicit quantitative ceilings on immigration, from which certain (important) categories of immigrants were exempted, and criteria defining eligibility for entry. In 1921, quantitative ceilings were first placed on immigration from the Eastern Hemisphere; and in 1968, by a provision of the 1965 Immigration Act, they were placed as well on Western Hemisphere immigration. As we shall see, several categories of persons (notably certain kinds of relatives of U.S. citizens) have been exempt from the numerical ceilings. Table 1.1 lists the major legislation governing immigration to the United States, together with selected laws

TABLE 1.1
Major U.S. Legislation
Pertaining to Criteria for Immigration and Naturalization: 1789–1989

Legislation	Date	Major Provision(s)
A. Pre-Restriction Era (1789–1874)		
Naturalization Act	1790	Requires 2-year residence in U.S. for naturalization
Naturalization Act	1795	Requires 5-year residence in U.S. for naturalization
Alien and Sedition Acts	1798	Empowers president to deport aliens considered dangerous to U.S.
Naturalization Act	1798	Requires 14-year residence in U.S. for naturalization
Act of April 14, 1802	1802	Restores naturalization provisions of 1795 Act
B. Restriction Era: Qualitative Restrictions (1875–1920)		
Immigration Act	1875	Bars prostitutes and convicts
Immigration Act	1882	Increases list of inadmissibles and imposes head tax
Chinese Exclusion Act	1882	Bars Chinese laborers; prohibits naturalization of Chinese persons
Alien Contract Labor Law	1885	Bars importation of contract labor
First Deportation Law	1888	Authorizes deportation of contract laborers
Immigration Act	1891	Increases list of inadmissibles; authorizes deportation of illegal aliens
Immigration Act	1903	Increases list of inadmissibles
Basic Naturalization Act	1906	Requires knowledge of English for naturalization
Immigration Act	1907	Increases list of inadmissibles (including unaccompanied children under 16)
[Gentlemen's Agreement]	1907	Restricts Japanese immigration
Immigration Act	1917	Increases and codifies list of inadmissibles; requires literacy for those over 16; bars Asia-Pacific Triangle aliens
C. Restriction Era: Qualitative Restrictions Plus Quantitative Restrictions on Eastern Hemisphere (1921–1964)		
First Quota Law	1921	Limits immigration to 3% of national origin of 1910 foreign-born: 357,000
National Origins Act	1924	Limits immigration to 2% of national origin of 1890 foreign-born: 164,000 In 1929, shifts quota formula to reflect national origin of white U.S. population in 1920: 154,000

TABLE 1.1 *(continued)*

Legislation	Date	Major Provision(s)
Philippine Independence Act	1934	Limits Filipino immigration to 50
Nationality Act	1940	Permits indigenous races of W.H. to naturalize
War Brides Act	1946	Facilitates immigration of spouses and children of military personnel
Internal Security Act	1950	Increases grounds for exclusion
Immigration & Nationality Act	1952	Establishes preference category system; retains national origins quotas; ceiling about 154,000 plus 2,000 from Asia-Pacific Triangle; eliminates all racial and gender bars to naturalization

D. Restriction Era: Qualitative Restrictions Plus Quantitative Restrictions on Both Hemispheres (1965–1989)

Legislation	Date	Major Provision(s)
Immigration Act	1965	Abolishes national-origins quotas; for E.H., establishes uniform per-country limit of 20,000 and preference-category system with overall ceiling of 170,000; for W.H., effective 1968, places overall ceiling of 120,000
Immigration & Nationality Act	1976	Extends per-country limit and preference-category system to W.H.
Worldwide Ceiling Law	1978	Brings both hemispheres under single worldwide ceiling of 290,000
Refugee Act of 1980	1980	Reduces worldwide ceiling to 270,000
Immigration Reform and Control Act	1986	Grants conditional legalization to certain aliens resident in the U.S.; imposes employer sanctions

NOTE: Legislation pertaining to the entry of refugees is summarized in Table 9.1 in Chapter 9.

governing naturalization and deportation.[1] Legislation pertaining to the admission of refugees is discussed in Chapter 9.

The history of immigration legislation in the twentieth century suggests that there have been five principal aims of immigration law: (1) to avoid large increases in the foreign-born population; (2) to avoid substantial

[1] For a history of U.S. immigration law, see Hutchinson (1981). For exposition and discussion of recent/current law, see Harper (1975) and Gordon and Rosenfield (1981). Two excellent introductions are, from a historical perspective, U.S. Select Commission on Immigration and Refugee Policy (1981b) and U.S. Congressional Research Service (1988) and, from a legal perspective, Weissbrodt (1984).

shifts in the country-of-origin composition of the foreign-born; (3) to facilitate the unification of immediate family relatives regardless of their place of birth; (4) to facilitate the acquisition of "scarce" labor skills by U.S. employers; and (5) to provide a refuge for displaced persons, chiefly those threatened by foreign governments. The unprecedented size of the inflows of immigrants from the Eastern Hemisphere between 1900 and 1920 was a primary motivation for the 1921 Quota Law and the 1924 National Origins Act, which placed numerical ceilings for the first time on the annual flow of immigrants from the Eastern Hemisphere. These laws also attempted to control the country-of-origin composition of the immigrant flow, according to formulae based on the "national origins" of the 1910 foreign-born population (1921 Act), the 1890 foreign-born population (the 1924 Act), and finally the entire white U.S. population of 1920 (effective in 1929, as provided by the 1924 Act). The impetus for this attentiveness to national origins can be seen in the rapid change that had occurred in the composition of the immigrants who came to the United States, without restriction, in the 1901–1910 period. The top half of Table 1.2 compares the origin-country composition of the resident foreign-born population in 1900 with that of the subsequent decadal flow of immigrants, by presenting the top five origin countries from each. In the 1900 foreign-born population, those persons born in four northern European countries and Canada make up over 70 percent of the total. In the 1901–1910 immigrant flow, however, the top three countries of origin are located in southern and eastern Europe, with immigrants from those countries representing 66 percent of all new immigrants. By formulating quotas according to the national origin of the resident white foreign-born population, the Congress was effectively placing restrictions on the flows of immigrants from Eastern and Southern Europe. These national origin quotas, of course, supplemented the restrictions on Asian immigration, already in place, that had begun with the Chinese Exclusion Act of 1882.

The immigration legislation of the 1920s was preceded by a commission established by a 1911 act of Congress (the Dillingham Commission) immediately following the large 1901–1910 flow of immigrants from the "new" origin countries. This commission was mandated to study the consequences of immigration, and, in particular, of the recent immigrants, and to propose reforms. In the contemporary period, it is interesting that Congress also established an immigration commission in 1978; the U.S. Select Commission on Immigration and Refugee Policy, at a time when the foreign-born population was growing at its largest rate since 1901–1910. And, as in the first decade of the century, the origin-country composition of immigrants arriving between 1970 and 1980 contrasted sharply with the origin-country composition of the foreign-born population of U.S. residents who had entered the United States in prior years. As the bottom half of Table 1.2

TABLE 1.2
Top Five Countries of Origin: Foreign-Born Populations
with at least Five Years of U.S. Residence
and Subsequent Decadal Immigrant Flows in 1900 and 1970

Foreign-Born Population		Ten-Year Immigrant Flow	
Country of Birth	Percentage of Total	Country of Birth	Percentage of Total
1900		*1901–1910*	
Germany	29.7	Austria-Hungary	24.4
Ireland	17.3	Italy	23.3
Canada	9.6	Russia	18.2
England	8.0	England	4.4
Sweden	5.9	Germany	3.9
1970		*1971–1980*	
Germany	11.3	Mexico	14.2
Italy	10.9	Philippines	7.9
Canada	10.7	Korea	6.0
Mexico	7.4	Cuba	5.9
Poland	6.3	Vietnam	3.8

SOURCE: U.S. Census of Population, Public Use Samples.

shows, only one country, Mexico, appears among the top five origin countries in both the resident foreign-born population of 1970 and the subsequent 1971–1980 immigrant flow, and that country goes from fourth largest among the foreign-born to the largest among the new immigrants after
1970.

Unlike the rapid shift in the composition of immigrants that had occurred in the 1901–1910 decade, due largely to events in Europe and to
changes in the costs of ocean voyages, the changes in composition in the
1971–1980 decade reflected changes in immigration law that had taken
place between 1965 and 1970. For example, the large influx of Cubans and
Vietnamese between 1970 and 1980 was due to circumstances in those
countries and to U.S. policies on the refugee status of these groups. More
pointedly, the appearance of Filipinos and Koreans among the top five
"sending" countries in that decade resulted largely from the abolition of the
national-origins quota system with the Immigration Act of 1965. This legislation replaced the old quotas with numerical country ceilings that were
equal across all Eastern Hemisphere countries; the change to a uniform
system of ceilings effectively eliminated the severe restrictions on immigration from Asia. The system of equal per-country limits on immigration was
extended in 1976 to the Western Hemisphere.

The contrast between the origin-country composition of the 1970 foreign-born population and that of the subsequent population of immigrants understates the change in that period in the origin-country composition of the U.S. foreign-born. Just as the size of the flow of immigrants between 1970 and 1980 did not exactly correspond to the change in the size of the foreign-born population in that decade, the origin-country composition of the immigrants arriving between 1971 and 1980 does not correspond to the change in origin-country composition of the resident foreign-born between 1970 and 1980. Figure 1.1 displays the proportions of immigrants arriving between 1970 and 1974 from Asia, Europe, and the Western Hemisphere, based on U.S. Immigration and Naturalization Service (INS) immigration data, and the shares represented by the same origin areas among the 1980 foreign-born who reported that they had entered the United States in the same period, from the 1980 census. As can be seen in Figure 1.1, the share of the Western Hemisphere foreign-born in 1980, at almost 50 percent, is almost 16 percent higher than the corresponding share among the immigrants, at 43 percent.

The discrepancies between both the size and composition of the 1971–1980 immigrant flows and those of the 1980 foreign-born population have been almost universally attributed to the influx of illegal immigrants. Illegal immigration is one consequence of qualitative restrictions (if persons ineligible under the law desire to live in the United States) and of quantitative restrictions (if numerical ceilings on the immigration of eligible persons are lower than the number who wish to reside in the United States). Thus, illegal immigration during the 1971–1980 decade also resulted in

FIGURE 1.1a
Immigrants Admitted in 1970–1974, by Area of Last Residence

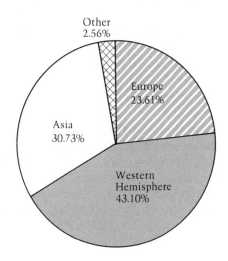

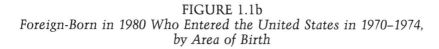

FIGURE 1.1b
*Foreign-Born in 1980 Who Entered the United States in 1970–1974,
by Area of Birth*

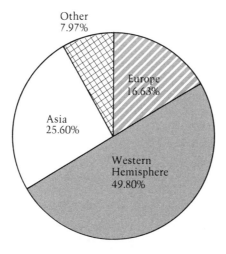

part from the 1965 Immigration Act, which for the first time placed an overall annual ceiling of 120,000 on Western Hemisphere immigration, beginning in 1968. It is no coincidence that one of the principal concerns of the Select Commission on Immigration and Refugee Policy was the formulation of measures to impede illegal immigration. And Congress passed legislation in 1986—the Immigration Reform and Control Act—concerned almost exclusively with reducing illegal immigration. Of course, illegal immigration is not the only factor producing the observed discrepancies between the size and composition of the 1971–1980 immigrant flows and those of the 1980 foreign-born population. As discussed in the Introduction, the foreign-born population includes not only immigrants but also persons in a wide variety of legal non-immigrant statuses whose origin-country composition might be distinct from that of legal immigrants.

Numerical ceilings, it should be noted, do not limit the total number of immigrants, quite apart from the possibility of their being illegally circumvented. On the one hand, numerical ceilings, since their inception in 1924 (on the Eastern Hemisphere), have never been applied to all immigrants but only to certain categories of immigrants; for example, the immigration of wives of U.S. citizens has never been restricted. On the other hand, numerical ceilings limit immigration only if the number of prospective immigrants exceeds the ceiling. Figure 1.2 displays graphically the Eastern Hemisphere numerical ceilings in existence from 1921 to 1978 and the annual number of immigrants from both the Eastern and Western hemispheres between

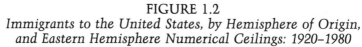

FIGURE 1.2

*Immigrants to the United States, by Hemisphere of Origin,
and Eastern Hemisphere Numerical Ceilings: 1920–1980*

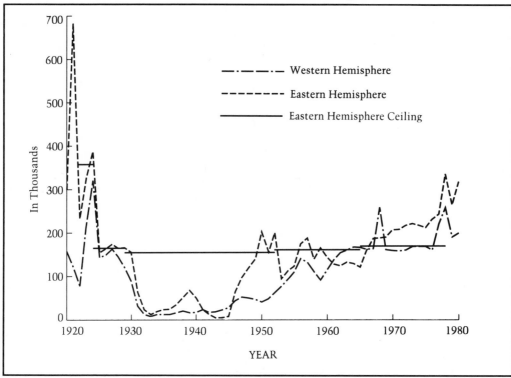

1920 and 1980. Between 1930 and 1960 the total number of immigrants from the Eastern Hemisphere was less than the numerical ceiling, and substantially so in the depression years of the 1930s. Eastern Hemisphere (legal) immigration exceeds the ceiling after 1970, however, mainly because of increases in the number of numerically unlimited legal immigrants, principally foreign-born persons marrying U.S. citizens.

Figure 1.3 displays the number of legal immigrants admitted each year to the United States between 1950 and 1988 according to whether the immigrants were numerically restricted. As can be seen, from about 1954 to 1968, before Western Hemisphere immigration was subjected to an overall numerical limit, the number of numerically unlimited immigrants exceeded the number of numerically limited immigrants. There is a sharp rise in the number and proportion of numerically restricted immigrants in 1968 because of the application of the ceiling to the Western Hemisphere; however, from 1968 on there is a steady decline in the proportion of numerically

FIGURE 1.3
Total Immigrants Admitted, by Quantitative Restrictions: 1950–1988

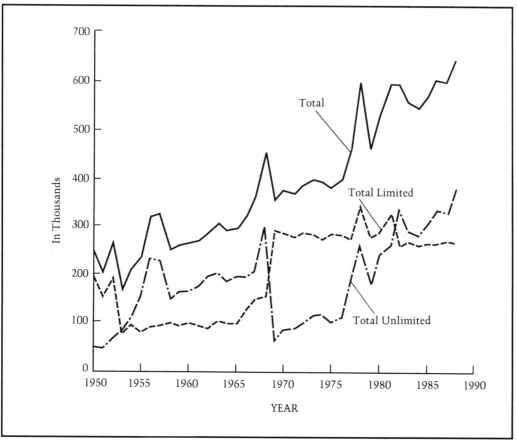

limited immigrants in total immigration, because of an increase in the number of immigrants obtaining visas in numerically unlimited categories. Starting in 1982, more immigrants are exempt from quantitative restrictions than are subject to them. In this sense, immigration is "out of control." We will examine in detail some of the reasons for this increase in "unlimited" immigration in Chapter 4, where we consider marriage and immigration. The decline in the share of numerically limited immigration in total immigration in recent years is due also to the admission of refugees, a class of immigrants treated quite differently from other immigrants. Laws pertaining to refugees and the recent experience of the two largest groups of refugees in the United States, those from Cuba and Indochina, are discussed in Chapter 9.

Allocating Visas

If the demand for U.S. visas granting foreign-born individuals the rights of permanent resident aliens exceeds or is expected to exceed the number of visas available under the numerical restrictions, then immigration law must provide some way of allocating the scarce visas among potential recipients. Table 1.3 presents the rationing systems in place, by hemisphere, since the initial immigration laws that imposed ceilings on immigrants from the Eastern Hemisphere. The table also reports those categories of immigrants entitled to an unlimited supply of visas, by hemisphere. For compactness it omits the history of immigrant visa allocations to the (small) category "special immigrant" (such as American Indians born in Canada, employees of missions abroad) and to the larger category of asylees and refugees; as well it omits national-origins quotas and country ceilings.[2]

The principal form of rationing the numerically restricted visas which has been used by the United States is based on a "preference" system in which priorities among visa applicants are established based on a single attribute of the potential immigrant. Since 1924, when the system was first instituted, there have been two basic attributes to which immigration law has been attentive: (1) the kinship of the foreign-born applicant to a U.S. citizen or permanent resident alien (legal immigrant) and (2) the labor market skill of the visa applicant. From 1924 to 1965–1968, potential immigrants with "scarce" skills were accorded the highest preference among numerically restricted immigrants—sharing the category with husbands and parents of U.S. citizens until 1952—while other numerically restricted kin were accorded lower preference. Of course, kinship of a certain type with a *U.S. citizen*—minor child, wife, husband (since 1952)—was not subject to a numerical limit during that period and continues to be exempt from numerical ceilings. After 1965, however, the skill of the immigrant was accorded a lower priority than was kinship.

In addition to the overall numerical ceilings on certain categories of immigrants beginning in 1924, the 1965 legislation placed ceilings of 20,000 for each country on the numerically limited categories of immigrants. The equality of the per-country ceilings was an antidote to the highly unequal national-origins quota system of earlier legislation, but also represents an attempt, not wholly successful as we discuss in the next section, to avoid both the dominance by few countries and rapid shifts in the country composition of immigration flows. That the overall and per-country numerical ceilings do currently limit immigration is evident from several pieces of information. First, the backlog of eligible (and approved)

[2]Table 1.3 grows out of an effort initiated by Lisa S. Roney, director of the INS Planning Staff, to summarize U.S. visa-allocation rules over time.

TABLE 1.3

Summary of U.S. Law Governing Immigrant Visa Entitlement 1924–1989, by Nativity and Kinship Ties to U.S. Citizens and Residents

Years Hemisphere	1924–1952		1952–1965/68		1965/68–1977		1978–1989	
	E.H.	W.H.	E.H.	W.H.	E.H.	W.H.	E.H.	W.H.
Kin of U.S. Citizen								
Husband	U∣1P[a]	U,NS	U	U,NS	U	U	U	U
Wife	U	U,NS	U	U,NS	U	U	U	U
Parent	1P	U,NS	2P	U,NS	U	U	U	U
Minor child	U	U	U	U	U	U	U	U
Adult unmarried child	NP	U,NS	4P/2P	U,NS	1P	L,NS	1P	1P
Adult married child	NP	U,NS	4P	U,NS	4P	L,NS	4P	4P
Sibling	NP	U,NS	4P	U,NS	5P	L,NS	5P	5P
Kin of U.S. Permanent Resident Alien								
Husband	NP	U,NS	3P	U,NS	2P	L,NS	2P	2P
Wife	2P	U,NS	3P	U,NS	2P	L,NS	2P	2P
Minor child	2P	U	3P	U	2P	L	2P	2P
Adult unmarried child	NP	U,NS	NP/3P	U,NS	2P	L,NS	2P	2P
Adult married child	NP	U,NS	NP	U,NS	NP	L,NS	NP,NS	NP,NS
Other Kin and Non-Kin								
Skilled	1P	U,NS	1P	U,NS	3P / 6P	L,NS	3P / 6P	3P / 6P
All others	NP	U,NS	NP	U,NS	NP	L,NS	NP,NS	NP,NS
Ceiling on Numerically Limited Visas (in thousands)	165/154	—	156	—	170	120	290 worldwide 270 since 1981	

NOTES:
1. The symbol U denotes an unlimited supply of visas. All other visas are numerically limited, and denoted either by the generic L, by the corresponding preference category (such as 1P), or by the residual nonpreference NP. The symbol NS denotes the case where no visa sponsorship is required; such persons may apply for an immigrant visa without the action of a U.S. citizen or permanent resident.
2. A slash between two visa categories indicates a change in the law during the period. A slash between two dates indicates different end-dates for some of the provisions in the table. The symbol ∣ indicates the possible relevance of both visa categories.

[a]Date of marriage determines the appropriate category.

visa applicants who are waiting for numerically limited visas exceeded 2.3 million by January 1989 (U.S. Department of State 1989). Second, the number of persons applying in January 1987 for the 10,000 visas awarded on a first-come, first-served basis to citizens of 36 countries, under the remedial provisions of the Immigration Reform and Control Act of 1986, exceeded 1 million; and over 3 million persons applied for the 20,000 visas to be distributed by lottery in FYs 1990 and 1991 to nationals of 162

---

[3]As noted in the Introduction, however, the provision did not restrict multiple applications.

countries. Third, under the two main "amnesty" provisions of the 1986 Act, over 3 million deportable (illegal) aliens applied for conditional legalization as of May 1989.

While the uniform per-country ceilings reflect the role of immigration law in preventing sharp changes in origin-country composition of the U.S. foreign-born, the kinship-based preference system may also act to constrain sharp changes in the origin-country composition of at least the numerically limited categories of immigrants. This is so because the principal means by which new immigrants qualify for visas is through their kinship to a member of the U.S. population. If close relatives are likely to come from the same country, then a kinship-based preference system preserves the origin-country composition of the foreign-born, or at least of recent immigrants. To the extent that foreign-born citizens and permanent resident aliens marry persons from their origin country, origin-country composition is also preserved. However, if there is a sharp but temporary change in the country-composition of immigrants because of a change in immigration law or the admission of a new refugee group, then the kinship-oriented preference system will *permanently* alter the country-of-origin composition of future immigration flows. The rise in the flow of Asian immigrants since 1968 reflects in large part these phenomena.

In summary, in the decade after enactment of the Immigration and Nationality Act of 1965, some of whose provisions took effect only in 1968, immigrant visas were allocated under a two-pronged system that provided (1) an unlimited number of visas to the "immediate relatives" of U.S. citizens (defined as the spouses, minor children, and parents of adult U.S. citizens) and to a small class of "special immigrants" (including such persons as former employees abroad of the United States and American Indians born in Canada); and, (2) up to 290,000 additional visas annually.[4] Until 1977, different selection rules for the 290,000 numerically limited visas were in effect for the Western and Eastern hemispheres. In the Western Hemisphere, 120,000 visas were granted on a first-come, first-served basis. In the Eastern Hemisphere, 170,000 visas were granted under the system of preference categories, in which up to 74 percent of the visas were received by the "close relatives" of U.S. citizens (defined as the adult children and the siblings of U.S. citizens) and by the spouses and children of permanent resident aliens, and with the additional proviso that no more than 20,000 visas be granted to the nationals of any single country.

The 1976 amendments to the Immigration and Nationality Act extended the preference-category and country-ceiling selection system to the Western Hemisphere; the Worldwide Ceiling Law of 1978 placed all numerically limited visas under a single worldwide ceiling of 290,000. The

[4]See Keely (1971, 1975) for a detailed and insightful exposition of the 1965 provisions.

Refugee Act of 1980 removed refugee visas from the preference-category system, reduced the worldwide ceiling to 270,000 (for immigrants in the numerically limited categories) and increased the kin-based share of visas to 80 percent.

Thus, under current law, no more than 20 percent of the 270,000 numerically limited visas (i.e., 54,000) may be allocated to occupation-based applicants and their family members (i.e., to persons who qualify under the provisions of the third- and sixth-preference categories and their spouses and minor children).[5] In fact, because the immediate family members (spouse, children) of immigrants who qualify under the occupational or skill criteria also acquire visas in those categories, the number of persons who become immigrants by dint of their skills is far less than 54,000. Between 1981 and 1988, less than 4 percent of all immigrants were "screened" with respect to labor market criteria.

Finally, the law's provision for the allocation of unused visas to "non-preference" applicants (i.e., applicants who do not qualify for the kin-based or skill-based visas) is academic, for the six preference categories have used all available visas since September 1978 (INS 1988, p. 143). Kinship with a U.S. citizen or legal immigrant is now the principal route to immigration to the United States.

Table 1.4 presents the INS (1988) summary of the current visa allocation system. Tables 1.5 and 1.6 report the INS (1988) summaries of recent immigration to the United States, by country of birth (FYs 1978–1988) and by class of admission (FYs 1982–1988), respectively.

The allocation of non-immigrant visas also plays a part in immigrant visa allocation. Non-immigrants resident in the United States may have a better chance than foreign-born persons still living abroad to acquire an immigrant visa. For example, they may more readily find a U.S. job that qualifies them for a skill-based visa or find a U.S. citizen to marry. Individuals who desire to live in the United States but do not qualify for an immigrant visa may qualify for a succession of non-immigrant visas, becoming *de facto* long-term (legal) residents. Table 1.7 reports the INS (1988) summary of non-immigrants admitted, by class of admission, for FYs 1978–1988. As can be seen, the number of non-immigrant visas granted has been steadily increasing since 1970.

Becoming a Permanent Resident Alien: The Immigrant and the Immigrant Sponsor

An important feature of the kinship or family unification criteria that dominate current immigration law is that the awarding of virtually every

---

[5]Throughout this book, the phrase "current law" will appear again and again. It refers to the immigration laws in effect as of early 1990.

TABLE 1.4
U.S. Immigrant Visa Allocation System, 1989

A. Immigration Subject to the Worldwide Limitation of 270,000 Annually

Preference	Provision	Percent/Number
First	Unmarried sons and daughters of U.S. citizens and their children	20% or 54,000
Second	Spouses and unmarried sons and daughters of permanent resident aliens	26% or 70,200*
Third	Members of the professions of exceptional ability and their spouses and children	10% or 27,000
Fourth	Married sons and daughters of U.S. citizens and their spouses and children	10% or 27,000*
Fifth	Brothers and sisters of U.S. citizens (at least 21 years of age) and their spouses and children	24% or 64,800*
Sixth	Workers in skilled or unskilled occupations in which laborers are in short supply in the United States and their spouses and children	10% or 27,000
Nonpreference	Other qualified applicants	Any numbers not used above

B. Immigration Exempt from the Worldwide Limitation

The major categories of immigrants exempt from the worldwide limitation of 270,000 annually are listed below:

Immediate relatives of U.S. citizens:
    Spouses
    Children (including orphans)
    Parents (of U.S. citizens at least 21 years of age)
Refugees and asylees adjusting to permanent residence
Special immigrants:
    Certain ministers of religion
    Certain former employees of the U.S. government abroad
    Certain persons who lost U.S. citizenship
    Certain foreign medical graduates
Babies born abroad to legal permanent resident aliens
Aliens who have continuously resided in the United States since January 1, 1972

SOURCE: INS, *1988 Statistical Yearbook*, pp. xiv–xv.

* Numbers not used in higher preferences may be used in these categories.

immigrant visa requires at least one U.S. *sponsor.* Indeed, even those immigrants who qualify under the occupational preferences must be petitioned for by a U.S. employer. The exceptions are refugees or asylees. Thus, the sponsor is as central an actor in the immigration process as is the immigrant.

TABLE 1.5

Immigrants Admitted, by Region and Selected Country of Birth: FYs 1978–1988

Region and Country of Birth	1978	1979	1980	1981	1982	1983	1984	1985	1986	1987	1988
All Countries	601,442	460,348	530,639	596,600	594,131	559,763	543,903	570,009	601,708	601,516	643,025
Europe	73,198	60,845	72,121	66,695	69,174	58,867	64,076	63,043	62,512	61,174	64,797
Austria	467	369	401	367	339	433	442	419	463	483	514
Belgium	439	395	426	467	559	538	537	538	620	636	581
Czechoslovakia	744	763	1,051	793	960	946	1,218	1,222	1,118	1,357	1,482
Denmark	409	414	504	506	463	513	512	478	554	537	558
Finland	358	327	356	317	346	311	264	290	322	331	390
France	1,844	1,705	1,905	1,745	1,994	2,061	2,135	2,187	2,518	2,513	2,524
Germany	6,739	6,314	6,595	6,552	a	a	a	a	a	a	a
Germany, West	a	a	a	a	6,467	6,725	6,747	7,109	6,991	7,210	6,645
Greece	7,035	5,090	4,699	4,361	3,472	2,997	2,865	2,579	2,512	2,653	2,458
Hungary	941	861	819	581	642	632	825	1,009	1,006	994	1,227
Ireland	1,180	982	1,006	902	949	1,101	1,223	1,397	1,839	3,060	5,058
Italy	7,415	6,174	5,467	4,662	3,644	3,225	3,130	3,214	3,089	2,784	2,949
Netherlands	1,153	1,145	1,169	999	1,053	1,152	1,242	1,217	1,261	1,230	1,187
Norway	423	431	403	331	342	409	375	361	354	326	397
Poland	5,050[b]	4,418[b]	4,725	5,014	5,874	6,427	9,466	9,464	8,481	7,519	9,507
Portugal	10,445	7,085	8,408	7,049	3,510	3,231	3,779	3,781	3,766	3,912	3,199
Romania	2,037	1,554	1,913	1,974	3,124	2,543	4,004	5,188	5,198	3,837	3,875
Soviet Union	5,161	2,543	10,543	9,223	15,462	5,214	6,088	3,521	2,588	2,384	2,949
Spain	2,297	1,933	1,879	1,711	1,586	1,507	1,393	1,413	1,591	1,578	1,483
Sweden	638	750	768	832	874	870	974	1,076	1,098	1,057	1,156
Switzerland	706	665	713	601	626	680	620	729	677	759	751
United Kingdom	14,245	13,907	15,485	14,997	14,539	14,830	13,949	13,408	13,657	13,497	13,228
Yugoslavia	2,621	2,171	2,099	2,048	1,418	1,382	1,569	1,662	2,011	1,827	1,941
Other Europe	851	849	787	663	931	1,140	719	781	798	690	738

TABLE 1.5 (continued)

Region and Country of Birth	1978	1979	1980	1981	1982	1983	1984	1985	1986	1987	1988
Asia	**249,776**	**189,293**	**236,097**	**264,343**	**313,291**	**277,701**	**256,273**	**264,691**	**268,248**	**257,684**	**264,465**
Afghanistan	180	353	722	1,881	1,569	2,566	3,222	2,794	2,831	2,424	2,873
Bangladesh	716	549	532	756	639	787	823	1,146	1,634	1,649	1,325
Burma	1,188	1,534	1,211	1,083	820	723	719	990	863	941	803
Cambodia	3,677	1,432	2,801	12,749	13,438	18,120	11,856	13,563	13,501	12,460	9,629
China	21,331	24,272	27,651	25,803	c	c	c	c	c	c	c
China, Mainland	c	c	c	c	27,100	25,777	23,363	24,787	25,106	25,841	28,717
Cyprus	408	323	279	326	276	265	291	294	307	331	286
Hong Kong	5,158	4,119	3,860	4,055	4,971	5,948	5,465	5,171	5,021	4,706	8,546
India	20,772	19,717	22,607	21,522	21,738	25,451	24,964	26,026	26,227	27,803	26,268
Indonesia	694	820	977	1,006	1,194	952	1,113	1,269	1,183	1,254	1,342
Iran	5,861	8,476	10,410	11,105	10,314	11,163	13,807	16,071	16,505	14,426	15,246
Iraq	2,188	2,871	2,658	2,535	3,105	2,343	2,930	1,951	1,323	1,072	1,022
Israel	3,276	3,093	3,517	3,542	3,356	3,239	3,066	3,113	3,790	3,699	3,640
Japan	4,028	4,063	4,225	3,896	3,903	4,092	4,043	4,086	3,959	4,174	4,512
Jordan	3,483	3,360	3,322	3,825	2,923	2,718	2,438	2,998	3,081	3,125	3,232
Korea	29,288	29,248	32,320	32,663	31,724	33,339	33,042	35,253	35,776	35,849	34,703
Kuwait	168	303	257	317	286	344	437	503	496	507	599
Laos	4,369	3,565	13,970	15,805	36,528	23,662	12,279	9,133	7,842	6,828	10,667
Lebanon	4,556	4,634	4,136	3,955	3,529	2,941	3,203	3,385	3,994	4,367	4,910
Malaysia	577	623	795	1,033	1,046	852	879	939	886	1,016	1,250
Pakistan	3,876	3,967	4,265	5,288	4,536	4,807	5,509	5,744	5,994	6,319	5,438
Philippines	37,216	41,300	42,316	43,772	45,102	41,546	42,768	47,978	52,558	50,060	50,697
Singapore	320	321	322	408	390	362	377	460	480	469	492
Sri Lanka	375	397	397	448	505	472	554	553	596	630	634
Syria	1,416	1,528	1,658	2,127	2,354	1,683	1,724	1,581	1,604	1,669	2,183
Taiwan	c	c	c	c	9,884	16,698	12,478	14,895	13,424	11,931	9,670
Thailand	3,574	3,194	4,115	4,799	5,568	5,875	4,885	5,239	6,204	6,733	6,888
Turkey	1,578	1,764	2,233	2,766	2,864	2,263	1,793	1,691	1,753	1,596	1,642
Vietnam	88,543	22,546	43,483	55,631	72,553	37,560	37,236	31,895	29,993	24,231	25,789
Yemen (Sanaa)	258	203	160	230	305	268	324	432	420	577	360
Other Asia	702	718	898	1,017	771	885	685	751	897	997	1,102

TABLE 1.5 (continued)

Region and Country of Birth	1978	1979	1980	1981	1982	1983	1984	1985	1986	1987	1988
Africa	**11,524**	**12,838**	**13,981**	**15,029**	**14,314**	**15,084**	**15,540**	**17,117**	**17,463**	**17,724**	**18,882**
Cape Verde	941	765	788	849	852	594	591	627	760	657	921
Egypt	2,836	3,241	2,833	3,366	2,800	2,600	2,642	2,802	2,989	3,377	3,016
Ethiopia	539	726	977	1,749	1,810	2,643	2,461	3,362	2,737	2,156	2,571
Ghana	711	828	1,159	951	824	976	1,050	1,041	1,164	1,120	1,239
Kenya	516	618	592	657	601	710	753	735	719	698	773
Liberia	333	327	426	556	593	518	585	618	618	622	769
Morocco	461	486	465	512	445	479	506	570	646	635	715
Nigeria	1,007	1,054	1,896	1,918	2,257	2,354	2,337	2,846	2,976	3,278	3,343
Sierra Leone	212	217	267	277	283	319	368	371	323	453	571
South Africa	1,689	2,214	1,960	1,559	1,434	1,261	1,246	1,210	1,566	1,741	1,832
Tanzania	301	401	339	423	304	364	418	395	370	385	388
Uganda	303	284	343	410	304	332	369	301	401	357	343
Other Africa	1,675	1,677	1,936	1,802	1,807	1,934	2,214	2,239	2,194	2,245	2,401
Oceania	**4,396**	**4,449**	**3,951**	**4,187**	**3,833**	**3,511**	**3,817**	**4,054**	**3,894**	**3,993**	**3,839**
Australia	1,565	1,400	1,480	1,281	1,367	1,273	1,308	1,362	1,354	1,253	1,356
Fiji	809	1,000	724	1,060	659	712	901	980	972	1,205	1,028
New Zealand	619d	599d	729d	666d	642	606	595	679	610	591	668
Tonga	706	809	453	588	561	481	555	669	510	545	434
Other Oceania	697	641	565	592	604	439	458	364	448	399	353

TABLE 1.5 (continued)

Region and Country of Birth	1978	1979	1980	1981	1982	1983	1984	1985	1986	1987	1988
North America	**220,784**	**157,579**	**164,772**	**210,427**	**158,057**	**168,487**	**166,706**	**182,045**	**207,714**	**216,550**	**250,009**
Canada	16,863	13,772	13,609	11,191	10,786	11,390	10,791	11,385	11,039	11,876	11,783
Mexico	92,367	52,096	56,680	101,268	56,106	59,079	57,557	61,077	66,533	72,351	95,039
Caribbean	91,361	74,074	73,296	73,301	67,379	73,306	74,265	83,281	101,632	102,899	112,357
Antigua-Barbuda	908	770	972	929	3,234	2,008	953	957	812	874	837
Bahamas, The	585	651	547	546	577	505	499	533	570	556	1,283
Barbados	2,969	2,461	2,667	2,394	1,961	1,849	1,577	1,625	1,595	1,665	1,455
Cuba	29,754	15,585	15,054	10,858	8,209	8,978	10,599	20,334	33,114	28,916	17,558
Dominica	595	1,009	846	721	569	546	442	540	564	740	611
Dominican Republic	19,458	17,519	17,245	18,220	17,451	22,058	23,147	23,787	26,175	24,858	27,189
Grenada	1,206	946	1,198	1,120	1,066	1,154	980	934	1,045	1,098	842
Haiti	6,470	6,433	6,540	6,683	8,779	8,424	9,839	10,165	12,666	14,819	34,806
Jamaica	19,265	19,714	18,970	23,569	18,711	19,535	19,822	18,923	19,595	23,148	20,966
St. Kitts & Nevis	1,014	786	874	867	1,039	2,773	1,648	769	573	589	660
St. Lucia	572	953	1,193	733	586	662	484	499	502	496	606
St. Vincent & Grenadines	679	639	763	799	719	767	695	693	635	746	634
Trinidad & Tobago	5,973	5,225	5,154	4,599	3,532	3,156	2,900	2,831	2,891	3,543	3,947
Other Caribbean	1,913	1,383	1,273	1,263	946	891	680	691	895	851	963
Central America	**20,153**	**17,547**	**20,968**	**24,509**	**23,626**	**24,601**	**24,088**	**26,302**	**28,380**	**29,296**	**30,715**
Belize	1,033	1,063	1,120	1,289	2,031	1,585	1,492	1,353	1,385	1,354	1,497
Costa Rica	1,575	1,467	1,535	1,359	1,272	1,182	1,473	1,281	1,356	1,391	1,351
El Salvador	5,826	4,479	6,101	8,210	7,107	8,596	8,787	10,156	10,929	10,693	12,045
Guatemala	3,996	2,583	3,751	3,928	3,633	4,090	3,937	4,389	5,158	5,729	5,723
Honduras	2,727	2,545	2,552	2,358	3,186	3,619	3,405	3,726	4,532	4,751	4,302
Nicaragua	1,888	1,938	2,337	2,752	3,077	2,983	2,718	2,786	2,826	3,294	3,311
Panama	3,108	3,472	3,572	4,613	3,320	2,546	2,276	2,611	2,194	2,084	2,486
Other North America	40	90	219	158	160	111	5	—	130	128	115

TABLE 1.5 (continued)

Region and Country of Birth	1978	1979	1980	1981	1982	1983	1984	1985	1986	1987	1988
South America	**41,764**	**35,344**	**39,717**	**35,913**	**35,448**	**36,087**	**37,460**	**39,058**	**41,874**	**44,385**	**41,007**
Argentina	3,732	2,856	2,815	2,236	2,065	2,029	2,141	1,844	2,187	2,106	2,371
Bolivia	1,030	751	730	820	750	823	918	1,006	1,079	1,170	1,038
Brazil	1,923	1,450	1,570	1,616	1,475	1,503	1,847	2,272	2,332	2,505	2,699
Chile	3,122	2,289	2,569	2,048	1,911	1,970	1,912	1,992	2,243	2,140	2,137
Colombia	11,032	10,637	11,289	10,335	8,608	9,658	11,020	11,982	11,408	11,700	10,322
Ecuador	5,732	4,383	6,133	5,129	4,127	4,243	4,164	4,482	4,516	4,641	4,716
Guyana	7,614	7,001	8,381	6,743	10,059	8,980	8,412	8,531	10,367	11,384	8,747
Peru	5,243	4,135	4,021	4,664	4,151	4,384	4,368	4,181	4,895	5,901	5,936
Uruguay	1,052	754	887	972	707	681	712	790	699	709	612
Venezuela	990	841	1,010	1,104	1,336	1,508	1,721	1,714	1,854	1,694	1,791
Other South America	294	247	312	246	259	308	245	264	294	435	638
Born on Board Ship	—	—	—	6	4	—	—	—	—	—	3
Unknown or Not Reported	—	—	—	—	10	26	31	1	3	6	23

SOURCE: INS 1988 *Statistical Yearbook*, Table 3.

NOTES:
[a] Prior to fiscal year 1982, data for East and West Germany are included in Germany.
[b] Excludes Danzig.
[c] Prior to fiscal year 1982, data for Mainland China and Taiwan are included in China.
[d] Includes Niue.
— Represents zero.

TABLE 1.6
Immigrants Admitted, by Type and Class of Admission: FYs 1982–1988

Class of Admission	1982	1983	1984	1985	1986	1987	1988
Total, All Immigrants	**594,131**	**559,763**	**543,903**	**570,009**	**601,708**	**601,516**	**643,025**
Total, numerically limited	**259,749**	**269,213**	**262,016**	**264,208**	**266,968**	**271,135**	**264,148**
New arrivals	206,312	221,587	224,750	226,505	228,522	239,941	234,586
Adjustments	53,437	47,626	37,266	37,703	38,446	31,194	29,562
Total, exempt from numerical limitations	**334,382**	**290,550**	**281,887**	**305,801**	**334,740**	**330,381**	**378,877**
New arrivals	108,364	115,212	119,879	129,860	147,588	147,054	143,299
Adjustments	226,018	175,338	162,008	175,941	187,152	183,327	235,578
Total, Numerically Limited	**259,749**	**269,213**	**262,016**	**264,208**	**266,968**	**271,135**	**264,148**
Total, 1st Preference	**6,604**	**6,892**	**7,569**	**9,319**	**10,910**	**11,382**	**12,107**
1st preference, unmarried sons/daughters of U.S. citizens	5,539	5,753	6,242	7,661	8,711	9,263	9,971
New arrivals (P11, A11)	4,670	4,980	5,417	6,656	7,829	8,516	9,280
Adjustments (P16, A16)	869	773	825	1,005	882	747	691
1st preference, children of P11, P16, A11, A16	1,065	1,139	1,327	1,658	2,199	2,119	2,136
New arrivals (P12, A12)	923	998	1,170	1,452	2,007	1,982	2,053
Adjustments (P17, A17)	142	141	157	206	192	137	83

TABLE 1.6 (continued)

Class of Admission	1982	1983	1984	1985	1986	1987	1988
Total, 2nd Preference	**113,070**	**116,623**	**112,309**	**114,997**	**110,926**	**110,758**	**102,777**
2nd preference, spouses of alien residents	39,567	39,731	37,643	40,549	38,384	34,528	29,898
New arrivals (P21)	29,711	33,797	33,948	35,788	34,057	16,074	17,889
New arrivals, conditional (C21)	X	X	X	X	X	16,454	11,003
Adjustments (P26)	9,856	5,934	3,695	4,761	4,327	1,546	843
Adjustments, conditional (C26)	X	X	X	X	X	454	163
2nd preference, unmarried sons/daughters of alien residents	64,843	67,539	64,711	61,263	57,311	58,270	54,123
New arrivals (P22)	57,549	62,441	61,313	57,558	53,635	54,599	52,435
· New arrivals, conditional (C22)	X	X	X	X	X	1,620	503
Adjustments (P27)	7,294	5,098	3,398	3,705	3,676	2,012	1,170
Adjustments, conditional (C27)	X	X	X	X	X	39	15
2nd preference, children of P22, P27, C22, C27	8,660	9,353	9,955	13,185	15,231	17,960	18,756
New arrivals (P23)	7,795	8,845	9,508	12,769	14,739	15,697	16,958
New arrivals, conditional (C23)	X	X	X	X	X	X	X
Adjustments (P28)	865	508	447	416	492	222	118
Adjustments, conditional (C28)	X	X	X	X	X	4	—
Total, 3rd Preference	**26,001**	**27,250**	**24,852**	**24,905**	**26,823**	**26,921**	**26,680**
3rd preference, professional or highly skilled immigrants	11,981	12,338	10,691	10,947	11,763	12,048	11,758
New arrivals (P31)	3,052	3,147	3,094	2,981	3,342	4,004	3,693
Adjustments (P36)	8,929	9,191	7,597	7,966	8,421	8,044	8,065
3rd preference, spouses of P31 and P36	6,794	7,141	6,637	6,602	7,209	7,309	7,325
New arrivals (P32)	1,953	2,048	2,079	2,158	2,290	2,767	2,620
Adjustments (P37)	4,841	5,093	4,558	4,444	4,919	4,542	4,705
3rd preference, children of P31 and P36	7,226	7,771	7,524	7,356	7,851	7,564	7,597
New arrivals (P33)	2,631	2,847	2,925	2,973	3,233	3,522	3,383
Adjustments (P38)	4,595	4,924	4,599	4,383	4,618	4,042	4,214

TABLE 1.6 (continued)

Class of Admission	1982	1983	1984	1985	1986	1987	1988
Total, 4th Preference	**19,465**	**20,948**	**14,681**	**18,460**	**20,702**	**20,703**	**21,940**
4th preference, married sons/daughters of U.S. citizens	5,511	5,933	4,258	5,376	5,947	5,839	6,227
New arrivals (P41, A41)	4,557	5,100	3,531	4,520	5,057	5,024	5,552
New arrivals, conditional (C41)	X	X	X	X	X	53	10
Adjustments (P46, A46)	954	833	727	856	890	741	662
Adjustments, conditional (C46)	X	X	X	X	X	21	3
4th preference, spouses of P41, P46, A41, A46, C41, C46	4,284	4,666	3,282	4,216	4,737	4,833	5,168
New arrivals (P42, A42)	3,842	4,261	2,933	3,806	4,298	4,372	4,850
New arrivals, conditional (C42)	X	X	X	X	X	77	21
Adjustments (P47, A47)	442	405	349	410	439	375	292
Adjustments, conditional (C47)	X	X	X	X	X	9	5
4th preference, children of P41, P46, A41, A46, C41, C46	9,670	10,349	7,141	8,868	10,018	10,031	10,545
New arrivals (P43, A43)	8,865	9,650	6,506	8,121	9,189	9,330	10,058
New arrivals, conditional (C43)	X	X	X	X	X	73	12
Adjustments (P48, A48)	805	699	635	747	829	613	473
Adjustments, conditional (C48)	X	X	X	X	X	15	2
Total, 5th Preference	**66,926**	**69,025**	**77,765**	**70,481**	**70,401**	**68,966**	**63,948**
5th preference, brothers or sisters of U.S. citizens	25,802	26,573	29,287	25,536	24,837	23,517	21,489
New arrivals (P51)	23,181	24,762	27,737	24,407	23,914	22,980	21,146
Adjustments, (P56)	2,621	1,811	1,550	1,129	923	537	343
5th preference, spouses of P51 and P56	13,124	13,998	15,951	14,861	15,321	14,910	14,497
New arrivals (P52)	12,161	13,245	15,266	14,391	14,937	14,676	14,336
Adjustments, (P57)	963	753	685	470	384	234	161
5th preference, children of P51 and P56	28,000	28,454	32,527	30,084	30,243	30,539	27,962
New arrivals (P53)	26,505	27,269	31,435	29,247	29,592	30,162	27,717
Adjustments (P58)	1,495	1,185	1,092	837	651	377	245

TABLE 1.6 (continued)

Class of Admission	1982	1983	1984	1985	1986	1987	1988
Total, 6th Preference	**25,181**	**28,218**	**24,669**	**25,990**	**26,802**	**26,952**	**26,927**
6th preference, needed skilled or unskilled workers	12,041	12,708	11,393	11,425	11,399	11,623	10,696
New arrivals (P61)	7,884	8,148	8,395	8,603	8,728	9,983	9,382
Adjustments (P66)	4,157	4,560	2,998	2,822	2,671	1,640	1,314
6th preference, spouses of P61 and P66	5,049	5,980	5,219	5,674	5,988	6,181	6,390
New arrivals (P62)	3,146	3,722	3,635	4,291	4,562	5,259	5,617
Adjustments (P67)	1,903	2,258	1,584	1,383	1,426	922	773
6th preference, children of P61 and P66	8,091	9,530	8,057	8,891	9,415	9,148	9,841
New arrivals (P63)	5,690	6,279	5,858	6,784	7,113	7,754	8,663
Adjustments (P68)	2,401	3,251	2,199	2,107	2,302	1,394	1,178
Total, Nonpreference[a]	**—**	**—**	**—**	**7**	**—**	**3,040**	**6,029**
Nonpreference, NP1 and NP6	—	—	—	7	—	3	—
Adjustments (NP6)	—	—	—	7	—	3	—
Nonpreference, NP5 and NP0, Act of 11/6/86	X	X	X	X	X	3,037	6,029
New arrivals (NP5)	X	X	X	X	X	2,926	5,725
Adjustments (NP0)	X	X	X	X	X	111	304
Total, Suspension of Deportation, Section 244	**197**	**176**	**161**	**1**	**391**	**2,394**	**3,734**
Adjustments other than crewmen (Z11)	197	176	161	[b]—	[b]389	2,394	3,731
Adjustments, crewmen (Z57)	—	—	—	1	2	—	3
Total, Private Law, Adjustments (Z41)	**4**	**12**	**4**	**16**	**3**	**12**	**1**
Total, Foreign Gov't Officials, Act of 9/11/57 Section 13 (Z91)	**1**	**20**	**6**	**32**	**10**	**7**	**5**

TABLE 1.6 (continued)

Class of Admission	1982	1983	1984	1985	1986	1987	1988
Total, Recaptured Cuban Numbers	2,300	49	X	X	X	X	X
Western Hemisphere aliens	2,262	48	X	X	X	X	X
New arrivals (SA1)	2,168	47	X	X	X	X	X
Adjustments (SA6)	94	1	X	X	X	X	X
Nonwestern Hemisphere aliens, spouses of							
SA1 and SA6	16	1	X	X	X	X	X
New arrivals (SA2)	12	1	X	X	X	X	X
Adjustments (SA7)	4	—	X	X	X	X	X
Nonwestern Hemisphere aliens, children of							
SA1 and SA6	22	—	X	X	X	X	X
New arrivals (SA3)	17	—	X	X	X	X	X
Adjustments (SA8)	5	—	X	X	X	X	X
Total, Exempt from Numerical Limitations	334,382	290,550	281,887	305,801	334,740	330,381	378,877
Total, Immediate Relatives of U.S. Citizens	168,398	177,792	183,247	204,368	223,468	218,575	219,340
Total, spouses of U.S. citizens	104,218	112,666	116,596	129,790	137,597	132,452	130,977
New arrivals (IR1)	52,314	58,307	61,394	66,215	74,662	31,855	23,699
New arrivals, conditional (CR1)	X	X	X	X	X	41,186	44,267
Adjustments (IR6)	46,954	49,042	50,259	57,878	56,883	17,744	11,497
Adjustments, conditional (CR6)	X	X	X	X	X	36,762	46,572
Adjustments, Northern Marianas Is., P.L. 94-241 (MR6)	X	X	X	X	X	46	3
Adjustments, entered as a fiance(e) (IF1)	4,950	5,317	4,943	5,697	6,052	1,919	X
Adjustments, entered as a fiance(e), conditional (CF-1)	X	X	X	X	X	2,940	4,939

TABLE 1.6 (continued)

Class of Admission	1982	1983	1984	1985	1986	1987	1988
Total, Children of U.S. Citizens	**28,735**	**30,429**	**32,080**	**35,592**	**40,639**	**40,940**	**40,863**
New arrivals (IR2, AR1)	18,451	18,875	19,135	21,298	25,332	20,748	20,874
New arrivals, conditional (CR2)	X	X	X	X	X	4,823	4,565
Adjustments (IR7, AR6)	4,055	3,958	4,097	4,480	4,767	3,078	3,754
Adjustments, conditional (CR7)	X	X	X	X	X	1,638	2,042
Adjustments, entered as child of a fiance(e) (IF2)	480	469	521	528	595	209	X
Adjustments, entered as child of a fiance(e), conditional (CF2)	X	X	X	X	X	315	505
Adjustments, Northern Mariana Is., P.L. 94-241 (MR7)	X	X	X	X	X	32	3
Total, orphans	5,749	7,127	8,327	9,286	9,945	10,097	9,120
Total, orphans adopted abroad	829	813	1,097	1,166	1,264	1,667	1,840
New arrivals (IR3)	781	781	1,047	1,092	1,190	1,610	1,792
Adjustments (IR8)	48	32	50	74	74	57	48
Total, orphans to be adopted	4,920	6,314	7,230	8,120	8,681	8,430	7,280
New arrivals (IR4)	4,912	6,306	7,226	8,114	8,676	8,420	7,257
Adjustments (IR9)	8	8	4	6	5	10	23
Total, Parents of Adult U.S. Citizens	**35,445**	**34,697**	**34,571**	**38,986**	**45,232**	**45,183**	**47,500**
New arrivals (IR5)	26,321	25,664	25,609	27,657	31,699	32,416	33,571
Adjustments (IR0)	9,124	9,033	8,962	11,329	13,533	12,767	13,929
Total, Special Immigrants	**4,940**	**3,175**	**2,338**	**2,551**	**2,992**	**3,646**	**5,120**
Total, persons who lost citizenship	**6**	**6**	**3**	**2**	**6**	**1**	**4**
Total, lost citizenship by marriage	3	5	2	1	4	1	1
New arrivals (SC1)	—	3	1	—	—	—	1
Adjustments (SC6)	3	2	1	1	4	1	
Total, lost citizenship by service in armed forces	3	1	1	1	2	—	3
New arrivals (SC2)	1	—	—	—	1	—	—
Adjustments (SC7)	2	1	1	1	1	—	3

TABLE 1.6 (continued)

Class of Admission	1982	1983	1984	1985	1986	1987	1988
Total, ministers, spouses and children	**2,059**	**1,734**	**1,540**	**1,853**	**2,060**	**2,041**	**2,207**
Total ministers	895	773	663	777	822	829	899
New arrivals (SD1)	396	364	334	443	480	458	447
Adjustments (SD6)	499	409	329	334	342	371	452
Total, spouses of ministers	378	324	315	383	428	423	453
New arrivals (SD2)	251	215	214	267	312	298	304
Adjustments (SD7)	127	109	101	116	116	125	149
Total, children of ministers	786	637	562	693	810	789	855
New arrivals (SD3)	566	443	411	522	622	564	621
Adjustments (SD8)	220	194	151	171	188	225	234
Total, employees of U.S. gov't abroad, spouses and children	**554**	**529**	**535**	**479**	**773**	**1,112**	**2,047**
Total, employees of U.S. government abroad	181	180	189	156	248	380	585
New arrivals (SE1)	175	177	186	152	244	377	583
Adjustments (SE6)	6	3	3	4	4	3	2
Total, spouses of employees of U.S. gov't abroad	120	107	115	101	168	254	454
New arrivals (SE2)	116	107	115	101	166	251	454
Adjustments (SE7)	4	—	—	—	2	3	—
Total, children of employees of U.S. gov't abroad	253	242	231	222	357	478	1,008
New arrivals (SE3)	250	241	230	219	354	477	1,008
Adjustments (SE8)	3	1	1	3	3	1	—

TABLE 1.6 (continued)

Class of Admission	1982	1983	1984	1985	1986	1987	1988
Total, Panama Canal Act of 9/29/79	**455**	**116**	**86**	**130**	**105**	**90**	**124**
Total, certain former emp. of the PC Co. and CZ gov't	42	8	9	7	5	2	6
New arrivals (SF1)	40	8	6	2	2	2	4
Adjustments (SF6)	2	—	3	5	3	—	2
Total, accompanying spouses or children of SF1 and SF6	93	19	12	10	6	4	16
New arrivals (SF2)	93	19	12	8	5	4	16
Adjustments (SF7)	—	—	—	2	1	—	—
Total, certain former emp. of U.S. gov't in Panama CZ	155	43	29	42	43	36	41
New arrivals (SG1)	152	39	29	41	42	34	39
Adjustments (SG6)	3	4	—	1	1	2	2
Total, accompanying spouses or children of SG1 and SG6	164	46	36	71	51	48	61
New arrivals (SG2)	161	43	34	71	51	48	61
Adjustments (SG7)	3	3	2	—	—	—	—
Total, certain emp. of PC Co. or CZ gov't on 4/1/79	1	—	—	—	—	—	—
Adjustments (SH6)	1	—	—	—	—	—	—
Total, foreign medical graduates, Act of 12/29/81	**1,866**	**790**	**174**	**87**	**48**	**28**	**7**
Total, foreign med. school grads., adjustments (SJ6)	906	360	89	44	23	11	4
Total, accompanying spouses or children of SJ6	960	430	85	43	25	17	3
New arrivals (SJ2)	1	8	2	1	—	3	3
Adjustments (SJ7)	959	422	83	42	25	14	3

TABLE 1.6 (continued)

Class of Admission	1982	1983	1984	1985	1986	1987	1988
Total, retired employees of intern'l org. and their families	**X**	**X**	**X**	**X**	**X**	**374**	**731**
Total, retired employees of international organizations	X	X	X	X	X	11	16
New arrivals (SK1)	X	X	X	X	X	6	7
Adjustments (SK6)	X	X	X	X	X	5	9
Total, accompanying spouses of SK1 or SK6	X	X	X	X	X	9	10
New arrivals (SK2)	X	X	X	X	X	2	4
Adjustments (SK7)	X	X	X	X	X	7	6
Total, unmarried children of SK1 or SK6	X	X	X	X	X	351	702
New arrivals (SK3)	X	X	X	X	X	35	131
Adjustments (SK8)	X	X	X	X	X	316	571
Total, surviving spouses of employees of intern'l org.	X	X	X	X	X	3	3
New arrivals (SK4)	X	X	X	X	X	1	—
Adjustments (SK9)	X	X	X	X	X	2	3
Total, Special K Classes	—	**2**	—	—	**21**	**6**	**X**
Total, Act of 10/24/62 (P.L. 87-555)	—	2	—	—	21	6	X
Total, beneficiaries of 4th preference petition	—	—	—	—	5	3	X
New arrivals (K25)	—	—	—	—	5	3	X
Total, spouses/children of bene. of 4th pref. petition	—	2	—	—	16	3	X
New arrivals (K26)	—	2	—	—	16	3	X

TABLE 1.6 (continued)

Class of Admission	1982	1983	1984	1985	1986	1987	1988
Total, Refugee and Asylee Adjustments	156,601	102,685	92,127	95,040	104,383	96,474	110,721
Refugee Relief Act of 1953, Act of 8/7/53 (Y64)	—	1	—	—	—	—	—
Hungarian parolees, Act of 7/25/58 (M93)	1	—	—	—	—	—	—
Refugee escapees, Act of 7/14/60 (M83)	2	—	—	—	—	—	1
Total, Cuban refugees, Act of 11/2/66	1,965	3,274	3,460	14,288	30,152	26,869	10,993
Cuban refugees (CU6)	1,910	3,092	3,192	14,057	29,715	26,618	10,468
Non-Cuban spouses or children of Cuban refugees (CU7)	55	182	268	231	437	251	525
Total, Indochinese refugees, Act of 10/28/77	13,666	3,122	875	166	136	83	42
Indochinese refugees (IC6)	13,620	3,012	845	142	135	83	39
Spouse or child of Indochinese refugees (IC7)	46	110	30	24	1	—	3
Refugee parolees, Act of 10/5/78 (R86)	48,826	13,409	7,657	3,766	1,720	866	437
Total, refugees, Act of 3/17/80	90,282	79,965	74,528	71,820	67,375	59,022	64,801
Refugees (RE6)	68,984	54,303	46,765	43,511	39,957	34,599	37,125
Spouses of refugees (RE7)	5,627	6,920	7,894	7,797	7,382	6,236	7,259
Children of refugees (RE8)	15,671	18,742	19,869	20,512	20,036	18,187	20,417
Total, asylees, Act of 3/17/80	1,859	2,914	5,607	5,000	5,000	5,000	5,445
Asylees (AS6)	1,407	1,797	3,735	3,333	3,433	2,992	3,553
Spouses of asylees (AS7)	190	444	782	702	663	847	790
Children of asylees (AS8)	262	673	1,090	965	904	1,161	1,102
Cuban/Haitian entrants, Act of 11/6/86 (CH6)	X	X	X	X	X	4,634	29,002

TABLE 1.6 (continued)

Class of Admission	1982	1983	1984	1985	1986	1987	1988
Total, Amerasians (P.L. 100-202, effective 12/21/87)	X	X	X	X	X	X	**319**
Amerasians, born in Vietnam from 1/1/62–1/1/76							
New arrivals (AM1)	X	X	X	X	X	X	126
Spouses or children of AM1 or AM6	X	X	X	X	X	X	126
New arrivals (AM2)	X	X	X	X	X	X	4
Mothers, guardians, or next-of-kin of AM1 or AM6	X	X	X	X	X	X	4
New arrivals (AM3)	X	X	X	X	X	X	189
							189
Total, other adjustments	**1,060**	**3,286**	**281**	**185**	**147**	**8,250**	**40,101**
Presumed admitted for lawful permanent residence (XB3)	2	—	4	22	8	6	2
Suspension of deportation—other than crewman, Section 244 (Z13)	12	8	19	15	21	47	38
Suspension of deportation—crewman, Section 244 (Z56)	—	1	2	1	1	1	—
Section 249, entered before 7/1/24 (Z33)	55	49	48	36	27	22	25
Section 249, entered 7/1/24-6/28/40 (Z03)	35	28	27	21	21	71	5
Section 249, entered 6/29/40-1/1/72[c] (Z66)	67	58	36	32	25	8,060	39,999
Private bill (Z43)	1	3	—	5	—	5	2
Section 13, Act of 9/11/57 (Z83)	—	—	—	—	1	—	12
Total, Investors, Act of 12/29/81	**881**	**616**	**128**	**52**	**40**	**35**	**12**
Investors (NP8)	477	319	62	32	24	15	5
Accompanying spouses or children of NP8 (NP9)	404	297	66	20	16	20	7
Individuals born under diplomatic status in U.S. (DS1)	5	6	2	1	3	4	6

TABLE 1.6 (continued)

Class of Admission	1982	1983	1984	1985	1986	1987	1988
Total, Virgin Islands non-immigrants, Act of 9/30/82	2	2,517	15	—	—	—	—
H-2 non-immigrants (V16)	1	1,325	7	—	—	—	—
Spouses or children of V16 (V17)	1	1,192	8	—	—	—	—
Total, other classes	3,383	3,610	3,894	3,657	3,729	3,430	3,276
Children born abroad to alien residents (NA3)	3,157	3,356	3,639	3,429	3,450	3,174	2,997
American Indians born in Canada (S13)	121	109	135	149	175	161	194
Children born subsequent to issuance of visa (XA3)	105	145	120	79	104	95	85

SOURCE: INS 1988 Statistical Yearbook, Table 4.

NOTES:

[a] Although nonpreference visas (NP1 and NP6) have been unavailable since 1978, there were 7 nonpreference immigrants admitted in fiscal year 1985 and 3 in fiscal year 1987. These cases were filed prior to 1978, were denied by the INS, but were appealed through the judicial system.

[b] The 389 suspension of deportation (Z11) immigrants reported in fiscal year 1986 include 192 immigrants who actually immigrated in fiscal year 1985.

[c] Prior to fiscal year 1987 aliens must have entered before 6/30/48 to be eligible for Section 249.

— Represents zero. X, Not applicable.

TABLE 1.7
Nonimmigrants Admitted, by Class of Admission: Fiscal Years 1978, 1981, 1984, and 1986–1988

Class of Admission[a]	1978	1981	1984	1986	1987	1988
All Classes[b]	**8,290,108**	**11,756,903**	**9,292,732**	**10,470,900**	**12,272,866**	**14,591,735**
Foreign Government Officials and Families	**83,786**	**84,710**	**89,357**	**93,726**	**91,657**	**98,927**
Ambassador, public minister, career diplomatic, or consular officer (A1)	15,437	NA	21,091	22,241	21,480	22,182
Other foreign government official or employee (A2)	66,915	NA	66,383	69,495	68,195	74,723
Attendant, servant, or personal employee of A1 and A2 classes (A3)	1,434	NA	1,883	1,990	1,982	2,022
Temporary visitors	**7,443,337**	**10,650,592**	**8,217,996**	**9,279,917**	**11,019,343**	**13,196,729**
For business (B1)	800,652	1,135,422	1,623,421	1,937,929	2,132,044	2,375,565
For pleasure (B2)	6,642,685	9,515,170	6,594,575	7,341,988	8,887,299	10,821,164
Transit Aliens	**273,123**	**214,218**	**238,411**	**243,859**	**264,138**	**299,138**
Alien in transit (C1)	186,423	NA	143,227	140,579	141,389	153,811
Alien in transit to the U.N. (C2)	301	NA	1,190	937	981	1,381
Foreign government official and family in transit (C3)	9,806	NA	7,293	7,434	6,824	6,612
Transit without visa (C4)	76,593	NA	86,701	94,909	114,944	137,334
Treaty Traders and Investors and Families	**50,431**	**80,802**	**90,510**	**103,714**	**114,083**	**125,555**
Treaty trader (E1)	NA	NA	61,690	68,932	73,395	75,785
Treaty investor (E2)	NA	NA	28,820	34,782	40,688	49,770

TABLE 1.7 (continued)

Class of Admission[a]	1978	1981	1984	1986	1987	1988
Students	187,030	240,805	227,394	261,081	262,409	312,363
Academic student (F1)	187,030	NA	222,406	255,529	256,335	305,868
Vocational student (M1)	[c]	NA	4,988	5,552	6,074	6,495
Spouses and Children of Students	19,667	31,056	29,071	27,149	26,177	25,540
Academic student (F2)	19,667	NA	28,487	26,622	25,709	25,062
Vocational student (M2)	[c]	NA	584	527	468	478
Representatives (and Families) to International Organizations	44,042	54,223	56,557	59,378	57,325	58,947
Principal of recognized foreign government (G1)	6,655	NA	8,121	8,107	8,077	8,401
Other rep. of recognized foreign government (G2)	7,675	NA	7,583	8,003	7,593	8,101
Rep. of nonrecognized foreign government (G3)	227	NA	267	326	284	360
International organization officer or employee (G4)	28,573	NA	39,456	41,491	39,927	40,593
Attendant servant or personal employee of rep. (G5)	912	NA	1,130	1,451	1,444	1,492
Temporary Workers and Trainees	42,979	44,770	68,730	85,359	97,334	113,424
Distinguished merit or ability (H1)	16,838	NA	42,473	54,426	65,461	77,931
Performing services unavailable in the U.S. (H2)	22,832	NA	23,362	28,014	28,882	32,966
Agricultural workers (H2A)	X	X	X	X	X	10,851
Nonagricultural workers (H2B)	X	X	X	X	X	22,115
Industrial trainee (H3)	3,309	NA	2,895	2,919	2,991	2,527

TABLE 1.7 (continued)

Class of Admission[a]	1978	1981	1984	1986	1987	1988
Spouses and Children of Temporary Workers and Trainees (H4)	8,294	10,110	10,831	13,710	16,211	19,673
Representatives (and Families) of Foreign Information Media (I1)	9,979	16,708	19,051	16,919	18,386	21,461
Exchange Visitors (J1)	53,319	80,230	94,008	130,416	148,205	166,659
Spouses and Children of Exchange Visitors (J2)	21,778	27,793	26,919	32,591	34,824	36,267
Fiances(ees) of U.S. Citizens (K1)	5,730	5,456	6,386	7,147	6,024	5,927
Children of Fiances(ees) of U.S. Citizens (K2)	687	742	753	923	757	688
Intracompany Transferees (L1)	21,495	38,595	62,359	66,925	65,673	63,849
Spouses and Children of Intracompany Transferees (L2)	18,521	26,449	41,264	41,093	41,088	37,846
NATO Officials and Families (N1-7)	5,910	7,124	7,792	6,969	7,340	8,545
Unknown	—	142,520	5,343	24	1,892	197

SOURCE: INS 1988 Statistical Yearbook, Table 44.

NOTES:

[a]See INS (1988), Glossary for detailed descriptions of classes of admission.

[b]Excludes classes of admission processed as non-immigrants in the following years: for all countries—1978—1,053,602 returning resident aliens; 1984—63,263 parolees (R1-3), 2,260 withdrawals (R4) and stowaways (R5), and 68,504 refugees (RF); 1986—67,483 parolees (R1-3), 17,547 withdrawals (R4) and stowaways (R5), and 51,165 refugees (RF); 1987—63,232 parolees (R1-3), 18,731 withdrawals (R4), and stowaways (R5), and 66,803 refugees (RF); 1988—94,918 parolees (R1-3), 17,060 withdrawals (R4), and stowaways (R5), and 80,382 refugees (RF).

[c]M1 and M2 were not classes of admission in 1978.

— Represents zero. NA, Not available. X, Not applicable. "Family," "immediate family" and "spouse and children" are defined as spouse and unmarried minor (or dependent) children.

For the (non-refugee/non-asylee) alien wishing to obtain an immigrant visa, given the unavailability of nonpreference visas, the first task is to find a U.S. person (natural or corporate) who desires that he/she live in the United States. That U.S. person (henceforth *petitioner*) then petitions the INS to establish the claim of the alien (henceforth *beneficiary*) to an immigrant visa. As discussed above and summarized in Table 1.4, there are two types of grounds for such a claim—kinship (of a certain type) and occupation.

If the claim is to be made on kinship grounds, then the petitioner files Form I-130, "Petition for Alien Relative," which establishes the kinship tie between the petitioner and beneficiary.[6] If the claim is to be made on occupational grounds, then the petitioner files Form I-140, "Petition for Prospective Immigrant Employee," which establishes the occupational tie, usually one in which the petitioner employs the beneficiary.[7] In this case, the labor certification process must also be complied with; the Labor Department must certify that the immigrant is in an occupation where there is a scarcity of available qualified U.S. citizen or permanent resident alien employees. The relevant form is ETA750A&B, "Application for Alien Employment Certification," for occupations not pre-certified.

If the beneficiary's claim to a visa is established by the INS and the visa office of the Department of State located in the area of origin of the beneficiary, then the beneficiary files for permanent residence. The procedure and the relevant forms differ somewhat depending on whether the prospective immigrant is abroad or in the United States. If in the United States, the beneficiary files Form I-485, "Application for Permanent Residence." At this time, the visa applicant also files Form G-325-A, a "Biographic Information" sheet. Also at this time, the visa applicant must submit evidence that he/she will not become a public charge in the United States. This evidence may consist of a personal financial statement or a letter from an employer or, alternatively, Form I-134, "Affidavit of Support," submitted by a U.S. person.[8]

As this brief sketch suggests, the awarding of virtually every immigrant visa requires that at least one U.S. sponsor—the petitioner who establishes the alien's claim to a visa—and possibly a second U.S. sponsor—the guarantor of financial support—play an active role in the immigration process.

[6]Copies of the principal forms discussed in this section are reproduced in the appendix to this chapter.

[7]In a small number of cases, a third-preference beneficiary is of such world renown that no sponsor is required, and the prospective immigrant himself/herself files Form I-140.

[8]If the visa applicant is abroad, the corresponding forms are OF-222, which establishes prima facie eligibility for an immigrant visa; OF-169, "Preliminary Questionnaire for Residence"; OF-230, "Application for Immigrant Visa and Alien Registration"; OF-179, "Biographic Data for Visa Purposes"; and OF-167, "Evidence Which May Be Presented to Meet the Public Charge Provisions of the Law."

To the extent that the population of visa sponsors selects who receives immigrant visas, the characteristics of visa sponsors, inclusive of their country of origin, may be as important as the characteristics of the immigrants they select. We examine the propensity of the foreign-born to be sponsors and the characteristics of sponsors, both native-born and foreign-born, in Chapters 4 through 6.

Framework for Examining the U.S. Foreign-Born Population

U.S. immigration laws set the rules under which foreign-born individuals or families may immigrate to the United States. But who actually immigrates depends as well on the choices of individuals or families born outside the United States and, as we have seen, on the choices of U.S. sponsors. In this section we are concerned with the *self*-selection process, with decisions to immigrate taken by potential immigrants and the decisions by U.S. immigrants to remain or to leave.

Who Immigrates

It is reasonable to assume that potential migrants decide to immigrate or to move when predicted or expected well-being in the potential destination (the United States) exceeds predicted or expected well-being in the home country, less all costs of the move. This view of migration is enshrined in the Latin saying, *Ubi bene ibi patria,* "Where one is well off, there is one's country."

Well-being is shaped by many factors, religious and political as well as material. Moreover, the prospective immigrant's future well-being in the origin and destination countries is further shaped by personal endowments and characteristics and by the ability to predict future well-being. Thus, the benefits from migration will differ across individuals, and across countries, because of differences in migration costs, differences in the amount and type of benefits, and differences in the availability of information.

To illustrate how the interplay between origin-country conditions, migration costs, the characteristics of potential immigrants, and U.S. immigration laws influences the composition of immigrants, we use the basic notion that immigrants self-select themselves based on the net gains from immigration to consider the factors that influence the initial skill level of immigrants. We assume that countries may differ in the rewards paid per unit of skill (skill returns), that earnings are equal to the level of skill multiplied by the skill return, and that well-being is higher the higher are earnings, all else being the same.

An immediate implication of these assumptions is that, for given costs of migration, if skills are rewarded less in an origin country than in the United States, those with higher skill levels reap the greatest gains from migration. In this case, while earnings may be higher in the United States for all skill levels, the differential between the earnings of origin-country and U.S. workers is highest for the most skilled workers. Now consider the effects of migration costs on the skill composition of immigrants. For given differences in the rewards to skills across the United States and an origin country, a decline in migration costs will (1) increase the flows of immigrants from that country, since now the net benefit to migration will have increased, and (2) decrease the average skill level of immigrants. The latter occurs because those with lower skills would have incurred no gain from migration prior to the decline in migration costs.

The substantial increase in the flows of immigrants from Europe that took place beginning in 1900 has been attributed to a decline in the costs of a transoceanic voyage at that time. If so, consideration of the self-selection mechanisms suggests that more low-skill immigrants will be represented among the new immigrants of that period compared with those immigrants who came to the United States in prior years. In Table 1.8 we display the average literacy rates for the 1900 and 1910 new entrants from Europe, subdivided among those new entrants coming from the top three sending countries in the 1901–1910 period—Austria-Hungary, Italy, Russia—and from the rest of Europe. As can be seen in the table, the percentage of new entrants able to read and write was lower among the immigrants from Austria-Hungary, Italy, and Russia in both 1900 and 1910. However, the percentage of immigrants from those countries who arrived between 1905 and 1910 represented over 65 percent of all European new entrants of that cohort compared with slightly less than 50 percent of European new entrants who arrived between 1895 and 1900, prior to the large increase in immigration. Indeed, the large increase in the number of low-literacy immigrants induced efforts by U.S. residents (of older immigrant vintages) to impose literacy requirements on future immigrants, efforts that were ultimately embodied in a 1917 law (1917 Immigration Act) that required literacy tests for immigrants over age 16, except in cases of religious persecution.

Differences in migration costs across countries also appear to be strongly related to skill differences among U.S. immigrants. Costs of migrating are conventionally thought to be higher the greater the distance between origin and destination. But the requirements of immigration laws also differentiate migrants in terms of the costs of migration. The almost complete exclusion of immigrants from Asia, for example, prior to the 1965 Immigration Act meant that in the years immediately following the law change few

TABLE 1.8

Percent Literate of European Recent Entrants Aged 25–44 in 1900 and 1910

| | 1900 Recent Entrants | | | 1910 Recent Entrants | | |
	Reads	Writes	Share	Reads	Writes	Share
Austria-Hungary, Italy, Russia	54.8	52.6	49.5	69.1	66.8	65.4
Other Europe	84.4	83.3	50.5	90.1	89.2	34.6
Total Europe	69.7	68.1	100.0	76.4	74.5	100.0

SOURCE: U.S. Census of Population, Public Use Samples.

Asian immigrants could take advantage of the family reunification provisions of the new law. As a consequence, most Asian immigration (with the exception of those immigrating under refugee status) immediately following the 1965 Act was in the occupational preference categories in which, generally, low skills (unless in "short supply") are screened out. In this case, an increase in immigration was accompanied by an increase in skill level, because of the selectivity of immigration law. As Asian countries are also located farther from the United States than are other countries, one should not be surprised to find that Asian immigrants tend to be more skilled than immigrants from other countries, with immigrants from Western Hemisphere countries, dominated by immigration from Mexico (for which migration costs are low and skills are rewarded considerably less than in many countries), exhibiting the lowest skill levels.

Tables 1.9 and 1.10 display the average years of schooling for the new-entrant foreign-born aged 25–34 in the 1960, 1970, and 1980 censuses; that is, those foreign-born who entered the United States within five years of the census enumeration. Consistent with the distance-migration costs hypothesis, and within both sex groups, new entrants from Asia have the highest schooling levels and those from the Western Hemisphere the lowest in all three census years. The temporal pattern of schooling attainment for female new entrants also appears to reflect the effects of the 1965 immigration reforms. Asian-born women in 1970 who arrived immediately after the law change (in 1965–1969) had a significantly higher average schooling level (by 18 percent) than did Asian-born women in 1960 who arrived before the law change. This schooling differential between the Asian new entrants of 1960 and 1970 is higher than that for either the European or Western Hemisphere new entrants between the two census years. The increase in schooling attainment for Asian female new entrants between 1970 and 1980 is not nearly so great as that between 1960 and 1970. This reflects the substantially larger proportion of 1980 new entrants from Asia who were refugees (27.2 percent of Asian immigrants entering between 1978

TABLE 1.9

Average Years of Schooling of Recent-Entrant Men Aged 25–34,
by Area of Origin and Census Year

Characteristic	1960		1970		1980	
Asia	14.2	(14.1)a	14.2	(27.3)	14.2	(37.0)
Europe	10.9	(47.1)	11.1	(31.6)	13.4	(12.0)
Western Hemisphere	8.1	(36.8)	9.5	(34.7)	9.2	(37.2)
Other	11.4	(1.96)	12.5	(6.39)	13.5	(13.7)
Total Recent Entrants	10.3	(100.0)	11.5	(100.0)	12.2	(100.0)
Native-Born	10.8		11.7		13.3	

SOURCE: U.S. Census of Population, Public Use Samples.

aPercentage of total male recent entrants aged 25–34.

TABLE 1.10

Average Years of Schooling of Recent-Entrant Women Aged 25–34,
by Area of Origin and Census Year

Characteristic	1960		1970		1980	
Asia	10.6	(17.2)a	12.5	(23.9)	13.2	(40.7)
Europe	9.8	(54.6)	10.3	(34.0)	12.7	(12.7)
Western Hemisphere	9.1	(25.8)	8.9	(36.2)	9.4	(34.7)
Other	9.5	(2.3)	10.2	(5.9)	12.3	(11.8)
Total Recent Entrants	9.8	(100.0)	10.3	(100.0)	11.7	(100.0)
Native-Born	10.6		11.2		13.0	

SOURCE: U.S. Census of Population, Public Use Samples.

aPercentage of total female recent entrants aged 25–34.

and 1980 came in under the provisions of special refugee programs). The skill patterns exhibited in Tables 1.9 and 1.10 thus suggest that both the distance of an origin country from the United States and the number of U.S. citizens and prior immigrants from an individual's country—the number of potential immigrant sponsors—influence the characteristics of immigrants.

As noted above, another important feature of U.S. immigration law is that it permits the unlimited immigration of the foreign-born spouses of U.S. citizens. Thus, a side effect of placing a U.S. military base in a given country is to increase opportunities for citizens of that country to immigrate, and hence the flow of immigrants to the United States, as we show in Chapter 6. Accordingly, residents of countries that host U.S. military bases face lower direct immigration costs than do inhabitants of other countries, and thus they do not "require" as high returns to immigration as U.S. immigrants from other countries. We more rigorously examine the effects of these and other country characteristics on the earnings of the U.S. foreign-born in Chapter 7.

Information and Emigration Selectivity

If information about the United States is imperfectly distributed around the world, a U.S. immigrant's expected and actual post-immigration benefits from migration may differ. Those immigrants from countries with highly imperfect information will presumably make more errors in their migration decisions. In particular, some individuals will underestimate their well-being in the United States and will therefore not migrate, while other individuals will mistakenly migrate, having overestimated the migration benefit. Therefore, a migrant group from a low-information country is likely to fare less well in the United States than would an otherwise similar migrant group from a country with generally superior information about the United States.

For the subset of immigrants whose U.S. experience falls short of expectations, given unchanged home-country circumstances, a return home may be desirable. Such U.S. immigrants then compare realized well-being in the United States with *post-return* well-being at home. They re-migrate if the move, net of re-migration costs, provides a benefit. And re-migration by immigrants appears to be an important phenomenon, as discussed in Chapter 3.

If the selectivity of emigration and of information costs is considered, the effects of distance on the skill level of those immigrants who *remain* in the United States is unclear. While a country's distance from the United States serves to screen for high-skill immigrants (to the extent that distance adds to the costs of migration), if distance also impedes information dissemination, then immigrants from more distant countries may also be less informed about the United States and fare less well there as a consequence. Moreover, distance also serves as an impediment to return migration. Thus, immigrants who are from distant countries but who are less successful than are other immigrants may be more likely to remain in the United States. The average "progress" of an immigrant entry cohort from a distant country may thus appear to be less rapid than that of a cohort from a country more proximate to the United States even though the average "quality" of the latter may be initially lower.

Of course, distance is only one of a large number of variables influencing the direct costs of migration and information acquisition. Investments in information dissemination, such as in networks that broker information, may also be undertaken where payoffs to such institutions are high. Moreover, individuals differ by more than just general or even specific skill levels, although these variables are at least in part measured directly in census data. Differences in concern for children, in ambition, in willingness to delay consumption until the future (invest), and in altruistic feelings toward other family members also exist, and immigration and emigration are selective with respect to these characteristics as well. In subsequent chapters we specify in more detail, where relevant, how the migration decisions of individuals and families facing the sometimes changing constraints and opportunities of U.S. immigration laws are reflected in the levels and changes in the "selected" characteristics of the U.S. foreign-born.

Appendix

Principal Forms
Used in the Process of Obtaining an Immigrant Visa

Form I-130	Petition for Alien Relative
Form I-140	Petition for Prospective Immigrant Employee
Form I-485	Application for Permanent Residence
Form G-325A	Biographic Information

U.S. Department of Justice
Immigration and Naturalization Service INS

Petition for Alien Relative

Instructions

Read the instructions carefully. If you do not follow the instructions, we may have to return your petition, which may delay final action. If more space is needed to complete an answer continue on separate sheet of paper.

1. Who can file?

A citizen or lawful permanent resident of the United States can file this form to establish the relationship of certain alien relatives who may wish to immigrate to the United States. You must file a separate form for each eligible relative.

2. For whom can you file?

A. If you are a citizen, you may file this form for:
1) your husband, wife, or unmarried child under 21 years old
2) your unmarried child over 21, or married child of any age
3) your brother or sister if you are at least 21 years old
4) your parent if you are at least 21 years old.

B. If you are a lawful permanent resident you may file this form for:
1) your husband or wife
2) your unmarried child

NOTE: If your relative qualifies under instruction A(2) or A(3) above, separate petitions are not required for his or her husband or wife or unmarried children under 21 years old. If your relative qualifies under instruction B(2) above, separate petitions are not required for his or her unmarried children under 21 years old. These persons will be able to apply for the same type of immigrant visa as your relative.

3. For whom can you *not* file?.

You cannot file for people in the following categories:

4. What documents do you need?

You must give INS certain documents with this form to show you are eligible to file. You must also give the INS certain documents to prove the family relationship between you and your relative.

A. For each document needed, give INS the original and one copy. However, because it is against the law to copy a Certificate of Naturalization, a Certificate of Citizenship or an Alien Registration Receipt Card (Form I-151 or I-551), give INS the original only. **Originals will be returned to you.**

B. If you do not wish to give INS the original document, you may give INS a copy. The copy must be certified by:
1) an INS or U.S. consular officer, or
2) an attorney admitted to practice law in the United States, or
3) an INS accredited representative (INS may still require originals).

C. Documents in a foreign language must be accompanied by a complete English translation. The translator must certify that the translation is accurate and that he or she is competent to translate.

5. What documents do you need to show you are a United States citizen?

A. If you were born in the United States, give INS your birth certificate.

B. If you were naturalized, give INS your original Certificate of Naturalization.

C. If you were born outside the United States, and you are a U.S. citizen through your parents, give INS:
   1) your original Certificate of Citizenship, or
   2) your Form FS-240 (Report of Birth Abroad of a United States Citizen).

D. In place of any of the above, you may give INS your valid unexpired U.S. passport that was initially issued for at least 5 years.

E. If you do not have any of the above and were born in the United States, see the instructions under 8, below.. *"What if a document is not available?"*

6. What documents do you need to show you are a permanent resident?

You must give INS your alien registration receipt card (Form I-151 or Form I-551). Do not give INS a photocopy of the card.

7. What documents do you need to prove family relationship?

You have to prove that there is a family relationship between your relative and yourself.

In any case where a marriage certificate is required, if either the husband or wife was married before, you must give INS documents to show that all previous marriages were legally ended. In cases where the names shown on the supporting documents have changed, give INS legal documents to show how the name change occurred (for example a marriage certificate, adoption decree, court order, etc.)

Find the paragraph in the following list that applies to the relative you are filing for.

A. An adoptive parent or adopted child, if the adoption took place after the child became 16 years old, or if the child has not been in the legal custody and living with the parent(s) for at least two years.

B. A natural parent if the United States citizen son or daughter gained permanent residence through adoption.

C. A stepparent or stepchild, if the marriage that created this relationship took place after the child became 18 years old.

D. A husband or wife, if you were not both physically present at the marriage ceremony, and the marriage was not consummated.

E. A husband or wife if you gained lawful permanent resident status by virtue of a prior marriage to a United States citizen or lawful permanent resident unless:
   1) a period of five years has elapsed since you became a lawful permanent resident; OR
   2) you can establish by clear and convincing evidence that the prior marriage (through which you gained your immigrant status) was not entered into for the purpose of evading any provision of the immigration laws; OR
   3) your prior marriage (through which you gained your immigrant status) was terminated by the death of your former spouse.

F. A husband or wife if he or she was in exclusion, deportation, rescission, or judicial proceedings regarding his or her right to remain in the United States when the marriage took place, unless such spouse has resided outside the United States for a two-year period after the date of the marriage.

G. A husband or wife if the Attorney General has determined that such alien has attempted or conspired to enter into a marriage for the purpose of evading the immigration laws.

H. A grandparent, grandchild, nephew, niece, uncle, aunt, cousin, or in-law.

If you are filing for your:

A. **husband or wife,** give INS:
   1) your marriage certificate
   2) a color photo of you and one of your husband or wife, taken within 30 days of the date of this petition. These photos must have a white background. They must be glossy, un-retouched, and not mounted. The dimension of the facial image should be about 1 inch from chin to top of hair in 3/4 frontal view, showing the right side of the face with the right ear visible. Using pencil or felt pen, lightly print name (and Alien Registration Number, if known) on the back of each photograph.
   3) a completed and signed Form G-325A (Biographic Information) for you and one for your husband or wife. Except for name and signature, you do not have to repeat on the G-325A the information given on your I-130 petition.

B. **child** and you are the **mother,** give the child's birth certificate showing your name and the name of your child.

C. **child** and you are the **father or stepparent,** give the child's birth certificate showing both parents' names and your marriage certificate. **Child** born out of wedlock and you are the **father,** give proof that a parent/child relationship exists or existed. For example, the child's birth certificate showing your name and evidence that you have financially supported the child. (A blood test may be necessary).

D. **brother or sister,** your birth certificate and the birth certificate of your brother or sister showing both parents' names. If you do not have the same mother, you must also give the marriage certificates of your father to both mothers.

E. **mother,** give your birth certificate showing your name and the name of your mother.

F. **father,** give your birth certificate showing the names of both parents and your parents' marriage certificate.

G. **stepparent,** give your birth certificate showing the names of both natural parents and the marriage certificate of your parent to your stepparent.

9. How should you prepare this form?

A. Type or print legibly in ink.

B. If you need extra space to complete any item, attach a continuation sheet, indicate the item number, and date and sign each sheet.

C. Answer all questions fully and accurately. If any item does not apply, please write "N/A"

10. Where should you file this form?

A. If you live in the United States, send or take the form to the INS office that has jurisdiction over where you live.

B. If you live outside the United States, contact the nearest American Consulate to find out where to send or take the completed form.

11. What is the fee?

You must pay $35.00 to file this form. **The fee will not be refunded, whether the petition is approved or not.** DO NOT MAIL CASH. All checks or money orders, whether U.S. or foreign, must be payable in U.S. currency at a financial institution in the United States. When a check is drawn on the account of a person other than yourself, write your name on the face of the check. If the check is not honored, INS will charge you $5.00.

Pay by check or money order in the exact amount. Make the check or money order payable to "Immigration and Naturalization Service". However,

A. if you live in Guam: Make the check or money order payable to "Treasurer, Guam", or

B. if you live in the U.S. Virgin Islands: Make the check or money order payable to "Commissioner of Finance of the Virgin Islands"

12. When will a visa become available?

When a petition is approved for the husband, wife, parent, or unmarried minor child of a United States citizen, these relatives do not have to wait for a visa number, as they are not subject to the immigrant visa limit. However, for a child to

H. **adoptive parent or adopted child,** give a certified copy of the adoption decree, the legal custody decree if you obtained custody of the child before adoption, and a statement showing the dates and places you have lived together with the child.

8. What if a document is not available?.

If the documents needed above are not available, you can give INS the following instead. (INS may require a statement from the appropriate civil authority certifying that the needed document is not available.)

A. Church record: A certificate under the seal of the church where the baptism, dedication, or comparable rite occurred within two months after birth, showing the date and place of child's birth, date of the religious ceremony, and the names of the child's parents.

B. School record: A letter from the authorities of the school attended (preferably the first school), showing the date of admission to the school, child's date and place of birth, and the names and places of birth of parents, if shown in the school records.

C. Census record: State or federal census record showing the name, place of birth, and date of birth or the age of the person listed.

D. Affidavits: Written statements sworn to or affirmed by two persons who were living at the time and who have personal knowledge of the event you are trying to prove; for example, the date and place of birth, marriage, or death. The persons making the affidavits need not be citizens of the United States. Each affidavit should contain the following information regarding the person making the affidavit: his or her full name, address, date and place of birth, and his or her relationship to you, if any; full information concerning the event; and complete details concerning how the person acquired knowledge of the event.

qualify for this category, all processing must be completed and the child must enter the United States before his or her 21st birthday.

For all other alien relatives there are only a limited number of immigrant visas each year. The visas are given out in the order in which INS receives properly filed petitions. To be considered properly filed, a petition must be completed accurately and signed, the required documents must be attached, and the fee must be paid.

For a monthly update on dates for which immigrant visas are available, you may call (202) 663-1514.

13. What are the penalties for committing marriage fraud or submitting false information or both?

Title 8, United States Code, Section 1325 states that any individual who knowingly enters into a marriage contract for the purpose of evading any provision of the immigration laws shall be imprisoned for not more than five years, or fined not more than $250,000.00 or both.

Title 18, United States Code, Section 1001 states that whoever willfully and knowingly falsifies a material fact, makes a false statement, or makes use of a false document will be fined up to $10,000 or imprisoned up to five years, or both.

14. What is our authority for collecting this information?

We request the information on the form to carry out the immigration laws contained in Title 8, United States Code, Section 1154(a). We need this information to determine whether a person is eligible for immigration benefits. The information you provide may also be disclosed to other federal, state, local, and foreign law enforcement and regulatory agencies during the course of the investigation required by this Service. You do not have to give this information. However, if you refuse to give some or all of it, your petition may be denied.

It is not possible to cover all the conditions for eligibility or to give instructions for every situation. If you have carefully read all the instructions and still have questions, please contact your nearest INS office.

U.S. Department of Justice (INS)

Petition for Alien Relative

DO NOT WRITE IN THIS BLOCK — FOR EXAMINING OFFICE ONLY

Case ID#	Action Stamp	Fee Stamp

A#

G-28 or Volag #

Section of Law:

☐ 201 (b) spouse   ☐ 203 (a)(1)
☐ 201 (b) child   ☐ 203 (a)(2)
☐ 201 (b) parent   ☐ 203 (a)(4)
     ☐ 203 (a)(5)

AM CON: _____

REMARKS:

Petition was filed on _____ (priority date)

☐ Personal Interview   ☐ Previously Forwarded
☐ Pet. ☐ Ben. "A" File Reviewed   ☐ Stateside Criteria
☐ Field Investigations   ☐ I-485 Simultaneously
☐ 204 (a)(2)(A) Resolved   ☐ 204 (h) Resolved

A. Relationship

1. The alien relative is my:

☐ Husband/Wife   ☐ Parent   ☐ Brother/Sister   ☐ Child

2. Are you related by adoption?

☐ Yes   ☐ No

3. Did you gain permanent residence through adoption?

☐ Yes   ☐ No

B. Information about you

1. Name (Family name in CAPS)   (First)   (Middle)

2. Address (Number and Street)   (Apartment Number)

(Town or City)   (State/Country)   (ZIP/Postal Code)

3. Place of Birth (Town or City)   (State/Country)

4. Date of Birth (Mo/Day/Year)

5. Sex
☐ Male
☐ Female

6. Marital Status
☐ Married   ☐ Single
☐ Widowed   ☐ Divorced

C. Information about your alien relative

1. Name (Family name in CAPS)   (First)   (Middle)

2. Address (Number and Street)   (Apartment Number)

(Town or City)   (State/Country)   (ZIP/Postal Code)

3. Place of Birth (Town or City)   (State/Country)

4. Date of Birth (Mo/Day/Year)

5. Sex
☐ Male
☐ Female

6. Marital Status
☐ Married   ☐ Single
☐ Widowed   ☐ Divorced

7. Other Names Used (including maiden name)

8. Date and Place of Present Marriage (if married)

9. Social Security number   10. Alien Registration Number (if any)

11. Names of Prior Husbands/Wives   12. Date(s) Marriage(s) Ended

13. Has your relative ever been in the U.S.?
☐ Yes   ☐ No

14. If your relative is currently in the U.S., complete the following:
He or she last arrived as a (visitor, student, stowaway, without inspection, etc.)

Arrival/Departure Record (I-94) Number   Date arrived (Month/Day/Year)

Date authorized stay expired, or will expire as shown on Form I-94 or I-95

15. Name and address of present employer (if any)

Date this employment began (Month/Day/Year)

16. Has your relative ever been under immigration proceedings?
☐ Yes   ☐ No   Where _____   When _____
☐ Exclusion ☐ Deportation ☐ Rescission ☐ Judicial Proceedings

---

7. Other Names Used (including maiden name)

8. Date and Place of Present Marriage (if married)

9. Social Security number   10. Alien Registration Number (if any)

11. Names of Prior Husbands/Wives   12. Date(s) Marriage(s) Ended

13. If you are a U.S. citizen, complete the following:
My citizenship was acquired through (check one)
☐ Birth in the U.S.
☐ Naturalization
Give number of certificate, date and place it was issued

Parents
Have you obtained a certificate of citizenship in your own name?
☐ Yes   ☐ No
If "Yes," give number of certificate, date and place it was issued

14a. If you are a lawful permanent resident alien, complete the following:
Date and place of admission for, or adjustment to, lawful permanent residence, and class of admission:

14b. Did you gain permanent resident status through marriage to a United States citizen or lawful permanent resident?   ☐ Yes   ☐ No

Form I-130 (Rev. 02-28-87) N

INITIAL RECEIPT	RESUBMITTED	RELOCATED		COMPLETED		
		Rec'd	Sent	Approved	Denied	Returned

73

C. (Continued) information about your alien relative

16. **List husband/wife and all children of your relative** (if your relative is your husband/wife, list only his or her children).

Name	Relationship	Date of Birth	Country of Birth

17. **Address in the United States where your relative intends to reside**

_____ _____ _____
(Number and Street)   (Town or City)   (State)

18. **Your relative's address abroad**

_____ _____ _____
(Number and Street)   (Town or City)   (Province)   (Country)

19. **If your relative's native alphabet is other than Roman letters, write his/her name and address abroad in the native alphabet:**

_____ _____ _____
(Name)

_____ _____ _____
(Number and Street)   (Town or City)   (Province)   (Country)

20. **If filing for your husband/wife, give last address at which you both lived together:**

				From		To	
				(Month)	(Year)	(Month)	(Year)

_____ _____ _____
(Name)   (Apt. No.)   (Town or City)   (State or Province)   (Country)

21. **Check the appropriate box below and give the information required for the box you checked:**

☐ **Your relative will apply for a visa abroad at the American Consulate in** _____
(City)   (Country)

☐ Your relative is in the United States and will apply for adjustment of status to that of a lawful permanent resident in the office of the Immigration and Naturalization Service at _____ . If your relative is not eligible for adjustment of status, he or she will

(City)   (State)

apply for a visa abroad at the American Consulate in _____

(City)   (Country)

(Designation of a consulate outside the country of your relative's last residence does not guarantee acceptance for processing by that consulate. Acceptance is at the discretion of the designated consulate.)

D. Other Information

1. If separate petitions are also being submitted for other relatives, give names of each and relationship.

2. Have you ever filed a petition for this or any other alien before?   ☐ Yes   ☐ No

If "Yes," give name, place and date of filing, and result.

Warning: The INS investigates claimed relationships and verifies the validity of documents. The INS seeks criminal prosecutions when family relationships are falsified to obtain visas.

Penalties: You may, by law be imprisoned for not more than five years, or fined $250,000, or both, for entering into a marriage contract for the purpose of evading any provision of the immigration laws and you may be fined up to $10,000 or imprisoned up to five years or both, for knowingly and willfully falsifying or concealing a material fact or using any false document in submitting this petition.

Your Certification

I certify, under penalty of perjury under the laws of the United States of America, that the foregoing is true and correct. Furthermore, I authorize the release of any information from my records which the Immigration and Naturalization Service needs to determine eligibility for the benefit that I am seeking.

Signature _____   Date _____   Phone Number _____

Signature of Person Preparing Form if Other than Above

I declare that I prepared this document at the request of the person above and that it is based on all information of which I have any knowledge.

_____   _____   _____

(Signature)   (Date)

(Print Name)   (Address)

Volag Number _____   G-28 ID Number _____

NOTICE TO PERSONS FILING FOR SPOUSES IF MARRIED LESS THAN TWO YEARS

Pursuant to section 216 of the Immigration and Nationality Act, your alien spouse may be granted conditional permanent resident status in the United States as of the date he or she is admitted or adjusted to conditional status by an officer of the Immigration and Naturalization Service. Both you and your conditional permanent resident spouse are required to file a petition, Form I-751, Joint Petition to Remove Conditional Basis of Alien's Permanent Resident Status, during the ninety day period immediately before the second anniversary of the date your alien spouse was granted conditional permanent residence.

Otherwise, the rights, privileges, responsibilities and duties which apply to all other permanent residents apply equally to a conditional permanent resident. A conditional permanent resident is not limited to the right to apply for naturalization, to file petitions in behalf of qualifying relatives, or to reside permanently in the United States as an immigrant in accordance with the immigration laws.

> **Failure to file Form I-751, Joint Petition to Remove the Conditional Basis of Alien's Permanent Resident Status, will result in termination of permanent residence status and initiation of deportation proceedings.**

NOTE: You must complete Items 1 through 6 to assure that petition approval is recorded. Do not write in the section below item 6.

1. Name of relative (Family name in CAPS)   (First)   (Middle)

2. Other names used by relative (Including maiden name)

3. Country of relative's birth   4. Date of relative's birth (Month/Day/Year)

5. Your name (Last name in CAPS)   (First)   (Middle)   6. Your phone number

Action Stamp

SECTION	DATE PETITION FILED
☐ 201 (b)(spouse)	
☐ 201 (b)(child)	
☐ 201 (b)(parent)	
☐ 203 (a)(1)	
☐ 203 (a)(2)	☐ STATESIDE
☐ 203 (a)(4)	CRITERIA GRANTED
☐ 203 (a)(5)	SENT TO CONSUL AT:

CHECKLIST

Have you answered each question?
Have you signed the petition?
Have you enclosed:

☐ The filing fee for each petition?
☐ Proof of your citizenship or lawful permanent residence?
☐ All required supporting documents for each petition?

If you are filing for your husband or wife have you included:

☐ Your picture?
☐ His or her picture?
☐ Your G-325A?
☐ His or her G-325A?

Relative Petition Card
Form I-130A (Rev. 02-28-87) N

77

U.S. Department of Justice
Immigration and Naturalization Service (INS)

Petition for Prospective Immigrant Employee

Instructions

Read the instructions carefully. If you do not follow the instructions, we may have to return your petition which may delay final action.

Definitions

Third Preference Immigrant - A prospective employee who is a member of the professions, or who because of exceptional ability in the sciences or arts will substantially benefit the national economy, cultural interest, or welfare of the United States, and whose services are sought by an employer.

Sixth Preference Immigrant - A prospective employee who is capable of performing skilled or unskilled labor, not of a temporary or seasonal nature, for which there is a shortage of employable and willing persons in the United States.

Schedule A - A list of occupations for which it has already been determined that a shortage of U.S. workers exists. This list can be found in Title 20 CFR 656.10.

1. Who can file?

A. You may file this form under Third Preference if you are:

1) the prospective employer, or
2) the prospective employee, or
3) any other person applying on the prospective employee's behalf.

C. You must document the prospective employee's qualifications:

1) If the prospective employee's qualifications are based on education, give INS:

a) diploma(s) and

b) a certified copy of school transcript(s).

2) If the prospective employee's qualifications are based on exceptional ability in the sciences or arts, give INS evidence of national or international recognition such as awards, prizes, specific products, publications, memberships in a national or international association that maintains standards of outstanding achievement in a specific field, etc.

3) If the prospective employee's qualifications are based on a profession requiring a license or other official permission to practice, give INS a copy of the license or other official permission.

4) If the prospective employee's qualifications are based on technical training or specialized experience, give INS affidavits or published material supporting this training or experience.

B. You may file this form under Sixth Preference only if you are the prospective employee's prospective employer.

If the petition is approved, the husband or wife and unmarried children under 21 years of age of the prospective employee will automatically be eligible to apply for a visa.

2. What documents do you need?

A. 1) In general, you must give INS certain documents with this form. For each document needed, give INS the original and one copy. **Originals will be returned to you.**

2) If you do not wish to give an original document, you may give INS a copy. The copy must be certified by:

a) an INS or U.S. consular officer, or

b) an attorney admitted to practice law in the United States, or

c) an INS accredited representative

(INS still may require originals).

3) Documents in a foreign language must be accompanied by a complete English translation. The translator must certify that the translation is accurate and that he or she is competent to translate.

B. You must give INS a completed Form ETA–750A&B "Application for Alien Employment Certification" bearing the Department of Labor's certification, unless the occupation is currently listed in Schedule A (see definitions).

5) For physicians or surgeons, also give INS:

a) the results of Parts 1 and 2 of the National Board of Medical Examiners Examination, the Visa Qualifying Examination, or Foreign Medical Graduate Examination in Medical Sciences.

b) evidence of competency in oral and written English.

D. The prospective employer must give INS documentary evidence that establishes ability to pay the offered wage (e.g., latest annual report, last U.S. tax return, profit/loss statement, etc.)

E. Affidavits - These must come from independent sources, such as the prospective employee's former employers or recognized experts familiar with the prospective employee's work. The affidavits must:

a) identify the person making the affidavit, showing the capacity in which he or she is testifying

b) give the places and the dates during which the prospective employee gained his or her experience

c) describe in detail the duties the prospective employee performed, the tools he or she used, how he or she was supervised, and any supervisory tasks that he or she performed. A mere statement, for example, that the prospective employee was employed as a baker, is not adequate.

d) show the date on which the affidavit was signed.

3. How should you prepare this form?

A. Type or print legibly in ink.

I-140

B. If you need extra space to complete any item, attach a continuation sheet, indicate the item number, and date and sign each sheet.

C. Answer all questions fully and accurately. If any item does not apply, please write "N/A".

4. Where should you file this form?

A. If you are in the United States, send or take the completed form and supporting documents to the INS office that has jurisdiction over the place of intended employment.

B. If you are outside the United States, contact the nearest American Consulate to find out where to send the completed form.

5. When will a visa become available?

The availability of an immigrant visa number depends on the number of aliens in the same visa classification who have an earlier priority date (date for which visas are available) on the visa waiting list.

Visa numbers are given out in the order in which Forms ETA-750A&B are filed with the Department of Labor or the order in which they are properly filed with INS in Schedule A cases. Since these numbers are limited each year, it is important to make sure the form is properly filed to put the prospective employee on the waiting list at the earliest possible date. To be properly filed, the form must be complete, the necessary documents must be signed, the necessary documents must be attached, and the fee must be paid. For a monthly update on dates for which immigrant visas are available, you may call (202) 632-2919.

refunded, **whether the petition is approved or not**. DO NOT MAIL CASH. All checks or money orders, whether U.S. or foreign, must be payable in U.S. currency at a financial institution in the United States. When a check is drawn on the account of a person other than yourself, write your name on the face of the check. If the check is not honored, INS will charge you $5.00.

Pay by check or money order in the exact amount. Make the check or money order payable to "Immigration and Naturalization Service". However,

A. if you live in Guam: Make the check or money order payable to "Treasurer, Guam", or

B. if you live in the U.S. Virgin Islands: Make the check or money order payable to "Commissioner of Finance of the Virgin Islands".

7. What are the penalties for submitting false information?

Title 18, United States Code, Section 1001 states that whoever willfully and knowingly falsifies a material fact, makes a false statement, or makes use of a false document will be fined up to $10,000 or imprisoned up to five years, or both.

8. What is our authority for collecting this information?

We request the information on this form to carry out the immigration laws contained in Title 8, United States Code, Section 1154(a). We need this information to determine whether a person is eligible for immigration benefits. The information you provide may also be disclosed to other federal, state, local, and foreign law enforcement and regulatory agencies during the course of the investigation required by this Service. You do not have to give this information. However, if you refuse to give some or all of it, your petition may be denied.

6. What is the fee?

You must pay $35.00 to file this form. **The fee will not be**

It is not possible to cover all the conditions for eligibility or to give instructions for every situation. If you have carefully read all the instructions and still have questions, please contact your nearest INS office.

U.S. Department of Justice
Immigration and Naturalization Service (INS)

Petition for Prospective Immigrant Employee

OMB # 1115-0061
Expires 4/86

DO NOT WRITE IN THIS BLOCK

Case ID#

A#

G-28 or Volag#

_____
(Priority Date)

Action Stamp

Fee Stamp

Petition was filed on.

Petition is approved for status under section:
- ☐ 203(a)(3)
- ☐ 203(a)(6)

Section 212(a)(14) certification
- ☐ Attached
- ☐ Sched. A. Group _____

A. Information about this petition

This petition is being filed for a:
- ☐ 3rd Preference Immigrant
- ☐ 6th Preference Immigrant

(See instructions for definitions and check one block only)

B. Information about employer

1. Name (Family name in CAPS) (First) (Middle)   or   (Company Name)

2. Address (Number and Street)

_____   _____   _____
(Town or City)   (State/Country)   (ZIP/Postal Code)

3. Address where employee will work (If different)
(Number and Street)

_____   _____   _____
(Town or City)   (State/Country)   (ZIP/Postal Code)

C. Information about prospective employee

1. Name (Family name in CAPS) (First)   (Middle)

2. Address (Number and Street)   (Apartment Number)

_____   _____   _____
(Town or City)   (State/Country)   (ZIP/Postal Code)

3. Place of Birth (Town or City)   (State/Country)

4. Date of Birth
(Mo/Day/Yr)

5. Sex
- ☐ Male
- ☐ Female

6. Marital Status
- ☐ Married ☐ Single
- ☐ Widowed ☐ Divorced

I-140

83

Form I-140 (08-01-85) N

---

4. **Employer is:** (check one)
   - ☐ an organization
   - ☐ a permanent resident
   - ☐ a U.S. citizen
   - ☐ a nonimmigrant

5. **Social Security Number**   or   **IRS employer ID number**

6. **Alien Registration Number** (if any)

7. **Description of Business** (Nature, number of employees, gross and net annual income, date established) (If employer is an individual, state occupation and annual income).

8. **Have you ever filed a visa petition for an alien employee in this same capacity?**
   - ☐ Yes   ☐ No   (If Yes, how many?)

9. **Are you and the prospective employee related by birth or marriage?**
   - ☐ Yes   ☐ No

10. **Are separate petitions being filed at this time for other aliens?**
   - ☐ Yes   ☐ No   (If Yes, list names)

11. **Title and salary of position offered**

12. Is the position permanent?   ☐ Yes   ☐ No

13. Is the position full-time?   ☐ Yes   ☐ No

14. Is this a newly-created position?   ☐ Yes   ☐ No
    (If No, how long has it existed?)

---

7. **Other names used** (including maiden name)

8. **Profession or occupation and years held**

9. **Social Security Number**   10. **Alien Registration Number** (if any)

11. **Name and address of present employer** (Name)

   (Number and Street)

   (Town or City)   (State/Country)   (ZIP/Postal Code)

12. **Date employee began present employment**

13. **If employee is currently in the U.S., complete the following:**
    He or she last arrived as a (visitor, student, exchange alien, crewman, stowaway, temporary worker, without inspection, etc.)

   Arrival/Departure Record (I-94) Number   Date arrived (Month/Day/Year)

   Date authorized stay expired, or will expire as shown on Form I-94 or I-95

14. **Has a visa petition ever been filed by or on behalf of this person?**
    - ☐ Yes   ☐ No   (If Yes, explain)

RESUBMITTED	RELOCATED		COMPLETED		
	Rec'd	Sent	Approved	Denied	Returned
INITIAL RECEIPT					

C. (continued) Information about prospective employee

15. List husband/wife and all children of prospective employee

Name	Relationship	Date of Birth	Country of Birth	Present Address

16. Employee's address abroad

_____ _____ _____
(Number and Street)   (Town or City)   (Province)   (Country)

17. If your employee's native alphabet is other than Roman letters, write his/her name and address abroad in the native alphabet:

_____ _____ _____
(Name)   (Number and Street)   (Town or City)   (Province)   (Country)

18. Check the appropriate box below and give the information required for the box you checked:

☐ The employee will apply for a visa abroad at the American Consulate in _____

_____
(City)   (Country)

☐ The employee is in the United States and will apply for adjustment of status to that of a lawful resident in the office of the Immigration and Naturalization

Service at _____ If the employee is not eligible for adjustment of status, he or she will apply
(City)   (State)

for a visa abroad at the American Consulate in _____

_____
(City)   (Country)

Warning: The INS investigates employment experience. If the INS finds that employment experience is false, the application is denied and the person responsible for providing false information may be criminally prosecuted.

Penalties: You may, by law, be fined up to $10,000, imprisoned up to five years, or both, for knowingly and willfully falsifying or concealing a material fact or using any false document in submitting this petition.

Your Certification

This petition may only be filed by one of the following:

I am
☐ the employer
☐ the prospective employee (only allowed for 3rd preference)
☐ a person filing on behalf of and authorized by the prospective employee (only allowed for 3rd preference)

I certify, under penalty of perjury under the laws of the United States of America, that the foregoing is true and correct. Furthermore, I authorize the release of any information from my records which the Immigration and Naturalization Service needs to determine eligibility for the benefit that I am seeking.

Print Name _____ Title _____

Signature _____ Date _____ Phone Number _____

Signature of Person Preparing Form if Other than Above

I declare that I prepared this document at the request of the person above and that it is based on all information of which I have any knowledge.

_____   _____   _____
(Print Name)   (Signature)   (Date)

_____   G-28 ID Number _____
(Address)
                                           Volag Number _____

I-140

85

U.S. Department of Justice

Immigration and Naturalization Service (INS)

Application for Permanent Residence

Instructions

Read the instructions carefully. If you do not follow the instructions, we may have to return your application, which may delay final action.

You will be required to appear before an Immigration Officer to answer questions about this application. You must bring your temporary entry permit (Form I-94, Arrival Departure Record) and your passport to your interview.

If you plan to leave the U.S. to any country, including Canada or Mexico, before a decision is made on your application, contact the INS Office processing your Application for Permanent Residence before you depart, since a departure from the U.S. without written authorization will result in the termination of your application.

1. Who can apply?

You are eligible to apply for lawful permanent residence if you are in the U.S. and you:

A. have an immigrant visa number immediately available to you (see below - "When will a visa become available?"), or

B. entered with a fiance(e) visa and have married within ninety days, or

C. have been granted asylum by the INS or an immigration judge one year or more ago, or

D. are a member of a class of "special immigrants" which includes certain ministers of religion, certain former employees of the United States government abroad, certain retired officers or employees of international organizations, certain immediate relatives of officers or

E. were in transit through the United States without a visa, or

F. were admitted as a crewman of either a vessel or an aircraft.

NOTE: If you are included under 2 above but have lived here continuously since before January 1, 1972 or are applying under the Cuban/Haitian provisions, you may still apply.

3. When will a visa become available?

If you are applying for a permanent residence as the relative of a U.S. citizen or lawful permanent resident, or as an immigrant employee, an immigrant visa petition (I-130 or I-140) must have been filed (or must be filed with your application). In addition, an immigrant visa number must be immediately available to you.

If you are the husband, wife, parent or minor unmarried child of a U.S. citizen, a visa is immediately available to you when your U.S. citizen relative's petition, Form I-130, for you is approved.

employees of international organizations, and certain physicians who were licensed to practice medicine in the United States prior to January 8, 1978, or

E. have resided continuously in the United States since before January 1, 1972, or

F. are filing a motion before an immigration judge, or

G. are a former foreign government official, or a member of the immediate family of that official, or

H. received the designation "Cuban/Haitian Entrant (Status Pending)" or are a national of Cuba or Haiti who arrived before January 1, 1982 who had an INS record established before that date, and who (unless you have filed for asylum prior to January 1, 1982) was not admitted to the U.S. as a nonimmigrant. You must apply prior to November 6, 1988.

2. Who may not apply?

You are not eligible for lawful permanent residence if you entered the United States and you:

A. were not inspected and admitted or paroled by a United States Immigration Officer, or

B. continued in or accepted unauthorized employment, on or before January 1, 1977, unless you are the spouse, parent, or child of a United States citizen, or

C. are not in legal immigration status on the date of filing your application, or have failed (other than through no fault of your own for technical reasons) to maintain continuously a legal status since entry into the United States, unless you are the spouse, parent, or child of a United States citizen, or

D. are an exchange visitor subject to the two-year foreign residence requirement, or

FORM I-485 (REV. 2-27-87)N

For all other applicants,, the availability of visa numbers is based on priority dates, which are determined by the filing of immigrant visa applications or labor certifications. When the priority date is reached for your approved petition, a visa number is immediately available to you. For a monthly update of the dates for which visa numbers are available, you may call (202)663-1514.

4. What documents do you need?

A. 1) For each document needed, give INS the original and one copy. **Originals will be returned to you.**

2) If you do not wish to give INS an original document, you may give INS a copy. The copy must be certified by:

a) an INS or U.S. consular officer, or

b) an attorney admitted to practice law in the United States, or

c) an INS accredited representative

(INS still may require originals)

3) Documents in a foreign language must be accompanied by a complete English translation. The translator must certify that the translation is accurate and that he or she is competent to translate.

B. You must also give INS the following documents:

1) Your birth certificate.

2) If you are between 14 and 79 years of age, Form G-325A (Biographic Information).

3) a) If you are employed, a letter from your present employer showing that you have employment of a permanent nature.

7. **Medical Examination**

Unless you are applying as a fiance(e) or dependent, or as an individual who has lived here continuously since before January 1, 1972, you will be required to have a medical examination in conjuction with this application. You may find out more from the INS office that will handle your application.

8. **How should you prepare this form?**

A. Type or print clearly in ink.

B. If you need extra space to complete any item, attach a continuation sheet, indicate the item number, and date and sign each sheet.

C. Answer all questions fully and accurately. If any item does not apply, please write "N/A".

9. **Where must you file?**

You must send or take this form and any other required documents to the INS office that has jurisdiction over the place where you live. You will be interviewed. You must bring your temporary entry permit (Form I-94, Arrival Departure Record), and your passport to your interview.

10. **What is the fee?**

You must pay $50.00 to file this form, unless you are filing under the Cuban/Haitian provisions. **The fee will not be refunded, whether your application is approved or not.** DO NOT MAIL CASH. All checks or money orders, whether U.S. or foreign, must be payable in U.S. currency at a financial institution in the United States. When a check is drawn on the account of a person other than yourself, write your name on the face of the check. If the check is not honored, INS will charge you $5.00.

b) If you are not employed in a permanent job, a Form I-134 (Affadavit of Support) from a responsible person in the United States or other evidence to show that you are not likely to become a public charge.

4) If your husband or wife is filing an application for permanent residence with yours, he or she also must give INS your marriage certificate and proof for both of you that all prior marriages have been legally ended.

5) If your child is filing an application for permanent residence with yours, he or she also must give INS your marriage certificate and proof that all prior marriages for you and your husband or wife have been legally ended, unless those documents are being submitted with your husband or wife's application.

C. If you entered the U.S. as a fiance(e), give INS your marriage certificate. If you are the child of a fiance(e), give INS your birth certificate and the marriage certificate for your parent's present marriage.

D. If you have resided in the United States continuously since before January 1, 1972, give INS documentary evidence of that fact. Some examples of records that can be used to prove residence are bank, real estate, census, school, insurance, or business records, affidavits of credible witnesses, or any other document that relates to you and shows evidence of your presence in the United States during this period.

E. If you have resided in the United States continuously since before July 1, 1924, INS may be able to create a record of your lawful admission as of the date of your entry. Therefore, if you have resided continuously in the United States since a date before July 1, 1924, it is very important to give evidence establishing that fact.

F.   If you are a foreign government official or a representative to an international organization, a member of the family, or a treaty trader or treaty investor or the spouse or child of that person, you must give INS Form I-508. Form I-508 waives all rights, privileges, exemptions, and immunities which you would otherwise have because of that status.

5.   Photographs

Give INS two color photographs of yourself taken within 30 days of the date of this application. These photos must have a white background. They must be glossy, un-retouched, and not mounted. The dimension of the facial image must be about 1 inch from the chin to the top of the hair; your face should be in ¾ frontal view, showing the right side of the face with the right ear visible. Using pencil or felt pen, lightly print your name on the back of each photograph.

6.   Fingerprints

Give INS a completed fingerprint card (Form FD-258) for each applicant between 14 and 79 years of age. Applicants may be fingerprinted by INS employees, other law enforcement officers, outreach centers, charitable and voluntary agencies, or other reputable persons or organizations. The fingerprint card (FD-258), the ink used, and the quality of the prints must meet standards prescribed by the Federal Bureau of Investigation. You must sign the card in the presence of the person taking your fingerprints. That person must then sign his or her name and enter the date in the spaces provided. It is important to give all the information called for on the card.

Pay by check or money order in the exact amount. Make the check or money order payable to "Immigration and Naturalization Service". However,

A.   if you live in Guam: Make the check or money order payable to "Treasurer, Guam", or

B.   if you live in the U.S. Virgin Islands: Make the check or money order payable to "Commissioner of Finance of the Virgin Islands".

11.   What are the penalties for submitting false information?

Title 18, United States Code, Section 1001 states that whoever willfully and knowingly falsifies a material fact, makes a false statement, or makes use of a false document will be fined up to $10,000 or imprisoned up to five years, or both.

12.   What is our authority for collecting this information?

We request the information on this form to carry out the immigration laws contained in Title 8, United States Code, Section 1255. We need this information to determine whether a person is eligible for immigration benefits. The information you provide may also be disclosed to other federal, state, local, and foreign law enforcement and regulatory agencies during the course of the investigation required by this Service. You do not have to give this information. However, if you refuse to give some or all of it, your application may be denied.

It is not possible to cover all the conditions for eligibility or to give instructions for every situation. If you have questions and still have questions, please contact your nearest INS office.

U.S. Department of Justice

Immigration and Naturalization Service (INS)

Application for Permanent Residence

OMB # 1115-0053

DO NOT WRITE IN THIS BLOCK

Case ID#	Action Stamp
A#	
G-28 or Volag#	

Fee Stamp

Section of Law

☐ Sec. 209(b). INA
☐ Sec. 214(d). INA
☐ Sec. 13. Act of 9/11/57
☐ Sec. 245. INA
☐ Sec. 249. INA

_____
Country Chargeable

Eligibility Under Sec. 245

☐ Approved Visa Petition
☐ Dependent of Principal Alien
☐ Special Immigrant
☐ Other _____

_____
Preference

A. Reason for this application

I am applying for lawful permanent residence for the following reason: (check the box that applies)

1. ☐ **An immigrant visa number is immediately available to me because**

    ☐ **A visa petition has already been approved for me** (approval notice is attached)

    ☐ **A visa petition is being filed with this application**

2. ☐ **I entered as the fiance(e) of a U.S. citizen and married within 90 days** (approval notice and marriage certificate are attached)

3. ☐ **I am an asylee eligible for adjustment**

4. ☐ **Other:** _____

B. Information about you

1. **Name** (Family name in CAPS)   (First)   (Middle)

2. **Address** (Number and Street)   (Apartment Number)

11. **On what date did you last enter the U.S.?**

12. **Where did you last enter the U.S.?** (City and State)

(Town or City)

3. **Place of Birth** (Town or City)   (State/Country)   (State/Country)   (ZIP/Postal Code)

4. **Date of Birth**   5. **Sex**   6. **Marital Status**
(Mo/Day/Yr)   ☐ Male   ☐ Married   ☐ Single
                     ☐ Female   ☐ Widowed   ☐ Divorced

7. **Social Security Number**   8. **Alien Registration Number** (if any)

9. **Country of Citizenship**

10. **Have you ever applied for permanent resident status in the U.S.?**
☐ Yes ☐ No
(If Yes, give the date and place of filing and final disposition)

20. **Have you ever been married before?**   ☐ Yes   ☐ No
If Yes.   (Names of prior husbands/wives)

21. **Has your husband/wife ever been married before?**   ☐ Yes   ☐ No
If Yes.   (Names of prior husbands/wives)

FORM I-485 (REV. 2-27-87)N

---

13. **What means of travel did you use?** (Plane, car, etc.)

14. **Were you inspected by a U.S. immigration officer?**
☐ Yes ☐ No

15. **In what status did you last enter the U.S.?**
(Visitor, student, exchange alien, crewman, temporary worker, without inspection, etc.)

16. **Give your name EXACTLY as it appears on your Arrival/Departure Record (Form I-94).**

17. **Arrival/Departure Record (I-94) Number**   18. **Visa Number**

19. **At what Consulate was your nonimmigrant visa issued?**   **Date** (Mo/Day/Yr)

(Date marriage ended)

(Country of citizenship)

(Date marriage ended)

(Country of citizenship)

91

22. List your present husband/wife, all of your sons and daughters, all of your brothers and sisters (If you have none, write "N/A")

Name	Relationship	Place of Birth	Date of Birth	Country of Residence	Applying With You?
					☐ Yes ☐ No
					☐ Yes ☐ No
					☐ Yes ☐ No
					☐ Yes ☐ No
					☐ Yes ☐ No
					☐ Yes ☐ No
					☐ Yes ☐ No
					☐ Yes ☐ No
					☐ Yes ☐ No
					☐ Yes ☐ No

23. List your present and past membership in or affiliation with every organization, association, fund, foundation, party, club, society or similar group in the United States or in any other country or place, and your foreign military service (If this does not apply, write "N/A")

A. _____ 19 _____ to 19 _____

B. _____ 19 _____ to 19 _____

C. _____ 19 _____ to 19 _____

D. _____ 19 _____ to 19 _____

E. _____ 19 _____ to 19 _____

F. _____ 19 _____ to 19 _____

G. _____ 19 _____ to 19 _____

24. Have you ever, in or outside the United States:

a) knowingly committed any crime for which you have not been arrested? ☐ Yes ☐ No

b) been arrested, cited, charged, indicted, convicted, fined, or imprisoned for breaking or violating any law or ordinance, including traffic regulations? ☐ Yes ☐ No

c) been the beneficiary of a pardon, amnesty, rehabilitation decree, other act of clemency or similar action? ☐ Yes ☐ No

If you answered Yes to (a), (b), or (c) give the following information about each incident:

Date	Place (City)	(State/Country)	Nature of offense	Outcome of case, if any

1) _____
2) _____
3) _____
4) _____
5) _____

25. Have you ever received public assistance from any source, including the U.S. Government or any state, county, city or municipality?

☐ Yes   ☐ No   (If Yes, explain, including the name(s) and Social Security number(s) you used.)

---

26. Do any of the following relate to you? (Answer Yes or No to each)

A. Have you been treated for a mental disorder, drug addiction, or alcoholism?   ☐ Yes ☐ No

B. Have you engaged in, or do you intend to engage in, any commercialized sexual activity?   ☐ Yes ☐ No

C. Are you or have you at any time been an anarchist, or a member of or affiliated with any Communist or other totalitarian party, including any subdivision or affiliate?   ☐ Yes ☐ No

D. Have you advocated or taught, by personal utterance, by written or printed matter, or through affiliation with an organization:

1) opposition to organized government   ☐ Yes ☐ No

2) the overthrow of government by force or violence   ☐ Yes ☐ No

3) the assaulting or killing of government officials because of their official character   ☐ Yes ☐ No

4) the unlawful destruction of property   ☐ Yes ☐ No

5) sabotage   ☐ Yes ☐ No

6) the doctrines of world communism, or the establishment of a totalitarian dictatorship in the United States?   ☐ Yes ☐ No

E. Have you engaged or do you intend to engage in prejudicial activities or unlawful activities of a subversive nature?   ☐ Yes ☐ No

F. During the period beginning March 23, 1933, and ending May 8, 1945, did you order, incite, assist, or otherwise participate in persecuting any person because of race, religion, national origin, or political opinion, under the direction of, or in association with any of the following:

1) the Nazi government in Germany   ☐ Yes ☐ No

2) any government in any area occupied by the military forces of the Nazi government in Germany   ☐ Yes ☐ No

3) any government established with the assistance or cooperation of the Nazi government of Germany   ☐ Yes ☐ No

4) any government that was an ally of the Nazi government of Germany   ☐ Yes ☐ No

G. Have you been convicted of a violation of any law or regulation relating to narcotic drugs or marijuana, or have you been an illicit trafficker in narcotic drugs or marijuana?   ☐ Yes ☐ No

93

H. Have you been involved in assisting any other aliens to enter the United States in violation of the law? ☐ Yes ☐ No

I. Have you applied for exemption or discharge from training or service in the Armed Forces of the United States on the ground of alienage and have you been relieved or discharged from that training or service? ☐ Yes ☐ No

J. Are you mentally retarded, insane, or have you suffered one or more attacks of insanity? ☐ Yes ☐ No

K. Are you afflicted with psychopathic personality, sexual deviation, mental defect, narcotic drug addiction, chronic alcoholism, or any dangerous contagious disease? ☐ Yes ☐ No

L. Do you have a physical defect, disease, or disability affecting your ability to earn a living? ☐ Yes ☐ No

M. Are you a pauper, professional beggar, or vagrant? ☐ Yes ☐ No

N. Are you likely to become a public charge? ☐ Yes ☐ No

O. Are you a polygamist or do you advocate polygamy? ☐ Yes ☐ No

P. Have you been excluded from the United States within the past year, or have you at any time been deported from the United States or have you at any time been removed from the United States at government expense? ☐ Yes ☐ No

Q. Have you procured or have you attempted to procure a visa by fraud or misrepresentation? ☐ Yes ☐ No

R. Are you a former exchange visitor who is subject to, but has not complied with, the two-year foreign residence requirement? ☐ Yes ☐ No

S. Are you a medical graduate coming principally to work as a member of the medical profession, without passing Parts I and II of the National Board of Medical Examiners Examination (or an equivalent examination)? ☐ Yes ☐ No

T. Have you left the United States to avoid military service in time of war or national emergency? ☐ Yes ☐ No

U. Have you committed or have you been convicted of a crime involving moral turpitude? ☐ Yes ☐ No

If you answered Yes to any question above, explain fully (Attach a continuation sheet if necessary):

27. ☐ Completed Form G-325A (Biographic Information) is signed, dated and attached as part of this application. Print or type so that all copies are legible.   ☐ Completed form G-325A (Biographic Information) is not attached because applicant is under 14 or over 79 years of age.

Penalties: You may, by law, be fined up to $10,000, imprisoned up to five years, or both, for knowingly and willfully falsifying or concealing a material fact or using any false document in submitting this application.

94

Your Certification

I certify, under penalty of perjury under the laws of the United States of America, that the above information is true and correct. Furthermore, I authorize the release of any information from my records which the Immigration and Naturalization Service needs to determine eligibility for the benefit that I am seeking.

Signature _____ Date _____ Phone Number _____

Signature of Person Preparing Form if Other than Above

I declare that I prepared this document at the request of the person above and that it is based on all information of which I have any knowledge.

_____ _____ _____
(Print Name)   (Signature)   (Date)

G-28 ID Number _____

Volag Number _____

_____
(Address)

Stop Here

*(Applicant is **not** to sign the application below until he or she appears before an officer of the Immigration and Naturalization Service for examination)*

I, _____ swear (affirm) that I know the contents of this application that I am signing including the attached documents, that they are true to the best of my knowledge, and that corrections numbered ( ) to ( ) were made by me or at my request, and that I signed this application with my full, true name:

_____
(Complete and true signature of applicant)

Signed and sworn to before me by the above-named applicant at _____ on _____
                                                                          (Month)   (Day)   (Year)

_____
(Signature and title of officer)

GPO : 1987 - 177-424

95

INSTRUCTIONS. USE TYPEWRITER. BE SURE ALL COPIES ARE LEGIBLE. Failure to answer fully all questions delays action.
Do Not Remove Carbons: If typewriter is not available, print heavily in block letters with ball-point pen.

★ U.S.GPO:1987-0-169-462

For sale by the Superintendent of Documents, U.S. Government Printing Office, Washington, D.C. 20402 (Per 100)

U.S. Department of Justice
Immigration and Naturalization Service

FORM G-325A

OMB No. 1115-0066
Approval expires 4-30-85

BIOGRAPHIC INFORMATION

(Family name)	(First name)	(Middle name)	□ MALE □ FEMALE	BIRTHDATE(Mo.-Day-Yr.)	NATIONALITY	FILE NUMBER A

ALL OTHER NAMES USED (Including names by previous marriages)

CITY AND COUNTRY OF BIRTH

SOCIAL SECURITY NO. (If any)

	FAMILY NAME	FIRST NAME	DATE, CITY AND COUNTRY OF BIRTH(If known)	CITY AND COUNTRY OF RESIDENCE.

FATHER
MOTHER(Maiden name)

HUSBAND(If none, so state) OR WIFE	FAMILY NAME (For wife, give maiden name)	FIRST NAME	BIRTHDATE	CITY & COUNTRY OF BIRTH	DATE OF MARRIAGE	PLACE OF MARRIAGE

FORMER HUSBANDS OR WIVES(if none, so state)

FAMILY NAME (For wife, give maiden name)	FIRST NAME	BIRTHDATE	DATE & PLACE OF MARRIAGE	DATE AND PLACE OF TERMINATION OF MARRIAGE

APPLICANT'S RESIDENCE LAST FIVE YEARS. LIST PRESENT ADDRESS FIRST.

STREET AND NUMBER	CITY	PROVINCE OR STATE	COUNTRY	FROM MONTH	YEAR	TO MONTH	YEAR
						PRESENT TIME	

APPLICANT'S LAST ADDRESS OUTSIDE THE UNITED STATES OF MORE THAN ONE YEAR

STREET AND NUMBER	CITY	PROVINCE OR STATE	COUNTRY	FROM MONTH	YEAR	TO MONTH	YEAR

96

APPLICANT'S EMPLOYMENT LAST FIVE YEARS. (IF NONE, SO STATE.) LIST PRESENT EMPLOYMENT FIRST

FULL NAME AND ADDRESS OF EMPLOYER	OCCUPATION(SPECIFY)	FROM		TO	
		MONTH	YEAR	MONTH	YEAR
				PRESENT TIME	

Show below last occupation abroad if not shown above. (Include all information requested above.)

THIS FORM IS SUBMITTED IN CONNECTION WITH APPLICATION FOR: | SIGNATURE OF APPLICANT

☐ NATURALIZATION ☐ STATUS AS PERMANENT RESIDENT

☐ OTHER (SPECIFY):

DATE

Are all copies legible? ☐ Yes

IF YOUR NATIVE ALPHABET IS IN OTHER THAN ROMAN LETTERS, WRITE YOUR NAME IN YOUR NATIVE ALPHABET IN THIS SPACE.

PENALTIES: SEVERE PENALTIES ARE PROVIDED BY LAW FOR KNOWINGLY AND WILLFULLY FALSIFYING OR CONCEALING A MATERIAL FACT.

APPLICANT: BE SURE TO PUT YOUR NAME AND ALIEN REGISTRATION NUMBER IN THE BOX OUTLINED BY HEAVY BORDER BELOW.

COMPLETE THIS BOX (Family name)   (Given name)   (Middle name)   (Alien registration number)

97

2

TAKING ROOT: NATURALIZATION

ADMISSION to permanent resident alien status marks the beginning of the immigrant career—of the process of social, economic, and political integration into the United States. For some immigrants, permanent residence status is indeed "permanent," lasting until death. For others, immigrant status is a transitory state culminating in either citizenship or emigration. In this chapter we examine naturalization and in the next chapter we consider emigration.

There are two reasons to begin a study of immigrant behavior with what for many immigrants is the end point of their immigrant status. First, as we have stressed, most immigrants are sponsored by U.S. citizens as a consequence of the family reunification provisions of immigration law. If we view immigrants as potential sponsors of new immigrants, then the sponsorship propensities of immigrants will be reflected in their naturalization behavior, as a principal benefit of citizenship is the expanded right to petition for foreign-born relatives. In addition to creating entitlements for naturalized citizen's parents (to a numerically unlimited visa) and for married children and siblings (plus their spouses and children), naturalization shifts the visa entitlement of the immigrant's spouse and minor children to the numerically unlimited category and that of non-minor unmarried children (and their children) to a higher preference category.

Second, the naturalization decision illustrates more clearly than do the other choices of immigrants the close relationship between the selection criteria of immigration laws and the behavior of the foreign-born residing in the United States. The decision to naturalize depends on the joint operation of many factors, including characteristics of the immigrant, such as age and sex, and characteristics of the country of origin, such as its attractiveness as a place to which to return and its laws governing dual citizenship. The selection criteria of U.S. immigration law influence naturalization not only through their influence on these characteristics of immigrants but also because they define the benefits of citizenship.

Our data on the 1971 immigrant cohort, for which we can compute naturalization rates within ten years of immigration, indicate that citizenship is not equally desired by all immigrants. Table 2.1 reports the percentage naturalized within ten years of admission to permanent resident status among the adults in the Fiscal Year (FY) 1971 immigrant cohort. These rates of naturalization are broken down by sex and country/region of origin for the ten countries with the largest proportion of immigrants in the cohort. The proportion naturalized after ten years ranges from close to zero for immigrants from Canada and Mexico to over 80 percent for male immigrants from Korea and the Philippines. Immigrants from European countries have moderately low naturalization rates (about 25 percent of the European-origin entry cohort naturalize), immigrants from countries with recent histories of political dislocations have higher naturalization rates (e.g., 42 percent, 58 percent, and 73 percent for males from Greece, Cuba, and the Republic of China, respectively), and immigrants from Asian countries have the highest naturalization rates.

In this chapter, we examine naturalization in three ways. We first focus on trends in the naturalization of immigrants, relying on data from the administrative records of the U.S. Immigration and Naturalization Service (INS). We then examine trends in the proportion naturalized among the foreign-born population, using data from the decennial censuses. Finally, we investigate the determinants of the propensity to naturalize, using our longitudinal sample from the 1971 immigrant cohort.

Preliminaries

Naturalization is the granting of U.S. citizenship to a person after birth. It confers the right to vote, authorizes the immigrant to engage in any occupation except those of President and Vice President of the United States,[1] and, under current immigration law, expands the right to sponsor the immigration of foreign-born kin. More generally, naturalization removes all restrictions based on alienage (e.g., restrictions on land ownership

[1]Both federal and state statutes restrict certain occupations to citizens.

TABLE 2.1

Percent Naturalized Within Ten Years After Admission,
of Adults in the FY 1971 Immigrant Cohort,
by Sex and Country and Region of Origin,
for Top Ten Origin Countries

Country or Region	Males		Females	
A. Country of Origin				
Canada	0.0	(3.3)[a]	2.9	(2.9)
China (Mainland)	72.5	(3.8)	63.8	(4.0)
Cuba	58.2	(5.3)	40.9	(5.6)
Greece	42.1	(5.5)	34.0	(4.2)
India	61.6	(8.2)	43.2	(3.1)
Italy	26.0	(7.0)	14.7	(5.7)
Korea	86.8	(3.6)	65.2	(5.8)
Mexico	4.2	(9.2)	3.8	(8.8)
Philippines	81.0	(6.0)	68.6	(10.2)
Portugal	23.9	(4.4)	26.1	(3.9)
B. Region of Origin				
Africa	46.4	(2.7)	56.5	(1.9)
Asia (excluding Middle East)	70.1	(26.9)	60.8	(31.3)
Caribbean and Central America	21.5	(29.3)	19.7	(30.3)
Europe	29.9	(29.7)	24.3	(29.7)
South America	24.0	(4.7)	25.5	(4.3)

SOURCE: U.S. INS FY 1971 Immigrant Cohort Sample.

[a]Percentage of total immigrants who are from the country or region of origin.

and on commercial radio operation), removes the risk of deportation (though deportation may follow denaturalization for cause), and confers the full rights and privileges associated with citizenship (except holding the two highest elective offices).

Under current law, eligibility to naturalize requires a five-year period of continuous residence in the United States subsequent to admission to legal permanent resident status (and physical presence in the United States for at least half of the five years immediately prior to filing the petition for naturalization),[2] knowledge of English,[3] knowledge of and attachment to

[2]The residency requirement is reduced or waived for certain categories of immigrants. These include (1) spouses of U.S. citizens, for whom the residency requirement is reduced to three years (if during the three years immediately prior to filing the petition they have lived "in marital union" with the citizen spouse), and spouses of certain U.S. citizens stationed abroad (such as employees of the U.S. government), for whom the residency requirement may be waived; (2) military personnel serving actively and honorably in the U.S. armed forces during specified periods of hostility, for whom the residency requirement may be reduced or waived, depending on length and place of service and the time elapsed between such service and the

the Constitution of the United States (demonstrated by examination), and explicit repudiation of the country of origin, expressed in the oath which all new citizens must take.[4] Note that under current law all qualifications for naturalization are amendable, that is, can be met if the immigrant chooses to do so. The last bars to naturalization based on race and sex were removed by the Immigration and Nationality Act of 1952.

The benefits and costs associated with naturalization suggest that the decision to naturalize will be influenced not only by an immigrant's decision to live permanently in the United States, but also by the following personal and contextual factors specifically relevant to naturalization: (1) the desire to sponsor the immigration of kin; (2) the extent to which employment opportunities are affected by citizenship status; (3) knowledge of English; (4) the extent of residual affection for the native country; and (5) age, which affects the length of time during which the post-naturalization employment, voting, and sponsorship privileges may be enjoyed.

U.S. law on immigration and nationality thus influences the individual immigrant's decision to naturalize and the aggregate volume of naturalization in at least four ways: (1) It prescribes the qualifications for naturalization. (2) By its quantitative restrictions on immigration, it sets bounds on the number of persons eligible to naturalize. (3) By the selective mechanisms embodied in its qualitative restrictions on immigration, it affects the characteristics of immigrants who enter and thus the propensity to naturalize. (4) By the sponsorship benefits associated with citizenship, it affects the benefits of naturalization. Accordingly, we would expect to observe the effects of a change in nationality law immediately after enactment and of a change in immigration law both immediately after enactment and also five years later, when the new immigrants (selected under the admission criteria of a new law) become eligible to naturalize.

---

petition; and (3) refugees, for whom special legislation has permitted part or all of the time between entry into the United States and admission to permanent resident status to count toward the residency requirement for naturalization. Note also that under certain conditions persons who are not "immigrants" (that is, have never been admitted to permanent resident alien status) may be naturalized through legislative or administrative action. Examples include battlefield grants of citizenship and the recent conferring of citizenship on residents of the Northern Mariana Islands (INS 1985, pp. xxxiv, xxxvii). Our focus, however, is on the naturalization of permanent resident aliens.

[3]Public Law 95-597, effective 2 November 1978, waives the knowledge-of-English requirement for persons aged 50 and over who have been in the United States as permanent resident aliens for at least 20 years. Prior to 1978, a similar waiver was granted to persons who as of 1952 were aged 50 and over and had lived in the United States for 20 years.

[4]The oath begins: "I hereby declare, on oath, that I absolutely and entirely renounce and abjure all allegiance and fidelity to any foreign prince, potentate, state or sovereignty, of whom or which I have heretofore been a subject or citizen. . . ." Note, however, that under certain circumstances immigrants who naturalize (and their children) may retain their initial nationality, becoming dual nationals. For example, the laws of the native country may not stipulate loss of nationality through foreign naturalization.

Immigration has been termed the "Great Experiment" and, indeed, changes in U.S. immigration laws do provide insights into human behavior. From 1968 to 1977, for example, the preference-category system of visa allocation, including the right of citizens to sponsor the immigration of "immediate" relatives, pertained only to Eastern Hemisphere countries while it pertained to both hemispheres after 1977. If kinship sponsorship rights are indeed viewed as important by immigrants, we would expect that prior to 1977 immigrants from Eastern Hemisphere countries would be significantly more likely to naturalize than immigrants from the Western Hemisphere, all else being the same, with Western Hemisphere naturalization rates increasing relative to those in the Eastern Hemisphere after 1977. We examine the results of this "experiment" below.

Trends in the Naturalization of Immigrants

Figure 2.1 depicts the total number of persons naturalizing, as recorded by the INS, in FYs 1945–1988, classified by the immigrant's hemisphere of birth. Naturalizations had reached an all-time high of 441,979 in FY 1944. The numbers for FYs 1945–1947 and 1954–1956—corresponding to the great pre-1985 peaks in Figure 2.1—include naturalizations in various theaters of war or areas occupied by U.S. armed forces, enabled by several pieces of legislation (U.S. Bureau of the Census 1975, pp. 101, 115). Following World War II annual naturalizations declined, so that by 1969 the number was 98,709—less than a quarter of the number for 1944. Between 1969 and 1986, however, there was a steady increase, mirroring the increase in the population of the foreign-born, with the number of naturalizations reaching 280,623 in FY 1986, but dropping to 242,063 by 1988 (the most recent year for which figures are available).

Figure 2.2 displays the number of persons naturalizing from three groups of countries of origin—in Europe, Asia, and the Western Hemisphere. From the mid 1950s to the early 1980s there was a steady decline in the naturalization of persons from Europe (with a slight upward trend after 1983); this decline coincides with the postwar recovery of Europe and signals a decline in eligible sponsors of European kin. However, there is an increasing trend in the number of immigrants naturalizing from Asia and from the Western Hemisphere.

The naturalization trends for Asia reflect two important changes in U.S. nationality law. First, an increase in naturalizations followed the removal of all racial qualifications in 1952. Second, there was a remarkable shift approximately six years after the 1965 amendments to the Immigration and Nationality Act, amendments which abolished restrictions on the immigration of persons from Asian countries. The number of naturaliza-

FIGURE 2.1
Persons Naturalized, by Hemisphere of Birth: 1945–1988

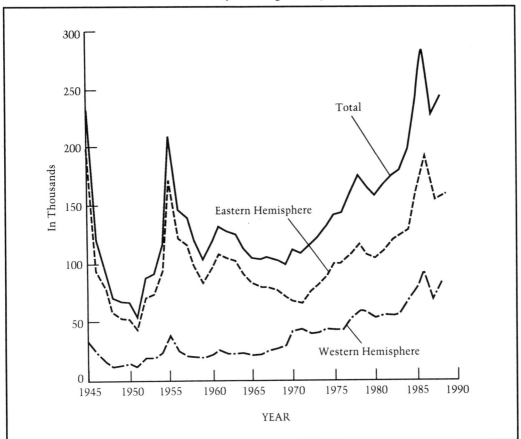

tions—which between 1961 and 1970 ranged from 12,200 to 17,729 per year—begins a steep increase, from 18,033 in 1971 to 90,844 in 1984 (a rate of approximately 5,600 annually). With the naturalization of recently eligible Indochinese immigrants, the number climbs even more sharply, to a peak of 139,181 in 1986.

The plot for the Western Hemisphere shows three abrupt shifts, corresponding to the two major law changes affecting natives of the Western Hemisphere. First, there is an increase between 1969 and 1970 of over 10,000 naturalizations; presumably, one response to the newly imposed quantitative restrictions was the naturalization of those wishing to sponsor the immigration of spouses, parents, or minor children. The graph is then approximately flat through 1976—with an average annual number of natu-

FIGURE 2.2
Persons Naturalized, by Region of Birth: 1945–1988

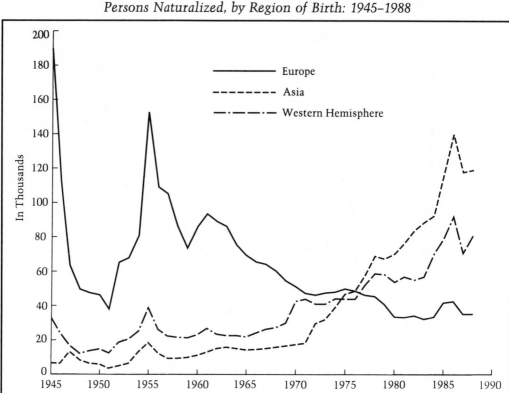

ralizations of 41,838 between 1970 and 1976—followed by the second abrupt increase of about 15,000 between 1976 and 1978; this coincides with the law change which extended to the Western Hemisphere the sponsorship privileges embodied in the preference category system. Between 1978 and 1983 the graph is again approximately flat, with an annual average of 55,213. But naturalization subsequently climbs, from 55,550 in 1983 to 91,712 in 1986—perhaps reflecting the naturalization of the immigrants selected under the post-1976 rules.

Trends in the Proportion Naturalized Among the Foreign-Born

Census data afford a different way of describing naturalization, enabling measurement of the proportion of the foreign-born population *currently resident* in the United States who report having been naturalized. Figure 2.3 depicts the proportion naturalized among the foreign-born aged 21 and over, for men in the census years 1890–1970 and for women beginning in 1920 (except for 1960, when the question on citizenship was not asked).[5] Data gaps notwithstanding, Figure 2.3 reveals a striking pattern: a decline in the proportion naturalized from 58 percent in 1890 to 45 percent in 1910; a subsequent increase, for both sexes, to peaks in 1950 of 78 percent for men and 71 percent for women; and a decline since 1950.[6]

The trends in the proportions naturalized calculated from census data must be interpreted with caution. As discussed in the Introduction, these figures reflect shifts in the proportion of the foreign-born population *eligible* to naturalize, and thus may not correspond to any historical changes in the propensities of immigrants to naturalize. For example, the greater the number of new immigrants and the greater the number of visitors (persons who are not permanent resident aliens), the lower will be the proportion naturalized, other things being the same. Thus, the high proportions naturalized at the turn of the century and again from the Depression years to the immediate post–World War II period, when immigration declined, may simply reflect the presence of fewer recent immigrants during those periods. Similarly, the lower proportions naturalized in 1910 and 1920 and again in 1970 and 1980 are undoubtedly related to the increases in the number of recent immigrants and, for the last two censuses, increases in the number of non-immigrants, including undocumented migrants.

For those census years for which Public Use Samples are available— 1900, 1910, 1970, and 1980—it is possible to examine the proportions naturalized by country of origin, again from among the foreign-born population currently resident in the United States. Proportions naturalized are

[5]Figure 2.3 is based on published historical tabulations (U.S. Bureau of the Census 1975). The purpose of the question on naturalization was to ascertain the maximum number of persons eligible to vote (Shryock and Siegel 1975, p. 272). Accordingly, before 1920, when the Nineteenth Amendment to the U.S. Constitution granted women the suffrage, the question was asked only of males aged 21 and over.

[6]It is widely believed that naturalization has been overreported in the censuses of 1950, 1970, and 1980 (Shryock and Siegel 1975, p. 274; U.S. Bureau of the Census 1960, 1974; Warren and Passel 1987). For example, while the proportion naturalized calculated from published data for the 1980 census (for foreign-born of all ages) is 50 percent, the data modifications proposed by Warren and Passel (1987) reduce it to 44 percent. On the other hand, the size of the foreign-born population may be overestimated and the number of native-born citizens underestimated (because of the wording of the questions on nativity and naturalization, as discussed in the Introduction).

FIGURE 2.3
*Proportion Naturalized of Foreign-Born Persons Aged 21 and Over,
by Sex: 1890–1970*

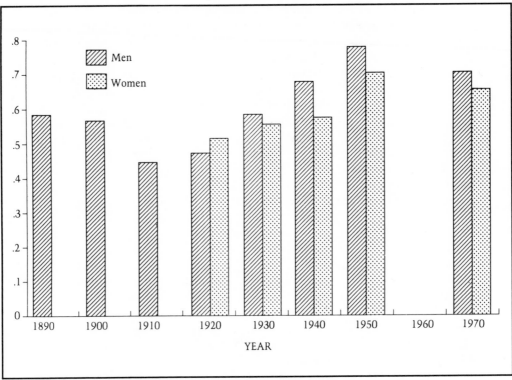

shown in Table 2.2 for the entire foreign-born population aged 21–65 and
for the top ten countries (as ranked by this measure), from among countries
providing more than 0.4 percent of the total sex-specific foreign-born population in the United States. The sample estimates indicate that the proportions of the adult foreign-born who were naturalized declined by about 10
percentage points between 1900 and 1910 and again between 1970 and
1980. However, the proportion of recent entrants also increased between
1900 and 1910 and again between 1970 and 1980. The latter increase,
however, is smaller than the earlier one, suggesting a shift upward in the
number of foreign-born persons who are not immigrants.

In 1900 and 1910 the proportions naturalized were highest for Western European and Scandinavian countries, while in 1970 and 1980 they are
highest for Eastern European countries. While it is tempting to conclude
that refugees from Eastern Europe have high naturalization propensities,
the absence of information on legal status in census data dictates caution.

As noted above, other things being the same, the percentage naturalized will be larger the smaller the ratio of non-immigrants to permanent resident aliens from each country. Thus, it is not surprising that Eastern-bloc countries are heavily represented in the top ten for 1970 and 1980, since there are relatively few visitors (or non-immigrants) in the United States from Eastern-bloc countries. Nor is it surprising that the proportion naturalized from among all foreign-born declined between 1970 and 1980, since the number of non-immigrants increased substantially during that period.[7]

Tracking the Naturalization Rates of Immigrant Cohorts

While the figures just shown are suggestive, they cannot be used readily either to calculate naturalization rates for entry cohorts (and age/sex/country-specific subsets of entry cohorts) or to analyze in a rigorous manner the determinants of the *propensity* to naturalize. Such analyses would require information on the population of persons eligible to naturalize—that is, on the population of permanent resident aliens.

Exact naturalization counts by fiscal year of admission to lawful permanent residence are difficult to obtain. This is due in part to the fact that the naturalization of some children is recorded separately,[8] in part to the fact that INS-published tabulations of immigration and naturalization use different referents for year of entry (fiscal year for immigration tables and calendar year for naturalization tables), and in part to the aggregation of some years of entry in the naturalization tables.

The U.S. Select Commission on Immigration and Refugee Policy (1981b, p. 264) reports the totals naturalized by the end of FY 1979 for cohorts reporting entry in calendar years since 1967. These figures indicate that 30, 25, and 32 percent of the calendar-year entry cohorts of 1967, 1968, and 1969, respectively, had naturalized by late 1979.[9]

A prospective study of immigrant cohorts would yield accurate naturalization rates and would enable estimation of behavioral models of the decision to naturalize. Useful designs would sample from several entry

---

[7]Two indications of the increase in non-immigrants are that (1) the number of new non-immigrants admitted more than doubled, from approximately 3.57 million in calendar year 1969 to 4.7 million in the first half of calendar year 1979 alone (INS 1969, 1970, 1979, Table 16); and (2) the number of non-immigrants residing in the United States in January 1970 and 1980 who were required to report their addresses and who did so increased by 61 percent, from 527,627 to 848,460 (INS 1970, Table 34; INS 1980, Table 18).

[8]The INS is devising new procedures for the collection and magnetic storage of data on derivative citizenship (INS 1985, p. vii).

[9]The cohorts may include children whose naturalization is recorded elsewhere or who are not yet eligible to naturalize and may include as well individuals who died or emigrated after entry.

TABLE 2.2

Top Ten Origin Countries Ranked by Percent Naturalized,
Among Foreign-Born Men and Women Aged 21–65 Years:
1900, 1910, 1970, and 1980

	Males			Females	
	Origin Country	Percent Naturalized		Origin Country	Percent Naturalized
A. 1900					
Ireland	69.3		Not recorded		
Bohemia-Moravia	67.8				
Wales	66.7				
Germany	65.4				
Netherlands	63.8				
Scotland	63.6				
Sweden	63.0				
Denmark	62.4				
Switzerland	62.2				
England	62.1				
F-B Population	53.7				
(% recent entrants)	(10.9)				
B. 1910					
Wales	74.7		Not recorded		
Germany	69.6				
Ireland	66.1				
Sweden	62.4				
Denmark	61.9				
England	59.5				
Norway	59.4				
Switzerland	58.2				
Scotland	57.5				
Netherlands	56.6				
F-B Population	43.5				
(% recent entrants)	(22.9)				
C. 1970					
Hungary	93.5		Russia	96.1	
Russia	86.0		Czechoslovakia	91.8	
Ukraine	85.7		Hungary	87.2	
Poland	84.0		Austria	86.0	
Turkey	83.3		Lithuania	82.4	
Lithuania	83.3		Romania	78.6	
Czechoslovakia	81.5		Belgium	78.6	
Romania	78.6		Poland	77.5	
Scotland	77.4		Ireland	77.5	
Ireland	76.9		Italy	71.7	
F-B Population	61.9		F-B Population	60.0	
(% recent entrants)	(18.4)		(% recent entrants)	(16.4)	

TABLE 2.2 *(continued)*

Males		Females	
Origin Country	Percent Naturalized	Origin Country	Percent Naturalized
D. 1980			
Ukraine	90.9	Austria	100.0
Czechoslovakia	83.3	Czechoslovakia	100.0
Poland	81.0	Hungary	83.3
Israel	75.0	Ireland	79.3
Panama	75.0	Scotland	76.0
Germany (West)	71.9	Italy	72.8
Italy	71.4	Germany (West)	71.6
Scotland	71.4	France	70.0
Ireland	71.4	Poland	69.6
Hungary	70.0	Israel	63.6
F-B Population	52.1	F-B Population	50.5
(% recent entrants)	(22.5)	(% recent entrants)	(17.3)

SOURCE: U.S. Census of Population, Public Use Samples.

NOTE: The countries of origin that are ranked according to percent naturalized are countries providing more than 0.4 percent of the total sex-specific foreign-born population.

cohorts (since naturalization may reflect the distinctive selection mechanisms associated with characteristics of a given cohort). In the next section we simulate such a longitudinal design by investigating the propensity to naturalize among the adult members of the FY 1971 immigrant cohort sample, for which we know the precise number of entrants and know as well some of their individual characteristics.

The Naturalization Behavior of the FY 1971 Cohort

The sample drawn from the FY 1971 immigrant cohort, described in the Introduction, provides a unique opportunity to study the decision to naturalize, since it provides a complete and exact naturalization history for the cohort over approximately a ten-year period. We will first describe the major features of the cohort sample's naturalization behavior and then report estimates of a model in which the probability of naturalizing is related to the characteristics of immigrants and their countries of origin.

Naturalization Rates

Thirty percent of all immigrants in the FY 1971 cohort sample had naturalized within ten years of admission, a figure very close to those obtained (25–32 percent) for the 1967–1969 immigrant cohorts studied by the Select Commission on Immigration and Refugee Policy. Because, as noted, the total immigrant sample includes children, who might have obtained derivative citizenship (recorded separately) or who were not yet eligible for independent naturalization, and includes aged persons who might have died, a more meaningful naturalization rate is obtained by restricting attention to those cohort sample members who were between the ages of 21 and 65 at admission to permanent residence. Of this latter group, 37 percent had naturalized by early 1981. Of course, some of the non-naturalized may have emigrated.

Figure 2.4 depicts cumulative naturalization rates by years since admission for all of the 1971 immigrants who were aged 21–65 at admission. As expected, the figure shows (1) the small increase in naturalizations at three years since admission, associated with the naturalization of persons for whom the residency requirement is reduced to three years (spouses of U.S. citizens), and (2) the large increase beginning at five years since admission, associated with fulfillment of the residency requirement for all cohort members. Also as expected, because of the greater family-reunification benefits accorded to citizens with origins (relatives) in the Eastern Hemisphere, the naturalization rates for persons from the Eastern Hemisphere are more than double those for persons from the Western Hemisphere. Of course, there may be other reasons for this difference, which we investigate below.

After the 1976 amendments to the Immigration and Nationality Act, which extended the preference-category system—and its visa entitlements for the adult children and the siblings of U.S. citizens—to the Western Hemisphere, we would expect to see an increase in the naturalization of Western Hemisphere persons. Figure 2.5 reveals a striking tendency toward convergence in the two hemisphere-specific hazard rates (the probability of naturalizing among non-naturalized immigrants) at about eight years after admission—that is, around December 1978, appropriately following the change in hemisphere entitlements which became effective in 1977.

The section of law under which a person obtains an immigrant visa is a potentially useful indicator of the propensity to naturalize. The immigrant visa imparts information which measures, or signals, the operation of factors potentially associated with naturalization—for example, age, attachment to the labor force, the desire to sponsor the immigration of kin, and affection for the country of origin. Accordingly, the following conjectures may be formulated:

(1) Persons admitted as the parent of a U.S. citizen may be assumed to

FIGURE 2.4
*Cumulative Naturalization Rates, by Hemisphere of Origin
and Years Since Admission: FY 1971 Cohort*

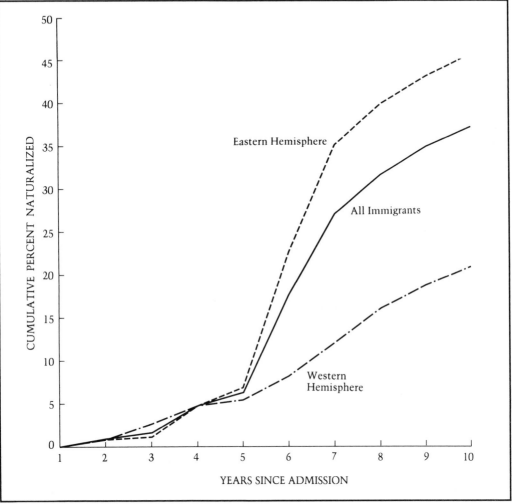

be, *ceteris paribus,* older than other immigrants, and hence would be expected to have a lower propensity to naturalize.

(2) Persons admitted in consequence of their being a spouse would benefit from the privilege of sponsoring blood kin but less so from the privilege of sponsoring a new spouse.

(3) Persons admitted as blood relatives might have fewer blood kin left to sponsor but enhanced desire to sponsor a spouse.

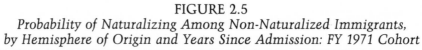

FIGURE 2.5
Probability of Naturalizing Among Non-Naturalized Immigrants,
by Hemisphere of Origin and Years Since Admission: FY 1971 Cohort

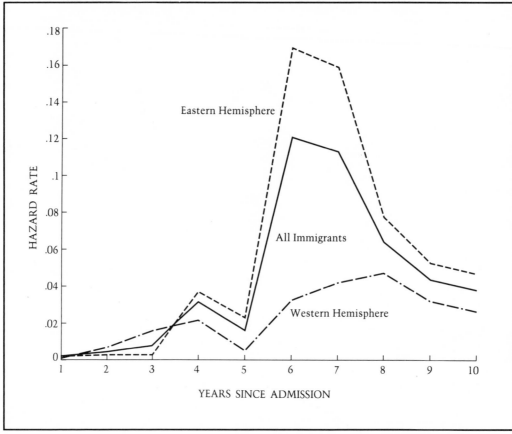

(4) Persons admitted with a skill-based visa (third- and sixth-preference category principals in the Eastern Hemisphere) and other persons required to obtain labor certification (from among Eastern Hemisphere non-preference applicants and numerically limited Western Hemisphere applicants) would be more likely to possess a greater attachment to the labor force and thus to partake more fully of the employment benefits associated with citizenship.

(5) Refugees would have lower attachment to their origin countries, especially if the conditions which provoked their exile are not likely to be changed soon.

(6) Refugee and occupation-based immigrants would benefit from the

TABLE 2.3

Percent Naturalized Within Ten Years After Admission,
of Adult Women in the FY 1971 Immigrant Cohort Sample,
by Type of Visa, Marital Status, and Hemisphere of Origin

Visa Type	All Women	Eastern Hemisphere		Western Hemisphere	
		Married	Single	Married	Single
Kin by Marriage					
Married to U.S. citizen	36.5	43.0	—	17.3	—
Married to U.S. permanent resident	45.3	45.3	—	—	—
Married to new skill immigrant	50.0	50.0	—	—	—
Married to new kin immigrant	52.2	52.2	—	—	—
Blood Kin					
Parent of U.S. citizen	15.6	19.0	21.4	0	0
Son/daughter of U.S. citizen	50.0	42.9	66.7	—	—
Son/daughter of U.S. permanent resident	44.4	—	44.4	—	—
Sibling of U.S. citizen	24.4	19.7	34.5	—	—
Non-Kin					
Skilled immigrant	73.3	75.0	72.2	—	—
Refugee	37.0	15.4	42.9	36.6	50.0
Non-preference immigrant	44.5	47.9	35.7	—	—
Native of the Western Hemisphere	17.2	—	—	14.3	24.3

SOURCE: U.S. INS FY 1971 Immigrant Cohort Sample.

NOTES: Percentages are based on sample cohort members who were aged 21 to 65 years at admission to permanent resident status (1,190 women). The skilled classification includes persons entering as principal applicants in the third and sixth preference categories. Hyphen entries indicate the absence of a visa category under the rules governing admission of adults in FY 1971.

full spectrum of kin sponsorship privileges—but those from the Western Hemisphere only after 1976.

In addition, married persons might consider that they as well as their children are better off if husband and wife have different nationalities. If so, we would observe lower naturalization rates among immigrants admitted as the spouses of U.S. citizens than among other immigrants, especially those admitted as the spouses of permanent resident aliens.

Tables 2.3 and 2.4 report the naturalization rates, within ten years of admission, for women and men, respectively, by selected visa category, marital status at entry, and hemisphere. The observed rates are consistent with the conjectures. Immigrants with skill-based visas have among the highest naturalization rates: 73 percent of women and 65 percent of men. Persons admitted as parents of U.S. citizens have the lowest naturalization rates: 16 percent of women and 12 percent of men (the sex difference possibly suggesting the operation of life expectancy). Refugee men have the expected high naturalization rates (59 percent), while refugee women have

TABLE 2.4

Percent Naturalized Within Ten Years After Admission,
of Adult Men in the FY 1971 Immigrant Cohort Sample,
by Type of Visa, Marital Status, and Hemisphere of Origin

Visa Type	All Men	Eastern Hemisphere		Western Hemisphere	
		Married	Single	Married	Single
Kin by Marriage					
Married to U.S. citizen	33.9	53.7	—	17.8	—
Married to U.S. permanent resident	58.3	58.3	—	—	—
Married to new skill immigrant	69.2	69.2	—	—	—
Married to new kin immigrant	33.9	33.9	—	—	—
Blood Kin					
Parent of U.S. citizen	11.8	9.1	0	33.3	0
Son/daughter of U.S. citizen	41.7	42.9	40.0	—	—
Son/daughter of U.S. permanent resident	28.2	—	28.2	—	—
Sibling of U.S. citizen	34.5	30.0	40.5	—	—
Non-Kin					
Skilled immigrant	64.8	69.8	53.8	—	—
Refugee	59.4	45.4	70.0	55.6	75.0
Non-preference immigrant	53.1	50.0	58.7	—	—
Native of the Western Hemisphere	15.0	—	—	14.4	17.6

SOURCE: U.S. INS FY 1971 Immigrant Cohort Sample.

NOTES: All percentages are based on sample cohort members who were aged 21 to 65 years at admission to permanent resident status (1046 men). The skilled classification includes persons entering as principal applicants in the third and sixth preference categories. Hyphen entries indicate the absence of a visa category under the rules governing admission of adults in FY 1971.

considerably lower rates (37 percent)—possibly reflecting occupational considerations. Within the refugee classification, single persons of both sexes and hemispheres have higher naturalization rates than married persons, consistent with the possibility that couples prefer to diversify their citizenship portfolio. Persons admitted as spouses of U.S. citizens have relatively low naturalization rates: 37 percent of women and 34 percent of men. And, as expected, if couples diversify their citizenship portfolio, these rates are lower than the corresponding rates for spouses of permanent resident aliens. Finally, the lowest naturalization rates, next to those of parents, are those of natives of the Western Hemisphere—consistent with the pre-1977 differential in sponsorship benefits.

Figure 2.6 plots cumulative naturalization rates, by years since admission, for three Eastern Hemisphere visa groupings: labor-certified (including nonpreference as well as third- and sixth-preference categories), siblings of U.S. citizens (fifth-preference principals), and spouses of permanent resident aliens (second-preference spouses). As expected from Tables 2.3 and

FIGURE 2.6
*Cumulative Naturalization Rates of Eastern Hemisphere Immigrants,
by Visa Category and Years Since Admission: FY 1971 Cohort*

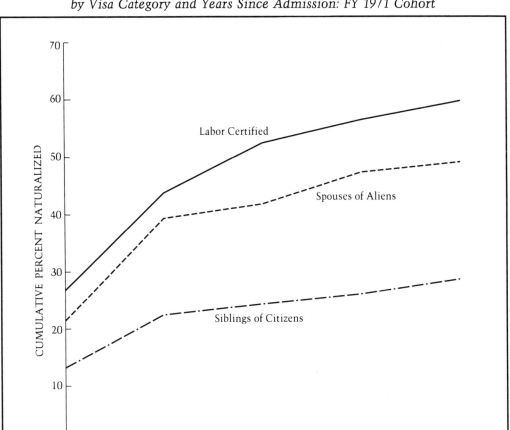

2.4, the labor-certified group has the highest naturalization rate, followed by the spouses of aliens, and, far below, the sibling group.

Figure 2.7 depicts the cumulative naturalization rates among spouses of U.S. citizens, by hemisphere and years since admission. The significantly higher rates for the Eastern Hemisphere immigrants presumably reflect, in part, the differential sponsorship privileges.

FIGURE 2.7
Cumulative Naturalization Rates
of the Immigrant Spouses of U.S. Citizens,
by Hemisphere of Origin and Years Since Admission: FY 1971 Cohort

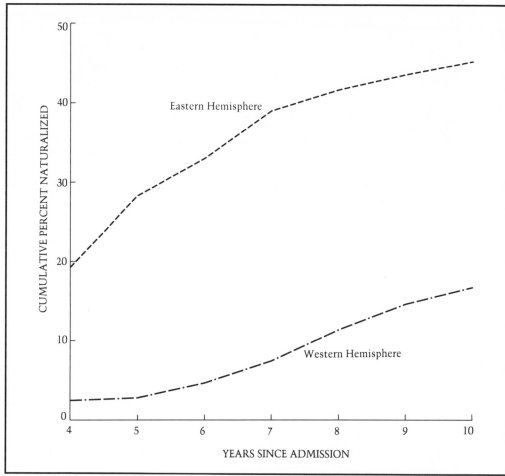

Determinants of Naturalization: A Multivariate Analysis

The preceding tables and figures do not readily permit an assessment of the separate and independent effects of visa categories, personal characteristics, and origin-country characteristics on immigrants' naturalization propensities. As noted in the Introduction, the linked immigration-naturalization records of the 1971 immigrant cohort include information on age, sex, marital status, country of birth, country of last permanent residence, country of chargeability (for numerically limited visas issued to natives of the Eastern Hemisphere), as well as detailed information on the provisions of the law under which the person became an immigrant and naturalized, and the month and year of naturalization. The merged microdata set thus provides a unique opportunity to study the determinants of naturalization in a true, longitudinal cohort analysis using data which permit multivariate analysis.

Many of the factors involved in the decision to naturalize can be represented by measured characteristics of the origin country and of the immigrant visa. Accordingly, we specify an equation in which the origin-country characteristics are GNP per capita, literacy rate, distance, centrally planned economy, English an official/dominant language, presence of U.S. military installations, and native-language broadcasts by the Voice of America. The included immigrant characteristics are age at entry, spouse of citizen, spouse of resident alien (second preference), sibling (fifth-preference principal), refugee, labor-certified (third-, sixth-, and nonpreference-category principals among Eastern Hemisphere immigrants, as well as labor-certified Western Hemisphere immigrants), spouse of sibling, and spouse of Eastern Hemisphere labor-certified immigrant. The omitted visa category includes first- and fourth-preference Eastern Hemisphere immigrants, parents of U.S. citizens, non-labor-certified nonpreference Eastern Hemisphere immigrants, and non-labor-certified Western Hemisphere immigrants.

We also include in the specification a dichotomous variable describing whether the immigrant is from the Eastern or Western Hemisphere, in order to test whether the difference in the family-reunification benefits from naturalization across hemispheres prior to 1977 affected naturalization propensities, net of the effects of the age of the immigrant and the characteristics of his/her origin country. The estimates are obtained separately for men and women.

Table 2.5 reports maximum-likelihood logit estimates[10] of the determinants of naturalization for women and men and the corresponding estimated naturalization probabilities, by the entry visa category of the immigrant.[11] For both men and women, as expected, the older the immigrant at

[10]When the dependent variable in an equation is binary, ordinary-least-squares procedures yield estimates whose standard errors are biased. To correct for such biases and hence obtain more precise estimates, it is customary to transform the equation, utilizing the cumulative distribution function associated with a tractable and otherwise pleasing distribution. The two most popular distributions used for this purpose are the normal, which leads to the "probit" model, and the logistic, which gives rise to the "logit" model. In addition, if the number and measurement properties of the regressors are such that not all "cells" (i.e., combinations of values of the regressors) are amply populated, then maximum-likelihood techniques must be used in order to obtain the logit estimates. Introductory exposition is available in Judge et al. (1985) and more detailed coverage in Maddala (1983).

[11]The estimated naturalization probabilities are based on the sample means.

TABLE 2.5
Determinants of Naturalization Within Ten Years After Admission
and Associated Naturalization Probabilities, in the FY 1971 Immigrant
Cohort, by Sex: Maximum-Likelihood Logit Estimates

Variable	Females		Males	
	Coefficient[a]	Probability[b]	Coefficient[a]	Probability[b]
Immigrant Characteristics				
Age at entry	−3.67		−3.24	
	(4.59)		(3.43)	
Sibling (5th preference)	−3.40	.240	2.77	.340
	(0.88)		(0.83)	
Spouse of citizen	.118	.331	.599	.425
	(0.46)		(2.33)	
Spouse of alien (2nd preference)	.334	.373	.990	.517
	(1.06)		(2.50)	
Labor certified (3rd, 6th preferences, Western Hemisphere)	.802	.454	.537	.418
	(3.07)		(2.28)	
Refugee	.0597	.313	.951	.506
	(0.142)		(2.26)	
Sibling spouse	1.35	.542	−.0338	.286
	(3.02)		(0.07)	
Labor-certified spouse	.205	.339	.537	.336
	(0.67)		(2.28)	
Origin-Country Characteristics				
GNP per capita ($\times 10^{-4}$)	−3.30		−3.36	
	(6.39)		(4.68)	
Literacy rate ($\times 10^{-2}$)	1.91		2.38	
	(3.26)		(4.39)	
Distance ($\times 10^{-4}$)	1.70		4.08	
	(1.72)		(3.88)	
Centrally planned economy	.876		.987	
	(2.46)		(2.52)	
English an official language	.386		.141	
	(1.51)		(0.47)	
U.S. military base present	−.0687		.526	
	(0.35)		(2.45)	
Voice of America broadcasts	.911		.471	
	(3.60)		(1.73)	
Western Hemisphere	−.833		.0939	
	(1.57)		(0.17)	
Constant	−1.74		−3.10	
	(2.19)		(3.95)	
Number in Sample	1,085		952	

SOURCE: U.S. INS FY 1971 Immigrant Cohort Sample.

[a]Maximum likelihood coefficient; absolute values of asymptotic t-ratios in parentheses.
[b]Probabilities computed at sample means.

entry the lower is the propensity to naturalize, presumably because there is less time in which to reap the benefits of naturalization.[12]

The estimates for both sex groups indicate that propensities to naturalize differ significantly by visa category, for given personal and origin-country characteristics. However, the rankings of naturalization probabilities across visa categories are quite different across female and male immigrants. For women, spouses of principals who are siblings of U.S. citizens have the highest naturalization probabilities; more than 50 percent naturalize five years after entry. For men entering in the same visa category, less than 29 percent naturalize within the same period, the lowest probability among the male immigrants. Similarly, refugees have the highest average probability of naturalizing among men (0.51), while female refugees have the next-to-lowest among all female immigrants (0.31). On the other hand, among principal immigrants who are not refugees, labor-certified immigrants have the highest and second-highest propensities to naturalize among women and men, respectively. The naturalization probabilities for the labor-certified female principals are statistically significantly higher than those for women entering as siblings, spouses of aliens, spouses of citizens, and refugees.

The results in Table 2.5 provide additional support for the hypothesis that one incentive for naturalizing is the right of family reunification, particularly among women. For that group, those immigrants who have the least number of their relatives already in the United States (spouses of siblings of citizens and the labor-certified) have the highest propensities to naturalize, while those who in all likelihood have most of their relatives already in the United States (siblings) have the lowest. Moreover, among Western Hemisphere immigrants, for whom family reunification was not a right conferred by naturalization until 1977, women were 17 percent less likely to naturalize prior to 1981, "controlling for" the proximity of the country to the United States and its standard of living. These patterns, however, are not evident in the estimates from the male immigrant sample.

Origin-country characteristics also influence the decision to naturalize. The results are consistent with the hypothesis that coming from a country in which English is an official/principal language facilitates naturalization, for which knowledge of the English language is a requirement. Female immigrants from such countries were 28 percent more likely to naturalize; male immigrants were 10 percent more likely to naturalize. Only the effect for females is statistically significant (10 percent level, one-tail test), however. For both male and female immigrants, those from countries receiving native-language broadcasts from the Voice of America were 23 and 43

[12]Based on estimates obtained from pooling the female and male samples, the hypothesis that the set of coefficients is identical for both sexes is rejected at the .01 level of significance (chi-squared test).

percent more likely, respectively, to naturalize. To the extent that those immigrants who have acquired more accurate information about the United States prior to immigration are most likely to succeed after immigration, this result suggests that Voice of America broadcasts, at least prior to 1981, may have been providing a realistic depiction of life in the United States, one which helps potential immigrants make a more informed decision about the selection of country of residence and citizenship. Or perhaps such signals are beamed to countries whose residents are most likely to become U.S. citizens, other things being the same.

The estimates also suggest that immigrants from high-GNP countries are significantly less likely to naturalize. Moreover, naturalization rates appear to be lower as well for immigrants from countries that are located closest to the United States, that are not centrally planned, and that have lower literacy rates. These results appear consistent with the hypotheses that lower costs of and greater possibilities for returning to the home country, higher levels of the attractiveness of the country of origin, and lower levels of information about the United States prior to immigration reduce the likelihood of an immigrant, whatever his/her entry visa, becoming a citizen of the United States.

Summary

Becoming a citizen of the United States entails costs and provides benefits. In addition to the residency and language requirements, naturalization demands the transfer of special loyalties, particularly if dual citizenship is barred. The benefits are commensurate. The new citizen not only is empowered to enter fully into life in a democracy, but also acquires occupational, licensing, and ownership rights and as well special privileges of sponsoring the immigration of kin.

For many immigrants the benefits of naturalization do not outweigh the costs. The most recent estimates of immigrant cohorts of the early 1970s indicate that less than 50 percent of immigrants ever become naturalized citizens, although approximately 70 percent of the resident foreign-born have naturalized. The discrepancy between the propensities of an original immigrant cohort to naturalize and the proportion of the foreign-born naturalized reflects the presence of non-immigrants in the foreign-born population and the emigration of many immigrants from the United States, a phenomenon we examine in the next chapter. Naturalization rates also differ strongly across country-of-origin groups, with Asian immigrants and refugees the most likely to naturalize, and border-country immigrants the least.

Because of the increase in the size of immigration flows since 1970, and the extension of sponsorship benefits to the Western Hemisphere, the number of persons becoming citizens through naturalization each year has grown at a rapid rate, from less than 100,000 in 1969 to over 280,000 in 1986. As the composition of the immigrant population by country of origin has changed, so has that of the annual cohorts of new citizens. In 1977, the number of naturalized citizens from Europe fell from its traditional first place to third place, exceeded by both the number from Asia and that from the Western Hemisphere. In 1988, more than 47 percent of immigrants becoming citizens were from Asia, 34 percent from Western Hemisphere countries, and 15 percent from Europe.

Differences in the likelihood of naturalizing among immigrants appear to depend on differences in the costs and benefits of doing so. Thus, we found that, all else being the same, immigrants from English-speaking countries are more likely to naturalize, as knowledge of English is a prerequisite for citizenship, while immigrants who enter the United States at older ages, and thus who have fewer years to enjoy the benefits of citizenship, are less likely to naturalize. One of the benefits of naturalization that appears to importantly affect immigrants' decisions to naturalize is the ability to sponsor immigrant kin. We found that immigrants who are less likely to have kin residing abroad (immigrants who themselves were sponsored by U.S. citizen relatives) are significantly less likely to naturalize. Moreover, the extension of the preference system to the Western Hemisphere, which made it possible for particular kinds of relatives to be sponsored by citizens, appears to have led to a marked increase in naturalization rates for Western Hemisphere immigrants. We further explore the effects of changes in the selection criteria of immigration law on the family reunification of immigrants in Chapters 4 and 5, where we look at "marital immigration" and the family reunification of immigrants, respectively.

3

TAKING LEAVE: EMIGRATION

NOT ALL IMMIGRANTS take root. Some find the new country less congenial than envisioned prior to immigration or the old country more endearing than previously appreciated. Others may be marked by "wanderlust" and go on to experiment in different climes. Still others may never have intended to live permanently in the United States, obtaining an immigrant visa merely because it was the only way to live and work legally and freely in the United States. For still others, disruptive emergencies (e.g., medical difficulties of aged parents) may precipitate an extended "visit" in the origin country, which, if it occurs prior to eligibility for naturalization and lasts longer than one year, may lead to loss of permanent resident status.[1]

For as long as there has been immigration to the United States there has been emigration from the United States. Possibly the most dramatic example involves the founding of Liberia by emigrant American blacks in the first half of the nineteenth century (Huberich, 1947). Excepting such historical landmarks and stories of well-known expatriates, however, little is known about emigration. The available information—historical accounts of transoceanic travel, data on place of birth collected by the decennial.

---

[1]Special rules (and associated documents) may permit the re-entry of a permanent resident alien after an absence from the United States of longer than one year. It should also be noted that a naturalized citizen who establishes permanent residence abroad within five years of naturalization is subject to revocation of naturalization.

censuses since 1850, and the emigration statistics recorded from 1908 to 1957—does appear to support two conjectures: that many immigrants to the United States have left the United States to make their permanent home elsewhere and that the likelihood of emigrating differs markedly across country-of-origin groups.

The first recorded number of foreign-born persons expressing their intention to permanently leave their permanent home in the United States was 395,073 in 1908, a year when immigrants numbered 782,870. In the ten years between the censuses of 1900 and 1910, a period during which almost 8.5 million persons immigrated to the United States, the foreign-born population increased by only 3.2 million persons. More recently, between 1960 and 1970, when the United States admitted 3.3 million new permanent resident aliens, the census-enumerated foreign-born population decreased by about 100,000 (from 9.7 million to 9.6 million).

There are three reasons why it is important to know both the number and characteristics of the foreign-born who leave the United States. First, studies of the number of illegal foreign-born have for the most part made use of information on the changes in the size of the population of the foreign-born to infer the size of the illegal population or its growth rate. But, apart from legal immigration and deaths (which are either counted in administrative data or which can be accurately predicted), the foreign-born population will change its size because of both the entry of illegal aliens and exits by the foreign-born, neither of which have been recorded in any administrative data since 1957. Counting the illegal population thus requires an estimate of the magnitude of emigration.

Second, comparisons of the characteristics of an immigrant cohort at one or more points in time have been used to make inferences about their progress or assimilation. But observed changes in the characteristics of an immigrant entry cohort reflect not only true changes in the characteristics but also selective emigration. For example, if the average schooling level of an entry cohort rises, this may be due to either or both the acquisition of schooling by the immigrants or the selective emigration of the less schooled. An evaluation of the "success" of immigrants or of immigration policy needs to distinguish between these two phenomena.

Finally, an assessment of the impact of immigration on the U.S. economy requires information on net immigration—immigrants less emigrants—rather than gross immigration. The effects of the immigration of 600,000 persons per year, for example, will be quite different if 50 percent as compared to, say, 10 percent of immigrants leave.

Severe data limitations hamper the study of emigration for recent years. Since the United States discontinued exit review in 1957 (U.S. Bureau of the Census 1975), there has been no direct measurement of the emigration of immigrants. Absent direct measurement, it is necessary to rely on the methods of demographic analysis, formulating estimates based on parsimonious combinations of available data and appropriate assumptions.[2] In this chapter, using data from both recent censuses and the annual registration of permanent resident aliens conducted from 1951 to 1980, we estimate the temporal patterns of emigration and the selectivity associated with emigration—that is, how a cohort of the foreign-born changes over time due to selective emigration.

Our analysis suggests that emigration continued to be high in the 1960s and 1970s. Emigration rose to 36 percent of gross immigration between 1960 and 1969 and to 44 percent between 1970 and 1979. Gross legal immigration figures thus appear to overstate substantially the potential impact of immigration. Because of the higher level of, and rising, emigration rates of European immigrants compared with Asian immigrants between 1960 and 1980, moreover, gross immigration figures understate the substantial shift in the origin-country composition of the net flow of immigrants in that period, with the proportion from European countries declining and that from Asian countries increasing.

Census data further indicate that there are dramatic changes over time in the proportions of male foreign-born entry cohorts that can be explained only by sex-selective emigration; the emigration rates of foreign-born men are substantially greater than those for women among all the foreign-born in the 1960s and among the Eastern Hemisphere foreign-born in the 1970s. Finally, there is evidence that emigrants may be more schooled than the average foreign-born population; average schooling levels for the female foreign-born from the Western Hemisphere and male foreign-born from the Eastern Hemisphere who immigrated around 1960 actually declined in the subsequent decade as a result of emigration.

Data on Emigration

There are two main ways to measure the size of the population of (naturalized and non-naturalized) legal immigrants as it changes over time. The first is to record all exits from permanent resident status and update a master file of all persons granted permanent residence.[3] Such "exits" are of three types: naturalization, death, and emigration. Of these, only naturalization is currently recorded; exit review was discontinued in 1957, and the death registry systems do not include information on immigration status.

---

[2]For valuable exposition of the pertinent components-of-population equations and examination of the available data, see Shryock and Siegel et al. (1975) and Siegel (1978).

[3]Of course, such a master file could be even more inclusive, including, for example, refugees prior to admission to permanent resident status.

The information on naturalization, moreover, is not currently used to update a computerized master file of immigrants.[4]

The second way to keep track of the immigrant population is to require periodic registration. The United States did so from 1951 to 1980—but only for non-naturalized aliens—in accordance with the provisions of the Internal Security Act of 1950 and the Immigration and Nationality Act of 1952. The U.S. Immigration and Naturalization Service (INS) conducted this registration program in January of each year, requesting that all aliens residing in the United States provide their names and addresses and other basic information (such as age, sex, country of nationality, current immigration status, and date of admission to current immigration status) on an official INS form/questionnaire (form I-53). Their *Annual Report* and *Statistical Yearbook* published selected summaries of these data, including tabulations by state of residence and country of origin.

The Alien Address Report Program (AARP) data system constitutes the sole source of data on the size of the permanent resident alien population (given that the census and other periodic population surveys do not collect information on immigration status). Unfortunately, neither its coverage rate nor the stability of that rate is known. Warren (1979) compared the 1970 AARP data with the 1970 census count of the alien population, but because the coverage of aliens in the census is itself unknown, he was able to conclude only that "the alien population was probably more completely counted in 1970 by the INS than by the Census Bureau" (p. 4). Nonetheless, AARP data can be combined with other data bases with suitable assumptions to enable estimation of the emigration of permanent resident aliens.[5]

Estimating the Emigration of Permanent Resident Aliens: 1960–1980

Aggregate Emigration

In this section we combine INS data on immigration, naturalization, and alien address registration in order to calculate annual changes in the

[4]It would be straightforward to link each year's set of naturalized persons with previous years' sets of new immigrants, for the period since magnetic-tape storage of these files began in the early 1970s. The relevant files, the New-Immigrant File and the Naturalization File, are prepared by the INS, principally through the Immigrant Data Capture (IMDAC) facility and the Naturalization Casework System (NACS); for further details, see INS (1987, pp. xxii, xxxviii, and xliv). Of course, it would not be necessary to update a master file for the entire populations of legal-immigrant cohorts; implementing this method for a random sample drawn from each year's immigrant cohort would yield valuable data.

[5]For further discussion of the AARP data, see Levine et al. (1985) and Woodrow (1988).

population of permanent resident aliens between 1960 and 1980.[6] The appendix to this chapter contains the components-of-population equations as well as the numerical estimating equations used to obtain these estimates.

As described in the appendix, the term "observed population of permanent resident aliens" denotes the number of persons who report their addresses to the INS, in January of a given year, under the AARP. The term "predicted population of permanent resident aliens" denotes the expected population, computed by adding to the previous year's observed population the number of new permanent resident aliens admitted during the year and subtracting the number who naturalized during the year. It follows that if during the preceding year there were no deaths and no emigration and if the number of immigrants who though resident fail to report their addresses remains constant, then the predicted and observed populations would exactly equal each other. Finally, the term "loss" denotes the difference between the observed and predicted populations; accordingly, the loss is due to mortality, emigration, and changes in non-response. Thus, as discussed in the appendix, the observed worldwide loss can be negative in the unlikely event that the number of non-responders in January of the previous year exceeds the sum of deaths and emigration during the preceding year and the number of non-responders in January of the current year.

This way of calculating the loss of permanent resident aliens is very simple and requires no assumptions about death rates or non-response rates. The observed loss, however, is an unrefined number, containing unknown proportions of its constituent elements (viz., emigration, death, non-response). As shown in the appendix, the loss overestimates emigration if non-response increases over time or if deaths occur and non-response is nondecreasing over time. To the extent that these assumptions are reasonable, the calculated loss may be regarded as the upper bound on emigration. Of course, it is possible for non-response in the previous year to exceed the sum of deaths in the past year and non-response in the current year—the condition for the loss to be a lower bound on emigration.[7]

Figure 3.1 reports the predicted and observed population of permanent resident aliens, from all countries of the world, for the 20 years from 1961 to 1980 (the final year of the AARP). As shown, the observed population of permanent resident aliens totaled 3,038,304 in January 1961, and increased

---

[6]Other attempts to estimate the volume of emigration for (selected age/origin-country/ entry cohorts of) permanent resident aliens and/or the broader foreign-born population are reported in Keely and Kraly (1978), Passel and Peck (1979), Warren (1979), Warren and Peck (1980), Jasso and Rosenzweig (1982), Kraly (1982), Hill (1985a), Warren and Kraly (1985), and Warren and Passel (1987).

[7]The loss is defined for permanent resident aliens and does not reflect the emigration of immigrants who naturalized.

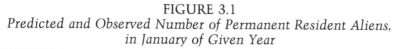

FIGURE 3.1
*Predicted and Observed Number of Permanent Resident Aliens,
in January of Given Year*

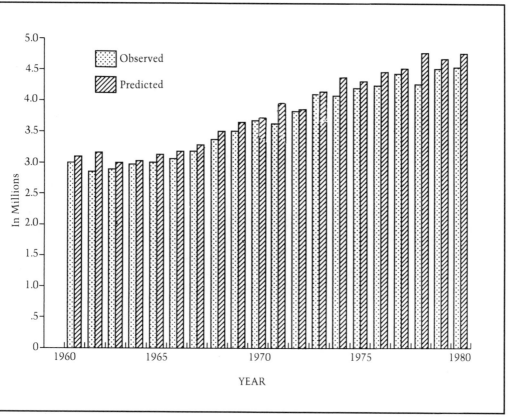

(nonuniformly) to 4,532,647 in January 1980. As expected, the predicted population exceeds the observed population in every one of the 20 years, and thus the annual loss (for all origin countries) is always positive.[8]

Figure 3.2 shows the magnitude of the loss of permanent resident aliens. The total reduction in the permanent resident alien population due to deaths and emigration ranges from less than 50,000 in 1961, 1970, 1972, and 1973 to almost 500,000 in 1978. The movements in the number of losses are extremely jagged, suggesting the operation of many disparate forces.[9]

[8]Since the predicted and observed populations are defined for January of a given year, the calculated loss results from losses during the preceding calendar year.

[9]As well, the jaggedness may be an artifact of the procedure used to convert fiscal-year

FIGURE 3.2

Annual Loss in the Observed Population of Permanent Resident Aliens

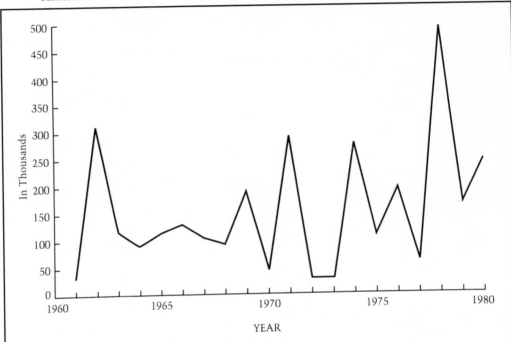

It is useful to view the annual loss alongside the number of new permanent resident aliens admitted each year. For, if it were the case that non-response changes little from year to year, then such comparison would show whether the flow of new immigrants offset the loss due to death and emigration. Figure 3.3 depicts the annual loss and the new immigrant flow for the years 1961 to 1980. Despite the jaggedness of the losses, the new immigrant flow exceeds the loss for all years except 1962.

As noted in the appendix, two further comparative measures may be defined. The first is the difference between the number of new immigrants and the loss of permanent resident aliens. This measure estimates net annual legal immigration. Its bias is opposite that of the loss, so that if the loss overestimates emigration then the estimated net inflow underestimates net immigration. The second measure, applicable whenever the loss is positive, is the ratio of the loss to the new immigrant flow. Applying these measures to the worldwide data, we find that the *net* annual immigration over the

figures into calendar-year figures, a procedure which assumes uniform flows within a fiscal year.

FIGURE 3.3
New Immigrant Flow and Annual Loss of Permanent Resident Aliens

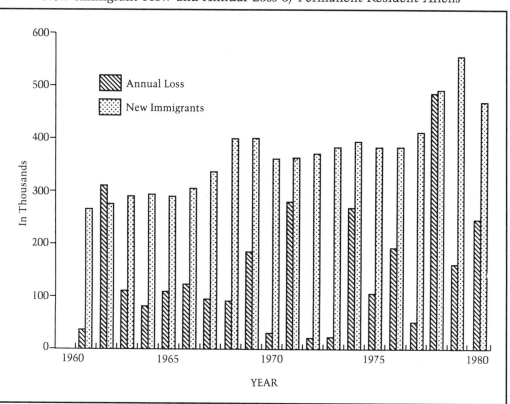

entire 20-year period averages about 221,000 compared with the average of 539,000 for gross immigrations. The average annual ratio of the loss to the new immigrant flow over the 20-year period is thus 41 percent.

Emigration by Origin Area

Because the worldwide data may mask important intraregion effects, we next examine the same series for three groups of origin countries, located in Europe, Asia, and the Western Hemisphere. Because of different definitions of the concept of region of origin in the available data—country of birth in the immigration and naturalization data series versus country of nationality in the AARP data series—region-specific estimates must be more cautiously interpreted than the corresponding worldwide estimates.

FIGURE 3.4

Predicted and Observed Number of Permanent Resident Aliens from Europe

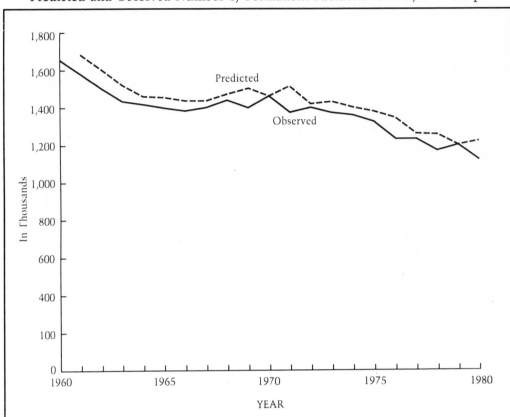

For example, it is possible that an observed loss may erroneously appear to be negative because of this definitional discrepancy.

Figures 3.4 and 3.5 indicate that the annual loss in the number of permanent resident aliens from Europe is substantial. Positive in every year except 1979, the loss averages 63,174 per year between 1961 and 1980—in some years exceeding the flow of new immigrants.

Figures 3.6 and 3.7 report the comparable data for permanent resident aliens from Asia. Between 1963 and 1977, the annual loss is small, both absolutely and relatively (with the possible exceptions of 1969 and 1974), and indeed is negative in three years—1968, 1973, and 1979. However, in 1978 and again in 1980 the loss is quite high, over 125,000 persons in each year. The fact that a negative loss (in 1979) follows a large positive loss suggests the possibility that the pro rata allocation used to convert fiscal-

FIGURE 3.5
*New Immigrant Flow and Annual Loss
of Permanent Resident Aliens from Europe*

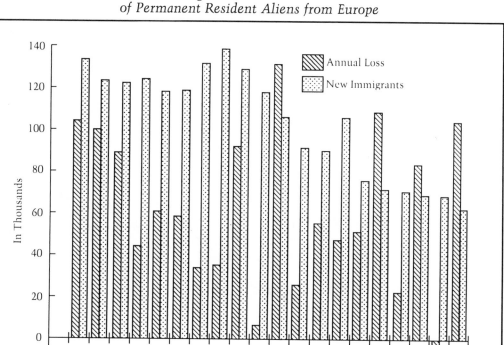

year figures to calendar-year figures (described in the appendix) may not accurately reflect the true volume of immigration and the other components of the loss equation. To smooth the data, we use five-year averages, to be calculated below.

Figures 3.8 and 3.9 suggest an upward trend in the loss of permanent resident aliens from the Western Hemisphere. The loss, which is positive in all years except two (1961 and 1973), doubles from an average annual loss of 45,910 between 1961 and 1970 to an average annual loss of 92,256 between 1971 and 1980.

The annual ratio of the loss to the new immigrant flow is shown in Figure 3.10 for the three groups of countries (omitting, of course, all observations for which the loss was negative). Except for the large ratio registered

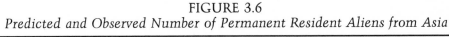

FIGURE 3.6
Predicted and Observed Number of Permanent Resident Aliens from Asia

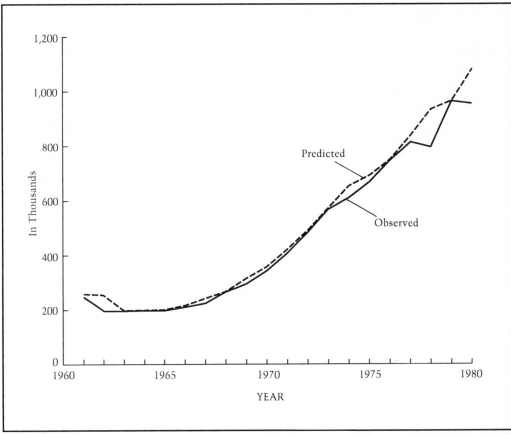

by the Asian countries in 1962, the largest ratios appear to be among the group of European countries.

It would be premature to attempt an explanation of the temporal and regional variation in the direction and magnitude of the observed loss of permanent resident aliens. A prerequisite would be a refined country-specific analysis, with particular attentiveness to the likelihood of a discrepancy between country of birth and country of nationality—a project beyond the scope of this book. Nonetheless, we may speculate that the increase in the Western Hemisphere loss between 1971 and 1980 may be due in part to the fact that Cubans, who would be expected to have low emigration, were moving out of the permanent resident alien pool (as they became natural-

FIGURE 3.7

New Immigrant Flow and Annual Loss of Permanent Resident Aliens from Asia

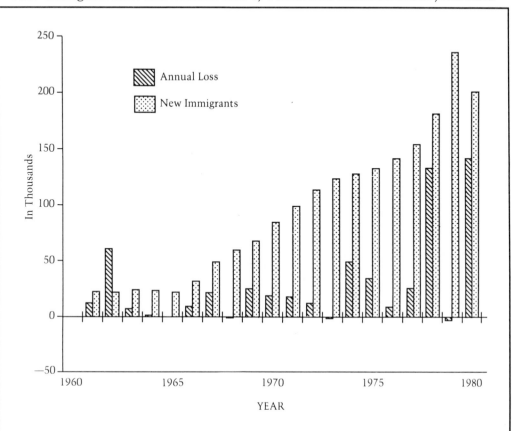

ized citizens) and, hence, no longer contributing downward pressure on the annual loss.[10]

As noted, all the figures are extremely jagged, making it difficult to discern a meaningful trend. In an effort to "smooth" the jaggedness, we compute five-year averages of the principal quantities discussed. Panel A of Table 3.1 reports the average annual loss for the four five-year periods between 1961 and 1980. As shown, the worldwide loss and all three region-specific loss figures increased across the last three periods; only the Western Hemisphere loss increased across all four periods. The European average

---

[10]This is not consistent with the anecdotal conjecture concerning the emigration of Cubans from the United States to such countries as Mexico and Spain—if such emigration occurs after naturalization.

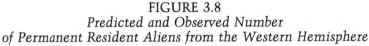

FIGURE 3.8
Predicted and Observed Number
of Permanent Resident Aliens from the Western Hemisphere

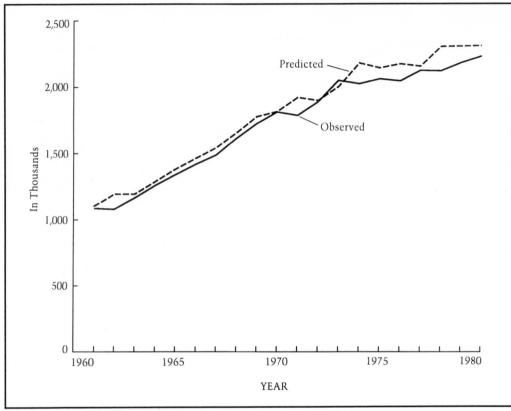

annual loss was substantial in the 1961–1965 period (over 80,000 persons), dropping to almost half that, and subsequently increasing to an average of about 63,000 during the 1970s. The average annual loss for the Asian group of countries increased moderately from about 13,000 in the 1966–1970 period to about 21,000 in the 1971–1975 period, and then to almost 60,000 in the 1976–1980 period. The Western Hemisphere loss hovered near 45,000 during the 1960s, increasing to over 69,000 in the first half of the 1970s and to 115,000 in the last half.

Panel B of Table 3.1 reports the average annual gross legal immigration and panel C the average annual estimated net immigration (i.e., the difference between the loss and the new immigrant flow). Panel C shows the dramatic decline in the average annual estimated net immigration from Europe and the dramatic increase in the estimated net immigration

FIGURE 3.9
New Immigrant Flow and Annual Loss
of Permanent Resident Aliens from the Western Hemisphere

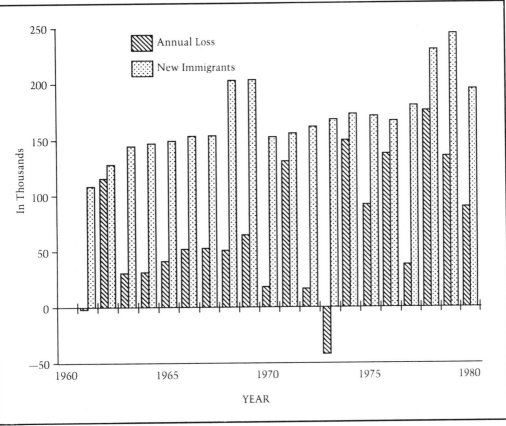

from Asia, across the four five-year periods from 1961 to 1980. While the estimated net inflow from Europe declined from an average annual high of over 80,000 in the 1966–1970 period to an average annual low of 6,527 in the most recent period, the estimated net inflow from Asia increased from an average annual low of 5,765 in the 1961–1965 period to an average annual high of 122,331 in the 1976–1980 period. The estimated net inflow from the Western Hemisphere appears remarkably constant at about 90,000 annually, the higher figures in the 1966–1970 period presumably reflecting the admission to permanent resident status of Cuban refugees.

Panels D and E of Table 3.1 report the loss as a proportion of the new immigrant flow. In panel D, the ratio is based on the five-year averages of the annual loss and inflow. Panel E reports the five-year averages of the

FIGURE 3.10
Ratio of Annual Loss to New Immigrant Flow, by Region of Origin

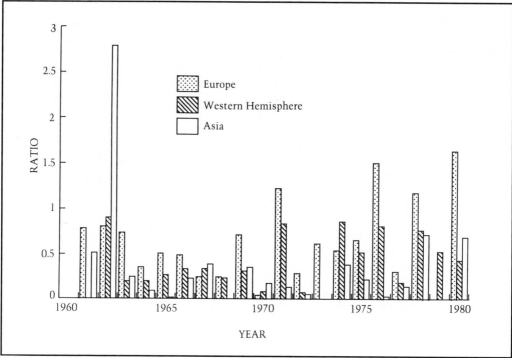

annual ratio for the worldwide case only, since, as discussed, a few of the region-specific observations had a negative annual loss. Both sets of worldwide figures indicate that the average ratio of losses to new immigrants was over 46 percent in the 1961–1965 period, declined to just under 30 percent in the next five-year period, and then increased to a high of 50 percent in the most recent period for which the requisite data are available. Since 1966, the highest loss-to-immigrants ratio has been among immigrants from Europe—over 90 percent in the most recent five-year period—followed by the Western Hemisphere, with over 56 percent, and by Asia, with almost 33 percent. The extremely high Europe figure may reflect the combined effects of emigration, deaths among elderly non-naturalized immigrants (presumably from early immigration waves), and lower levels of recent immigration flows.

These results suggest not only that net immigration is substantially lower than gross immigration but also that the discrepancy between the two differs considerably by region of origin. Because of apparent reinforcing area-specific trends in emigration, the rise in gross immigration flows

TABLE 3.1
Five-Year Averages of Annual Loss of Permanent Resident Aliens,
New Immigrants, Net Increment to Population of Permanent Resident
Aliens, and Ratio of Loss to New Immigrants, by Region of Origin:
Calendar Years 1961–1980

	1961–1965	1966–1970	1971–1975	1976–1980
A. Average Annual Loss in Population of Permanent Resident Aliens				
Europe	80,054	45,994	63,243	63,404
Asia	16,217	13,293	20,890	59,899
Western Hemisphere	44,177	47,643	69,218	115,295
Worldwide	132,400	108,671	148,116	237,646
B. Average Annual Flow of New Permanent Resident Aliens				
Europe	124,689	128,071	91,326	69,932
Asia	21,982	57,252	118,397	182,230
Western Hemisphere	136,456	174,122	166,358	203,948
Worldwide	286,932	366,610	385,969	470,430
C. Average Annual Net Increment to Population of Permanent Resident Aliens				
Europe	44,634	82,076	28,083	6,527
Asia	5,765	43,958	97,507	122,331
Western Hemisphere	92,280	126,479	97,140	88,653
Worldwide	154,532	257,939	237,853	232,785
D. Ratio of Average Loss to Average Flow of New Immigrants				
Europe	.642	.359	.692	.907
Asia	.738	.232	.176	.329
Western Hemisphere	.324	.274	.416	.565
Worldwide	.461	.296	.384	.505
E. Average Annual Ratio of Loss to New Immigrants				
Worldwide	.464	.297	.385	.500

SOURCE: INS *Annual Reports* and *Statistical Yearbooks.*

NOTES: The annual loss is calculated as the difference between the predicted population of permanent resident aliens in January of a given year and the population observed in the Alien Address Report Program. The loss thus reflects mortality, emigration, and non-response. See text for definitions and computational equations.

from Asia and the Western Hemisphere in recent decades (relative to that from Europe) understates the trends in the relative proportions of foreign-born persons from those areas residing in the United States. Comparison of the figures in panels B and C indicates that while the average annual flows of immigrants from Asia and the Western Hemisphere during the 1976–1980 period exceeded those from Europe by factors of 2.6 and 2.9, respectively, the average annual estimated *net* inflows from Asia and the Western Hemisphere exceeded those from Europe by factors of 18.7 and

13.6, respectively. Put differently, while persons from Europe accounted for 14.9 percent of *gross* legal immigration during the period 1976–1980, the estimated *net* legal immigration from Europe was only 2.8 percent of the total. In contrast, the Asian proportions of the gross inflow and net inflow were 38.7 and 52.6 percent, respectively; the Western Hemisphere proportions of the gross inflow and net inflow were 43.4 and 38.1 percent, respectively.[11]

Emigration Selectivity: Sex and Schooling

As the foregoing suggests, not all immigrants are equally likely to emigrate. The decision to leave the United States—like the decision to enter it and the decision to become a U.S. citizen—is likely to be related to the immigrant's characteristics and to the set of opportunities presented by the United States as well as by the origin country. It is likely therefore that emigration is not only selective but also *differentially* selective by country of origin and/or by entry vintage. For example, it is possible that among immigrants from country A the most skilled leave the United States, while among immigrants from country B the least skilled do so.

One way to search for emigration selectivity is to compare at two points in time the "immutable" characteristics of a cohort of the foreign-born who entered within a certain time period. As described in the Introduction, information in the Public Use Samples drawn from the U.S. censuses of 1960, 1970, and 1980 enables construction of approximations of age-specific cohorts of *recent entrants*, defined as foreign-born persons who report entering the United States in the five-year period prior to the census.

The only immutable characteristic provided by census data is sex. Substantial changes in the sex ratio of an immigrant cohort thus signal the importance of selective emigration. A "quasi-immutable" characteristic provided by the census data is schooling attainment: it can surely rise over time for an individual but it cannot decrease. Decreases in schooling attainment levels for an immigrant cohort thus also signal emigration selectivity. In this section we therefore investigate emigration selectivity by examining changes in the sex ratio and in years of schooling completed for foreign-born entry cohorts.

Panel B of Table 3.2 reports the sex ratios (measured as the ratio of females to males) in 1960 and 1970 for both age-specific cohorts of native-

[11]It would be difficult to interpret these dramatic differences between Asia and the Western Hemisphere and Europe as due to a greater propensity among Europeans to fail to register their addresses in the AARP.

TABLE 3.2
Decadal Cohort Change in Ratios of Women to Men,
by Age and Nativity: 1900–1910, 1960–1970, and 1970–1980

| Age at Start of Decade | 1900 | | | 1910 | | |
| | | 1900 New Entrants | | | 1900 New Entrants | |
	Native-Born	Eastern	Western	Native-Born	Eastern	Western
A. Age-Specific Cohorts of Native-Born and Recent Entrants in 1900						
20–24	1.05	1.08	1.52	0.97	0.69	1.81
25–29	1.06	0.58	0.88	0.98	0.50	1.14
30–34	0.95	0.44	0.83	0.92	0.48	0.88
35–39	0.98	0.40	0.75	0.99	0.55	1.00
40–44	0.92	0.41	1.75	0.94	0.56	2.00
20–44	1.01	0.65	1.11	0.96	0.58	1.28

| Age at Start of Decade | 1960 | | | 1970 | | |
| | | 1960 New Entrants | | | 1960 New Entrants | |
	Native-Born	Eastern	Western	Native-Born	Eastern	Western
B. Age-Specific Cohorts of Native-Born and Recent Entrants in 1960						
20–24	1.03	1.76	0.93	1.01	2.24	1.72
25–29	1.02	1.42	0.77	1.03	1.71	1.17
30–34	1.01	1.27	0.86	1.03	1.37	0.94
35–39	1.05	1.25	0.75	1.09	1.18	1.18
40–44	1.06	1.00	0.82	1.04	1.10	0.99
20–44	1.03	1.38	0.83	1.04	1.56	1.19

| Age at Start of Decade | 1970 | | | 1980 | | |
| | | 1970 New Entrants | | | 1970 New Entrants | |
	Native-Born	Eastern	Western	Native-Born	Eastern	Western
C. Age-Specific Cohorts of Native-Born and Recent Entrants in 1970						
20–24	1.04	0.74	1.08	1.01	1.38	1.23
25–29	1.03	1.09	1.51	1.00	1.23	1.26
30–34	1.01	1.05	1.12	1.05	1.10	1.28
35–39	1.04	1.00	1.16	1.00	1.14	1.13
40–44	1.03	0.96	1.22	1.06	0.93	1.30
20–44	1.03	0.96	1.27	1.02	1.19	1.24

SOURCE: U.S. Census of Population, Public Use Samples.

born persons and of recent entrants aged 20–44 from the Eastern and Western hemispheres. For all five age groups, the native-born exhibit the classical pattern of slightly more females than males. Against the background of the "natural" sex ratios of the native-born, the levels and the movements in the foreign-born sex ratios appear dramatic. Although differences at entry are not the primary concern in this chapter, the strong differences by hemisphere in the ratio of females to males among the foreign-born cannot be overlooked. Among natives of the Eastern Hemisphere, the 1960 recent-entrant age cohorts are predominantly female, and this tendency is more pronounced the younger the age; for example, among persons aged 20–24 in 1960, there are 176 females for every 100 males. The situation is reversed for the Western Hemisphere; in all of the age groups, there are more males than females.[12]

The passage of ten years does not preserve the foreign-born cohorts' sex ratios. It *increases* the female-male sex ratio for every hemisphere-age group except one (which remains virtually unchanged). Some of the increases are quite large. In the youngest (20–24) age group, the number of females per 100 males increased between 1960 and 1970 from 176 to 224 in the Eastern Hemisphere cohort and from 93 to 172 in the Western Hemisphere cohort.

While among the foreign-born from the Eastern Hemisphere the *increase* in the female-male sex ratio declines with age, perhaps reflecting the greater mobility of the young, among Western Hemisphere cohorts such an age pattern is not clearly discernible. Figure 3.11 shows the summary sex ratios for the three nativity groups in the broad age range of 20–44. It would appear unambiguous that the female foreign-born who entered between 1955 and 1960 tended to emigrate far less than male immigrants in the decade of the 1960s, unless census coverage of the foreign-born changed differentially by sex between the 1960 and the 1970 censuses or there are large discrepancies between the 1960 definition of the cohort (resided abroad five years earlier) and the 1970 definition of the cohort (entered in 1955–1959).[13]

The comparable figures for the 1970 recent-entrant cohorts appear in panel C of Table 3.2. These groups appear to behave rather differently from the 1955–1959 recent entrants. In every age group, the sex ratios for the Eastern Hemisphere entry cohorts are greater in 1960 than in 1970, while those for the Western Hemisphere entry cohorts are greater in 1970 than in 1960. Indeed, two of the Eastern Hemisphere ratios are less than one in 1970, and the Western Hemisphere cohorts now contain more women than men.

In the ensuing 1970–1980 decade, the Eastern Hemisphere cohorts become more predominantly female (with the exception of the 40–44 age group whose sex ratio declines slightly), as they did for the 1960 recent entrants. The Western Hemisphere cohorts, however, exhibit a mixed pat-

---

[12]We shall have more to say about this hemisphere difference in the sex ratio when we consider marriage in Chapter 4.

[13]We rule out sex changes by individuals.

FIGURE 3.11
*1960–1970 Decadal Cohort Change
in Ratios of Women to Men Aged 20–44 in 1960,
for Native-Born and Recent Entrants, by Hemisphere of Origin*

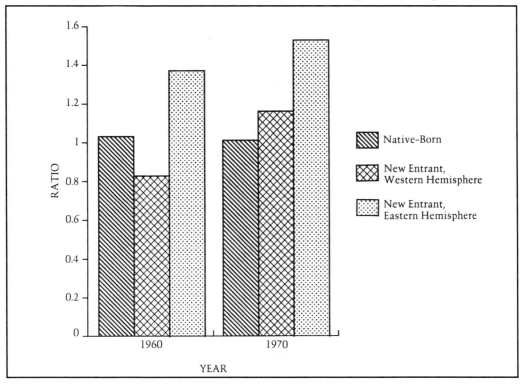

tern. Two of the age cohorts display reduced sex ratios, one of them (the 25–29 age group) markedly so. Thus, the summary sex ratios for the entire 20–44 age group, shown in Figure 3.12, indicate that in the aggregate only the Eastern Hemisphere 1970 recent-entrant cohorts became more "feminized" between 1970 and 1980.

These results suggest both the greater emigration propensities among foreign-born males and the operation of age and period of entry. Since both date of entry and age at entry reflect the selection mechanisms embodied in U.S. law as well as conditions in the origin country, these results reinforce the view that origin-country conditions and U.S. immigration law are fundamentally relevant to the migration process: they affect not only who comes to the United States, but also who stays.

The importance of historical period is underscored by comparison of the sex ratio in the three most recent censuses with the sex ratio in 1900 and its change over the ensuing decade. Panel A of Table 3.2 reports the

FIGURE 3.12
*1970–1980 Decadal Cohort Change
in Ratios of Women to Men Aged 20–44 in 1970,
for Native-Born and Recent Entrants, by Hemisphere of Origin*

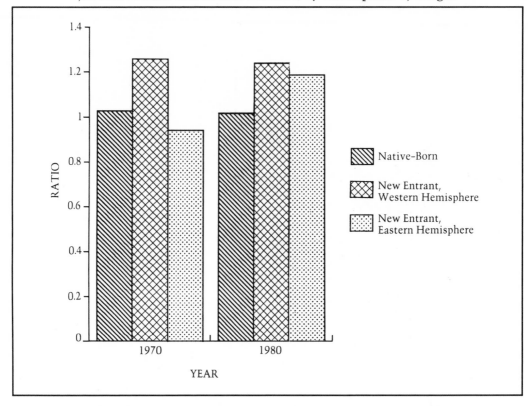

age-specific sex ratios for the native-born and for recent entrants, again by hemisphere. As is well known, the 1900 recent entrants were overwhelmingly male, the sex ratio exceeding unity for only the youngest (20–24) age group among the Eastern Hemisphere cohorts and for the youngest and oldest (40–44) age groups among the Western Hemisphere cohorts. For example, among Eastern Hemisphere recent entrants aged 35–39, there are 40 females for every 100 males. Ten years later, the Western Hemisphere cohorts have become more predominantly female, in the oldest age group there now being twice as many females as males. Among Eastern Hemisphere 1900 recent entrants, however, the sex ratio tends to increase slightly for the three oldest age groups and decrease dramatically for the youngest age group. Since the sex ratio among the native-born decreases slightly among the three youngest age groups, a portion of the decrease in the Eastern Hemisphere's sex ratio may reflect mortality among young women.

Barring such sex-specific mortality, the figures suggest that emigration by Eastern Hemisphere recent entrants was predominantly female, while the Western Hemisphere cohorts exhibit the pattern of male emigration characteristic of recent decades.

As noted, the temporal changes in a cohort's schooling attainment may also be a useful indicator of emigration selectivity, as a decrease in the average years of completed schooling may signal emigration by the better-educated, if census coverage does not selectively improve for the less educated. Tables 3.3 and 3.4 report the decadal change in years of school completed for the 1960–1970 and 1970–1980 periods for cohorts aged 25–34 in 1960 and 1970, respectively, separately by sex, among the native-born and recent entrants. These cohort changes are also depicted in Figures 3.13–3.16. The patterns appear to differ by sex. Among women, while the average schooling of the native-born increased slightly from 10.6 to 10.7 years between 1960 and 1970, average schooling declined slightly for the foreign-born recent entrants. When these changes in the schooling of female foreign-born recent entrants are decomposed by region of origin, it appears that only among Western Hemisphere immigrants did schooling levels decrease. Among men, however, the opposite appears to be the case: average schooling increased only for the Western Hemisphere recent entrants (and for the native-born), declining for the other origin groups. These results suggest that at least among the 25–34 age group that entered around 1960, the better-educated among Western Hemisphere women and among Eastern Hemisphere men may have emigrated.

As Table 3.4 reports, the picture is quite different for the 1970 recent entrants. For both females and males, schooling increases during the decade for all nativity groups. Such a schooling increase is consistent with both emigration of less educated persons and a true increase in schooling. Hence, no emigration inference can be drawn from the schooling behavior of the 1970 recent entrants.

As noted earlier, the indications of differential emigration selectivity by decade suggest again the part played by U.S. immigrant selection laws in shaping each immigrant cohort and the possible biases that may arise when such selectivity is not recognized. Moreover, the results suggest that inferences about the adjustment patterns of male immigrants based on census data are likely to be more biased by nonrandom emigration than inferences about the patterns of female immigrants, given the apparently greater emigration propensities of foreign-born males in the 1960–1970 and 1970–1980 decades. In addition, emigration rates appear to be increasing, making future inferences about how immigrants fare in the United States even less reliable in the absence of new data sources.[14]

---

[14]In Chapter 7 we compare in some detail cross-sectional, aggregate cohort change and longitudinal estimates of immigrant adjustment with respect to earnings attainment.

TABLE 3.3
1960–1970 Decadal Cohort Change in Average Years of Schooling Completed Among Recent-Entrant and Native-Born Men and Women Aged 25–34 in 1960, by Area of Origin

Area of Origin	1960		1970	
A. Females				
Asia	10.6	(17.2)[a]	10.7	(15.6)
Europe	9.8	(54.6)	9.9	(53.6)
Western Hemisphere	9.1	(25.8)	8.5	(26.7)
Other	9.5	(2.3)	9.9	(4.0)
Total 1960 recent entrants	9.8	(100.0)	9.7	(100.0)
Native-born	10.6		10.7	
B. Males				
Asia	14.2	(14.1)	13.9	(10.8)
Europe	10.9	(47.1)	10.3	(52.3)
Western Hemisphere	8.1	(36.8)	8.5	(33.7)
Other	11.4	(2.0)	11.1	(3.2)
Total 1960 recent entrants	10.3	(100.0)	10.1	(100.0)
Native-born	10.8		11.0	

SOURCE: U.S. Census of Population, Public Use Samples.

[a]Percentage of cohort from area of origin.

TABLE 3.4
1970–1980 Decadal Cohort Change in Average Years of Schooling Completed Among Recent-Entrant and Native-Born Men and Women Aged 25–34 in 1970, by Area of Origin

Area of Origin	1970		1980	
A. Females				
Asia	12.5	(23.9)[a]	14.1	(22.9)
Europe	10.3	(34.0)	11.8	(27.8)
Western Hemisphere	8.9	(36.2)	10.5	(43.9)
Other	10.2	(5.9)	11.9	(5.5)
Total 1970 recent entrants	10.3	(100.0)	11.7	(100.0)
Native-born	11.2		12.4	
B. Males				
Asia	14.2	(27.3)	16.3	(24.6)
Europe	11.1	(31.6)	11.8	(26.0)
Western Hemisphere	9.5	(34.7)	9.9	(41.9)
Other	12.5	(6.4)	13.2	(7.4)
Total 1970 recent entrants	11.5	(100.0)	12.2	(100.0)
Native-born	11.7		12.9	

SOURCE: U.S. Census of Population, Public Use Samples.

[a]Percentage of cohort from area of origin.

FIGURE 3.13
*1960–1970 Decadal Cohort Change in Schooling Attainment
Among Native-Born and Recent-Entrant Women Aged 25–34 in 1960,
by Area of Origin*

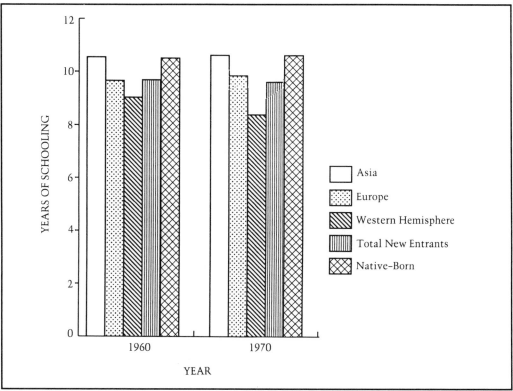

Summary

Our examination of alien registration data for the 20 years between
1961 and 1980 suggests that up to 1.2 million permanent resident aliens
may have left the United States between 1960 and 1969 and up to 1.9
million between 1970 and 1979, decades when new immigrants numbered
3.3 million and 4.3 million, respectively. Thus, more than 40 percent of
immigrants may have left the United States in the 1960–1979 period. Even
if we assume high death rates and high rates of non-response and non-
registration, the remaining emigration is substantial.

Moreover, the emigration of the foreign-born appears to be selective—
beyond the expected low emigration of refugees. Men appear to have higher
emigration rates than women. Persons from Europe appear to have the

FIGURE 3.14
*1960–1970 Decadal Cohort Change in Schooling Attainment
Among Native-Born and Recent-Entrant Men Aged 25–34 in 1960,
by Area of Origin*

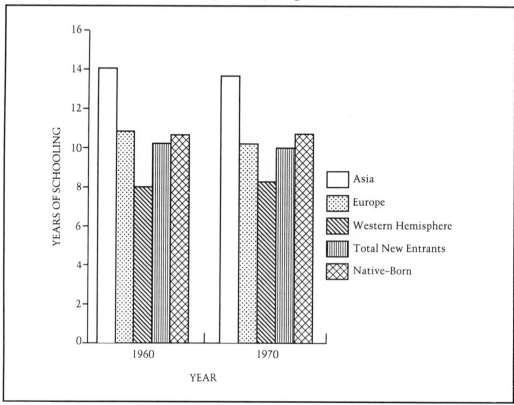

highest propensity to leave the United States, and persons from Asia the lowest, with Western Hemisphere immigrants in an intermediate place. As a consequence, data on gross immigration flows, used in almost all analyses of immigration, tend to understate the relative decline in the proportions of recent immigrants from Europe. Net immigration figures display a much greater growth in the volume of Asian immigration than of European immigration in recent years than do gross immigration data.

The data also suggest many other characteristics of emigration selectivity—by sex, age, schooling, period of entry, and region of origin. For example, if we restrict attention to those persons who entered the United States in the 1955–1960 period and who were aged 25–34 in 1960, among Western Hemisphere women and Eastern Hemisphere men, those with higher levels of schooling appeared to have emigrated at higher rates between 1960 and 1970.

FIGURE 3.15
*1970–1980 Decadal Cohort Change in Schooling Attainment
Among Native-Born and Recent-Entrant Women Aged 25–34 in 1970,
by Area of Origin*

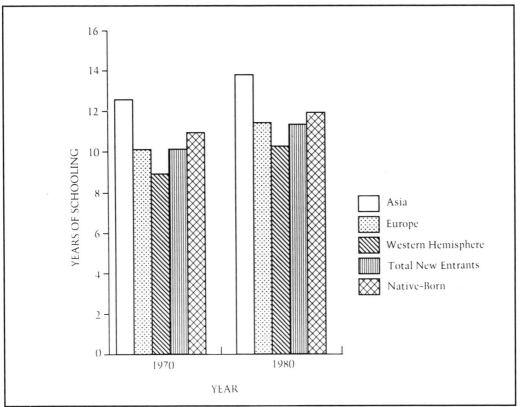

FIGURE 3.16
1970–1980 Decadal Cohort Change in Schooling Attainment
Among Native-Born and Recent-Entrant Men Aged 25–34 in 1970,
by Area of Origin

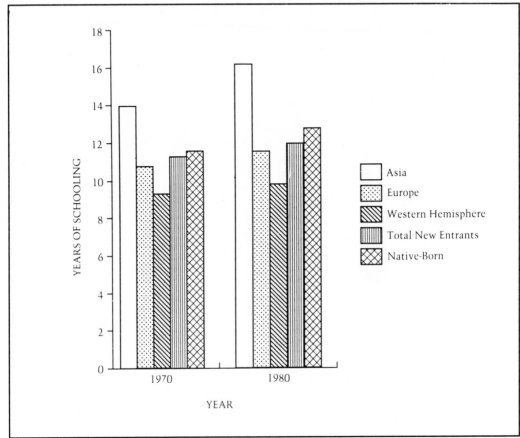

Appendix
Estimating Emigration

Components-of-Population Equations

To begin, we express the true number of permanent resident aliens at time t (for convenience, we fix the time units at one year) by the following components-of-population equation:

$$(3.1) \qquad \text{true } P_t = \text{true } P_{t-1} + I_{t-1} - C_{t-1} - D_{t-1} - E_{t-1},$$

where *true* P_t denotes the number of permanent resident aliens residing in the United States in January of year t, I_{t-1} denotes the number of immigrants (new permanent resident aliens) admitted during the preceding calendar year, C denotes the number of permanent resident aliens who became citizens during the year, D denotes the number of permanent resident aliens who died during the year, and E denotes the number of permanent resident aliens who emigrated during the year.[15]

While we cannot observe *true* P_t, we can observe the number of permanent resident aliens who, complying with the provisions of the Immigration and Nationality Act, reported their addresses to the INS in January of each year. This population may be represented by the following components-of-population equation:

$$(3.2) \qquad \text{obs } P_t = \text{true } P_t - N_t,$$

where N_t denotes the number of permanent resident aliens who do not report their addresses to the INS.

Substituting equation (3.1) into equation (3.2) yields:

$$(3.3) \qquad \text{obs } P_t = \text{true } P_{t-1} + I_{t-1} - C_{t-1} - D_{t-1} - E_{t-1} - N_t.$$

Since equation (3.2) holds at any time t, including time $t - 1$, so that

$$(3.4) \qquad \text{true } P_{t-1} = \text{obs } P_{t-1} + N_{t-1},$$

it follows that equation (3.3) can be restated:

$$(3.5) \quad \text{obs } P_t = \text{obs } P_{t-1} + I_{t-1} - C_{t-1} - D_{t-1} - E_{t-1} + N_{t-1} - N_t$$

Administrative records of the INS provide three of the terms in this expression: the *obs* P, I, and C terms. Hence, it is possible to define a measure of the predicted stock of permanent resident aliens and a measure of the observed loss—based entirely on quantities observed by the INS.

[15]For fuller discussion of the basic components-of-population equations, see Shryock and Siegel (1975) and Siegel (1978).

We define the predicted stock of permanent resident aliens at time t by:

$$(3.6) \qquad pred\ P_t = obs\ P_{t-1} + I_{t-1} - C_{t-1}.$$

It then follows that the loss L in permanent resident aliens observed from January to January may be written:

$$(3.7) \qquad L_{t-1} = pred\ P_t - obs\ P_t.$$

Substituting (3.5) and (3.6) into (3.7) shows that the loss has four components—deaths during the year, emigration during the year, and the number of non-responders in both the current and the preceding year:

$$(3.8) \qquad L_{t-1} = E_{t-1} + D_{t-1} - N_{t-1} + N_t.$$

Thus, the observed loss L, which can be calculated directly, is exactly equal to the sum of emigration and deaths during the year in the special case where the number of permanent resident aliens who did not report their addresses the previous January equals the number who do not report their addresses the current January. The observed loss is negative whenever the number of non-responders in the previous year exceeds the sum of deaths and emigration during the preceding year and non-responders in the current year. Such a situation would be highly unlikely.[16]

To examine the relationship between the observed loss and the volume of emigration, we write the conditional inequalities:

$$(3.9) \qquad L_{t-1} \begin{cases} < & E_{t-1} & \text{iff} & D_{t-1} - N_{t-1} + N_t & < & 0 \\ = & E_{t-1} & \text{iff} & D_{t-1} - N_{t-1} + N_t & = & 0 \\ > & E_{t-1} & \text{iff} & D_{t-1} - N_{t-1} + N_t & > & 0 \end{cases}$$

Thus, the loss overestimates emigration if non-response increases over time or if deaths occur and non-response is nondecreasing over time. In contrast, the loss underestimates emigration if non-response the preceding year exceeds the sum of deaths in the preceding year and non-response in the current year.

The observed loss L can be used to calculate two further measures: the estimated annual net immigration and an annual ratio of the loss to the new immigrant flow.

---

[16]However, as will be seen below, there are two data-related reasons why estimates of the loss may be negative.

Numerical Estimates of the Components of Population

To estimate the predicted stock of permanent resident aliens, we use information published in the INS *Annual Report* and *Statistical Yearbook* on the total number of new permanent resident aliens (the G-188 file), on the number of naturalizations (the G-173 file), and on the number of persons who obtained derivative citizenship (the G-172 file).

Two problems arise in obtaining numerical estimates of the elements in equations (3.6) and (3.7) above. The first involves comparability of the reporting period, and the second involves comparability of the concept used for region of origin. With respect to the first, the annual registration of aliens occurred during the month of January, dictating use of calendar-year referents for the immigration and citizenship components. The published data, however, are for fiscal-year referents. Prior to 1977, fiscal years in the United States began on the first of July. Effective with FY 1977, the government changed to an October start of the fiscal year; FY 1977 started in October 1976. A special transition quarter covers the missing three months of 1976. The auxiliary computational equation used to obtain calendar-year measures of the immigration and citizenship components, where K denotes any of the three data series, is as follows:

$$(3.10) \qquad K_{t-1}^{CY} = \begin{cases} .5\ K_{t-1}^{FY} + .5\ K_t^{FY}, & t < 77 \\ .5\ K_{t-1}^{FY} + K^{TQ} + .25\ K_t^{FY}, & t = 77 \\ .75\ K_{t-1}^{FY} + .25\ K_t^{FY}, & t > 77 \end{cases}$$

For example, to compute the predicted stock of permanent resident aliens in January 1975, we estimate the number of new immigrants admitted during CY 1974 as the sum of those admitted in January–June 1974 (estimated as half of those admitted in FY 1974) and those admitted in July–December 1974 (estimated as half of those admitted in FY 1975).

Equation (3.10) was used to calculate all the figures used to estimate *pred P*$_t$, with one exception: we were unable to obtain figures for derivative citizenship during the transition quarter. The result of this lack of information is to bias upward the predicted stock of permanent resident aliens in 1977 and hence to bias upward the observed loss (and the estimated emigration). However, since the number of derivative citizenships is quite small (the full-year figures for FY 1976 and 1977 are 9,632 and 10,579, respectively), the magnitude of the bias is less than 3,000 worldwide, an almost negligible quantity.

The second problem, comparability of region of origin, arises only in estimation for subworld segments. The address-report tabulations, for the years beginning in 1961 and continuing to the last round in 1980, report only the country of nationality; prior to 1961, the data for some years include region of birth. However, in the other required series, country of nationality is provided only in the naturalization tabulations and is absent from the derivative-citizenship and immigration tabulations. Thus, we are unable to estimate all the equation terms using a uniform concept of region of origin. Since tabulations by country of birth are published for all the data series required except the AARP data, we use the birth concept for everything except the address registration. This discrepancy, of course, has no effect on our results for total predicted stock or total worldwide loss. It can, however, affect the accuracy of our results for regions of the world. Since most cases involving a discrepancy between country of birth and country of nationality involve the British Empire, the potential for error is low in the period since 1960. For example, while in 1945 all 19,970 persons who naturalized and who reported their country of birth as Canada reported their country of nationality as other than Canada (presumably the British Empire), in 1965 the naturalization tabulations report 7,017 persons born in Canada and 8,489 claiming Canada as the country of former nationality. Of course, the reader may think of other special cases.

4

THE MARRIAGE MARKET
AND THE MELTING POT

A MONG THE rights that are considered basic in the United States is the right to marry almost any person of one's choosing[1]—including a foreigner—and to live with that person in the United States. Official U.S. commitment to the principle of free marital choice is reflected in its signing the Helsinki Accords of 1975 (which called for the easing of restrictions on marriages to foreigners and for the reunification of families) and in the relatively massive governmental efforts to secure the emigration from the Soviet Union (also a signatory of the Helsinki Accords) of approximately 100 "divided spouses."[2] Perhaps the most concrete embodiment of this commitment is in U.S. immigration law, which provides special privileges for a citizen's sponsorship of a foreign spouse[3] and for the immigrant spouse's subsequent naturalization.

[1]The qualifier is made necessary by a residual set of restrictions on the choice of spouse, such as age and degree of consanguinity.

[2]The term "divided spouses" is used in the popular press to denote married couples who are forced to live apart because of national restrictions on emigration and/or immigration. The *New York Times* has carried extended accounts of these persons, of the activities of the U.S. government on their behalf, and of the outcomes of these activities. This term is not often used about marriages involving non-Soviet spouses; however, the easing of certain marriage restrictions in South Africa in early 1986 also received extensive press coverage.

[3]The U.S. immigration law was not always so generous. In particular, the law was until 1952 gender-attentive, admitting without numerical restriction the wives of U.S. citizens but the husbands of U.S. citizens only if the marriage had taken place before a certain date (the

There is another perspective—besides that of the rights of U.S. citizens—from which one may look at the spouse provisions of U.S. immigration law. As competition for scarce visas increases, and many persons are either otherwise ineligible under immigration law or must wait many years for a visa, marriage to a U.S. citizen may become an increasingly attractive means of immigration.

Indeed, immigration through marriage is an important and growing component of immigration flows. In 1986, for example, 31 percent of all adults granted permanent residence in the United States—almost 132,000 persons—were admitted as the spouses of U.S. citizens.[4] The comparable figures in 1979 and 1969 were 26 and 17 percent, respectively. If we include the number of persons who enter the United States with a non-immigrant-fiancé-of-U.S.-citizen visa (K visa) and subsequently marry the U.S. citizen and become permanent resident aliens (IF1 class of admission), the 1986 figure rises to 32 percent—almost a third of all adult immigrants. Further, if we remove from the base adult population those immigrants adjusting from refugee/asylee status, the proportion admitted as spouses of U.S. citizens increases to almost 39 percent.[5]

That a U.S. immigrant visa is currently an object of value in courtship in the international marriage market is vividly exemplified by marriage advertisements published in foreign newspapers. Consider, for example, the *Times of India* for Sunday, 31 July 1983, which contains over 200 advertisements for marriage partners. The advertisements highlight characteristics of the individual seeking a mate as well as characteristics desired in a prospective mate. Alongside information on age, height, and caste origin, elaborated with such particulars as "status family," "earning five figures," and "highly cultured family having established business," there appear references to U.S. experience. The latter range from "educated in USA," being "well settled in USA," and "proposing to immigrate USA" to explicit mention of U.S. citizenship and U.S. permanent resident status. Following are three of these advertisements:

- Parents of Computer Engineer USA, 25, Tamil Protestant Christian, post graduate, smart, handsome youth, green card holder, invite corre-

---

date was originally set at 1 June 1928, later changed to 1 July 1932, and by 1952 was at 1 January 1948). Those more recently married foreign husbands competed for first-preference visas within the national origins quotas. Since some of the quotas were small (e.g., 307 for Greece and 3,845 for Italy), several countries had backlogs for immigrant visas (these countries included Greece, Portugal, Romania, Spain, and Turkey).

[4]This calculation, based on published INS tabulations, defines adults as persons aged 20 and over and assumes that new spouse-immigrants are themselves at least 20 years old (INS 1988, Tables 4 and 11; corresponding tables in earlier issues).

[5]The number of refugees and asylees aged 20 and over who were admitted to permanent residence in FY 1986 is constructed from Tables 25 and 31 (INS 1986).

spondence from parents of committed very fair, slim, beautiful girls with excellent background, full particulars.

- Wanted Tall, Handsome Doctor for beautiful, U.S. citizen brilliant Khatri girl 22, expecting career in medicine, 160 cms. Send particulars with photo. . . .
- Smart, Handsome, Leuva Patel Doctor 25/168, invites correspondence from green card holder girl, caste no bar.

These advertisements indicate that in making marital arrangements explicit consideration is accorded possession of a U.S. visa or U.S. citizenship; legal residence in the United States is weighed along with caste origin, physical traits, schooling, occupation, and other attributes more conventionally considered relevant to mate selection.

There are other indications that popular notice has been taken of the possibility that marriage may be an element in an immigration strategy. The *New York Times Sunday Magazine* of 11 May 1986 carried an article titled "The Mail-Order Marriage Business," discussing how U.S. citizens "order" spouses, usually brides, from foreign countries, in particular Asian countries (Belkin 1986). A recent "Dear Abby" column[6] led with a cautionary letter to American women contemplating marriage to a foreign man: "What kind of visa does he have? If he already has a green card, he's probably a good bet. Some men marry American women just to get permanent resident status in this country." It is possible that similar warnings, addressed to U.S. men, may be found in publications for U.S. personnel stationed overseas.

Marriage to a U.S. citizen may also be thought to hasten immigrant adjustment, providing for the alien a built-in "native caseworker," as well as a "citizen-advocate" before the state. In addition, the offspring of such mixed-origin marriages will reside in a family environment less dominated by non-U.S. traditions than will offspring of two foreign-born parents. The marital choices of the foreign-born are thus an important component of the "melting pot." To the extent that a higher proportion of the foreign-born are marrying U.S. citizens now than was true in the past, patterns of immigrant adjustment may differ from those observed in earlier decades.

Of course, not all of the foreign-born married to U.S. citizens became immigrants by such marriages. Immigrants who are unmarried at entry also become participants in the U.S. marriage market, as U.S. residents and possibly as U.S. citizens.

This chapter utilizes both census and INS data to (1) examine the role of U.S. immigration law in determining the number of foreign-born persons

---

[6]The syndicated column appeared in the *Minneapolis Star and Tribune*, 20 May 1986. The heading in this edition read, "Here are some points to consider if marrying a man from a foreign country."

who enter the United States through marriage and the origin-country characteristics and gender of such immigrants; (2) examine mate selection by the foreign-born, in terms of their spouses' origin-country characteristics and earnings potential; and (3) compare the stability of marriages in the foreign-born and native-born populations.

Marriage as a Route to Immigration

If the propensity of the foreign-born to marry U.S. citizens is assumed to be derived in part from the demand for scarce U.S. immigrant visas, a number of implications arise concerning the trends one would expect to observe in the number of "spouse-of-U.S.-citizen" visas over the last decades and the country composition of such immigrants. For example, other things being the same, the lower the probability that a foreign-born person can obtain an immigrant visa under non-spouse provisions, the greater the probability that he or she will seek to marry a U.S. citizen. That is, in general, persons who do not meet eligibility criteria—do not, for example, have the right kind of blood kin in the United States or the right skills—or whose co-nationals are in great numbers seeking immigration (such that country visa ceilings are binding) would be more likely to find attractive a U.S. partner. This in turn suggests that between 1952 and 1968 the possibility of immigration would not have played a significant part in marriages involving natives of the Western Hemisphere, since immigration from that area was virtually unconstrained.

Of course, the *opportunities* to meet a potential U.S. mate are not randomly distributed. If men are more likely to travel abroad than women, then we would expect that U.S. citizen men would meet foreign wives in other countries and that U.S. citizen women would meet foreign husbands in the United States. The U.S. men most likely to live abroad long enough to engage in a courtship are military personnel. The foreign men most likely to reside in the United States with sufficient time to search for mates or to arrange marital contracts are students. Accordingly, the immigrant wives of U.S. citizens would be disproportionately drawn from among countries which host U.S. military installations and the number of immigrant husbands of U.S. citizens would reflect the origin country's number of students in the United States.

The origin country's distance from the United States may also play a part. Net of other factors, the lower the direct cost of travel, the greater the likelihood of travel. Thus, other things the same, there would be greater travel—and hence greater mating opportunities—between the United States and other Western Hemisphere countries than between the United States and Eastern Hemisphere countries. And if the presumed sex differential in travel is mitigated somewhat by proximity, then there would be more women travelers in the United States from the Western Hemisphere than from the Eastern Hemisphere.

Trends in the Immigration of Spouses of U.S. Citizens

Figure 4.1 depicts the number of immigrants admitted as spouses of U.S. citizens between 1950 and 1985, for three region-of-birth groups.[7] While the number from Europe remained relatively constant at less than 20,000 annually during that period, the number from Asia and from the Western Hemisphere increased substantially. In the 20 years prior to 1968, the number of spouses from Asia hovered near 10,000 annually, presumably largely reflecting marriages of U.S. military personnel stationed in such Asian countries as Japan, Korea, and the Philippines (a proposition we examine more systematically below). The subsequent increase to 19,701 in 1973 and to 33,929 in 1985 presumably reflects both marriages of naturalized U.S. citizens (whose immigration was made possible by the 1965 amendments) and the increase in U.S. military forces associated with the Indochinese hostilities.

In the Western Hemisphere, the increase in marriage-related visas was both dramatic and seemingly responsive to the two major law changes affecting Western Hemisphere immigration. Two distinct increases are discernible in Figure 4.1. First, there was an increase from a few hundred a year—471 in 1968—to 19,605 in 1971 (a more than 40-fold increase) and to 31,944 in 1974. After a decline (possibly reflecting economic conditions in the United States) to 23,747 in 1976, there was a second increase, reaching 61,329 in 1985. These figures are consistent with the view that the number of marriages to U.S. citizens responds to changes in immigration law: the increase after 1968 may be a response to the then newly placed hemispheric numerical limitation, while the increase after 1977 may be a response to changes in the criteria for the selection of immigrants occurring in 1978.

Another way to view the dramatic shifts in the number of spouses of U.S. citizens is to examine trends for the two Western Hemisphere countries which border the United States. Table 4.1 reports the number of gender-specific spouse-of-U.S.-citizen immigrants for FYs 1968, 1969, 1976,

[7]Starting in 1986, the published cross-tabulations of country of birth by class of admission include in the same group both persons adjusting from a fiancé visa and persons admitted as spouses of U.S. citizens. Thus, the spouse series cannot, for subworld segments, be extended into 1986 using published data alone. The total worldwide number of adjustments from a fiancé visa hover at about 5,000 per year in the period 1982–1988 (Table 4, INS *1988 Statistical Yearbook*).

FIGURE 4.1
*Immigrants Admitted as Spouses of U.S. Citizens,
by Region of Birth and Year of Admission: 1950–1985*

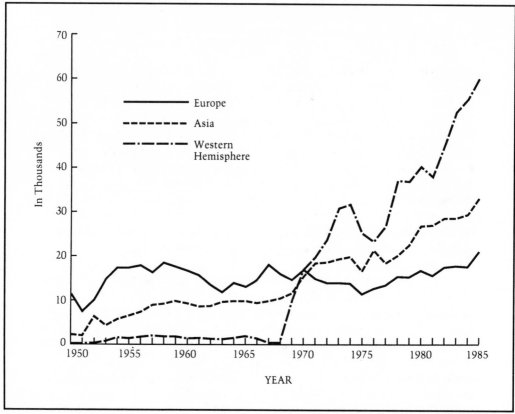

and 1977. The large increases between 1968 and 1969—for example, from 4 to 1,348 for Canadian wives—and between 1976 and 1977—for example, from 1,618 to 7,660 for Mexican husbands—suggest again the effects of policies which, first, set a ceiling on immigration (for certain types of immigrants) and, second, reduced the number of visas available to non-kin entrants from 120,000 to approximately 24,000.

The trends in the gender-specific number of admissions for wives and husbands are reported in Figures 4.2 and 4.3, respectively, for the same three region-of-birth categories between 1950 and 1979.[8] The figures indicate that while the number of wives from Europe declined from a high of 14,384 in 1967 to 10,247 in 1979, the number from Asia increased from

[8]Published tabulations of the gender-specific figures are not available after 1979.

TABLE 4.1
Immigrants Admitted as Spouses of U.S. Citizens
in FYs 1968, 1969, 1976, and 1977: Canada and Mexico

Country	FY 1968		FY 1969	
	Wives	Husbands	Wives	Husbands
A. Before and After Imposition of a Numerical Ceiling				
Canada	4	4	1348	575
Mexico	2	0	3397	3052

Country	FY 1976		FY 1977	
	Wives	Husbands	Wives	Husbands
B. Before and After Shift to Preference-Category System of Visa Allocation				
Canada	575	347	1813	1221
Mexico	1001	1618	4729	7660

SOURCE: INS *Annual Reports* and *Statistical Yearbooks.*

7,000 to almost 16,000—more than doubling—over the same period. The number of wives from the Western Hemisphere increased from virtually none through 1968 to 20,578 in 1978. If we rank-order the region-of-origin groups in 1979, we see that the largest group of wives is from the Western Hemisphere, the second largest from Asia, and the smallest from Europe. However, the numbers do not differ very much, the difference between the smallest and the largest contingent being less than 9,000.

The pattern for husbands is rather different. As Figure 4.3 shows, the number of husbands from Asia equalled the number from Europe in the early 1970s and by 1979 exceeded it by 2,191. In contrast, the number of Western Hemisphere husbands reached a peak of 16,863 in 1974 and, following a decline to 12,180 in 1976, increased again to 18,486 in 1979. While the rank-ordering of the husbands' groups in 1979 is the same as that for the wives, the difference between the Asian and the European contingents is minor, slightly over 2,000, while the difference between the Asian and the Western Hemisphere groups is 11,060.

The volume of spouse immigrants also differs by sex. The number of immigrants admitted as wives of U.S. citizens exceeded that admitted as husbands of U.S. citizens from 1950 to 1979, the latest year for which sex-specific figures are published (Figure 4.4). But this predominance of wives appears to be chiefly characteristic of Eastern Hemisphere spouse immigration. The sex-and-hemisphere-specific numbers and the hemisphere-specific proportion female shown in Figures 4.5 and 4.6, respectively, indicate that while Western Hemisphere spouses are about evenly divided among men and women, Eastern Hemisphere spouses of U.S. citizens are predominant-

FIGURE 4.2
*Immigrants Admitted as Wives of U.S. Citizens,
by Region of Birth and Year of Admission: 1950–1979*

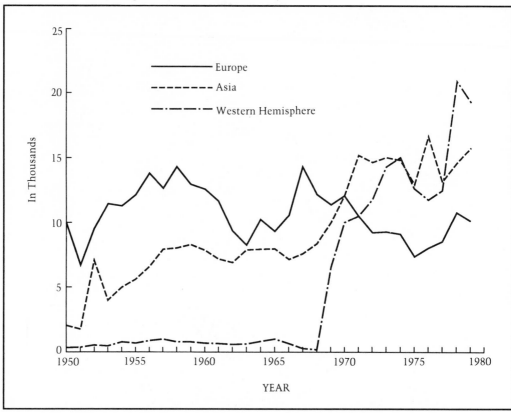

ly female. Figure 4.6, however, suggests a mild trend toward a diminished proportion female among Eastern Hemisphere spouses.

Table 4.2 reports the hemisphere-specific numbers of immigrants admitted as wives and husbands of U.S. citizens in FY 1979, the last year for which such data are published. Of the 37,380 Western Hemisphere spouses, 51 percent are women; in contrast, of the 43,401 Eastern Hemisphere spouses, 64 percent are women.

At least through 1979, male U.S. citizens were more likely than female U.S. citizens to sponsor foreign spouses; in 1979 the numbers, respectively, were 46,902 and 33,879. Hence, in order to understand the cross-hemisphere sex differential, it is necessary to examine gender-specific patterns. The numbers in Table 4.2 indicate that of the male U.S. citizens who married (and sponsored) foreigners, 60 percent chose wives from the East-

FIGURE 4.3
*Immigrants Admitted as Husbands of U.S. Citizens,
by Region of Birth and Year of Admission: 1950–1979*

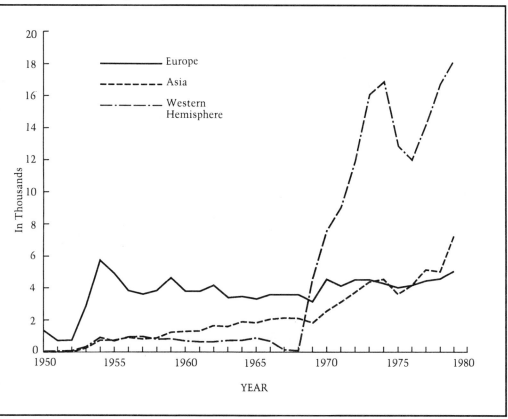

ern Hemisphere. In contrast, of the female U.S. citizens who married (and sponsored) foreigners, only 45 percent chose husbands from the Eastern Hemisphere. These marked gender-specific proclivities in foreign mates suggest (1) that marriageable U.S. men are more likely to travel to the Eastern Hemisphere than to the Western Hemisphere and/or that among marriageable foreign females in the United States, a majority are from the Eastern Hemisphere; and (2) that marriageable U.S. women are more likely to travel to the Western Hemisphere than to the Eastern Hemisphere and/or that among marriageable foreign males in the United States, a majority are from the Western Hemisphere.

FIGURE 4.4
*Immigrants Admitted as Spouses of U.S. Citizens,
by Sex and Year of Admission: 1950–1979*

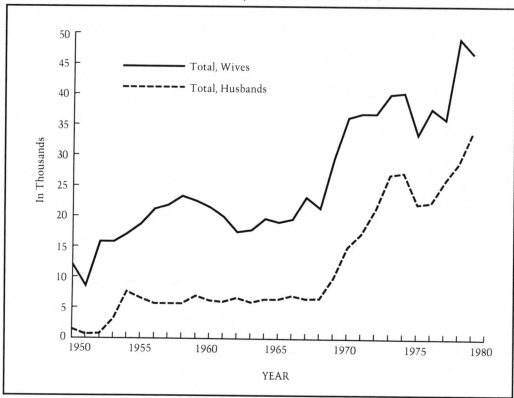

Trends in the Proportion Married Among Recent Entrants

Another way to examine the effects of immigration restriction on marital behavior is to compare the proportion married within age-specific groups of persons enumerated in the U.S. Census who report entry in the last five years with the proportion married among native-born persons of the same age. Table 4.3 and Figures 4.7 and 4.8 report the percent married for men and women aged 20–44 enumerated in the censuses of 1960, 1970, and 1980, for native-born and hemisphere-specific recent entrants. As is well known, the proportion married among the native-born has declined markedly since 1960: for women, from 84 percent in 1960 to 64 percent in 1980; for men, from 78 percent in 1960 to 60 percent in 1980.

The marriage rates for the foreign-born recent entrants aged 20–44 differ from those of their native-born counterparts in several ways. First, all

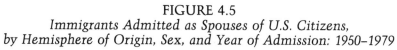

FIGURE 4.5
*Immigrants Admitted as Spouses of U.S. Citizens,
by Hemisphere of Origin, Sex, and Year of Admission: 1950–1979*

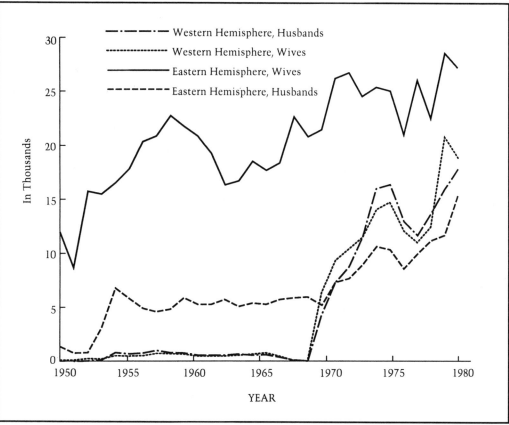

recent-entrant groups display a lower proportion married than the native-born except one—Eastern Hemisphere women in 1980—consistent with the numbers admitted as spouses of U.S. citizens shown in Figure 4.5. Second, while between 1960 and 1970 the proportion married fell for all recent-entrant groups, between 1970 and 1980 only that among Western Hemisphere recent-entrant men declined. The remaining three recent-entrant groups—that is, all the women and the Eastern Hemisphere men—experienced an increase in the proportion married between 1970 and 1980. Thus, it would appear that immigration policies, which facilitate the immigration of spouses and of family members, are manifested in the trend toward greater proclivities for marriage among the foreign-born than the native-born.

163

FIGURE 4.6
Proportion Female Among Immigrants
Admitted as Spouses of U.S. Citizens,
by Hemisphere of Origin and Year of Admission: 1950–1979

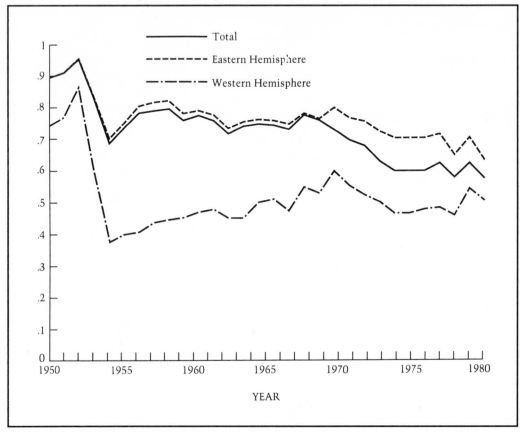

Table 4.3 also reports the ratio of the men's proportion married to the women's proportion married by census year; Figure 4.9 displays these trends graphically. Some interesting findings emerge. First, the figures show that the proportion married is always lower among men than among women. This is consistent with the greater numbers of wives admitted as spouses of U.S. citizens, as seen in Figure 4.5 and in Table 4.2. Second, while the ratio increases slightly across the 20-year period for the native-born, it follows U-shaped patterns for the two hemisphere-specific recent-entrant groups, patterns which are, moreover, opposite. For the Eastern Hemisphere groups, the ratio declines slightly between 1960 and 1970 and then increases slightly, to about its 1960 level, by 1980. For the Western Hemi-

TABLE 4.2
Immigrants Admitted as Spouses of U.S. Citizens in FY 1979,
by Sex and Hemisphere of Birth

Region of Birth/Sex	Wives	Husbands	Total
Western Hemisphere	18,894	18,486	37,380
Eastern Hemisphere	28,008	15,393	43,401
Total	46,902	33,879	80,781

SOURCE: Tables 6, 6A, INS *1979 Statistical Yearbook.*

NOTE: Figures are based on published INS tabulations for persons admitted with a spouse visa; they do not include the 4,123 persons who became permanent residents after marrying a U.S. citizen, having entered with a fiancé visa.

TABLE 4.3
Proportion Married of Native-Born and Hemisphere-Specific
Recent-Entrant Men and Women Aged 20–44: 1960–1980

Sex	Native-Born	Recent Entrants	
		E.H.	W.H.
A. 1960			
Male	.776	.596	.603
Female	.840	.798	.733
Ratio (Male/Female)	.924	.747	.823
B. 1970			
Male	.732	.464	.575
Female	.778	.641	.591
Ratio (Male/Female)	.941	.724	.973
C. 1980			
Male	.605	.550	.557
Female	.639	.733	.638
Ratio (Male/Female)	.947	.750	.873

SOURCE: U.S. Census Public Use Samples.

sphere groups, on the other hand, the ratio increases rather strongly between 1960 and 1970 and then declines to a level in 1980 higher than its 1960 level. These results suggest, mildly, that the preference-category system of visa allocation, whose inception was between 1960 and 1970 for the Eastern Hemisphere and between 1970 and 1980 for the Western Hemisphere, provided an impetus for the immigration of married women relative to married men.

FIGURE 4.7

Percent Married Among Native-Born and Recent-Entrant Women Aged 20–44, by Hemisphere of Origin: 1960–1980

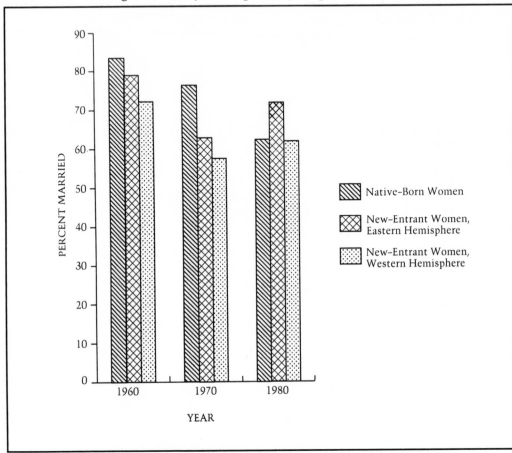

Determinants of Spouse-Immigrant Flows

Evidence from the 1971 Immigrant Cohort: The data on the FY 1971 cohort of legal immigrants enable a more precise examination of the determinants of the number of immigrants admitted as the spouses of U.S. citizens by country. As noted above, it is possible that features of the origin country—for example, whether it hosts a U.S. military installation, its proximity to the United States, and its attractiveness to tourists—may affect the number of women and men who immigrate as the spouses of U.S. citizens.

FIGURE 4.8

*Percent Married Among Native-Born and Recent-Entrant Men
Aged 20–44, by Hemisphere of Origin: 1960–1980*

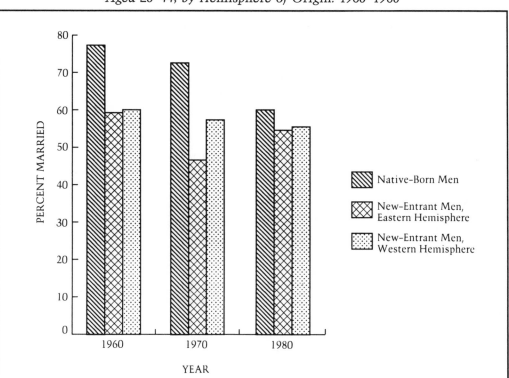

Table 4.4 reports estimates from an analysis of the determinants of the country-specific number of husbands and wives of U.S. citizens admitted in FY 1971. The explanatory variables include the set of potentially relevant country characteristics discussed and used in previous chapters.

The results indicate that the determinants of the number of male and female spouses differ in several ways. First, the set of country characteristics included in the equation explains almost 42 percent of the variation in the number of female spouses but no more than 13 percent in the number of male spouses. Second, as expected, some of the country characteristics influence differentially the immigration as spouses of males and females.

The most powerful determinant of the number of wives is the presence of a U.S. military base in the country of origin; such presence adds on average almost 1,500 immigrants admitted as wives of U.S. citizens per year (and thus 1,500 additional female immigrants per year). To appreciate the

FIGURE 4.9
*Ratios of Married Men to Married Women
Among Native-Born and Recent Entrants Aged 20–44,
by Hemisphere of Origin: 1960–1980*

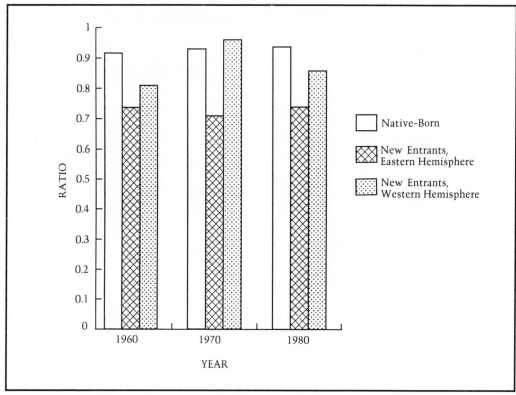

magnitude of this estimate, consider that in FY 1971 the total number of immigrants admitted as wives of U.S. citizens was 36,960 and that the country-specific number, among countries included in the INS *1971 Annual Report* (Table 6), ranged from a low of 5 for Burma to a high of 4,815 for the Philippines, a country with a substantial U.S. military presence.[9] Of the other determinants of the number of wives, only population size and Voice of America broadcasts approach statistical significance; both coefficients are positive, suggesting that information about the United States increases its attractiveness to potential wives and that the larger the potential number of visa applicants the greater the number of persons who enter by the spouse

[9]The next largest figure was 4,250 for Mexico—which does not host a U.S. military base but shares a long land border with it—followed by 3,033 and 3,003, respectively, for Korea and Germany, both countries the sites of major U.S. military installations.

TABLE 4.4
Determinants of the Number of Persons
Admitted as Wives and Husbands of U.S. Citizens in FY 1971:
Ordinary Least Squares Estimates

Variable	Wives		Husbands	
	(1)	(2)	(1)	(2)
GNP per Capita	.0200	.0126	−0.0368	−0.0661
	(0.46)	(0.23)	(0.95)	(1.39)
Literacy Rate	7.13	7.65	4.71	6.76
	(1.20)	(1.20)	(0.89)	(1.20)
Centrally Planned	−395.9	−431.9	−373.7	−515.1
	(1.11)	(1.11)	(1.18)	(0.14)
Population Size	.00167	.00172	.00129	.00151
	(1.77)	(1.76)	(1.54)	(1.75)
Western Hemisphere	—	−87.5	—	−343.8
		(0.24)		(1.06)
Distance from U.S.	−0.0254	−0.0368	−0.0854	−0.130
(miles)	(0.60)	(0.57)	(2.25)	(2.28)
English an	153.8	146.3	3.15	−26.1
Official Language	(0.67)	(0.63)	(0.02)	(0.13)
U.S. Military Base	1487.3	1470.7	31.5	−33.6
	(5.59)	(5.31)	(0.13)	(0.14)
Voice of America	433.8	444.4	12.5	54.2
Broadcasts	(1.65)	(1.65)	(0.05)	(0.23)
Constant	−640.4	−581.1	329.9	562.9
	(1.29)	(1.04)	(0.75)	(1.14)
F	5.45	4.78	0.93	0.95
R^2	.417	.417	.108	.125

SOURCE: U.S. INS FY 1971 Immigrant Cohort Sample.

NOTES: Estimates are based on 70 countries. Absolute values of t-ratios appear in parentheses under corresponding parameter estimates.

route. That distance of the origin country is irrelevant to the number of wives of U.S. citizens is consistent with the fact that the U.S. government absorbs transportation costs for the spouses of military personnel.

In contrast, the number of husbands—of whom the worldwide total in FY 1971 was 17,340, or about half the number of wives—appears to be largely responsive to two factors: the country's distance and population size. The greater the distance, the smaller is the number of male immigrants entering through marriage to a U.S. citizen; this finding is consistent with the figures in Table 4.2, discussed above.

Note that the direction of the effects is the same for both sexes for all variables except GNP per capita, which is not statistically significant for either, and the presence of a military base, which is not a statistically significant determinant of the number of men immigrating as husbands of U.S. citizens.

TABLE 4.5

Determinants of Proportion Female Among Immigrants
Admitted as Spouses of U.S. Citizens in the FY 1971 Cohort:
Weighted Least Squares Estimates

Variable	Coefficient
GNP per Capita ($\times 10^{-4}$)	0.251
	(2.34)
Literacy Rate	0.00501
	(2.56)
Centrally Planned	0.175
	(1.61)
Western Hemisphere	0.177
	(1.51)
Distance ($\times 10^{-4}$)	0.615
	(3.08)
English an Official Language	−0.0598
	(1.08)
U.S. Military Base	0.185
	(6.94)
Constant	−0.232
	(1.12)
R^2	0.543
F	11.20

SOURCE: U.S. INS FY 1971 Immigrant Cohort Sample.

NOTES: Estimates are based on 73 countries. Absolute values of t-ratios appear in parentheses under corresponding parameter estimates.

Another way to examine sex differences in the proclivity to gain immigration through marriage is to investigate the determinants of the country-specific proportion female from among natives of that country admitted to the United States as spouses of U.S. citizens in the FY 1971 cohort. Table 4.5 reports estimates of a proportion-female equation. The set of explanatory variables is again the set of country characteristics; and the estimation procedure employed is weighted least squares (WLS), where the weights represent the origin-country population. The country variables jointly explain a substantial 54 percent of the variation in the proportion of immigrant spouses who are female.

The estimates again indicate that the presence of a military base substantially increases the proportion female of a country's spouse-immigrants. Countries with a centrally planned economy and countries at a great distance from the United States are also associated with a higher proportion female among the spouse-immigrants, suggesting that travel to such countries may be more likely among U.S. men than among U.S. women.[10] The results also indicate that the higher the country's per capita GNP and literacy rate, the greater is the proportion female. Finally, the results suggest (though at borderline statistical significance) that, net of distance, military bases, and other factors, Western Hemisphere countries tend to have a greater proportion female among their spouse-immigrants—reversing the observed hemisphere-wide proportions (see Figure 4.7) and thus underscoring the importance of country characteristics.

Visa Backlogs and Use of the Spouse Route to Immigration: One way to measure the legal-immigration prospects of citizens of given countries is by the State Department's annual visa backlogs count, that is, the number of applicants for numerically limited visas, who are registered at consular offices abroad, for whom a sponsor's petition has already been approved, and who are waiting their turn. This count, which is cross-classified by preference category and country of chargeability, is made on January 1 of each year. The total worldwide number waiting as of January 1980 was 1,088,063 (U.S. Select Commission 1981b, pp. 376–378); these persons were nationals of 169 countries. If we ignore the preference-category and country-ceiling effects on allocation, this means that the supply of numerically limited visas for the next four years was already "mortgaged." But demand across countries varies considerably, so that, while some countries (e.g., Benin) were not even on the list, two (Mexico and the Philippines) had backlogs in excess of 250,000.

If the marriage route represents a detour around other visa restrictions, then we would expect to find (1) a very strong correlation between the backlog size and the volume of spouse immigrants and (2) a similar pattern in the determinants of both the backlogs and the spouse immigrants. To test these propositions, we examine the 1980 country-specific backlogs and the country-specific volume of spouse-of-U.S.-citizen immigrants admitted in 1981. Unfortunately, neither series permits sex-specific analyses.

The correlation between the 1980 backlogs and the 1981 spouse immigrants, calculated on the full set of 195 countries, is .87—indicating rather strongly that both may be manifestations of or responses to the same underlying conditions.

Table 4.6 reports the results of analyses of the determinants of both backlogs and spouse immigrants. A striking finding is that the direction of the effects of all the country characteristics is the same in both equations except for two factors, neither of which approaches statistical significance in either equation. Substantively, the results are what one would expect, given the findings reported in Table 4.4 and given the unfortunate pooling

[10]Of course, these results are not inconsistent with the proposition that travelers to the United States from such countries are preponderantly female.

TABLE 4.6
Determinants of Visa Backlogs in 1980
and Spouses of U.S. Citizens Admitted in 1981:
Weighted Least Squares Estimates

Variable	Visa Backlogs as of January 1980	Spouses of U.S. Citizens FY 1981
GNP per Capita	−9.786	−0.331
	(2.58)	(1.72)
Literacy Rate	204.6	−0.183
	(0.40)	(0.01)
Centrally Planned	−5251.3	−1232.6
	(0.24)	(1.09)
Population Size	.149	.00421
	(3.80)	(2.12)
Distance (miles)	−8.165	−0.645
	(2.26)	(3.51)
English an Official Language	−25925.9	−1207.1
	(1.50)	(1.38)
U.S. Military Base	45692.2	2011.3
	(2.17)	(1.88)
Voice of America Broadcasts	−2848.2	402.8
	(0.13)	(0.36)
Constant	59613.5	5296.8
	(1.20)	(2.11)
F	6.80	2.03
R^2	.480	.216

SOURCE: Visa Office, U.S. Department of State; INS *1981 Statistical Yearbook.*

NOTES: Estimates are based on 68 countries. The weighting variable is the country-of-origin population. Absolute values of *t*-ratios appear in parentheses under corresponding parameter estimates.

of the two sexes. That is, effects which in the sex-specific analyses reported in Table 4.4 were the same sign for both males and females tend to maintain that sign in the pooled analysis shown in Table 4.6; effects which were signed differently by sex now tend to display the more dominant effect (visible in the magnitude of the coefficient and in the levels of statistical significance).

These results appear to indicate that both backlog formation and marriage to U.S. citizens "obey the same rules." The suggestion is clear: marriage provides a way to achieve immigration when it would otherwise be quite difficult.

Indeed, the correspondence between the backlog and the spouse-immigrant results suggests another interesting proposition: namely, that, to the extent that illegal immigration, too, obeys the same rules—responds to the same underlying features of a given country—as do backlogs and marriage, the personal and country characteristics of the spouses of U.S. citizens provide a way to predict the characteristics of illegal migrants. We would not be surprised to find—were it possible to analyze the determinants of illegal flows in the same way that we have analyzed backlogs and marriage—that the signs and magnitudes of the coefficients characterizing the effects of origin-country conditions do not differ greatly.[11]

Mate Selection and the Characteristics of the Spouses of the Foreign-Born

Census data enable examination of the characteristics of the spouses of the enumerated foreign-born. It is thus possible to address questions concerning trends since 1900 in the proportions of the foreign-born who marry persons from their same country of origin (homogamy) or who marry U.S. citizens. Table 4.7 reports these characteristics for four of the census microdata sets used in this book—1900, 1960, 1970, and 1980. The figures show that the cross-time patterns are almost the same for both women and men. The percentage of the foreign-born married to foreign-born declined dramatically between 1900 and 1960 and subsequently began an equally dramatic increase; in 1900, for example, 79 percent of the husbands of the female foreign-born were also foreign-born, while in 1960 more than 50 percent were native-born. By 1980, however, the proportion foreign-born among the spouses of female foreign-born had risen to 62 percent. The two other measures—percentage from the same country of origin and with the same parental nativity—follow the same pattern: a decline to 1960 and a subsequent increase. Thus, while in 1960 only one third of the spouses of female foreign-born were from the same country of origin, in 1980 this figure had risen to over one half. These patterns suggest a reversal after 1960 of an assimilationist trend.

Of course, the figures in Table 4.7 reflect both mating opportunities in the United States and the influence of changes in the constraints on entry

[11]This proposition in turn leads to another. It would appear that the spouse provisions of U.S. immigration law represent an eminently *democratic* solution to the problem of setting immigration ceilings while containing illegal immigration. Ordinary U.S. citizens, in this view, perform a *screening* function. Any foreigner who passes the "marriage test" is granted an immigrant visa. Portes (1983:18) puts it well: All that is needed to immigrate are "the favors of a single American." This view is consistent with the fact that numerically unlimited visas are granted to the spouses *only* of U.S. citizens and not of permanent resident aliens—the latter not possessing the faculties required for screening potential citizens.

TABLE 4.7

Characteristics of Spouses of Married Foreign-Born Aged 25–44,
by Census Year and Sex: 1900, 1960–1980

Characteristics of Spouses	Census Year			
	1900	1960	1970	1980
A. Spouses of Female Foreign-Born				
Percent foreign-born	79.0	46.6	52.8	62.2
Percent same country of origin	70.9	32.9	42.7	51.2
Percent same parental nativity	81.3	41.9	49.1	—
Percent naturalized citizens	52.1	—	22.5	24.6
Percent citizens	74.7	—	68.7	62.4
B. Spouses of Male Foreign-Born				
Percent foreign-born	68.7	49.9	64.2	70.1
Percent same country of origin	61.8	36.7	49.9	59.8
Percent same parental nativity	78.9	48.1	56.7	—
Percent naturalized citizens	—	—	21.0	28.7
Percent citizens	—	—	57.2	51.9

SOURCE: U.S. Census Public Use Samples.

NOTES: Information on parental nativity was not obtained in 1960. Information on naturalization was not obtained in 1960; in 1900 it was obtained only for males aged 21 years and older. Thus, the percentage of citizens in 1900 and 1960 is greater than or equal to one minus the percentage of foreign-born.

associated with U.S. immigration law. The marital status at entry of the foreign-born may be importantly related to the characteristics of their spouses. Indeed, we would expect that persons who enter single will face a set of potential mates more predominantly native-born than the set faced by persons who selected a mate prior to immigration. Thus, exogamy with respect to nativity should be higher among immigrants who are single at entry.

Table 4.8 reports the characteristics of the spouses of foreign-born aged 25–64 at three census years—1900, 1970, and 1980—classified by whether the foreign-born person married before or after entry. (Such classification is not possible with the 1960 data for those persons who had been in the United States more than five years.) The figures indicate that, as expected, marital status at entry is strongly related to homogamy. In all comparisons, those foreign-born persons who married after entry had greater propensities

TABLE 4.8

Characteristics of Spouses of Married Foreign-Born Aged 25–64,
by Marriage Before and After Entry, by Census Year and Sex:
1900, 1970, 1980

Characteristics of Spouses	1900		1970		1980	
	Before	After	Before	After	Before	After
A. Spouses of Female Foreign-Born						
Percent foreign-born	88.9	75.5	68.7	43.9	77.3	60.6
Percent same country of origin	82.3	66.2	56.2	32.7	67.3	45.1
Percent same parental nativity	87.2	78.7	n.a.	n.a.	n.a.	n.a.
Percent naturalized citizens	56.7	60.4	32.3	23.7	27.7	24.0
Percent citizens	68.7	86.4	62.8	78.6	50.1	62.6
Percent in category	36.4	63.7	67.4[a]	11.7[a]	65.7[a]	13.6[a]
B. Spouses of Male Foreign-Born						
Percent foreign-born	96.3	62.5	89.3	49.7	91.0	67.2
Percent same country of origin	91.9	54.5	70.3	37.6	80.6	53.9
Percent same parental nativity	94.1	74.7	n.a.	n.a.	n.a.	n.a.
Percent naturalized citizens	0.0	0.0	33.7	25.7	25.6	22.0
Percent citizens	3.7	37.5	43.1	75.0	34.0	51.7
Percent in category	23.8	76.2	47.0	24.3	45.5	23.6

SOURCE: U.S. Census Public Use Samples.

[a]Because of the coding of date of entry in 5-year intervals in the 1970 and 1980 censuses, some married foreign-born cannot be unambiguously classified as having married before or after entry.

to marry persons who differed from them in nativity, parental nativity, and country of origin. For example, in 1970 almost 90 percent of the wives of foreign-born males who married prior to entry were also foreign-born; in contrast, less than 50 percent of the foreign-born men who entered prior to marriage married foreign-born women. The figures also show, however, the same pattern evident in Table 4.7—an attenuation of out-group mating between 1970 and 1980, even among those who marry after entry.

What determines whether or not an immigrant, unmarried at entry, marries someone from his or her native country? The probability that a foreign-born woman who is single at entry marries a husband from the same country of origin may be specified as a function of her age at marriage and duration in the United States prior to marriage; of whether the country of origin is English-speaking; and of opportunities in the United States for

TABLE 4.9

Determinants of Probability of Marriage to Husband
from Same Country of Origin, Among Foreign-Born Women Aged 25–64
Who Marry After Entering the United States, from 1900 to 1980:
Maximum-Likelihood Probit Estimates, with Selection Correction

Variable	Census Year		
	1980	1970	1900[a]
Age at Marriage	.0194	.0259	.0292
	(2.30)[b]	(2.34)[b]	(4.12)
Years in U.S. Prior to Marriage	−.0304	−.0404	−.0570
	(2.50)	(6.03)	(9.93)
Percentage of U.S. Population from	.0292	.00174	.00686
Same Country of Origin	(4.25)	(0.14)	(1.14)
Ratio of Males to Females in U.S.	.911	.707	.477
Population from Same Origin	(4.04)	(4.84)	(2.85)
Country			
English an Official Language of	−.121	−.312	−.274
Country of Origin	(1.07)	(2.86)	(2.97)
Constant	−1.41	−1.44	−.161
	(4.60)	(2.19)	(0.63)
Chi-squared	84.3	77.1	147.1
N	703	953	1370

SOURCE: U.S. Census Public Use Samples.

[a]Not selectivity-corrected.

[b]Asymptotic t-values, corrected for selectivity, in parentheses.

meeting potential mates from her country of origin—represented by two
variables, the percentage of the total population from her country of origin
and the sex ratio among her U.S.-resident co-nationals. Table 4.9 reports
maximum-likelihood probit estimates of the probability of marrying a person from the same country of origin, corrected for potential selectivity
biases associated with selecting a sample of women who married after entry, for three samples of foreign-born women aged 25–64 who were enumerated in the censuses of 1900, 1970, and 1980.

The results are remarkably consistent across the different historical
periods and indicate that the longer the duration in the United States, the
lower the probability of marrying a co-national. Similarly, coming from
an English-speaking country is negatively associated with marrying a co-
national (though not statistically significantly so in 1980). Moreover, the
range of opportunities for meeting persons from the same country of origin
strongly influences the propensity to marry endogamously. Finally, the
higher the age at marriage the greater is the probability of marrying a person

from the same country of origin. These results provide strong evidence that mate selection, conditional upon marital status at entry, is associated in predictable ways with knowledge of English, availability of co-national prospective mates, and duration of search. Indeed, the decline in immigrant flows between 1900 and 1960, and thus the reduction in the number of an immigrant's co-nationals in the United States, in part explains the fall in homogamy among immigrants unmarried at entry between those dates. The rise in homogamy between 1970 and 1980 also appears to mirror the rise in the relative size of the foreign-born population over that period.

A question that naturally follows concerns the characteristics of the mates chosen by those foreign-born who enter the United States unmarried. While censuses typically do not collect data on the attributes of persons which make them desirable mates, they do contain information on one important attribute of a husband—his earnings. Accordingly, it is possible to look further at the marriages of female foreign-born who marry after entry. Table 4.10 reports estimates of the determinants of the log of husband's earnings, again corrected for the selectivity associated with using a sample based on marital status at entry, for those women aged 20–64 in 1980 who married after entry and whose spouse is present at the census enumeration. Four specifications are estimated. All include as determinants the wife's age and age-squared in 1980, age at marriage, years in the United States prior to marriage, and whether English is an official/dominant language of her country of origin. The four specifications differ with respect to inclusion of four additional factors: the wife's schooling and her origin country's per capita GNP, literacy rate, and distance from the United States.

The results indicate that the U.S. experience of a foreign-born woman and the characteristics of her country of origin importantly affect the kind of husband she "obtains," at least as measured by his earnings. Other things being the same, in particular her age and schooling, the longer the period of time she spent in the United States prior to marriage, the higher are her husband's earnings. His earnings appear to vary nonmonotonically with her current age—presumably reflecting similar variation with *his* age—being at their maximum when her age is between approximately 37 and 41. The higher her level of schooling, the greater are his earnings. On the other hand, the older she is at marriage, the lower his earnings. These results are robust to changes in specification.

With respect to the origin-country characteristics, when English language is the sole country characteristic in the equation and wife's schooling is omitted, it appears to be positively associated with husband's earnings. However, introduction of the wife's schooling or of the other three country characteristics virtually eliminates the positive effect of coming from an English-speaking country. Controlling for wife's schooling, age, age at mar-

TABLE 4.10

Determinants of Log of Earnings of Husbands
of Foreign-Born Spouse-Present Women Aged 20–64 in 1980
Who Married After Entering the United States

Variable/Specification	(1)	(2)	(3)	(4)
Characteristics of Wife				
Years in U.S. prior to	.0202	.0144	.0220	.0145
marriage	(2.33)	(1.69)	(2.53)	(1.66)
Age at marriage	−.0128	−.0134	−.0129	−.0122
	(1.54)	(1.63)	(1.53)	(1.47)
Age	.129	.113	.132	.119
	(4.89)	(4.33)	(4.98)	(4.55)
Age squared ($\times 10^{-2}$)	−.172	−.137	−.172	−.156
	(4.48)	(3.59)	(4.05)	(3.72)
Schooling attainment	—	.0448	—	.0460
		(5.47)		(4.53)
Characteristics of Wife's Country of Origin				
GNP per capita, 1978	—	—	.113	.983
($\times 10^{-5}$)			(0.63)	(0.52)
Literacy rate, 1975	—	—	.471	.505
($\times 10^{-2}$)			(1.62)	(1.74)
Distance ($\times 10^{-4}$)	—	—	.229	.135
			(1.88)	(0.10)
English an official	.130	.00462	.0418	−.0213
language	(1.83)	(0.07)	(0.51)	(0.27)
Lambda	.540	.317	.449	.489
	(2.36)	(1.47)	(1.25)	(1.36)
Constant	6.81	6.62	6.36	6.04
	(13.71)	(13.42)	(10.65)	(9.79)
F	8.41	10.97	6.60	8.11

SOURCE: U.S. Census Public Use Samples.

NOTE: The number of observations is 615.

riage, and U.S. experience, only the origin-country's literacy rate is unambiguously associated with husband's earnings.

Marital Stability

Marital Stability and Immigration Through Marriage

Are the foreign-born who follow the marriage route to immigration more likely to divorce than other foreign-born? To the extent that courtship and mating may be characterized as a "matching" exercise in which a balance is sought between the two prospective partners' bundles of desirable and undesirable attributes, the immigration-sponsorship element may artificially (and temporarily) induce a balance.[12] That is, a potential foreign partner's attributes may "equal" the U.S. citizen's attributes *counting his/her visa-conferring faculty*. However, if one ignores this attribute, then the foreign partner would be likely to be of higher "quality" than the U.S. mate. This means that once immigration has occurred, and the benefits associated with the visa are fully conferred on the immigrant, the immigrant will be able to improve his/her marital status (in terms of mate characteristics) by re-entering the (U.S.) marriage market no longer requiring a visa. Moreover, an immigrant visa is not, like wealth or social position, a good that a spouse can confer gradually or continuously over a long period of time; rather it is dispensed all at once and early in the marriage. The subtle balance that produced the mating is rendered unequal in the initial marital adjustment period. Thus, there may be, other things being the same, greater marital disruption among marriages in which the marriage conferred an immigration benefit even when such marriages are not fraudulent.

Moreover, marital instability may be greater for the foreign-born than the native-born even for those immigrants who enter already married to non-U.S. citizens. Marital disruption may be a part of the immigrant adjustment process, if such adjustments are stressful and impose costs on the marriage and/or if immigration confers (in an unanticipated way) unequal benefits on the marital partners.

The ideal way to examine propositions about marital stability and immigrant adjustment would be to compare the divorce rates, by duration of marriage, of cohorts of legal immigrants of differing entry visas (with attention paid to the censoring associated with emigration) with each other and with those of cohorts of the native-born. Unfortunately, such a study has never been attempted, and the requisite data do not exist. A preliminary look is possible, however, by examining the divorce rates among the subset of members of the FY 1971 immigrant cohort who had naturalized by early 1981. Table 4.11 reports the percent divorced at naturalization by sex and by entry visa for immigrants who were already married at admission. The entry-visa groups are classified by type of kin, including non-kin. Although the percentages are small, they do suggest that those men who entered as the husbands of U.S. citizens (and who naturalized) have higher divorce rates than any other category of immigrants, while those women who entered as the wives of U.S. citizens (and who naturalized) had the second-highest divorce rates. Relatively high divorce rates are also observed for (naturalized) women who were siblings of U.S. citizens and for (naturalized) men who entered as numerically limited natives of the Western Hemisphere.

---

[12]Attention is focused on "real" marriages. That is, we are not concerned with explicitly "false" marriages such as that of W. H. Auden to Erika Mann, contracted in order to rescue her from Nazi Germany.

TABLE 4.11

Percent Divorced at Naturalization from Among FY 1971 Immigrants
Who Were Married at Admission, by Type of Visa

Visa Type	Women	Men
Kin by Marriage		
Married to U.S. citizen	5.9	14.5
Married to U.S. permanent resident	3.8	3.6
Married to new skill immigrant	3.4	0
Married to new kin immigrant	4.2	0
Blood Kin		
Parent of U.S. citizen	0	0
Son/daughter of U.S. citizen	0	0
Sibling of U.S. citizen	11.1	0
Non-Kin		
Skilled immigrant	0	0
Refugee	0	4.0
Non-preference immigrant	0	1.8
Native of the Western Hemisphere	4.2	13.6

SOURCE: U.S. INS FY 1971 Immigrant Cohort Sample.

NOTES: Percentages are based on the number of immigrants who were aged 21 to 65 at admission to permanent residence, who were married at admission, and who had naturalized by early 1981 (337 women and 306 men). The classification, "married to U.S. citizen," includes both persons admitted to permanent residence with spouse visas and persons who married after entering with a fiancé visa.

Census data do not provide information on the immigrant visas of the foreign-born or, for divorced or separated persons, any information on former spouse(s). However, the probability that an (ever-married) foreign-born person will be divorced or separated at the time of the census, by date of entry, can be computed, and the determinants of this probability, in terms of both personal and country-of-origin characteristics, can be estimated. Similarly, from INS data on visa-specific immigration flows by country, the determinants of the probability that an adult immigrant enters as a spouse of a U.S. citizen, in terms of country-of-origin characteristics, can also be estimated.

The ability to make these estimates permits an indirect test of the influence of entry route on marital stability. Presumably, the association between the marital stability of an immigrant and his/her origin-country characteristics reflects at least in part the influence of country characteristics on the selection of the entry route. Thus, we might expect that those variables tending to increase (decrease) the probability that an immigrant has entered as a citizen's spouse will also tend to be associated with a greater (lesser) probability of marital disruption. The effects of the presence of U.S. military personnel provide the clearest example. Based on our previous results, we know that women from countries with a U.S. military base are substantially more likely, everything else being the same, to enter as citizens' spouses. If marital disruption is higher among foreign-born women from such countries, it may be inferred that such immigrants tend to have higher marital dissolution rates.

The interpretation of the influence of the origin-country military base variable on the marital instability of foreign-born women is clearest, since this country-of-origin characteristic does not importantly affect the number of immigrants entering through routes other than that associated with marriage to a U.S. citizen.[13] However, it should also be true that the effects of all of the other origin-country characteristics on the probability that an immigrant enters as a citizen's spouse should be mirrored in the determinants of marital disruption for the foreign-born—if citizens' spouses have the most unstable marriages. Unfortunately, however, marital disruption may result in the emigration of foreign-born spouses, and such emigration cannot be determined from census data. As well, the prospects (costs and opportunities) of re-migration may influence marital dissolution. The association between origin-country characteristics and the marital status of the foreign-born recorded in the census will thus also reflect the decision by the divorced or separated to remain in the United States, the direct influence of re-migration prospects on marital stability, and the influence of immigration selectivity associated with the (constrained) choice of the immigration visa.

Table 4.12 reports estimates of the effects of country characteristics on (1) the probability that a foreign-born woman is divorced or separated at the time of the census survey, for given personal characteristics, based on a sample of ever-married foreign-born women aged 20–64 in 1980; and (2) the probability that an adult female immigrant entering in 1971 entered as the wife of a U.S. citizen, based on 70 origin countries for which the requisite data were available. The origin-country characteristics are similar to those used in the prior analyses.

The estimates indicate that the set of country characteristics explains a statistically significant proportion of the variability in the probabilities of both marital disruption and immigrating as the wife of a U.S. citizen. More important, with the exception of the distance variable, all of the signs of the origin-country characteristic coefficients are identical across the two equations: women from countries with a U.S. military base, with higher levels of per capita GNP and higher rates of literacy, and/or with a centrally planned economy are more likely both to immigrate as spouses of U.S. citizens and

---

[13]This is shown in Chapter 5.

TABLE 4.12

Determinants of Being Divorced or Separated
Among Ever-Married Foreign-Born Women, Aged 20–64 in 1980,
and of the Proportion of FY 1971 Adult Women Immigrants
Admitted as Wives of U.S. Citizens

Characteristic	Divorce/Separation	Wife of Citizen
Personal Characteristics		
Age	.0560	—
	(2.27)	
Age squared ($\times 10^{-3}$)	−.553	—
	(1.88)	
Years in the United States	.0415	—
	(3.28)	
Years in U.S. squared ($\times 10^{-3}$)	−.905	—
	(3.15)	
Country-of-Origin Characteristics		
GNP per capita ($\times 10^{-4}$	.220	4.70
	(1.35)	(3.25)
Literacy rate ($\times 10^{-2}$)	−.631	−1.48
	(2.09)	(2.80)
Centrally planned	.220	.521
	(1.73)	(1.60)
Western Hemisphere	.255	3.87
	(1.47)	(5.76)
Distance ($\times 10^{-4}$)	−.448	5.98
	(1.48)	(6.89)
English an official language	.0886	.0683
	(0.96)	(0.31)
U.S. military base	.249	4.44
	(2.37)	(19.71)
Constant	−2.53	−6.21
	(4.34)	(8.29)
Chi-squared	65.45	—

SOURCE: U.S. Census Public Use Samples; INS *1971 Annual Report.*

NOTES: The divorce/separation equation is estimated on a random sample of foreign-born women (n=2073) using the maximum-likelihood probit specification; asymptotic t-values in parentheses under the corresponding coefficient. The proportion citizen-wife equation is estimated on country-level data (n=70).

to be divorced or separated after entry, for given years in the United States.[14] Coming from a country where English is an official/dominant

---

[14]Thus, enshrining the mate-selection right—however ethically correct it may appear—may, when combined with other national policies and other features of the international scene, give rise to a new and unintended effect: the conjunction of numerically unlimited visas

language, however, affects neither probability. As expected, the strongest correlate is the military base variable: the estimates suggest that women from a country with a U.S. military base are more than twice as likely to have immigrated as wives of U.S. citizens and are 20 percent more likely to be divorced or separated after entry as women from countries otherwise identical.[15]

Marital Dissolution and Time in the United States

The estimates from the census sample of foreign-born women reported in Table 4.12 also indicate that age and duration in the United States, for given country characteristics, influence in a nonmonotonic way the probability of being divorced or separated. This probability increases with age for women up to approximately age 51, and declines for women at older ages. Similarly, it increases for durations in the United States up to approximately 23 years and then declines. These age and duration patterns must be interpreted cautiously, however, since they are consistent with both an entry-cohort interpretation—such that current remnants of particular entry cohorts and birth cohorts have higher or lower marital-disruption propensities—and an assimilationist or aging interpretation.

To explore further, and more appropriately, how time in the United States influences marital dissolution among foreign-born women and to compare the intertemporal patterns of marital dissolution among foreign-born and native-born women, Table 4.13 presents the changes in cumulative rates of divorce across adjacent censuses for age-specific cohorts of ever-married native-born and recent-entrant women aged 20–44; Figure 4.10 depicts the cohort changes graphically for the entire 20–44 age group. Again, these cohort changes must be interpreted cautiously—for the foreign-born because of the unknown influence of emigration and for both the native- and foreign-born between 1970 and 1980 because of the unknown change in the population coverage of the census across the decade.

A number of patterns emerge in Table 4.13 and Figure 4.10. First, for

---

for the immigration of spouses with numerically limited visas for the immigration of others may, in periods of high demand for immigrant visas, engender an immigration strategy in which marriage plays a key role. To the extent that the combination of visa scarcity and family-reunification policies promote *mariages de convenance,* such policies may undermine the very thing they were designed to protect: namely, the integrity of the institution of marriage. On the other hand, by reducing illegal immigration, the marriage provisions may be serving a collective good.

[15]The one anomalous result—that greater distance of the origin country from the United States is associated with a higher probability of a woman immigrating as a U.S. citizen spouse but with a lower probability of her being divorced or separated post entry—may be the result of the influence of emigration: higher costs of emigration may increase the cost of marital dissolution.

TABLE 4.13
Decadal Cohort Change in Percent Ever Divorced
for Ever-Married Native-Born and Recent-Entrant Women, by Age:
1960–1970 and 1970–1980

Age in 1960	Native-Born		Recent Entrants	
	1960	1970	1960	1970
20–24	9.3	19.0	3.8	12.5
25–29	12.1	19.3	7.4	14.6
30–34	14.6	20.8	11.1	20.8
35–39	16.7	22.1	15.2	20.2
40–44	17.6	20.3	18.1	24.5
20–44	14.5	20.4	9.7	16.9

Age in 1970	Native-Born		Recent Entrants	
	1970	1980	1970	1980
20–24	11.9	31.5	3.1	19.1
25–29	16.8	30.6	7.1	15.7
30–34	21.6	29.9	11.4	22.0
35–39	17.5	26.6	10.9	18.7
40–44	20.8	25.1	17.0	22.1
20–44	17.6	29.0	8.4	19.0

SOURCE: U.S. Census Public Use Samples.

all five-year age groups except the 40–44 age group in 1960, the recent-entrant foreign-born ever-married women are substantially less likely to have been divorced than their native-born counterparts, and this differential increased slightly from 1960 to 1970: less than 10 percent of recent-entrant ever-married foreign-born women aged 20–44 had been divorced in 1960 and only 8 percent of recent-entrant women had been divorced in 1970; the comparable rates for native-born women aged 20–44 were 14 and 18 percent in 1960 and 1970, respectively. Across each of the two decades, 1960–1970 and 1970–1980, all (excepting the 40–44 cohort in 1960) of the age cohorts of both recent-entrant and native-born women experienced an increase in cumulative divorce rates of about the same absolute magnitude. For example, cumulative divorce rates rose by 7 percentage points (from 10 to 17 percent) over the 1960–1970 decade for recent-entrant women in 1960 and by 11 percentage points (from 8 to 19 percent) for recent-entrant women in 1970. The corresponding decadal increases in cumulative divorce rates for the native-born were 6 and 11 percentage points, respectively.

Thus, the proportion of recent-entrant ever-married women obtaining a divorce in their first decade after entry appears to have been similar to that for similarly aged native-born women over the same ten-year period. Post-

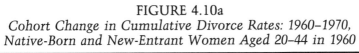

FIGURE 4.10a
Cohort Change in Cumulative Divorce Rates: 1960–1970,
Native-Born and New-Entrant Women Aged 20–44 in 1960

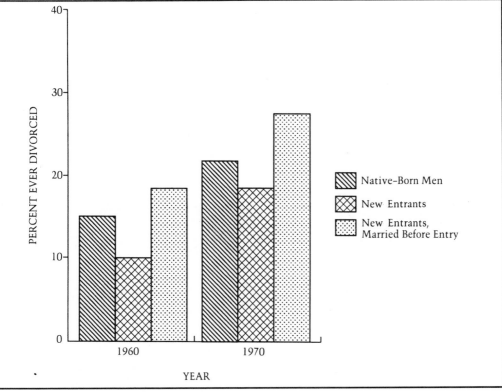

immigration marital instability among foreign-born women appears to be no greater than that among native-born women on average, although we have seen that marital stability differs among the foreign-born women by country of origin and by the visa category under which they entered the United States.

Summary

Whatever one's view on whether or not U.S. immigration policy should be as attentive to marriage markets as to labor markets, marriage has in recent years become the principal route to immigration to the United States. Since 1970 the number of persons immigrating through marriage has been increasing by 7 percent per year, and by 1988 more than one-third of

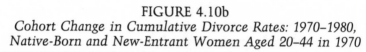

FIGURE 4.10b
Cohort Change in Cumulative Divorce Rates: 1970–1980,
Native-Born and New-Entrant Women Aged 20–44 in 1970

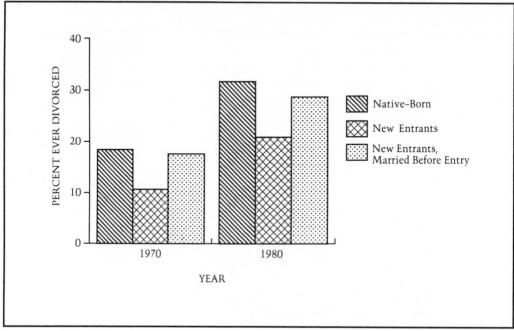

all adult immigrants who did not adjust from refugee/asylee status obtained their visas by marrying a U.S. citizen. In part this rapid rate of increase has been fueled by a substantial increase in the number of native-born U.S. citizens of marriageable age (18–25) since 1970 because of the "baby boom." But there is no doubt that increases in marital immigration were propelled in part by the restrictions on other types of immigration.

The available data provide strong evidence that the imposition of numerical limits on the availability of immigrant visas has been followed by substantial increases in the numbers of immigrant spouses, particularly in the Western Hemisphere. The data also indicate, moreover, that the number of spouse-immigrants from a given country is highly correlated with the number of persons approved but still waiting for a numerically limited visa; and both the size of immigrant visas backlogs and the number of marital immigrants appear responsive to the same characteristics of the country of origin.

Among U.S. citizens, men are more likely than women to sponsor foreign spouses. Among those U.S. citizens who sponsor foreign spouses, men are more likely to find their mates in the Eastern Hemisphere. Not surprisingly, American men show a marked tendency to find brides in countries which host U.S. military installations—undoubtedly the reason that the large majority of immigrants from West Germany and South Korea are women. These are domestic consequences of the role of the United States as the world's "policeman" that are often overlooked.

In the foreign-born population, of which legal immigrants are a subset, the proportion married to another foreign-born person declined from over 70 percent in 1900 to less than 50 percent in 1960, but has subsequently increased. In 1980 the proportions of foreign-born married men and women with foreign-born spouses were 70 and 62 percent, respectively. The reduction in the proportions of the foreign-born married to native-born U.S. citizens, which suggests a diminished role of marriage in the "melting pot," is in part the result of the increase in the size and geographical concentration of the foreign-born population since 1960.

While marital disruption appears to be no greater among the foreign-born than among the native-born, among the foreign-born it appears to be related to the characteristics of their immigration. Factors which increase the number of immigrant wives of U.S. citizens from a given country also increase the probability that a foreign-born woman is divorced or separated at the time of the census. Data on the 1971 immigrant cohort indicate that among cohort members who were married at admission and who naturalized by 1981, the highest divorce rates were those of men who had immigrated as the husbands of U.S. citizens.

5

FAMILY REUNIFICATION
AND FAMILY STRUCTURE

T HE WORD "NEPOTISM" has been used to describe the selection criteria
of recent and current U.S. immigration laws. And, indeed, except for
the skilled persons who enter as principals in the third- and sixth-
preference categories—categories whose total number of visas, including
visas for the spouses and minor children of the skilled principals, may not
exceed 54,000 annually—all of the 270,000 numerically limited visas are,
under current law, awarded on the basis of a kinship tie to a citizen or
permanent resident alien of the United States.[1] Moreover, in FYs
1981–1988 the number of third- and sixth-preference principals averaged
only 22,848 per year. In addition, the numerically exempt visas are primarily allocated to relatives, the number of non-kin "special immigrant" principals—such as ministers of religion, former employees of the U.S. government abroad, and American Indians born in Canada—averaging well under·
2,000 annually. Thus, approximately 95 percent of the persons who qualify
for admission to legal permanent residence under non-refugee provisions of
U.S. immigration law do so on the basis of their familial relationship to
another immigrant or to a U.S. citizen.

Of the immigrants entering because of their family relationship to a

---

[1]The law's provision for the allocation of unused visas to "nonpreference" applicants (i.e.,
applicants who do not qualify for the kin-based or skill-based visas) is academic, for the six
preference categories have used all available visas since September 1978 (INS 1988, pp. xvi,
143).

resident alien or U.S. citizen, a large proportion are blood relatives of the U.S. sponsor. In the years 1980–1984, for example, of the 2.8 million immigrants admitted, 6.1 percent were the foreign-born parents of U.S. citizens, 14.0 percent were the foreign-born brothers or sisters of U.S. citizens, and their spouses and children, and 19.5 percent were the foreign-born children of either permanent resident aliens or U.S. citizens. Thus, almost 40 percent of all immigrants are "reuniting" with their blood relatives in the United States.

The family-reunification nature of most non-refugee immigration allowed under current law suggests two questions. First, what proportion of resident aliens who become U.S. citizens take advantage of the reunification entitlement? Second, does this kin-oriented policy actually affect the living arrangements of immigrants in the United States? In particular, do sponsored siblings, adult children, and parents live with their sponsors? Has the increased emphasis in immigration law on family reunification produced an increase in extended-family household structures among immigrants?

In this chapter we examine the immigration of the three kinds of adult blood relatives—parents, siblings, and sons and daughters—whose immigration current law facilitates. As discussed in Chapter 1, parents of adult U.S. citizens are exempt from numerical limitations, while siblings and adult offspring must compete for numerically limited visas. Siblings of U.S. citizens (and their spouses and minor children) must compete for 64,800 visas annually.[2] Current law allows up to 54,000 visas annually for the unmarried adult offspring of U.S. citizens and their children (under the first preference) and approximately 27,000 visas annually for the married children of U.S. citizens and their spouses and children (under the fourth preference), although the first- and fourth-preference categories have never used all available visas. Indeed, the number of adult offspring admitted annually under both preferences has never come close to the number allotted; only 5,721 to 12,107 first-preference visas were issued each year between 1981 and 1988, while the number of fourth-preference immigrants ranged from 14,681 to 21,940 inclusive of family members.

The fact that the first- and fourth-preference categories have unused visa slots does not signal a dearth of adult sons and daughters of U.S. citizens wishing to immigrate (or U.S. citizen parents willing to sponsor them). Rather, the unused visa slots are the result of the country ceilings on numerically limited immigration (20,000 annually for independent countries and 600 for dependencies). Thus, the visa backlog figures for January 1989 indicate that a total of 27,785 persons were waiting for first-prefer-

---

[2]Under current law, 24 percent of the 270,000 worldwide visas are allocated to siblings of U.S. citizens and their spouses and children. To this number are added any visas not used by the preceding four preference categories (which together are allowed 66 percent, or 178,200 visas).

ence visas and another 133,266 for fourth-preference visas. As would be expected, the figures show that the two countries with the largest overall backlogs, Mexico and the Philippines, account for 74 percent of the first-preference backlog and 80 percent of the fourth-preference backlog.[3] Country ceilings also limit sibling immigration, although there are no unused visas in this category.

We begin by describing in more detail trends in the immigration of parents and siblings. Next we examine the determinants of the country-specific flows of parents, siblings, and adult sons and daughters. In particular, we attempt to estimate the probability that a naturalized U.S. citizen will sponsor either a parent, sibling, or child, or all three. Finally, we assess the extent to which sponsorship of kin is reflected in living arrangements and household structure in the United States.

The Immigration of Parents of U.S. Citizens

As Table 1.3 shows, the precise character of the visa entitlement accorded to the parents of U.S. citizens has differed across hemisphere, over time, and by the age of the citizen offspring. Between 1924 and 1965, a person from the Eastern Hemisphere who was the parent of an adult U.S. citizen was entitled to a high preference for an immigrant visa (within the national-origin quotas applicable to Eastern Hemisphere immigrants).[4] Meanwhile, in the Western Hemisphere, where applicants were not subject to numerical restrictions, the parent of a minor U.S. citizen was exempt from any labor-certification requirement. The 1965 amendments to the Immigration and Nationality Act imposed numerical ceilings on the Western Hemisphere and removed the parents of *adult* U.S. citizens from the numerically limited category. Thus, the years between 1965 and 1968 represent an important transition period. Eastern Hemisphere parents who earlier had to compete for visas could now enter immediately. Western Hemisphere immigrants, who now had to compete for visas, could find in appropriate parenthood a means of obtaining a numerically exempt visa.

Figure 5.1 depicts the number of persons admitted as parents of adult U.S. citizens between 1954 and 1988, by hemisphere of birth. Since the parent category began to exist for the Western Hemisphere only in 1966, the graph for the latter group begins then. The figures reveal several important features. The Eastern Hemisphere plot shows the expected jump, from

---

[3]As of January 1989, Mexico has 3,280 and 39,191 active visa registrants for first- and fourth-preference categories, respectively (Visa Office data). The corresponding figures for the Philippines are 17,228 and 67,705.

[4]The parent relationship was accorded first preference prior to the McCarran-Walter Act (1952), second preference afterward.

FIGURE 5.1
Immigrants Admitted as Parents of U.S. Citizens,
by Region of Birth and Year of Admission: 1954–1988

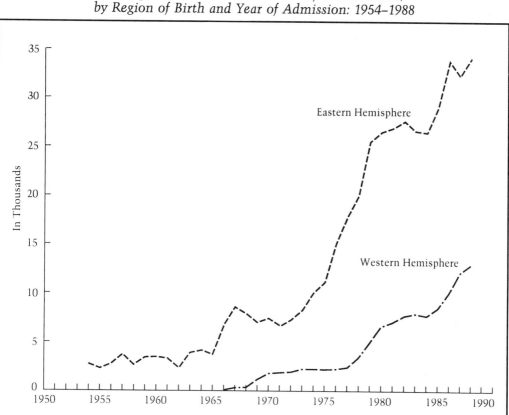

3,799 in 1965 to 8,626 in 1967—more than doubling—as the parent category became numerically unlimited. Following a decline to 6,705 in 1971, the volume increased rapidly to 26,129 in 1979, remaining at approximately that level through 1983 and subsequently increasing to 34,333 in 1988. The initial increase after 1965 may be attributed to the clearing of backlogs. The increases since 1971, however, would appear to reflect sponsorship of parents by newly naturalized citizens, whose own immigration became possible only in 1965.

The line-plot for the Western Hemisphere shows two critical points (Figure 5.1). The first occurs in 1968, when the number of parents begins to increase, from 133 in 1968 to 1,774 in 1970. The second occurs in 1977, when parent immigration begins a new increase, from 2,471 in 1977 to 13,167 in 1988. The first critical point coincides with the newly placed numerical restrictions on immigration from the Western Hemisphere. The second coincides with the placing of the Western Hemisphere under the preference-category system. It is possible that the latter increase reflects new pressure by other family members who could now become eligible for an immigrant visa if a U.S. citizen's parent immigrated. For example, consider the aunt of a U.S. citizen; suppose that the aunt very much wants to move to the United States but is ineligible under the law. If the U.S. citizen sponsors his/her parent, then the parent can (upon naturalizing) sponsor the citizen's-aunt/parent's-sister (under fifth preference).[5] This example illustrates how restricting eligibility to "immediate" relatives can lead to the immigration of increasingly distant family members. This "chaining" of immigration is the focus of the next chapter.

Figure 5.2 shows the total volume of parent immigration and the hemisphere shares. The increase since 1965 has been quite rapid, the total volume of parent immigration in 1988 exceeding 47,000. As the graphs show, the Eastern Hemisphere accounts for a substantial portion of parent immigration—72 percent in 1988.

The Immigration of Siblings of U.S. Citizens

The immigration from Eastern Hemisphere countries of the brothers and sisters of adult U.S. citizens was allowed as part of a nonpreference category between 1924 and 1952, when it became part of the fourth-preference category (which also included the adult children of U.S. citizens). The 1965 amendments established a special category (fifth-preference) solely for siblings and their spouses and minor children. Meanwhile, persons from the Western Hemisphere who were siblings of U.S. citizens received no special family-reunification consideration between 1968 (when numerical restrictions were placed on Western Hemisphere immigration) and 1976. The 1976 amendments, however, accorded them visa entitlement under the fifth-preference category.

Published tabulations enable construction of several data series for siblings: (1) sibling principals (from the Eastern Hemisphere) in the period from 1957 to 1969; (2) all fifth-preference visa recipients (i.e., the sibling principals together with their spouses and children) in the period since 1966, separately by hemisphere; and (3) worldwide totals for each of the

---

[5]Given that naturalization requires knowledge of English, such pressures would be intensified for parents (of U.S. citizens) who know English, and hence for nationals of countries where English is spoken.

FIGURE 5.2
Total Immigrants Admitted as Parents of U.S. Citizens,
by Region of Birth and Year of Admission: 1954–1988

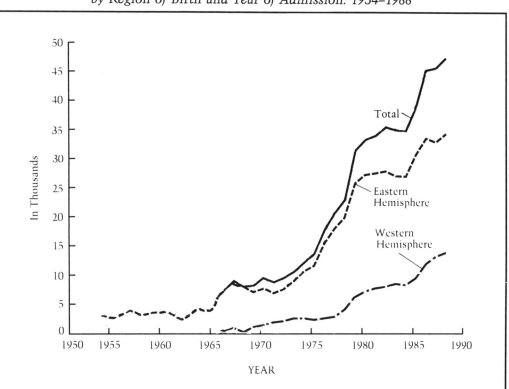

three types of fifth-preference entrants—sibling principals, spouses of siblings, and children of siblings—in the years since the 1976 amendments.

Figure 5.3 depicts the number of Eastern Hemisphere sibling principals who immigrated between 1957 and 1969. The number increases dramatically after 1965, from 1,532 in 1965 to 22,570 in 1969. Of course, this reflects the new and large fifth-preference category and the abolition of the national-origins quotas.

Figure 5.4 reports the longer series for siblings together with their families and incorporates the Western Hemisphere immigration established by the 1976 amendments. Prior to 1977, the Eastern Hemisphere fifth-preference category was allocated 40,800 visas (i.e., 24 percent of the 170,000 Eastern Hemisphere ceiling) plus any visas not used in the four higher preferences. The number thus fluctuated between 40,000 and 60,000 annually. With the extension of the preference-category system to the Western

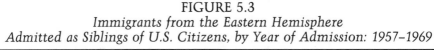

FIGURE 5.3
*Immigrants from the Eastern Hemisphere
Admitted as Siblings of U.S. Citizens, by Year of Admission: 1957–1969*

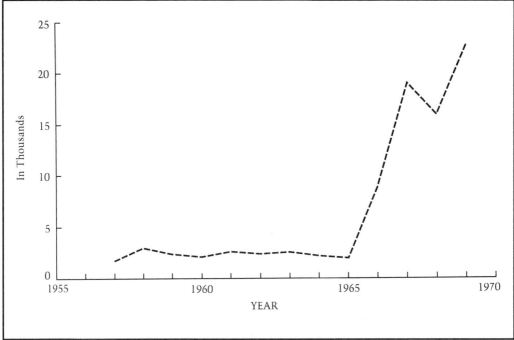

Hemisphere and the subsequent (1978) worldwide ceilings, nationals from both hemispheres began to compete for the new worldwide allotment of 69,600 fifth-preference visas (plus visas unused in the higher preferences), which by the provisions of the Refugee Act of 1980 was reduced to 64,800 (or 24 percent of the worldwide ceiling of 270,000). Figure 5.4 shows the effect of the new competition on the Eastern Hemisphere sibling immigration; it declined from a high of 72,311 in 1978 to 42,118 in 1982, subsequently hovering near 47,000. Meanwhile, Western Hemisphere sibling immigration increased rapidly to 25,143 in 1978 and hovered near 30,000 until reaching 31,555 in 1981; since then it declined to 21,714 in 1983, and to 16,716 in 1988.

The decline in fifth-preference admissions since 1978 is more vivid in Figure 5.5, which shows the total and the hemisphere shares. The decline—from 97,454 in 1978 to 63,948 in 1988—is of interest, because it appears to be a decline in the number of visas allocated to the fifth-preference category (i.e., the sum of its own allocation, 64,800 since 1980, and unused visas in the first- through fourth-preference categories) and hence is proba-

FIGURE 5.4
*Immigrants Admitted as U.S. Citizens' Siblings
and Siblings' Spouses and Children,
by Hemisphere of Origin and Year of Admission: 1966–1988*

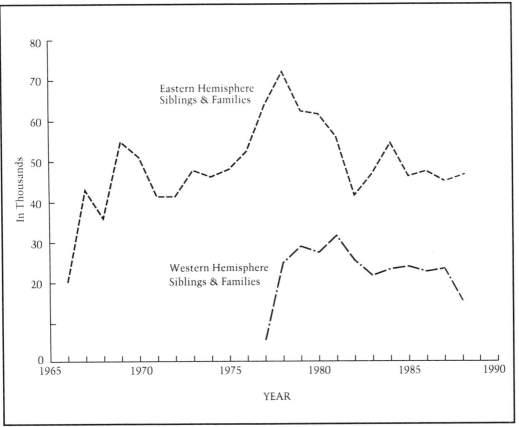

bly due to the decrease in unused visas in the four higher preferences. The decline in unused visas in the four higher preferences, in turn, is most likely due to the sharp demand for second-preference visas among Western Hemisphere persons—that is, an increase in marriages of permanent resident aliens to foreign-born persons who are not also permanent resident aliens (or naturalized citizens).

Demand for immigration among siblings of U.S. citizens has grown enormously—the backlog for fifth-preference visas increasing from 507,756 in 1980 to 1,469,231 in 1989. The growth in this category reflects in part the immigration of refugees, most of whom were admitted without relatives in the United States. The fifth-preference backlog for Vietnam in

FIGURE 5.5

*Total Immigrants Admitted as U.S. Citizens' Siblings
and Siblings' Spouses and Children,
by Hemisphere of Origin and Year of Admission: 1966–1988*

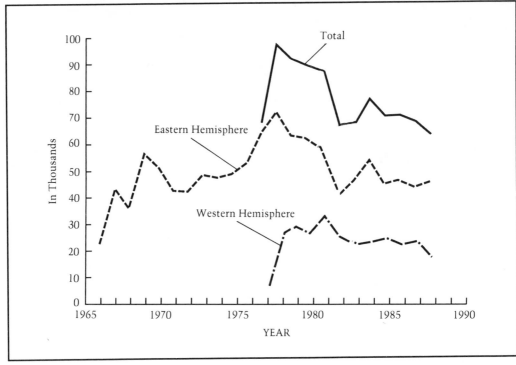

1980 totaled 13,980; by 1986 it had grown to 69,060, and by 1989 to 90,997. In the interval, the annual number of fifth-preference immigrants from Vietnam never reached 2,000; the number of new, naturalized citizens from Vietnam—persons eligible to sponsor their siblings—however, has numbered over 10,000 in every year beginning with 1982, reached 30,840 in 1986, and numbered 21,636 in 1988.

As the waiting period for a visa lengthens, the sibling-immigrant's age at entry would be expected to increase, together with his or her likelihood of being married. Of course, as the probability of being married increases, the backlogs increase as well. Available data enable an initial glimpse of these processes. Figure 5.6 reports the ratio of spouse-of-sibling immigrants to sibling principals in FYs 1978–1988. If all married siblings obtain visas for their spouses and if all spouses enter with their principals, then this ratio exactly represents the proportion married of the new immigrants admitted by virtue of being the siblings of U.S. citizens. To the extent that the two

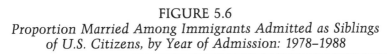

FIGURE 5.6
*Proportion Married Among Immigrants Admitted as Siblings
of U.S. Citizens, by Year of Admission: 1978–1988*

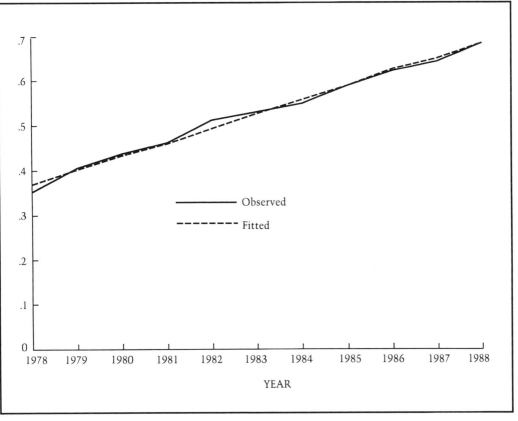

conditions are not exactly met, the ratio represents an approximation (albeit a reasonable approximation) to the proportion married. The plot indicates a steady increase in the proportion of the foreign-born siblings of U.S. citizens who are married, from 36 percent in 1978 to 67 percent in 1988. The increase is remarkably constant at about 3 percentage points per year; fitting a line by least squares produces an R^2 of .99. The fitted line is superimposed on the observed line in Figure 5.6.

Interestingly, the average number of children among the married siblings—approximated by the ratio of children-of-siblings immigrants to spouses-of-siblings immigrants—has remained almost constant during the 1978–1988 period, at about two children (depicted in Figure 5.7). Given the lengthening of the waiting period for fifth-preference visas, this constancy

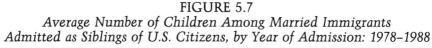

FIGURE 5.7

Average Number of Children Among Married Immigrants
Admitted as Siblings of U.S. Citizens, by Year of Admission: 1978–1988

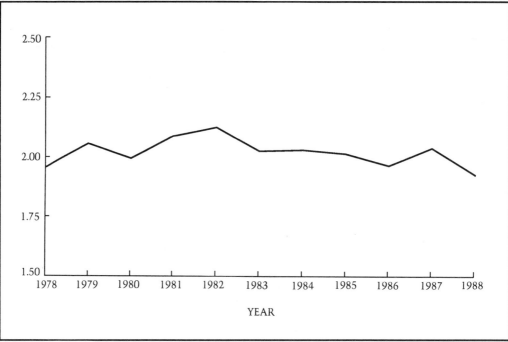

suggests that potential immigrants tend to have fewer children than their compatriots or delay childbearing—issues we examine in Chapter 10.

The combined number of siblings immigrating and seeking to immigrate far exceeds the number of foreign-born parents of U.S. citizens who accept the numerically exempt visa to which they are entitled. If the same set of U.S. citizens has both potential parent-immigrants and sibling-immigrants, then these figures reflect the fact that each citizen is likely to have more siblings-cum-spouses-and-children than parents, although it is also possible that parents have less desire to immigrate than siblings. The size of the fifth-preference backlog and its apparent rapid increase suggests that parents indeed manifest a much lower propensity to immigrate than their children. Consider, for example, the following recent figures. The number of immigrants who gained permanent residence as the parents of U.S. citizens in FY 1985 was 38,986. That same year the number of persons who became immigrants as sibling principals was 25,536; this number represents 36 percent of the total fifth-preference immigration. In January 1986 the fifth-preference backlog totaled 1,210,656. If we approximate the number of siblings in the backlog by applying the corresponding proportion among the FY 1985 immigrants—36 percent—then the estimated number of siblings in the backlog is 438,633. Summing the siblings in the backlog with the sibling immigrants, we obtain 464,169, which approximates the number of siblings who sought to immigrate in FY 1985. This calculation suggests that for every parent who immigrated in 1985, there were almost 12 siblings who wished to do so—including, of course, siblings who had been in the backlog for several years. Because the siblings' spouses and children also use up visas and because of the fifth-preference ceiling, however, the number of siblings who actually immigrated in FY 1985 was about two thirds the number of parent-immigrants.

Determinants of Flows of Family Immigrants: Sponsorship Rates and Country Conditions

The worldwide and hemisphere-specific figures presented above may mask important differences between countries in the number of persons who enter with different types of visas. What determines the number of family-reunification immigrants by visa type? In addition to the factors associated with the decision to immigrate discussed in previous chapters— the attractiveness of the origin country, the quantity and quality of information about the United States, the direct costs of migrating—a further determinant of kinship-based immigration may be identified: the number of naturalized citizens in the United States from each origin country, who represent the potential sponsors of family-based immigrants.

To assess the quantitative importance of country-specific conditions and to estimate the proportion of naturalized citizens who actually make use of reunification entitlements, we perform a multivariate analysis of the determinants of the three types of blood relatives of interest—adult sons and daughters, siblings, and parents—who immigrated in FY 1971. The explanatory variables include the relevant country characteristics measured for the immediate pre-immigration (i.e., decision-making) period as well as the numbers of naturalized citizens from the origin-country, classified by their length of time in the United States. Duration and origin-country-specific numbers of naturalized citizens are sample estimates of the number of persons enumerated in the U.S. 1970 census who report being naturalized citizens of the United States and who report entering the United States in 1960–1964, 1955–1959, and 1950–1954, respectively.[6]

---

[6]The 1970 census information on the numbers of naturalized foreign-born represents the correct measure of the number of naturalized citizens at a given point in time who may petition for relatives living outside the United States. However, as discussed in previous chap-

Table 5.1 reports ordinary-least-squares (OLS) and two-stage-least-squares (TSLS) estimates of the determinants of the flows of adult immigrants who obtain U.S. visas as a result of being (adult) children, siblings, or parents of U.S. citizens.[7] The set of origin-country and U.S. citizen variables accounts for 45 to 61 percent of the cross-country variation in these visa-specific, kin-based immigration flows. In the adult-children and siblings equations, only the naturalized citizens arriving in the United States from five to ten years prior to the 1970 census survey (i.e., the 1960–1964 entry cohort) are positively and statistically significantly related to the 1971 flow of "family-reunification" immigrants, suggesting that most reunification of this type occurs within a decade of an immigrant cohort's entry.[8] Negative associations between the cohorts of naturalized citizens who entered in 1950–1954 and the immigration flows in 1971 suggest a depletion over time of the stock of home-country parents, children, and siblings eligible to immigrate. The point estimates for the 1960–1964 citizen-cohort represent sponsorship rates, that is, the rates at which naturalized citizens sponsor family-based immigrants. The preferred TSLS estimates indicate that every 100 *naturalized* citizens in the United States with an average duration of stay of 7.5 years sponsor the immigration of 5 adult sons and daughters, 11 adult siblings, and 3 parents *per year* from their origin country over the

---

ters, the accuracy of the counts of naturalized citizens may not be high, possibly owing in part to the foreign-born (particularly recent immigrants, legal or illegal) misunderstanding a poorly worded question. Alternatively, we could have measured the cohort-specific, origin-country-specific 1970 numbers of naturalized citizens by summing the naturalization counts in the INS *Annual Report* for each immigrant entry cohort from 1950 to 1970 by country of origin. But even if these counts were perfectly accurate, such an INS-based measure would not take into account either mortality among or emigration by the naturalized, phenomena which are, however, incorporated in the 1970 census count.

[7]The family-reunification equations are vulnerable to two sources of bias: (1) measurement error, as noted above, in the naturalized-citizen population variables; and (2) potential correlation of the naturalized-citizen population variables and the equation stochastic term. Thus, OLS estimation will yield biased estimates of the coefficients. To correct for both kinds of biases, we employ two-stage least squares, using as instruments lagged, exogenous origin-country characteristics which pertain to the 1950–1965 period and which, when available, are the counterparts to those 1970s country-specific variables included in the equations. Reliable country-specific data are more sparse for the pre-1960 period than for the post-1960 period. In order not to reduce the size of the country data set, we employ in the first-stage equation a set of dummy variables corresponding to missing observations for particular variables rather than eliminate countries because of one or another missing variable for the pre-1960 period. Consistency of the relevant *second*-stage estimates (i.e., the family-reunification equations shown in Table 5.1) is retained, without sacrificing sample size.

[8]Both the stock (population) and the flow variables are drawn from 1-in-100 samples. Hence, the coefficients of the stock variables describe the increase in the number of immigrants associated with a unit increase in the number of naturalized citizens. In contrast, the coefficients of the country-characteristic dummy variables describe the associated increase in terms of the 1 percent sample; the effect in numbers of new immigrants is thus equal to the coefficient multiplied by a factor of 100.

TABLE 5.1
Determinants of the Number of Legal Immigrants Admitted in FY 1971,
by Relationship to U.S. Citizens: OLS and TSLS Estimates

| | Eastern Hemisphere | | | | All Countries | |
| | Sons and Daughters | | Siblings | | Parents | |
Variable	OLS	TSLS	OLS	TSLS	OLS	TSLS
Naturalized Citizens of the United States in 1970, by Entry Cohort						
Naturalized citizens,	.0453	.0488	.145	.106	.00519	.0321
Entered 1960–1964	(4.32)[a]	(2.91)[b]	(3.13)[a]	(1.38)[b]	(1.28)	(1.15)
Naturalized citizens,	−.00883	−.00588	−.0196	.0127	.0167	.0237
Entered 1955–1959	(2.10)	(0.82)	(1.05)	(0.39)	(3.68)	(1.53)
Naturalized citizens,	−.00335	−.00738	−.0176	−.0396	−0.00854	−0.0358
Entered 1950–1954	(1.66)	(2.07)	(1.97)	(2.40)	(2.37)	(0.89)
Origin-Country Characteristics						
GNP per capita (×10⁻³)	−.110	−.0949	−.480	−.436	−0.311	.186
	(1.74)	(1.39)	(1.72)	(1.39)	(3.08)	(0.25)
Literacy Rate (×10⁻²)	.187	−.354	.489	−.692	1.799	−.559
	(0.25)	(0.41)	(0.15)	(0.17)	(1.43)	(0.16)
Distance (×10⁻⁴)	−.241	−.112	−6.10	−5.99	.668	2.27
	(0.21)	(0.09)	(1.22)	(1.10)	(0.70)	(0.96)
Centrally Planned	.0326	.505	−.217	.185	−0.707	−0.641
	(0.06)	(0.74)	(0.83)	(0.06)	(0.92)	(0.36)
English official	−.0406	.0152	−1.57	−1.53	−0.391	−0.446
language	(0.11)	(0.04)	(0.93)	(0.83)	(0.82)	(0.51)
U.S. military base	−1.29	−1.34	−2.59	−1.10	−0.0322	.793
	(2.35)	(1.92)	(1.07)	(0.34)	(0.06)	(0.38)
Voice of America	−.836	−1.02	−3.19	−3.62	−1.436	.0875
broadcasts	(2.18)	(2.35)	(1.88)	(1.82)	(2.54)	(0.03)
Population Size (×10⁻⁷)	.886	.547	−.136	−.591	−0.531	0.382
	(0.04)	(0.03)	(0.15)	(0.06)	(2.68)	(1.00)
Constant	.860	1.18	7.16	8.15	.594	−1.029
	(1.05)	(1.31)	(1.98)	(1.96)	(0.57)	(0.37)
F	4.95	3.68	3.85	2.80	8.23	1.68
R^2	.511	—	.448	—	.609	—
N		64		64		67

SOURCES: U.S. Census Public Use Samples; U.S. INS FY 1971 Immigrant Cohort and Immigrant Cohort Sample.

NOTES: In 1971 the preference-category system applied only to the Eastern Hemisphere; hence the siblings and adult-children equations are estimated only for Eastern-Hemisphere countries. Absolute values of t-ratios and of asymptotic t-ratios appear in parentheses beneath the OLS and TSLS estimates, respectively.

five-year period following the date at which most of the cohort could have first naturalized after immigrating.

While the estimates indicate that, as for children and siblings, the naturalized citizens who have resided in the United States for five to ten years are responsible for the largest country-specific number of parents who immigrated in FY 1971, the estimated sponsorship rate coefficient is not measured very precisely; moreover, the estimated sponsorship rate for the earlier 1955–1959 entry cohort of naturalized citizens approaches respectable levels of statistical significance and is also positive. Thus, it would appear that the reunification of immigrants with their parents is a more prolonged process than the reunification of immigrants with their foreign-born siblings. It is possible that the parents take a longer time to make the immigration decision; alternatively, it is possible that this type of reunification increases in attractiveness as the parent grows older. However, consistent with the trends reviewed above, the estimates indicate that fewer parents immigrate than siblings even if one sums them over a ten-year period.

A causal relationship may exist between the size of the population of naturalized citizens from a country and future immigration flows from that country even in the absence of statute-based family-reunification entitlements. Prior flows of immigrants may facilitate information exchange and immigrants may aid their compatriots in settlement. To discriminate between family-reunification sponsorship effects and linkages that extend beyond family boundaries, we employ the same variables to estimate the determinants of the flow of non-family immigrants—the labor-certified immigrants. Estimates (not shown) of the effects of the number of naturalized citizens from the origin country on the immigration of this group are not statistically significantly different from zero, indicating that these general national ties are significantly less important than direct, statute-based family linkages. We feel confident in interpreting the results in Table 5.1, therefore, as estimates of family-reunification-based sponsorship rates associated with recently naturalized U.S. citizens.

The set of origin-country characteristics also influences the flow of family migrants; in all equations the set of the country variables explains a statistically significant proportion of the variance in the immigration flows (F-test, .01 significance level). For given potential petitioners in the United States, flows of children and siblings appear to be lower from countries with higher levels of per-capita GNP, although the coefficients are statistically significant only at the 10 percent level of significance (one-tail test). It is not possible to discern whether the negative effect of origin-country GNP on the immigration of these categories of immigrants is due to smaller family size in high-GNP countries or to the greater reluctance of eligible individuals to emigrate from such countries. In contrast, the origin-country's GNP does not appear to be related to the immigration of parents, suggesting the operation of more purely familial mechanisms in their immigration.

A noteworthy feature of Table 5.1 is the negative or zero effect of the presence of a U.S. military base on the immigration of blood relatives in 1971; as noted in Chapter 4, the presence of such bases does add to the total immigration through marriage. Of the other variables, distance does not appear to be a significant deterrent to these family migrants. Nor is the size of the population or the literacy rate of the origin country an important determinant of the magnitude of family immigration, once the size of the naturalized-citizen population (potential sponsors) from that country residing in the United States is taken into account. Finally, Voice of America broadcasts appear to reduce the flow of offspring and siblings (while being irrelevant to the immigration of parents).

The Effects of Family Reunification on Family Structure

We have seen how U.S. immigration law eased the immigration of parents of adult U.S. citizens in 1965–1968 and the immigration of siblings of adult U.S. citizens, first in 1965 for Eastern Hemisphere applicants and 12 years later for Western Hemisphere prospective immigrants. The available INS data cannot reveal the true increase in the immigration of parents and siblings, since they do not indicate the parental and sibling status of those who earlier entered by prefamily reunification criteria. However, to the extent that the law provided a new immigration entitlement, it is likely that there would have been an increase in the immigration of these kin groups; to the extent that such an increase has occurred, we might also expect to find a parallel increase in the numbers of *recent-entrant* parents and siblings who reside with their sponsors.

Is the household structure of the foreign-born different from that of the native-born? Have these differences, if any, changed over time, reflecting the changes in immigration law? Are differences in family structure across nativity groups temporary or do they persist? While not providing information on sponsorship per se, U.S. Census data can be used to assess the extent to which recent-entrant foreign-born persons live in households to whose heads they are related as parent, parent-in-law, sibling, or sibling-in-law. Changes across censuses in the proportion of foreign-born recent entrants displaying such co-residence would reflect the effects of immigration law. Moreover, the matched year-of-entry cohort groups across the 1960 and 1970 censuses and the 1970 and 1980 censuses permit an examination and comparison of the cohort changes in family structure for the native- and foreign-born.

Table 5.2 reports, for three age-specific groups and by hemisphere, the percentage of recent entrants in 1960, 1970, and 1980 who live in households in which they are the parent or the parent-in-law of the household head. There is an increase for every group but one over the 20-year period (the proportion of Eastern Hemisphere recent entrants over age 65 residing with a son/daughter or a son/daughter-in-law declined between 1960 and 1970 from over 51 percent to almost 48 percent, but subsequently increased to over 55 percent in 1980).

TABLE 5.2
Percent Parents or Parents-in-Law Residing with Household Heads,
Among Recent Entrants, by Age, Hemisphere of Origin, and Census Year: 1960–1980

Age	1960		1970		1980	
	Eastern	Western	Eastern	Western	Eastern	Western
45–54	3.46	5.37	4.15	7.02	7.79	10.16
55-64	18.60	20.21	20.41	24.92	30.23	25.00
65+	51.50	40.91	47.97	47.88	55.44	50.35

SOURCE: U.S. Census of Population, Public Use Samples.

Figure 5.8 summarizes the recent-entrant information for the entire group aged 45 and over and incorporates parallel information for the native-born. The results clearly suggest that while among the native-born the level of co-residence of parents and adult children is low and the trend is decreasing, among recent-entrant foreign-born the level is higher and the trend strongly increasing: while the proportion of native-born persons exhibiting "intergenerational" co-residence declines from 4.5 percent to 2 percent from 1960 to 1980, the Eastern (Western) Hemisphere proportions rise from 15 (12) percent to 27 (33) percent.

FIGURE 5.8
Percent Parents or Parents-in-Law Residing with Household Heads,
Among Recent Entrants and Native-Born Aged 45+,
by Hemisphere of Origin and Census Year: 1960–1980

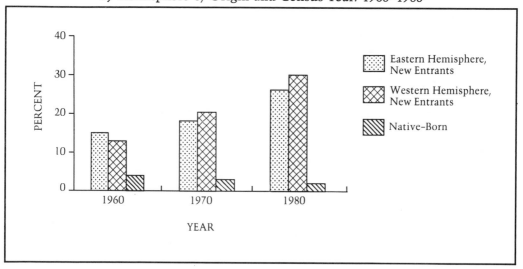

TABLE 5.3
Percent Siblings or Siblings-in-Law Residing with Household Heads,
Among Recent Entrants, by Age, Hemisphere of Origin, and Census Year: 1960–1980

	1960		1970		1980	
Age	Eastern	Western	Eastern	Western	Eastern	Western
25–34	2.69	4.33	2.86	4.53	5.21	8.28
35–44	2.21	4.11	4.14	3.74	3.92	7.51
45–54	2.05	5.37	4.14	3.86	4.52	6.67

SOURCE: U.S. Census of Population, Public Use Samples.

Table 5.3 repeats the same analysis for recent-entrant foreign-born persons who report being the sibling or sibling-in-law of the head of the household in which they reside. The figures suggest a strong responsiveness of "horizontal family extension" to the increases in sibling entitlements provided by U.S. immigration law. Between 1960 and 1970 co-residence of siblings increases for all three age-specific Eastern Hemisphere groups, approximately doubling for the 35–44 and 45–54 age groups, while the proportions decline slightly for two of the Western Hemisphere groups. However, between 1970 and 1980 (the period following the extension of sibling entitlements to the Western Hemisphere foreign-born) all three Western Hemisphere age groups display an almost twofold increase in sibling co-residence rates, while there is little change in the Eastern Hemisphere rates for the two 35–54 age groups. Thus, the figures are consistent with the hemisphere-specific changes in immigration law over that period. Moreover, these co-residential patterns are not displayed by the native-born.

Figure 5.9 summarizes the sibling co-residence data for all persons aged 25–54, again including the native-born. As with the results for parents, both the level and trend in sibling co-residence differ between recent immigrants and the native-born. The incidence of horizontal family extension is much greater for the foreign-born recent entrants than for the native-born in each census year; and the trend is increasing for the foreign-born groups while it is decreasing for the native-born. By 1980, the proportion of persons aged 25–54 who are a sibling of a co-resident household head is less than 1 percent for the native-born (down from 1.3 percent in 1960), while the comparable proportion is 7.9 percent for the Western Hemisphere recent entrants, up from 4.3 percent in 1960.

Do the co-residential patterns displayed by the foreign-born recent entrants persist, or do they merely reflect immigrant transitions to independence? Tables 5.4–5.7 display the decadal cohort change, by age and sex, in kinship co-resident rates for the 1960 and 1970 recent entrants. The tables indicate that the proportions of the foreign-born of either sex who reside

FIGURE 5.9

Percent Siblings or Siblings-in-Law Residing with Household Heads,
Among Recent Entrants and Native-Born Aged 25–54,
by Hemisphere of Origin and Census Year: 1960–1980

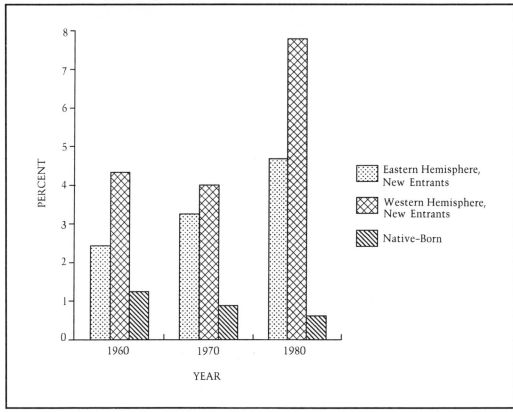

with and are parents of the household head remain substantially higher
than those of the native-born, even after ten years. For example, in 1960 the
proportion of recent entrants aged 55–64 who are mothers or mothers-in-
law of and who are residing with the household head was 27.9 percent.
After ten years the proportion for this cohort (in 1970) was 30.5 percent.
The comparable rates for the native-born cohort aged 55–64 in 1960 were
4.7 and 6.9 percent, respectively. Between 1970 and 1980, the proportion
of the 1970 recent entrants aged 55–64 who are co-resident mothers or
mothers-in-law of the head remains close to 30 percent, while that for the
comparable native-born age cohort rises from 2.8 percent to only 3.8 percent. The incidence of intergenerational extension of foreign-born households does not appear to converge to that of the native-born after ten years.

TABLE 5.4
1960–1970 Decadal Cohort Change in Percent Recent-Entrant
and Native-Born Women Residing with Household Head,
by Relationship to Head, and Age in 1960

Age in 1960	Sister or Sister-in-Law		Mother or Mother-in-Law	
	1960	1970	1960	1970
	1960 Recent Entrants			
25–34	2.19	0.50	0.00	0.13
35–44	2.88	1.36	0.13	1.63
45–54	3.39	3.14	6.10	8.64
55–64	4.33	2.30	27.88	30.46
	Native-Born			
25–34	0.87	0.65	0.04	0.23
35–44	1.17	1.34	0.16	0.74
45–54	1.81	2.25	1.28	2.75
55–64	2.92	3.48	4.70	6.94

SOURCE: U.S. Census of Population, Public Use Samples.

The immigration of the parents of U.S. citizens appears also to be manifested in the co-residence of these parents with their children in the United States.

In contrast, the proportions of persons who are siblings of and reside with the household head, initially higher for the recent entrants than for

TABLE 5.5
1960–1970 Decadal Cohort Change in Percent Recent-Entrant
and Native-Born Men Residing with Household Head,
by Relationship to Head, and Age in 1960

1960	1960	1970	1960	1970
	1960 Recent Entrants			
25–34	4.35	0.58	0.00	0.08
35–44	2.89	0.77	0.00	0.31
45–54	2.53	0.26	1.84	2.63
55–64	3.74	1.57	10.28	7.09
	Native-Born			
25–34	1.36	0.76	0.00	0.03
35–44	1.13	1.31	0.04	0.18
45–54	1.41	1.43	0.26	0.53
55–64	1.71	1.56	1.26	1.97

SOURCE: U.S. Census of Population, Public Use Samples.

TABLE 5.6
1970–1980 Decadal Cohort Change in Percent Recent-Entrant
and Native-Born Women Residing with Household Head,
by Relationship to Head, and Age in 1970

Age in 1970	Sister or Sister-in-Law		Mother or Mother-in-Law	
	1970	1980	1970	1980
	1970 Recent Entrants			
25–34	3.04	0.48	0.08	0.24
35–44	3.78	1.38	0.64	2.30
45–54	3.61	3.37	8.79	10.12
55–64	3.45	4.90	30.34	26.96
	Native-Born			
25–34	0.82	0.43	0.03	0.26
35–44	0.65	0.84	0.23	0.80
45–54	1.34	1.37	0.74	1.76
55–64	2.24	2.63	2.75	3.75

SOURCE: U.S. Census of Population, Public Use Samples.

TABLE 5.7
1970–1980 Decadal Cohort Change in Percent Recent-Entrant
and Native-Born Men Residing with Household Head,
by Relationship to Head, and Age in 1970

Age in 1970	Brother or Brother-in-Law		Father or Father-in-Law	
	1970	1980	1970	1980
	1970 Recent Entrants			
25–34	3.95	0.96	0.98	0.58
35–44	4.13	1.03	0.08	1.71
45–54	4.44	1.46	1.87	2.91
55–64	2.15	0.00	11.66	10.20
	Native-Born			
25–34	0.76	0.45	0.03	0.00
35–44	1.31	0.81	0.18	0.26
45–54	1.43	1.01	0.53	0.69
55–64	1.55	1.55	1.97	1.29

SOURCE: U.S. Census of Population, Public Use Samples.

the native-born, appear to converge with those of the native-born within a decade in both the 1960–1970 and 1970–1980 periods. The family reunification of siblings through immigration is not manifested in household living arrangements in as persistent a way as it is for parents.

It is tempting to speculate about the reasons why a relatively high proportion of the foreign-born who entered the United States when relatively old (over age 40) reside with their adult children even ten years after entry, in contrast to native-born of the same age. In part this may reflect traditional household patterns in the origin country. However, older immigrants may be less willing than younger migrants to invest in the new skills needed to be self-sufficient in the United States, since the lifetime payoffs are less. Moreover, selectivity may also be operating; only those parents of U.S. citizens living abroad who are less independent, by choice or by necessity, may choose to immigrate. And, finally, most older native-born U.S. citizens receive or are eligible to receive Social Security income, which for the elderly foreign-born will be low if they entered the United States (and its work force) at an advanced age.

Summary

To safeguard the integrity of families, U.S. immigration law enables the immigration of three types of adult blood relatives of adult U.S. citizens—parents, sons and daughters, and siblings. In this chapter we examined trends in the number of U.S. citizens and relatives who make use of these family-reunification entitlements and assessed their effects on the household structure of the foreign-born.

Because parent visas are exempt from numerical limitations, it is possible to know exactly the number of citizen-and-parent pairs who seek the parent's immigration. That number increased from less than 5,000 in 1965 to almost 39,000 in 1985 and to 47,500 in 1988. Adult offspring of U.S. citizens compete for numerically limited visas under the first- (if unmarried) and fourth-preference (if married) categories. The number of immigrant visas awarded to them increased gradually to over 15,000 in 1987 and to over 16,000 in 1988, with another 17,000 and 18,000 awarded to their spouses and children in the two years, respectively. Meanwhile, more than 161,000 offspring and immediate families were approved and waiting for a visa as of January 1989; if the composition of the backlogs resembles that of the immigrant population, then over 75,000 were the adult sons and daughters of U.S. citizens.

The number of citizen-and-offspring pairs seeking the offspring's immigration is small compared with that of citizen-and-sibling pairs. The fifth-preference category, for siblings of U.S. citizens and their spouses and children, has not only used all available visas but also has accumulated a large backlog. The number of visas awarded to siblings in 1985 and 1986 hovered near 25,000, declining to 21,489 in 1988, with another 42,000 to 45,000 awarded to their spouses and children each year. The backlog, however, grew to almost 1.5 million by 1989, of whom, again if backlog composition resembles that of the immigrant population, over half a million were the siblings of U.S. citizens.

Information on both the relatives who immigrated and those in the visa backlogs indicates that for every citizen-and-parent pair who sought and achieved the parent's immigration in 1985, there were 1.3 citizen-and-offspring pairs seeking the offspring's immigration and 12 citizen-and-sibling pairs seeking the sibling's immigration. However, because visas are also awarded to family members and because of the numerical limitations, for every 100 parents who entered in 1985, 33 offspring and 66 siblings entered.

Multivariate analyses suggest, however, that relatively few naturalized citizens make use of family reunification visa entitlements. We estimate that each naturalized citizen sponsors, on average, only 0.25 adult children, 0.55 adult siblings, and 0.15 parents within ten years after entry. Part of the reason for these low rates is that many of the naturalized citizens are themselves brought in by U.S. citizen relatives. The implications of this "chaining" of immigration, resulting from family reunification provisions, are considered in more detail in the next chapter. Our multivariate analyses also suggest that the immigration of parents may be more purely the result of familial mechanisms than that of siblings and adult offspring. For example, while the propensity of the latter to immigrate appears to be related to the origin country's per capita GNP, that of parents does not.

The provisions of immigration law that facilitate the immigration of relatives of U.S. citizens does appear to result in a household structure for the U.S. foreign-born that is strikingly more "extended" than that of the native-born. The incidence of co-residence by native-born parents and adult children and/or adult siblings has been low and the trend decreasing from 1960 to 1980. Among the recent-entrant foreign-born, however, the incidence of both "vertical" and "horizontal" extension is higher and the trend strongly increasing over the same period. Furthermore, the trends in sibling co-residence mirror hemisphere-specific changes in U.S. immigration law; in particular, the foreign-born from the Western Hemisphere exhibited an almost twofold increase in sibling co-residence between 1970 and 1980, the period when the sibling sponsorship entitlement was extended to the Western Hemisphere.

Sponsoring the immigration of a sibling does not permanently increase the likelihood that sponsor and immigrant will live together. In contrast, sponsoring the immigration of a parent may strongly reflect the wish of the citizen-parent pair to live together permanently. Co-residence rates of parents and adult children remain high after more than a decade in the United States, while rates of adult siblings converge with those of the native-born as length of residence in the United States increases.

6

SPONSORSHIP,
FAMILY REUNIFICATION,
AND THE IMMIGRATION MULTIPLIER

A S WE HAVE seen, for the overwhelming majority of persons around the world who desire to immigrate to the United States, the attainment of a legal immigrant visa depends on a kinship tie (of a certain kind) to a person already a citizen or permanent resident alien of the United States. Over one third of all non-refugee/asylee adult immigrants achieve permanent residence as the spouses of U.S. citizens.[1] Eighty percent of all numerically limited visas are designated for relatives of citizens or permanent resident aliens;[2] and more than half of the remaining 20 percent are awarded to the spouses and children of the principals who immigrate on the basis of their relationship to a U.S. citizen or resident alien.[3] In FY 1988 some 341,000 U.S. citizen-relative or U.S. resident-relative pairs sought jointly a relative's immigration.[4]

---

[1]Indeed, in FY 1986 immigrants admitted as the spouses of U.S. citizens constituted 38.6 percent of all non-refugee/asylee immigrants aged 20 and over.

[2]The number of relatives awarded numerically limited visas may exceed 80 percent, if not all visas in the (occupation-based) third-preference category are used. Conversely, if not all 216,000 visas are used by relatives, the remainder may be awarded to nonpreference applicants; as noted in Chapter 1, this has not occurred since 1978.

[3]The average for FYs 1984–1988 was 56 percent.

[4]We say the request is made "jointly" by sponsor and prospective immigrant because the decision is made jointly and the application process requires the action of both persons. Of course, each files a separate set of documents, and may do so at a different time and with a different office, as discussed in Chapter 1.

An important consequence of these family-reunification entitlements is that each new immigrant becomes a potential immigrant sponsor. More fundamentally, each native-born sponsor of an immigrant (and as well the U.S. government, through "sponsorship" of refugees and of some "special immigrants" who require neither relative nor employer) generates not only the currently sponsored immigrant but also the set of potential future immigrants associated with the current immigrant. In principle, one new immigrant could sponsor the eventual immigration of almost the entire population of the world through the "chaining" of migration via family reunification entitlements.[5] The realization of these potential immigration flows depends, however, on the decisions by each new immigrant to remain in the United States and to naturalize and on the joint decisions with his or her relatives residing abroad to utilize the entitlement. And we have seen that many immigrants do not remain in the United States and fewer than half ever become citizens.

In this chapter we estimate the *actual* total number of immigrants that are eventually sponsored as a result of the admission of one original immigrant, taking into account the chaining entailed by the family-reunification provisions of immigration law. That is, we estimate how immigration actually "multiplies" through chaining, making use of our estimates of naturalization and sponsorship rates, and their determinants, reported in previous chapters.

One important aspect of sponsorship and chain migration is the nativity of the sponsor, because of its implications for the relationship between past immigration and future immigration. If all sponsors are immigrants, then the size and composition of today's immigrant population importantly affect future immigration flows through chaining. If, on the other hand, all

[5]The potential explosiveness of this *hypothetical* multiple-strand chain characterizing the reproduction of immigrants has not gone unnoticed. The chairman of the U.S. Select Commission on Immigration and Refugee Policy, the Rev. Theodore M. Hesburgh, has argued (U.S. Select Commission 1981b): "The inclusion of a preference for brothers and sisters of adult U.S. citizens creates a runaway demand for visas. . . . The reason is simple. Once any person enters the country under any preference and becomes naturalized, the demand for the admission of brothers and sisters increases geometrically. . . . To illustrate the potential impact, assume one foreign-born married couple, both naturalized, each with two siblings who are also married and each new nuclear family having three children. The foreign-born married couple may petition for the admission of their siblings. Each has a spouse and three children who come with their parents. Each spouse is a potential source for more immigration, and so it goes. It is possible that no less than 84 persons would become eligible for visas in a relatively short period of time." In Hesburgh's hypothetical case, the excess growth arises from the combination of the sibling entitlement with the spouse entitlement, or, put differently, from the attentiveness of the family-reunification provisions of U.S. immigration law to both marital and blood ties. That is, if the second generation consisted exclusively of the earlier immigrant's own siblings, these new immigrants would in most cases have no further siblings or parents to entitle; it is the spouses of the siblings of the earlier immigrant who would appear to account for much of the third generation.

sponsors are native-born U.S. citizens, then current immigration has no direct bearing on future immigration.[6] In the second part of this chapter we therefore examine the characteristics of the sponsors of immigrants, inclusive of their nativity, based on a recent study (1988a) conducted by the U.S. General Accounting Office (GAO), which is the first to examine the sponsors of a probability sample of immigrants. Among the questions we address are the following: Which immigrants have the highest rates of sponsorship? Is the immigration multiplier explosive? What proportions of sponsors are native-born citizens? Are native-born or foreign-born citizens more likely to sponsor new immigrants? Are men or women more likely to sponsor immigrants and, if so, of what type? When native-born U.S. citizens marry foreign-born spouses, do they gravitate to certain countries to find their mates?

The Family-Reunification Immigration Multiplier

The family-reunification provisions of immigration law have resulted in large backlogs of persons *eligible* for visas who must wait many years to receive them—2,328,479 persons as of January 1989. And the potential explosiveness of the "multiplier effect" of these provisions has been of great concern to policymakers. Little or no systematic evidence exists on the actual magnitude of the effect of the immigration of an immigrant on the future flows of immigrants, however, because there have been no attempts to trace the "progeny" of any immigrant cohort through record linkage or sampling. In this section we estimate indirectly the magnitude of the immigration multiplier using available data sources.

To rigorously define the immigration multiplier, it is necessary to consider and define two more basic concepts: that of an *original immigrant* and that of an *original sponsor.* Original immigrants are those immigrant principals sponsored by a native-born U.S. citizen, an employer, or the U.S. government, and the principals' accompanying family members (viz., spouse and minor children). An original sponsor is the person who sponsors an original immigrant. Under current law, there are four main kinds of original sponsors: native-born U.S. citizens who marry a foreign-born person; native-born U.S. citizens who have foreign-born blood relatives; individuals and groups who employ foreign-born persons; and the U.S. government, which "sponsors" the immigration of some persons in the "special

---

[6]Note, however, that temporary residence in the United States may also play a part in kinship-based immigration. For example, as the number of non-immigrants increases, the likelihood that a family abroad has a U.S.-born member increases; that U.S.-born member may, as an adult, exercise the right to live in the United States and to sponsor the immigration of kin.

immigrant" class (such as American Indians born in Canada) as well as refugees. While every immigrant can trace his/her immigration descent back to an original sponsor, only those immigrants who are not original immigrants can trace descent back to an original immigrant. Note that each original sponsor starts a new immigration line.[7]

The number of immigrants *directly* sponsored by an immigrant during his/her lifetime is the *immigrant sponsorship rate.* This rate will clearly depend on the immigrant's location in the immigration "genealogical chain." Thus, for example, immigrants brought in as siblings, under the fifth-preference category, are unlikely to have siblings or parents wishing to immigrate, since these family members will have been sponsored by their (sibling) sponsor. Fifth-preference immigrant principals are likely to have low sponsorship rates. In contrast, an unmarried immigrant entering in a non-kin category (skilled, refugee, etc.) will be expected to have the highest sponsorship rate, since he or she can sponsor parents, siblings, and a future spouse. Married persons who can confer entitlement on parents and siblings are likely to have the next highest sponsorship rates. This group includes three kinds of original immigrants—married non-kin immigrant principals (skilled, refugee, etc.), their accompanying family members, and immigrants entering as the spouses of native-born U.S. citizens—as well as accompanying family members of nonoriginal immigrant principals.[8]

Having defined the immigrant sponsorship rate, we define the *immigration multiplier* as the *total* number of immigrants directly or indirectly sponsored by one original immigrant. The magnitude of the multiplier may differ by the original immigrant's class of admission and other characteristics—for example, by whether the original immigrant is a principal or is instead an accompanying family member. Thus, for example, the number of immigrants attributable to an original marital event may differ from the number attributable to an original employment event or refugee event.

If the composition of an immigrant cohort characterized by the propor-

[7]For example, each Vietnamese person awarded permanent residence under a "refugee" visa category (i.e., "sponsored" by the U.S. government) represents the beginning of a new immigration line in Vietnam. As an indicator of the growth of such immigration lines, consider that while in 1980 the backlogged Vietnamese relatives of U.S. citizens and permanent resident aliens numbered 20,318, by 1986 this number had grown to 97,276 and by 1989 to 121,628. (The number of Vietnamese awaiting visas in non-kin preference categories is very small; in 1989 it was 256.)

[8]Future research might investigate the distinctive operation of blood and marriage ties. One avenue concerns the connection between sponsor's nativity and the nature of the relationship between sponsor and sponsored immigrant. We would expect that native-born sponsors would largely sponsor spouses, while foreign-born sponsors would sponsor both spouses and blood relatives. But sponsorship of blood kin by native-born persons may be an increasingly important phenomenon. For example, as the number of non-immigrants increases, the likelihood that a family living abroad has one U.S.-born member increases; similarly, many Canadian and Mexican families have U.S.-born members, the result of birth in a hospital on the U.S. side of the border.

tion who are original immigrants differs by country of origin, then aggregate sponsorship rates may differ markedly, since original immigrant principals have a greater pool of potential relatives to sponsor than nonoriginal immigrant principals. But, because the multiplier may extend intertemporally over a long genealogical chain and span a variety of links (e.g., single siblings leading to immediate-relative spouses leading to siblings and parents), the multiplier may still be identical across country-of-origin groups. Reports of actual or intended sponsorship rates for a sample of immigrants at one point in time are thus not sufficient either to compute the magnitude of the immigration multiplier or to forecast it.

The appropriate method for measuring the size of the immigration multiplier is to begin with a sample of original immigrants—those immigrant principals sponsored by native-born U.S. citizens, or immigrating via the skill-based preference categories or as refugees, and so on, and their accompanying family members—and then to count the number of immigrants they sponsor and the immigrants sponsored by those immigrants, and so on.[9] This "ideal" prospective design has two major limitations for predictive or policy purposes, however. First, the process of sponsorship takes time. For example, for many immigrants, five years of residence are required before it is possible to naturalize, and naturalization is a prerequisite for most sponsorship. It would thus take many decades before the full magnitude of the multiplier could be assessed. Second, and relatedly, each multiplier thus computed would characterize one particular cohort of (original) immigrants. It would not necessarily be generalizable to future cohorts, since both world circumstances and immigration laws are unlikely to have remained unchanged since the cohort of original immigrants arrived in the United States.

One method of circumventing the length of time required to compute an actual multiplier is to assume that the sponsorship rates exhibited within visa categories for an immigrant cohort are the same as the sponsorship rates of the future immigrants to be sponsored by the original immigrants in the cohort. That is, the sponsorship rates of family-reunification (non-

---

[9]Like other aspects of the process by which an immigrant adjusts to the United States— the decision to remain in the United States; the decision to naturalize; the social, economic, and linguistic integration—the transformation of an immigrant into a sponsor occurs over time. Consequently, in order to estimate quantities associated with the immigration multiplier, the ideal research design would longitudinally track the sponsorship activities of random samples of immigrants. A wealth of information could be obtained simply by producing an annual sponsor file, containing the basic identifier (the A-number) for both those sponsors who are themselves immigrants and the immigrants they are sponsoring, and subsequently linking the administrative records of new immigrants and their immigrant sponsors, as discussed in Jasso and Rosenzweig (1987) and U.S. General Accounting Office (1988b).

original) immigrants in the cohort can be combined with those of the original immigrants in the cohort to create a synthetic multiplier.

The synthetic-cohort method is the method we apply, making use of our 1971 immigrant cohort and the estimated naturalization and sponsorship rates reported in Chapters 2 and 5. The estimation procedure is based on the identity that, for those visa categories requiring the sponsor to be a U.S. citizen, the sponsorship rate at each year after immigration (duration) is equal to the product of the probability that the immigrant has naturalized by that date and the probability that a naturalized immigrant sponsors an immigrant of a given visa category. Thus, estimates of the duration-specific propensities to naturalize and of the duration-specific propensities for naturalized citizens to bring in relatives are jointly sufficient to estimate the set of duration-specific sponsorship rates for any immigrant class. In Chapter 2, we used the longitudinal data describing the 1971 immigration cohort to obtain the probability of each cohort member naturalizing in the first decade of permanent residence, by sex and by immigrant class of admission. In Chapter 5 and in Jasso and Rosenzweig (1986a) we reported estimates of visa-specific immigration flows per naturalized citizen obtained by combining aggregate immigration data, country-of-origin data, and census data on the numbers of naturalized immigrants, by country, residing in the United States. We now combine these estimates to calculate the sex-specific/visa-specific sponsorship rates.

The estimated sponsorship rates embody several further assumptions. First, we assume that earlier immigrants who are themselves siblings of U.S. citizens or adult children of U.S. citizens would not petition for additional siblings. Second, we assume that never-married immigrants and newly married spouses of citizens or permanent resident aliens would have no adult children living abroad. Third, to avoid double-counting, we assume that a married couple can have only one set of adult children living abroad; thus the multipliers associated with the petitioning of adult children through the first- and fourth-preference categories are attributed to the earlier principal immigrant.[10]

Tables 6.1 and 6.2 report the estimated sex-specific/visa-specific immigrant sponsorship rates and also show the visa-category types of the sponsored immigrants. For example, the estimates indicate that during the first ten years of permanent residence, a female immigrant admitted as the sibling of a U.S. citizen would sponsor 0.038 adult offspring, 0.110 spouses, and 0.024 spouses-of-adult-offspring, for a total of 0.172 adult immigrants.

---

[10]A more detailed discussion of procedures is found in Jasso and Rosenzweig (1986a; 1989).

TABLE 6.1
Estimated Sponsorship Rates:
Number of Adult Immigrants Admitted in Period T to T + 10
per Female Immigrant Admitted at Time T, by Visa Category

| | Adult Immigrants (T, T + 10) | | | | | |
| | Principals | | | Spouses of Principals | | |
Female Immigrants (T)	Sibling	Adult Offspring	Spouse	Sibling	Adult Offspring	Total
Principals						
Sibling of citizen	—	.0378	.110	—	.0235	.171
Adult offspring of citizen	—	.0605	.0650	—	.0372	.163
Spouse of citizen	.185	—	.0250	.120	—	.315
Spouse of alien	.209	—	.0100	.136	—	.355
Labor-certified	.254	.0454	.215	.165	.0281	.708
Spouses of Principals						
Sibling spouse	.302	—	.0520	.197	—	.551
Adult-offspring spouse	.209	—	.0076	.136	—	.353
Labor-certified spouse	.190	—	.000	.124	—	.314

SOURCE: U.S. INS FY 1971 Immigrant Cohort Sample; U.S. Census Public Use Samples.

Two findings in Tables 6.1 and 6.2 are worth noting. First, the highest sponsorship rates are found among the labor-certified immigrants—0.59 for men and 0.71 for women. This is due to the relatively high naturalization rates of these immigrants and the greater likelihood that few of their relatives are already residing in the United States. Second, the sibling category (fifth preference) contributes most to the estimated sponsorship rates. For the labor-certified immigrants, the sibling category constitutes 59 and 65 percent of the total adult sponsorship rate for men and women, respectively; for spouses of citizens and aliens, 55 and 63 percent.

The results in Tables 6.1 and 6.2 refer to the sponsorship of adult immigrants. Thus, they must be augmented to include the accompanying children of the sponsored immigrants. Data from the FY 1971 immigrant cohort sample indicate that there are on average 0.95 children for each sibling principal and 0.78 children for each adult offspring of U.S. citizens (first- and fourth-preference categories). Table 6.3 reports the estimated sponsorship rates, inclusive of children, for immigrants of given sex and entry category. As shown, the sponsorship rates in the first decade rise to a range of 0.18–0.87 for men and 0.21–0.98 for women. As before, the highest rates are for labor-certified immigrants. Note that since the ratio of children to principals is highest among fifth-preference immigrants, the

TABLE 6.2
Estimated Sponsorship Rates:
Number of Adult Immigrants Admitted in Period T to T + 10
per Male Immigrant Admitted at Time T, by Visa Category

| | Adult Immigrants (T, T + 10) | | | | | |
| | Principal | | | Spouses of Principals | | |
Male Immigrants (T)	Sibling	Adult Offspring	Spouse	Sibling	Adult Offspring	Total
Principals						
Sibling of citizen	—	.0540	.0790	—	.0314	.164
Adult offspring of citizen	—	.0396	.0850	—	.0231	.148
Spouse of citizen	.235	—	.0540	.135	—	.424
Spouse of alien	.299	—	.000	.172	—	.471
Labor-certified	.241	.0675	.100	.138	.0393	.585
Spouses of Principals						
Sibling spouse	.164	—	.0276	.0945	—	.286
Adult-offspring spouse	.254	—	.0066	.146	—	.406
Labor-certified spouse	.194	—	.000	.111	—	.305

SOURCE: U.S. INS FY 1971 Immigrant Cohort Sample; U.S. Census Public Use Samples.

proportionate contributions of the sibling category to the sponsorship rates are even higher when these are inclusive of children.

The estimated sponsorship rates can be used to calculate multipliers for the original immigrants. Of all the entry categories in Tables 6.1–6.3, only the labor-certified immigrants and their spouses can be unambiguously classified as *original* immigrants. For example, those who entered as the spouse of a U.S. citizen may include both original and nonoriginal immigrants—depending on the nativity of the sponsor. Thus, we can calculate the multipliers only for the labor-certified immigrants and their spouses.

To compute the multiplier, we sum the estimated sponsorship rates across succeeding *generations* of immigrants by first calculating the total number of immigrants sponsored by the sponsored (nonoriginal) immigrants of each generation in their first decade of residence.[11] For example, if we assume that, except for a spouse, the immigrants sponsored by a female

[11]For example, each of the (up to) K kinds of immigrants brought in by the labor-certified original immigrant then brings in (up to) K kinds of immigrants, and each of these in turn brings in (up to) K kinds of immigrants, and so on. In our research, K was equal to five, with sponsorship rates estimated for sponsored immigrants entering as (1) spouses of U.S. citizens, (2) adult offspring of U.S. citizens (first- and fourth- preference categories), (3) siblings of U.S. citizens (fifth-preference category), (4) spouses of offspring (fourth-preference category), and (5) spouses of siblings.

TABLE 6.3

Estimated Sponsorship Rates, Inclusive of Children Accompanying
Sponsored Immigrants, in the First Decade
of the Sponsoring Immigrant's Permanent Residence,
by Entry Category and Sex of Sponsoring Immigrant

Entry Category	Male	Female
Principals		
Sibling of citizen	.207	.201
Adult offspring of citizen	.179	.210
Spouse of citizen	.647	.506
Spouse of alien	.755	.554
Labor-certified immigrant	.867	.984
Spouses of Principals		
Spouse of sibling of citizen	.442	.838
Spouse of adult offspring of citizen	.648	.551
Spouse of labor-certified immigrant	.489	.495

SOURCE: U.S. INS FY 1971 Immigrant Cohort Sample; U.S. Census Public Use Samples.

labor-certified immigrant are divided equally among both sexes, the estimates indicate that the second generation of immigrants in her line would
total .32. Notice that although she almost reproduced herself—bringing in
0.98 immigrants (Table 6.3)—the immigrants she sponsored would not
similarly reproduce themselves, since, unlike her, they were entering in
categories with lower propensities for sponsorship.

Table 6.4 reports the computed sponsorship rates and the total multiplier for three generations for each of the four original immigrant groups.
As can be seen, the sponsorship rates diminish rapidly across generations, so
that the three-generation multiplier, given in the last column, would differ
only trivially from subsequent-generation multipliers if the calculations
were carried out for more than three generations. Thus, the two-generation
multiplier for a female labor-certified immigrant equals 1.30, the (almost)
one immigrant she sponsors herself and the 0.32 immigrants sponsored by
her progeny, while the three-generation multiplier is only 1.39.

The rapid attenuation in the multiplier across immigrant generations
implies that the actual multipliers are not explosive, at least for this cohort
of original immigrants, and are substantially lower than the potential multipliers. However, the multipliers for labor-certified principals are over one;
for every immigrant of this type who immigrates, yet another immigrant
receives a visa within a span of 20 years. Even the multipliers for the
spouses of principals in the "skill" categories, who do not add to the flow
of visa entitlements through marriage, are not trivial; each original-immi-
grant spouse results in over 0.6 additional immigrants over the same period.

TABLE 6.4
Estimated Immigration Multipliers,
by Type of Original Immigrant and by Generation

Original Immigrant	Generation			Total
	1	2	3	
Female Labor-Certified Principal	0.98	0.32	0.09	1.40
Male Labor-Certified Principal	0.87	0.23	0.07	1.16
Female Spouse of Labor-Certified Principal	0.50	0.12	0.04	0.65
Male Spouse of Labor-Certified Principal	0.49	0.11	0.03	0.63

SOURCE: U.S. INS FY 1971 Immigrant Cohort Sample; U.S. Census Public Use Samples.

Some of the limitations of these multiplier estimates are discussed in Jasso and Rosenzweig (1986a) and by Passel and Woodrow (in U.S. Congress 1987), Warren et al. (in U.S. Congress 1987), and Goering (1988). First, the indirect-estimation technique can be applied only to visa categories requiring a citizen sponsor. Second, because of small cell sizes, sponsorship rates are not calculated for sponsorship of or by parents. Third, because of both the small size of the sample and age-related constraints on naturalization and sponsorship, sponsorship rates cannot be calculated inclusive of the sponsorship of children or by immigrant children after they grow up (although, as discussed above, the sponsorship rates were augmented to take account of accompanying children). It is doubtful that any of these additions would substantially alter the estimates in Table 6.4. Fourth, the estimates of the naturalization and sponsorship rates are based on a maximum duration of ten years. If naturalization is a more prolonged process, or there are major lags in post-naturalization sponsorship, then the estimates may understate sponsorship rates for all visa categories and thus understate the actual multiplier. It does appear, however, that, except for changes in the law which alter the incentives to naturalize, most naturalizations occur within ten years of immigration; and the recent GAO study (1988a) suggests that immigrants who become sponsors do so as soon as possible. Finally, the estimated visa-specific sponsorship rates and the multipliers are based on the choices made by one immigrant cohort in a particular historical period. It is possible that the set of sponsorship rates assumes a distinctive pattern for each new cohort of immigrants, particularly given changes in immigration laws. This problem is inherent in all studies using the synthetic-cohort method, of course.

Choosing the Chosen:
U.S. Citizen Sponsors of Spouses and Parents

In this section we utilize the GAO sample of sponsors, combined with INS published information on immigration, to draw inferences, many for the first time, about the characteristics of both the sponsors and those they sponsor. Because GAO published tabulations (1988a) enable reconstruction of the GAO sample, we are able—without access to the original data—to obtain estimates of the proportions native-born and naturalized among the sponsors of spouses and parents and of the corresponding country distributions.

The GAO investigators defined the population of interest as the set of all persons who immigrated to the United States in FY 1985 as "exempt immediate relatives"—that is, as spouses, parents, and minor children of U.S. citizens. This population consists of 198,143 persons, of whom 124,093 are spouses and 38,986 are parents. Cross-tabulation by country of birth and class of admission is provided in INS (1985, Table IMM 2.3). The GAO sample highlighted the ten countries which represented the top origin countries for the entire class of immediate relatives in FY 1985 (spouses, parents, children), collapsing the rest of the sample into a residual category.[12] The ten countries were Canada, Mainland China, Colombia, the Dominican Republic, the Federal Republic of Germany, India, Korea, Mexico, the Philippines, and the United Kingdom. This set of GAO-identified countries omits two countries which are in the top ten for spouses—Iran and Haiti—including in their stead two countries which are not even in the top 12—Mainland China and India. Similarly, the GAO country set omits three countries which are in the top ten for parents—Iran, Taiwan, and Vietnam—including in their stead three which are not even in the top 13—Canada, the Federal Republic of Germany, and the United Kingdom. Thus, we are unable to describe the nativity of the sponsors of Iranian and Haitian spouses or of Iranian, Taiwanese, and Vietnamese parents, despite their large representation among sponsored spouses and parents, respectively.

We focus on the immigration of spouses and parents, omitting from consideration the immediate-relative children immigrants, for two reasons: (1) the GAO report does not distinguish between "own" children and adopted orphans and hence the "blood" relatives cannot be identified, and (2) the extent to which children are decision-making agents is not clear.[13]

---

[12]The GAO sample is a stratified random sample from the population of immediate relatives. Eleven strata were defined, representing the top ten countries and a residual category.

[13]As indicated in INS (1985, Tables IMM 2.3 and IMM 2.5), 9,286, or 26 percent, of the 35,064 children in the GAO population were adoptive children.

The FY 1985 Citizen-and-Spouse Pairs

In FY 1985, a total of 124,093 immigrants were admitted as the spouses of U.S. citizens. The first column of Table 6.5 reports the observed number of spouse immigrants, for all countries which are either among the top ten sources of entering spouses or parents or among the ten countries separately identified in the GAO report. As shown, the leading sources of foreign mates for U.S. citizens were Mexico, which provided 28,957 spouses; the Philippines, which provided 11,409 spouses; and the United Kingdom, Canada, and West Germany, which provided, respectively, 5,141, 4,452, and 4,368 spouses. The shares for the top five countries are shown in the first column of Table 6.6; these range from 23.3 percent for Mexico and 9.2 percent for the Philippines to 3.5 percent for West Germany. The next five countries, in order, were Korea, the Dominican Republic, Iran, Colombia, and Haiti, with shares ranging from 3.5 to 2.2 percent for Korea and Haiti, respectively. As already noted, Iran and Haiti are not identified in the GAO report, being replaced by India and Mainland China, which rank 13th and 17th, respectively, in spouse shares.

TABLE 6.5

Immigrants Admitted as Spouses of U.S. Citizens in FY 1985, by Estimated Nativity of Sponsor, and Approved Visa Applicants (Visa Backlog) in January 1986: Top Countries of Origin

Country	All Spouses	Sponsor Native-Born	Sponsor Naturalized	Visa Backlog
Canada	4,452	4,257	195	19,790
China, Mainland	1,449	693	756	112,843
Colombia	3,341	2,636	705	22,726
Dominican Republic	3,708	2,712	996	37,332
Germany, Federal Republic of	4,368	4,156	212	1,252
Haiti	2,729	—	—	18,948
India	1,709	1,386	323	142,734
Iran	3,552	—	—	14,796
Korea	4,292	3,219	1,073	134,778
Mexico	28,957	22,569	6,388	366,820
Philippines	11,409	6,461	4,948	362,695
Taiwan	1,078	—	—	69,397
United Kingdom	5,141	4,906	235	21,995
Vietnam	270	—	—	97,539
Total	124,093	99,635	24,458	1,903,475

SOURCES: U.S. INS *1985 Statistical Yearbook*; U.S. GAO (1988a) *Report*; U.S. Department of State, *1986 Report of the Visa Office.*

TABLE 6.6

Top Five Countries of Origin of Immigrants
Admitted as Spouses of U.S. Citizens in FY 1985,
by Estimated Nativity of Sponsor, and Countries' Share
of Approved Visa Applicants (Visa Backlog) in January 1986

| | Percentage of Spouses | | | Visa Backlog | |
| | All Spouses | Sponsor Native-Born | Sponsor Naturalized | Percentage Share | Rank |
Country					
Canada	3.59	4.27	—	1.04	17
Germany, Federal Republic of	3.52	4.17	—	0.07	76
Mexico	23.33	22.65	26.12	19.27	1
Philippines	9.19	6.48	20.23	19.05	2
United Kingdom	4.14	4.92	—	1.16	15
Other	56.22	57.50	53.65	59.41	—

SOURCES: U.S. INS *1985 Statistical Yearbook;* U.S. GAO (1988a) *Report;* U.S. Department of State, *1986 Report of the Visa Office.*

NOTES: As discussed in the text, only the top two countries of crigin of the spouses of naturalized U.S. citizens can be unambiguously established from the GAO data.

To determine the nativity of the sponsors of these spouses, we apply the country-specific proportions of native-born and naturalized citizens observed in the GAO sample to the corresponding country-specific INS-recorded populations. This procedure yields estimates of the number of native-born and foreign-born sponsors of spouses, for the GAO-identified countries of birth of the immigrant spouses. These estimates, reported in the second and third columns of Table 6.5, indicate that the proportion native-born among the full set of sponsors of spouses is 80.3 percent. This estimate, which is valid for FY 1985, is the first estimate of its kind ever obtained. The GAO sample makes it possible to assert that utilization of the spouse-sponsorship entitlement is primarily a native-born phenomenon. Thus, in 1985 four fifths of the sponsors of spouses were *original* sponsors: almost 100,000 native-born citizens started a new immigration "line." The remaining 24,000 forged new links in the line of the original sponsor to whom they trace immigration descent.

Of course, it is not surprising that most of the spouse visa entitlements are used by native-born citizens, since they outnumber the foreign-born (as of 1980) by a ratio of 15 to 1. Indeed, if we deflate the sponsorship numbers by the population sizes of the native-born and foreign-born, we see that a foreign-born resident is almost four times more likely to sponsor an immigrant spouse than is a native-born citizen.

The native-born and naturalized sponsors differ with respect to their source of mates. Column 2 of Table 6.5 provides the estimated number of spouses sponsored by native-born U.S. citizens; the shares for the top five countries appear in Table 6.6. Figure 6.1 depicts the top five origin countries of the spouses of native-born sponsors.

Given that two countries among the top ten sources of mates—Iran and Haiti—are not separately identified in the GAO sample, it is important to ask whether either could have been among the top five sources of mates for the native-born (Table 6.6 and Figure 6.1). To answer this question, we compare the estimated number of spouses sponsored by native-born for the GAO set of countries with the true number of total spouse immigrants observed for Iran and Haiti. The total number of spouses from Iran (3,552) is less than the estimated number from West Germany (4,156). Hence, we are confident that, subject only to sampling variability, the countries shown in Table 6.6 and Figure 6.1 are indeed the top five countries favored by native-born U.S. citizens as the source of foreign mates.

Thus, 22.7 percent of the spouses sponsored by native-born U.S. citizens are from Mexico, followed by 6.5 percent from the Philippines, 4.9 percent from the United Kingdom, 4.3 percent from Canada, and 4.2 percent from West Germany. Some of these proportions differ from those for the total spouse population, suggesting different patterns by sponsor's nativity. For example, while 6.5 percent of the native-born sponsors found mates from the Philippines, the corresponding share among the entire set of sponsors is 9.2 percent. Of course, the countries in which the 100,000 original sponsors started the new immigration lines become the countries where new visa entitlements arise.

Column 3 of Table 6.5 reports the estimated country-specific number of spouses sponsored by naturalized U.S. citizens. These numbers range from a high of 6,388 spouses from Mexico to a low of 195 spouses from Canada. To determine the top five source countries of mates for naturalized U.S. citizens, we first assess the reasonableness of the GAO-based estimates of the top five source countries. Comparison of the GAO-based estimates of the number sponsored by naturalized citizens with the total INS-recorded spouse immigrants indicates that Mexico and the Philippines are unambiguously the top two sources; their shares are reported in column 3 of Table 6.6. However, the results are ambiguous for the other three countries estimated to be in the top five—Korea, the Dominican Republic, and Mainland China. If all the spouses from Iran (which is not identified in the GAO sample) were sponsored by naturalized U.S. citizens, then Iran would outrank Korea, taking third place among the source countries of spouses for the naturalized. By this reasoning, the true recorded numbers of spouse immigrants indicate that a large set of countries could theoretically outrank Korea, including Haiti, France, Greece, Italy, Israel, Japan, Lebanon, Nigeria, Jamaica, and others.

FIGURE 6.1
*Top Five Origin Countries of Persons
Immigrating as Spouses of Native-Born U.S. Citizens: FY 1985*

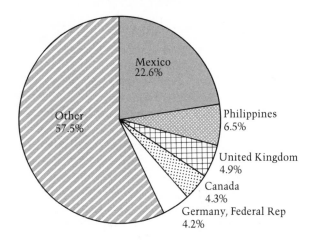

A far larger proportion of naturalized citizens than of the native-born—46 versus 29 percent—find their mates in Mexico and the Philippines (Table 6.6). This appears largely due to the fact that the share of spouses from the Philippines among the naturalized is over three times that among the native-born. Beyond the top two countries, the lack of overlap in the third through fifth top places suggests different patterns across native-born and naturalized sponsors.

Among native-born U.S. citizens the leading source countries for spouses are the two contiguous countries—Canada and Mexico—and three countries where the United States has a substantial military presence—the Philippines, the United Kingdom, and West Germany. Although the number of marriageable young persons may differ across military installations, it is useful to examine military strength. At midyear 1982, the largest country-specific number of active-duty U.S. military personnel (stationed on land) was 249,481 in West Germany, followed by 48,865 in Japan, 38,801 in South Korea, 25,294 in the United Kingdom, and 14,500 in the Philippines.[14] Thus, the three noncontiguous countries among the top five providing spouses for native-born U.S. citizens are among the top five in U.S. military personnel. Further, the country in sixth place among the origin countries for spouses of native-born is South Korea, so that four of the top

[14]These figures are reported in U.S. Department of State (1983).

TABLE 6.7
Percent Native-Born and Naturalized U.S. Citizen Sponsors
of Immigrants Admitted as Spouses of U.S. Citizens in FY 1985,
by Immigrant's Country of Origin: GAO-Based Estimates

Country	Sponsor Native-Born	Sponsor Naturalized	N
Canada	95.62	4.38	4,452
China, Mainland	47.83	52.17	1,449
Colombia	78.90	21.10	3,341
Dominican Republic	73.14	26.86	3,708
Germany, Federal Republic of	95.15	4.85	4,368
India	81.10	18.90	1,709
Korea	75.00	25.00	4,292
Mexico	77.94	22.06	28,957
Philippines	56.63	43.37	11,409
United Kingdom	95.43	4.57	5,141
All Countries	80.29	19.71	124,093

SOURCES: U.S. INS *1985 Statistical Yearbook;* U.S. GAO (1988a) *Report;* U.S. Department of State, *1986 Report of the Visa Office.*

six source countries are also four of the top five hosts of U.S. military bases.[15]

So far, we have viewed immigration from the perspective of the United States. *Whom do Americans marry? What are the countries of origin of spouse immigrants to the United States? Where do Americans start new immigration lines?* But, of course, the foreign countries involved have their own ways of regarding the marriage and migration events. From their perspective an interesting question might be: What proportion of our young people marrying U.S. citizens marry native-born U.S. citizens? To answer this question, we report in Table 6.7, for each country identified in the GAO report, the percentage shares by sponsor nativity. As shown, except for the Philippines and Mainland China, between 73 and 96 percent of the spouses leaving each country leave as the spouses of native-born U.S. citizens. The proportions of Chinese and Filipino spouses marrying native-born U.S. citizens are 48 and 57 percent, respectively. The countries with the largest proportions of their spouse-immigrants marrying native-born U.S. citizens are Canada, West Germany, and the United Kingdom—all over 95 percent.

We have discussed spouse sponsorship patterns in relation to U.S. mili-

[15]Note, however, that the estimated number of Korean spouses sponsored by native-born U.S. citizens is 3,219, which is less than the total admitted from Iran (3,552), so that Iran could outrank Korea. Korea's rank would then be seventh rather than sixth.

tary installations and travel behavior, which raises an obvious question: Are there sex-specific sponsorship/country/nativity patterns? Unfortunately, the information published in the GAO report does not permit unambiguous classification of the sponsor by sex. We can, however, establish lower and upper bounds on the number of sponsors of each sex, by sponsor's nativity and spouse's country of origin. Because the cell sizes for the naturalized sponsors of spouses are small, we calculate the lower and upper bounds only for the native-born sponsors. For example, our estimates show that of the estimated 4,156 native-born sponsors of West German spouses, the number of women lies in the range 212–688 and the number of men lies in the range 3,468–3,944. That is, the proportion male ranges from 83 to 95 percent, and the proportion female is the mirror image (5 to 17 percent).

Table 6.8 reports the minimum and maximum proportion male among the native-born U.S. citizens who sponsored spouses from each of the countries identified in the GAO report. The lower bound ranges from 13 percent for India to 92 percent for Korea; the upper bound ranges from 48 percent for Mexico to 100 percent for Korea and the Philippines. The discrepancy between the lower and upper bounds ranges from 4.5 percentage points for Mainland China to 60 percentage points for India. The discrepancies are less than 25 percentage points for the United Kingdom, Mexico, Korea, West Germany, and Canada, in addition to China. The proportion male among the native-born sponsors is unambiguously greater than half for all origin countries except Mexico, the Dominican Republic, and India; and for the latter two countries the proportion male could be greater than half. Thus, only in the case of Mexico is it possible to conclude that the majority of its citizens who leave to reside in the United States as the spouses of native-born U.S. citizens are male.

The minimum and maximum estimates can also be used to calculate each country's share of the brides and grooms of native-born U.S. citizens. For simplicity, we restrict attention to the case where all the GAO countries uniformly exhibit either the minimum or maximum possible of each sex. Columns 1 and 2 of Table 6.9 report the estimated country shares of the foreign-bride population, based on the minimum-male and maximum-male bounds. The two sets of estimates yield the same top five countries and, except for the countries in fourth and fifth place, the same ordering. The top origin country for brides is Mexico, providing 13–18 percent of brides of native-born U.S. citizens, followed by the Philippines, providing 10–11 percent, and West Germany, providing 7–9 percent. Korea and the United Kingdom round out the top five, with shares of 5–7 and 6–7 percent, respectively. The top five countries provide almost 47 percent of all brides.

The corresponding estimates for the bridegrooms of native-born U.S. citizens are reported in columns 3 and 4 of Table 6.9. These suggest both a greater dominance by a single country and a larger dispersion of bride-

TABLE 6.8
Estimated Minimum and Maximum Percent Male
Among the Native-Born U.S. Citizen Sponsors of Immigrant Spouses,
by Immigrant's Country of Origin: FY 1985

| Country | Percent Male | |
	Minimum	Maximum
Canada	56.86	73.86
China, Mainland	59.09	63.64
Colombia	55.45	82.18
Dominican Republic	35.71	66.33
Germany, Federal Republic of	83.44	94.90
India	13.33	73.33
Korea	91.67	100.00
Mexico	23.58	48.11
Philippines	63.83	100.00
United Kingdom	54.79	73.29
Other	33.53	49.71

SOURCES: U.S. INS *1985 Statistical Yearbook;* U.S. GAO (1988a) *Report;* U.S. Department of State, *1986 Report of the Visa Office.*

TABLE 6.9
Top Five Origin Countries of Persons Immigrating as Brides
and as Grooms of Native-Born U.S. Citizens:
Estimated Percent in FY 1985

| Country of Birth | Brides of U.S. Citizens | | Grooms of U.S. Citizens | |
	Min.-Male	Max.-Male	Min.-Female	Max.-Female
Canada	—	—	2.8	3.1
Colombia	—	—	1.2	—
Dominican Republic	—	—	2.3	2.9
Germany, Federal Rep.	8.8	6.6	—	—
Korea	7.4	5.4	—	—
Mexico	13.4	18.2	29.4	28.7
Philippines	10.4	10.8	—	3.9
United Kingdom	6.8	6.0	3.3	3.7
Other	53.2	53.1	61.0	57.7

SOURCES: U.S. INS *1985 Statistical Yearbook;* U.S. GAO (1988a) *Report;* U.S. Department of State, *1986 Report of the Visa Office.*

NOTE: As described in the text, these estimates of the country-specific shares of brides and grooms of U.S. citizens are based on the estimates of the minimum and maximum proportions male and female among the native-born U.S. citizen sponsors (shown in Table 6.8).

grooms among the remaining origin countries; the top five countries provide 42 percent. The set of top five countries is not stable, only one country—Mexico—maintaining its rank across both lower-bound and upper-bound estimates, with a 29 percent share under both estimates. In second place is the Philippines in one estimate and the United Kingdom in another—with shares of less than 4 percent.

These results provide further evidence that while both men and women, among native-born U.S. citizens, find spouses from Mexico, women do so to a far greater extent. Moreover, except for Mexico, all the top five countries where U.S. men find brides are countries which host U.S. military installations. While the smallest share among the top five countries where U.S. men find brides exceeds 5 percent, no country (except Mexico) provides as many as 4 percent of the bridegrooms for U.S. women.

The FY 1985 Citizen-and-Parent Pairs

The immigrants admitted in FY 1985 included 38,986 parents of U.S. citizens. Column 1 of Table 6.10 reports the observed country-specific number of parent immigrants, for all countries which are either among the top ten sources of entering spouses or parents or among the ten countries identified in the GAO report. The largest contingent of parent immigrants—8,020—comes from the Philippines; this is followed by 4,615 from Mainland China, 4,350 from India, 3,907 from Korea, and 2,464 from Mexico. The shares for the top five countries are shown in Table 6.11. These range from the Philippine share of almost 21 percent to the Mexican share of over 6 percent; as shown, the top five origin countries account for 60 percent of all the parent immigrants. The next five countries, in order, are Iran, Taiwan, Vietnam, the Dominican Republic, and Colombia (Table 6.10), with shares ranging from nearly 4 percent for Iran to nearly 2 percent for Colombia. As noted above, the GAO report does not separately identify Iran, Taiwan, and Vietnam, replacing them with the United Kingdom, West Germany, and Canada, whose ranks are 17th, 33rd, and 34th.

A priori we would expect that most of the parents would be sponsored by naturalized U.S. citizens. Estimates based on the GAO sample indicate that nearly 96 percent of the sponsors are indeed former immigrants. The estimated number of parents sponsored by native-born and naturalized citizens, respectively, are 1,686 and 37,300 (Table 6.10). Thus, sponsorship of parents is overwhelmingly a naturalized-citizen phenomenon. Put differently, less than 5 percent of parents are original immigrants, and less than 5 percent of the sponsors of parents are original sponsors. The remaining 96 percent are forging new links in the immigration line of an original sponsor.

Columns 2 and 3 of Table 6.10 provide estimates of the country-

TABLE 6.10

Immigrants Admitted as Parents of U.S. Citizens in FY 1985,
by Estimated Nativity of Sponsor, and Approved Visa Applicants
(Visa Backlog) in January 1986: Top Countries of Origin

Country	All Parents	Sponsor Native-Born	Sponsor Naturalized	Visa Backlog
Canada	185	82	103	19,790
China, Mainland	4,615	32	4,583	112,843
Colombia	657	0	657	22,726
Dominican Republic	661	30	631	37,332
Germany, Federal Republic of	187	31	156	1,252
Haiti	354	—	—	18,948
India	4,350	36	4,314	142,734
Iran	1,432	—	—	14,796
Korea	3,907	0	3,907	134,778
Mexico	2,464	329	2,135	366,820
Philippines	8,020	501	7,519	362,695
Taiwan	825	—	—	69,397
United Kingdom	354	27	327	21,995
Vietnam	796	—	—	97,539
Total	38,986	1,686	37,300	1,903,475

SOURCES: U.S. INS *1985 Statistical Yearbook;* U.S. GAO (1988a) *Report;* U.S. Department of State, *1986 Report of the Visa Office.*

specific number of parents sponsored by native-born and naturalized citizens, respectively. Figure 6.2 depicts the top five origin countries of parents sponsored by naturalized U.S. citizens. Table 6.11 shows that in no case do the shares of the top five countries differ by as much as one percentage point across the full set of sponsors and the naturalized subset.

As noted above, the classification by sponsor's nativity cannot be made for the origin countries which fall in sixth through eighth place—Iran, Taiwan, and Vietnam. We again assess the accuracy of the estimated top five list by comparing the estimated numbers of native-born and naturalized sponsors with the total INS-recorded number of sponsors. Because the total number of sponsors of (the sixth-place) Iranian parents (1,432) is less than the estimated number of naturalized sponsors of (the fifth-place) Mexican parents (2,135), we are confident that, subject only to sampling variability, the countries shown in Table 6.11 and Figure 6.2 are the top five countries of origin of the parents of naturalized sponsors.

This same procedure, however, yields the conclusion that the apparent top source of parents of native-born citizens (Table 6.10)—the Philippines—could be outranked by several countries not separately identified in the GAO report: Iran, Pakistan, Taiwan, Vietnam, Jamaica, and Guyana.

TABLE 6.11
Top Five Countries of Origin
of Immigrants Admitted as Parents of U.S. Citizens in FY 1985,
by Estimated Nativity of Sponsor, and Countries' Share
of Approved Visa Applicants (Visa Backlog) in January 1986

| Country | Percentage of Parents | | | Visa Backlog | |
	All Parents	Sponsor Native-Born	Sponsor Naturalized	Share	Rank
China, Mainland	11.84	—	12.29	5.93	5
India	11.16	—	11.57	7.50	3
Korea	10.02	—	10.47	7.08	4
Mexico	6.32	—	5.72	19.27	1
Philippines	20.57	—	20.16	19.05	2
Other	40.09	—	39.79	59.41	—

SOURCES: U.S. INS 1985 Statistical Yearbook; U.S. GAO (1988a) Report; U.S. Department of State, 1986 Report of the Visa Office.

NOTE: As discussed in the text, the top countries of origin of the parents of naturalized U.S. citizens cannot be unambiguously established from the GAO data.

Accordingly, we cannot establish unambiguously the top five origin countries of parents of native-born U.S. citizens.

The sponsorship of parents, which is an overwhelmingly naturalized-citizen phenomenon, is also an overwhelmingly Asian phenomenon. As shown in Table 6.11 and Figure 6.2, the top source country—the Philippines—provides one fifth of all parents, the top four countries (all Asian countries) together provide over half of the parents, and the fifth country (Mexico) has a share almost half that of the fourth country (Korea).

While both the absolute number and the relative share of parents sponsored by native-born citizens are small, the reader may nonetheless wish to examine the information in column 2 of Tables 6.10 and 6.11. Of the ten countries identified by the GAO report, the Philippines registers the largest share, almost 30 percent (or 501 parents). This is followed by a Mexican share of over 19 percent (or 329 parents), and very small shares (less than 5 percent each) for Canada (82), India (36), and Mainland China (32). Who are these parents of native-born U.S. citizens? It seems reasonable that the Mexican and Canadian parents are persons who resided in border areas and one of whose children was born in a U.S. hospital. It is possible that parents from nonborder countries were living in the United States at the time of the offspring's birth, possibly in some non-immigrant status; whether they had remained in the United States or instead left and subsequently sought re-entry, these data cannot say.

As in the case of spouses, it is also of interest to view the parent-immi-

FIGURE 6.2
Top Five Origin Countries of Persons
Immigrating as Parents of Naturalized U.S. Citizens: FY 1985

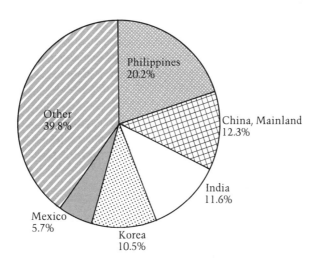

grant phenomenon from the perspective of the origin country. What proportion of those who leave as parent-visa holders are the parents of native-born U.S. citizens? Table 6.12 reports the within-country percentage shares by sponsor's nativity, for each country identified in the GAO report. As shown, the largest within-country share of parents sponsored by native-born U.S. citizens is that of Canada, at 44.3 percent. Other within-country shares are very small—for example, those of China and India, at 0.7 and 0.8 percent, respectively.

If there is a surprise in Table 6.12, it is the relatively small proportion of the Mexican parent-immigrants who are sponsored by native-born U.S. citizens—13.4 percent. We can only speculate as to the reason. If the widespread view that substantial numbers of Mexican families have for half a century had U.S.-born children is correct, then these parents' low representation among parent immigrants suggests that perhaps such parents continue to reside in border areas where they have all the advantages of both sides of the border and hence no desire to immigrate to the United States. Alternatively, it is possible that those parents with U.S.-born children are precisely the ones most benefited by the Mexican economy and least likely to leave Mexico.

TABLE 6.12
Percent Native-Born and Naturalized U.S. Citizen Sponsors
of Immigrants Admitted as Parents of U.S. Citizens in FY 1985,
by Immigrant's Country of Origin: GAO-Based Estimates

Country	Sponsor Native-Born	Sponsor Naturalized	N
Canada	44.32	55.68	185
China, Mainland	0.69	99.31	4,615
Colombia	0.00	100.00	657
Dominican Republic	4.54	95.46	661
Germany, Federal Republic of	16.58	83.42	187
India	0.83	99.17	4,350
Korea	0.00	100.00	3,907
Mexico	13.35	86.65	2,464
Philippines	6.25	93.75	8,020
United Kingdom	7.63	92.37	354
All Countries	4.32	95.68	38,986

SOURCES: U.S. INS *1985 Statistical Yearbook;* U.S. GAO (1988a) *Report;* U.S. Department of State, *1986 Report of the Visa Office.*

Sponsorship and the Demand for Immigration

It is a commonplace that the countries with the largest number of immigrants to the United States also have the largest visa backlogs. Does the sponsorship data make it possible to further refine that observation? Tables 6.5, 6.6, 6.10, and 6.11 also report the country-specific numbers, proportions, and shares of the visa backlogs, as of January 1986. These indicate that of the four sponsor-immigrant groups defined by sponsor's nativity and immigrant's visa type, only one—parents sponsored by naturalized U.S. citizens—yields the same set of top five countries as the visa backlogs. This suggests that the mechanisms involved in naturalized-citizen sponsorship of parents may more strongly resemble the mechanisms producing the demand for immigration than the mechanisms associated with the other three sponsor-immigrant combinations. In particular, except for marriages to persons from Mexico and the Philippines, sponsorship rates of spouses by native-born U.S. citizens depart dramatically from the backlog ordering. The countries providing the third through fifth largest shares of spouses of native-born U.S. citizens—the United Kingdom, Canada, and West Germany—rank, respectively, 15th, 17th, and 76th in the backlogs. Thus, it would appear that, in the aggregate, the marriage of persons from those three countries to U.S. citizens is not migration-driven. No firm conclusions, however, can be drawn for Mexico and the Philippines.

Summary

For every immigrant admitted to the United States, a potential flow of future immigrant entitlements is generated. The magnitude of this potential flow and its composition varies by the circumstances of the current immigrant's entry—in particular, by whether the immigrant is entering under the family-reunification provisions of U.S. law and, if so, whether as blood or marriage kin. For example, a single immigrant entering in a skilled category can sponsor parents, siblings, and a future spouse, while a married immigrant entering as a sibling is not likely to sponsor a spouse and can sponsor at least one sibling less.

While immigrant spouses can in principle provide fresh and unique entitlement to a full set of blood relatives (parents, children, siblings), immigrant parents provide supplementary entitlement to a subset of the sponsor's relatives as well. Among the new set of relatives are those not entitleable under immigration law by the parent's sponsor: namely, the sponsor's grandparents, aunts, and uncles. Of course, the new immigrant can also sponsor a spouse; a widowed parent who marries a foreign-born person can seek the new spouse's immigration through second-preference (immediately) or the numerically unlimited immediate relative provision (subsequent to naturalization). The "immediate" family reunification provisions of immigration law thus do not limit immigration solely to the immediate family of immigrants.

But not all immigrants become sponsors—many do not naturalize—and not all sponsorable relatives wish to immigrate; moreover, except for parents, spouses, and children, all relatives are subject to numerical ceilings. Thus, the number of actual immigrants sponsored by a current immigrant of a given type—the immigrant sponsorship rate—is far smaller than the potential number. Our estimates, based on our findings with respect to immigrant naturalization rates and the visa-specific sponsorship rates of naturalized citizens, indicate that the highest sponsorship rates are for immigrant principals who enter by dint of skills, a not unexpected result given that such immigrants are likely to have the least number of relatives already residing in the United States. For each of those immigrants we estimate that slightly over one additional visa entitlement for another immigrant is created within a span of 20 years. To the extent that a large proportion of refugees are similar to third- and sixth-preference (labor-certified) immigrants, in that most of their immediate family is abroad, the additions of a large number of refugees in the late 1970s and in the 1980s could therefore have important implications for the future growth of visa entitlements and thus the size of the waiting list for visas.

Immigrants are not the major users of the numerically exempt family reunification provisions of immigration law, although they have the highest *rates* of utilization. The limited data currently available indicate that a substantial majority of the immigrant spouses of U.S. citizens (80 percent in 1985) were sponsored by native-born U.S. citizens. As would be expected, however, the native-born sponsored only a tiny proportion of the immigrant parents of U.S. citizens (less than 5 percent in 1985). Thus, it is native-born citizens who, principally, initiate the growth, via the multiplier, of new visa entitlements. The top five countries where the native-born sponsors of spouses started new "immigration lines" in 1985 were the two contiguous countries—Mexico (the origin country of 23 percent of the spouses) and Canada—and three countries which host U.S. military installations—West Germany, the United Kingdom, and the Philippines. The data also indicate, however, that sponsorship of parents is primarily an Asian phenomenon; sponsorship of Mexican parents by native-born U.S. citizens is of trivial proportions.

It is possible to view native-born or "original" sponsors of spouses or blood relatives as themselves having acquired their sponsorship faculties directly from an action of the U.S. government. Young, marriageable Americans sent abroad in the service of their country become potential sponsors, as do children of exchange visitors and foreign students brought to the United States by the U.S. government. The exercise of sponsorship faculties, the resultant subsequent entitlement of a long line of potential immigrants, and the visa backlogs may thus be intimately linked to policies and activities of the United States ostensibly not relevant to immigration.

7

IMMIGRANTS IN THE U.S. ECONOMY

THE ECONOMIC status of new immigrants to the United States, their post-immigration economic progress, and their effects on the employment, earnings, and well-being of the native-born have been central concerns of both policymakers and researchers, almost to the exclusion of other aspects of immigrant experience. As we have seen, few immigrants are awarded a visa on the basis of their potential contributions to the economy; eligibility to immigrate is based most often on a kinship tie to a U.S. citizen. Yet the decision to immigrate is surely influenced by earnings prospects and/or experience in the United States.

Despite the interest in the question of how immigrants fare, inclusive of how they affect the welfare of the native-born, answers remain somewhat elusive owing, principally, to data deficiencies. With respect to patterns of immigrant progress, the chief problem is that there is no data set, of a size large enough to support a reliable analysis, which follows a probability sample of individual "immigrants" over time. As we have noted, the major available data bases—the U.S. censuses and Current Population Surveys (CPSs)—are cross-sectional.[1] The samples from them contain only

---

[1]With few exceptions (based on samples of small subsets of entering immigrants, such as Hirschman 1978, North 1978, and Portes and Bach 1980), research has utilized either cross-sectional data (e.g., in the work of Chiswick 1978 and in Reimers 1983) or a set of cross-sections (Borjas 1985), drawn from U.S. censuses and Current Population Surveys.

the *survivors* of immigrant entry cohorts (cohorts which may have been trimmed by emigration from the United States, which we have shown to be both numerically important and nonrandom). As a consequence, comparisons in a given year of the foreign-born who entered the United States in different time periods reflect the operation of emigration selectivity mechanisms, the effects of different lengths of residence in the United States, and initial (at-entry) differences in the cohorts associated, for example, with differential entry criteria due to changes in immigration policy. Comparisons of one entry cohort at different points in time, in adjacent censuses, for example, still confound the experience of a typical or average immigrant with a change in the composition of the entire cohort due to emigration.

Moreover, the principal data sets that provide information on earnings also do not provide information on *immigrants* per se—the focus of policy discussions concerning admission criteria—but rather on the broader population of foreign-born persons, which may include legal non-immigrants (such as foreign correspondents, students, and representatives of foreign firms) and illegal aliens. Because legal status places important constraints on the ability to earn income, this problem is particularly acute in studying the economic well-being of the foreign-born.

In this chapter, we first examine where in the economy the foreign-born, inclusive of illegal immigrants, have had the greatest impact. We then review evidence provided by census data on (1) how the average economic statuses of the foreign-born population and of immigrant entry cohorts have changed between 1960 and 1980 and (2) how the average economic status of different entry cohorts evolves over time. We also examine trends in income inequality, participation in public welfare programs, homeownership, self-employment, and labor force participation among the new additions to the foreign-born population compared with the native-born and assess how these economic characteristics are altered as the foreign-born acquire experience in the United States. In addition, we investigate the role of emigration in altering the economic characteristics of an immigrant cohort and the effects of the immigrant's experience and legal status in the United States on his/her economic status based on an intensive analysis of the 1971 longitudinal Immigration and Naturalization Service (INS) cohort sample. Finally, we test whether information on origin-country conditions can help explain the observed differentials in earnings among immigrants from different countries as they influence who comes to the United States and, among those who come, who stays.

The Effects of Immigration on the Economy: Who Gains and Who Loses?

The Foreign-Born in the Work Force: Industry, Occupation, Geographical Area

Generally speaking, any change from any source in an economic system renders some people better off and others worse off, even if the aggregate change is beneficial. Immigration—the addition of new persons to the population and work force of the United States—is no different. Thus, one way to examine the effects of immigration is to ask who gains and who loses. If we regard each person as a consumer of goods produced, as an owner of investable capital, and as an "owner" of particular or general skills, then the net impact of immigration on each individual will depend on the effects of immigration on (1) the supply (prices) of consumer goods that he/she consumes, (2) the returns to any capital owned, and (3) the returns to his/her particular skills. We discuss each in turn, examining the census data for insights into each effect.

With respect to the prices of consumer goods, an increase in the number of workers increases the relative supply of goods whose production technology is "intensive" in workers (relative to capital), which results in reductions in the relative prices of such goods. To the extent that immigrant workers bring specialized skills to the economy, different from those of the native-born work force, there will also be reductions in the relative prices of goods making intensive use of such skills. Consumers of these goods thus benefit. How has immigration actually affected prices? Unfortunately, there is little direct information on the effects of changes in the composition of the labor force on price levels and relative prices. However, the census contains information on the industries in which individuals work, which provides a hint about which consumer goods are intensive in foreign-born labor skills.

Table 7.1 provides the top ten industries in 1960, 1970, and 1980 ranked by the percentage of the work force that is foreign-born. Across all years, it is clear that consumers of shoes, shoe services, and apparel benefited from the presence of foreign-born workers. The work force in these industries has been at least 20 percent foreign-born over the 1960–1980 period. In 1980 we can also surmise that the cost of residential housing construction has been tempered by the presence of foreign-born workers, who make up 15 percent of the work force in wood housing construction. Shoes and clothing are staple goods consumed by everyone; the benefits of immigration for consumers are thus diffused widely and are probably distributed evenly across income groups.

TABLE 7.1
Top Ten Industries, by Percentage of Workforce Foreign-Born: 1960–1980

1960		1970		1980	
Industry	Percent Foreign-Born	Industry	Percent Foreign-Born	Industry	Percent Foreign-Born
Leather Tanning	35.1	Shoe Repair Shops	28.1	Non-Shoe Leather Product Mfg.	26.5
Shoe Repair Shops	24.6	Dressmaking shops	23.1	Wholesale Durables, Not Specified	20.7
Non-Shoe Leather Product Mfg.	20.9	Apparel Wholesaling	18.5	Manufacturing, Not Specified	19.7
Apparel Mfg.	20.9	Apparel Mfg.	17.3	Apparel Mfg.	19.2
Metal Product Mfg.	20.0	Fisheries	15.7	Screw Machine Product Mfg.	17.0
Dressmaking Shops	18.3	Barber Shops	15.3	Electronics Mfg.	15.8
Textile Mfg.	17.8	Leather Tanning	15.2	Transportation Services	15.7
Food Product Mfg.	17.3	Incidental Transp. Services	15.2	Leather Tanning	15.4
Water Transport Services	16.8	Horticulture Services	14.5	Wood Housing Construction	15.0
Miscellaneous Textile Mfg.	16.7	Hardware Retail	14.3	Toy, Sporting Goods Mfg.	13.8

Table 7.2 reports the top ten occupations ranked by the percentage of workers who are foreign-born from the 1900, 1910, 1960, 1970, and 1980 censuses of population. A remarkable feature of this table is the stability of the rankings over the 80-year period. Tailors head the list in 1900, 1910, 1960, and 1970 and are still as high as second in 1980. Indeed, the proportion of tailors who are foreign-born was almost constant from 1900 to 1960, at approximately 65 percent, but fell to 44 percent in 1970 and to 30 percent in 1980. The dominance of foreign-born workers among tailors, jewelers, and dressmakers evident in Table 7.2 suggests that the costs of the specialized services provided by such workers have been attenuated by immigration. But because such services now most likely serve those native-born citizens with higher incomes, it is higher-income consumers who probably have benefited the most.

One prominent change in the occupational rankings evident in Table 7.2 is the appearance of physicians as the third most intensive occupation in foreign-born workers in 1980. With over 20 percent of physicians foreign-born, it is possible that immigration has reduced somewhat the rising cost of medical care. However, to the extent that the total supply of physicians has been kept constant by licensing restrictions requiring training in U.S. medical facilities and by limitations on the number of such facilities, consumers may not have reaped the full benefits.

With respect to the effects of immigration on the earnings or employ-

TABLE 7.2
Top Ten Occupations, by Percentage of Workforce Foreign-Born,
by Decade: 1900, 1910, 1960–1980

1900		1910	
Occupation	Percent Foreign-born	Occupation	Percent Foreign-born
Tailors	64.9	Tailors	65.3
Shoemakers	59.2	Bakers	63.5
Bakers	53.8	Machine Feeders	62.0
Saloon Keepers	53.0	Peddlers	61.4
Gardeners	50.8	Stevedores	58.8
Textile Workers, n.e.c.	50.8	Miners	56.4
Stonecutters	50.6	Construction Workers	55.9
Peddlers	49.5	Textile Workers (pressing)	52.5
Coal Miners	45.0	Laborers, not Construction	51.3
Miners, n.e.c.	44.5	Shoemakers	50.0

1960		1970	
Occupation	Percent Foreign-born	Occupation	Percent Foreign-born
Tailors	67.1	Tailors	43.6
Shoemakers	27.3	Shoemakers	32.6
Sailors	26.1	Foreign-Language Teachers	25.8
Charwomen and Cleaners	23.3	Dressmakers	23.1
Dressmakers	23.2	Architects	18.6
Bakers	22.2	Textile Sewers	18.2
Blacksmiths	21.7	Ushers	17.9
Textile Sewers	21.5	Jewelers	17.8
Metal Rollers	21.2	Bakers	17.7
Building Superintendents	21.0	Fishermen	17.5

1980	
Occupation	Percent Foreign-born
Jewelers	29.6
Tailors	27.5
Dressmakers	22.4
Physicians	22.1
Tile setters	21.7
Textile Sewers	20.7
Electronics Assemblers	20.3
Milling Operators	20.0
Woodwork Operators	20.0
Biological Scientists	19.5

ment of native-born workers, economic theory suggests that, at least in the short run, an increase in the number of workers of a particular type will lower the earnings of other workers of that type and/or workers similar to or highly substitutable in production for such workers. If all immigrants are jewelers, for example, then the wages and earnings of native-born jewelers would be lower as a result of immigration; if all immigrants are persons with minimal skills, then the lowest-skill groups in the native-born work force are the most likely to be adversely affected. The occupational and skill composition of the foreign-born thus provides some information about those native-born workers who might be most harmed *as workers* by immigration. In 1980, the proportions of native-born and foreign-born workers who were classified in managerial or professional (22.7 versus 21.2 percent) occupations and precision production, craft, and repair occupations (13.0 versus 12.9 percent) were almost identical, but a higher proportion of foreign-born workers than native-born workers were in the service sector (10.1 versus 12.9 percent), and a lower proportion in technical, sales, and administrative support occupations (24.6 versus 30.3 percent). The aggregated breakdown of occupations thus appear somewhat similar for the two populations, with no striking winners or losers in the labor market.

Table 7.3, which provides the top ten detailed (three-digit) occupations for the new-entrant foreign-born, for all foreign-born, and for all native-born workers in 1900, 1960, 1970, and 1980, also does not suggest any dramatic dissimilarities in occupational composition. An exception is that in every period the proportion of foreign-born who are farmers is far smaller than among the native-born, and in the 1960–1980 period there is a significantly higher proportion of foreign-born workers who are hired farm laborers, particularly among the new-entrant foreign-born.

Table 7.4 reports the distribution of schooling attainment levels for adult (aged 25–64) native-born and the new-entrant foreign-born by area of origin for 1960, 1970, and 1980. These figures provide a less benign picture of the effects of immigration for those concerned about income inequality. In each successive year, a significantly higher proportion of the new-entrant foreign-born than native-born had attended school for less than eight years, and even less than five years. And there is a dramatic increase among new entrants from the Western Hemisphere between 1970 and 1980 in the proportion of adults with less than five years of schooling. In 1980, 48.9 percent of Western Hemisphere new entrants had less than a grammar-school education compared with only 5.5 percent of the native-born and 36.4 percent of Western Hemisphere new entrants in 1970. If economic theory is correct, this immigration of mainly low-skilled workers would clearly have depressed the wages of low-skilled native-born workers.

Is there direct evidence that the wages of some native-born workers are adversely affected by immigration? Two recent comprehensive reviews of

TABLE 7.3
Top Ten Occupations of Recent Entrants,
All Foreign-Born and Native-Born Men Aged 20–64, by Census Year

Recent Entrants		All Foreign-Born		Native-Born	
Occupation	Percent	Occupation	Percent	Occupation	Percent
		1900			
Laborers, Unspec.	27.0	Laborers, Unspec.	14.6	Farmers	39.8
Farm Workers	6.9	Farmers	13.7	Farm Family Laborers	17.5
Miners, Not Oil, Coal	5.7	Farm Workers	4.9	Farm Workers	15.9
Coal Miners	5.7	Carpenters	3.3	Laborers, Unspec.	14.5
Farmers	3.6	Miners, Not Oil, Coal	3.0	Service Workers	7.4
Laborers, Steel	3.3	Coal Miners	2.7	Private Household Workers	4.8
Laborers, Railroad	3.0	Truck Drivers	2.1	Carpenters	3.6
Tailors	2.7	Tailors	2.0	Salesmen, Unspec.	3.2
Blacksmiths	2.1	Machinists	1.5	Teachers	3.1
Shoemakers	1.9	Laborers, rail	1.5	Clerical	3.0
		1960			
Farm Workers	11.1	Managers, n.e.c.	9.7	Managers, n.e.c.	8.7
Operatives, n.e.c.	7.4	Operatives, n.e.c.	7.9	Operatives, n.e.c.	7.7
Salesmen	4.0	Laborers, n.e.c.	5.3	Laborers, n.e.c.	5.7
Janitors	3.4	Salesmen, n.e.c.	4.3	Farmers	4.9
Laborers, Unspec.	3.1	Farm Workers	3.6	Salesmen, n.e.c.	4.7
Managers, n.e.c.	3.1	Foremen	3.2	Truck Drivers	4.0
Mechanics, n.e.c.	2.8	Mechanics, n.e.c.	3.2	Mechanics, n.e.c.	2.7
Physicians	2.6	Farmers	2.3	Clerical, n.e.c.	2.7
Writers	2.0	Cooks	2.1	Foremen, n.e.c.	2.6
Barbers	1.7	Carpenters	2.0	Carpenters	2.0
		1970			
Physicians	5.7	Managers, n.e.c.	6.2	Managers, n.e.c.	6.5
Managers, n.e.c.	3.7	Janitors	2.8	Foremen, n.e.c.	3.3
Machine Opers., n.e.c.	3.5	Foremen, n.e.c.	2.6	Truck Drivers	3.2
Machine Opers., misc.	3.2	Carpenters	2.3	Farmers	2.5
Farm Workers	2.7	Cooks	2.3	Janitors	1.9
Construction Laborers	2.5	Farm workers	2.2	Carpenters	1.9
Draftsmen	2.2	Physicians	2.0	Mechanics, Auto	1.6
Janitors	2.2	Machine Opers., Misc.	1.9	Machine Opers., n.e.c.	1.6
Dishwashers	2.0	Machine Opers.	1.4	Sales Clerks, Retail	1.6
Mechanics, Auto	1.7	Mechanics, Auto	1.3	Craftsmen, n.e.c.	1.5
		1980			
Managers, n.e.c.	5.6	Managers, n.e.c.	6.5	Managers, n.e.c.	6.9
Farm Workers	4.3	Janitors	3.3	Truck Drivers	3.3
Janitors	3.9	Machine Opers., Unsp.	2.9	Supervisors, Prod.	2.7
Assemblers	3.2	Farm Workers	2.7	Non-Construction Laborers	2.2
Supervisors, Sales	2.8	Cooks	2.6	Janitors	2.0
Cooks	2.6	Assemblers	2.3	Carpenters	2.0
Machine Opers., Unspec.	2.6	Physicians	2.2	Supervisors, Sales	1.8
Construction Laborers	2.6	Supervisors, Prod.	2.2	Farmers	1.6
Physicians	2.4	Supervisors, Sales	2.0	Auto Mechanics	1.6
Non-Constr. Laborers	1.9	Construction Laborers	1.9	Machine Opers., Unspec.	1.5

TABLE 7.4

Schooling Distributions for Native-Born and New Entrants Aged 25–64, by Area of Origin and Census Year

Category	1960			1970			1980		
	New Entrants		Native-Born	New Entrants		Native-Born	New Entrants		Native-Born
	Western	Eastern		Western	Eastern		Western	Eastern	
Less Than 5 Yrs	20.7	8.2	5.3	13.0	10.0	3.4	33.3	8.3	1.7
Less Than 8 Yrs	40.9	19.1	17.1	36.4	21.3	10.8	48.9	25.7	5.5
More Than 12 Yrs	14.6	25.9	18.4	16.7	39.6	23.1	16.4	47.2	36.7
Four Yrs College	7.9	13.8	8.8	9.0	27.3	11.9	9.2	21.4	18.8
Percent Share	28.4	71.6	—	40.0	60.0	—	35.1	64.9	—

the growing literature concerned with this question (Greenwood and Mc-Dowell 1988; U.S. Department of Labor 1989) conclude that the negative effects of immigration on the wages of native-born workers are small, and appear to be confined to either low-wage native-born or foreign-born workers. The wages of some highly skilled workers are found to be higher as a result of immigration in some studies.

Almost all of the empirical findings on the impact of immigration on wages and employment are based on studies that measure these effects based on the relationship between the numbers (or proportion) of foreign-born workers and the wages of other groups across areas (states, SMSAs) of the United States. And, indeed, the presence of the foreign-born varies greatly across locations. Table 7.5 reports the top ten states ranked by the shares of the new-entrant and foreign-born populations residing in them. In 1980, 43 percent of the foreign-born and 47 percent of new entrants were located in California and New York. However, the concentration of a large proportion of the foreign-born in a few states is not a new phenomenon, as it is seen in 1900 as well, when 39 percent of all new entrants and 28 percent of all the foreign-born resided in two states (New York and Pennsylvania). In the 1960–1980 period, moreover, the geographical concentration has remained fairly stable, with, however, California receiving an increasing share of all the foreign-born over the period. Indeed, between 1970 and 1980, there was more than a 50 percent increase in the share of the new-entrant foreign-born residing in California.

Table 7.5 suggests the geographic areas where the initial impacts of immigration on labor markets are experienced. However, to the extent that the work force is geographically mobile, disparities in (real) wages across areas, adjusted for natural amenities and costs of consumption, are dissipated over time. With domestic workers migrating from low-wage to high-wage areas, the area-specific impact on wages of any local labor market events is minimized. Indeed, the 1980 census indicates that 24.6 percent of native-born citizens had changed their county of residence within the five years preceding the census; 12.9 percent had changed their state of residence. The cross-sectional studies of the determinants of wages, of which local immigration is one, thus could understate the direct effects of immigration on the wage rates of workers in the economy. Indeed, in a perfectly mobile society, there are (almost) no real wage differentials across areas for workers with identical skill levels, but there could still be important effects on *aggregate*, skill-specific wage levels due to immigration.

Finally, capital equipment and financial resources are also important factors of production that are owned by native-born citizens. An increase in the size of the domestic labor force brought about by immigration, or any other source, raises the return to capital and increases the incomes of owners of capital. Workers with skills complementary to capital (e.g., computer

TABLE 7.5
Top Ten States, by Share of New-Entrant and Foreign-Born Populations and by Census Year

New Entrants			Foreign-Born		
State	Share	Ratio to Native-Born Share	State	Share	Ratio to Native-Born Share
1900					
New York	25.0	2.99	New York	18.4	2.21
Pennsylvania	14.2	1.74	Pennsylvania	9.2	1.13
Massachusetts	10.7	3.68	Illinois	8.4	1.45
New Jersey	6.0	2.76	Massachusetts	7.9	2.72
Hawaii	4.3	43.8	Minnesota	5.3	2.93
Illinois	3.7	0.63	Michigan	5.0	1.93
Minnesota	3.5	1.98	New Jersey	9.8	1.92
Michigan	3.5	1.35	Wisconsin	4.8	2.23
Ohio	3.2	0.57	Ohio	4.8	1.98
Connecticut	3.1	3.10	California	3.5	0.85
1960					
California	22.7	2.67	New York	23.5	2.75
New York	19.5	2.29	California	13.7	1.61
Illinois	6.6	1.19	Illinois	7.1	1.29
New Jersey	5.1	1.60	New Jersey	6.4	1.99
Texas	4.5	0.83	Pennsylvania	6.1	0.97
Florida	4.3	1.54	Massachusetts	5.9	2.19
Massachusetts	3.7	1.37	Michigan	5.5	1.27
Michigan	3.4	0.78	Ohio	4.0	0.73
Ohio	3.4	0.62	Texas	3.2	0.58
Pennsylvania	3.1	0.48	Connecticut	2.9	2.21
1970					
California	21.0	2.24	New York	20.8	2.50
New York	20.4	2.45	California	18.1	1.93
Florida	7.4	2.29	New Jersey	6.5	1.92
New Jersey	6.6	1.95	Illinois	6.1	1.11
Illinois	5.8	1.07	Florida	5.5	1.71
Texas	4.5	0.80	Massachusetts	5.1	1.88
Massachusetts	4.4	1.64	Michigan	4.6	1.06
Michigan	3.2	0.72	Pennsylvania	4.4	0.75
Pennsylvania	2.7	0.46	Texas	3.7	0.66
Ohio	2.3	0.44	Ohio	3.2	2.60
1980					
California	33.4	3.51	California	25.2	2.64
New York	13.9	1.95	New York	17.3	2.43
Texas	7.8	1.26	Florida	7.7	1.91
Illinois	6.1	1.22	Texas	5.8	0.94
Florida	5.9	1.45	Illinois	5.8	1.17
New Jersey	3.7	1.21	New Jersey	5.4	1.76
Massachusetts	2.6	0.94	Massachusetts	3.5	1.48
Washington	2.0	1.09	Michigan	2.9	0.70
Pennsylvania	1.8	0.34	Pennsylvania	2.8	0.53

operators) also benefit. If capital is mobile domestically, then areas experiencing the greatest influx of new workers would also experience an inflow of capital; jobs go to workers as much as workers go to jobs (apart from the workers adding to the local demand for goods and services). If capital is mobile internationally and/or if domestic savings respond positively to the higher returns to investment, then immigration may also increase the total level of investment in the economy. There is little evidence, however, of the effects of immigration on capital investment or savings, neither of which are recorded in census data.

In sum, the effects of immigration on the earnings, incomes, and welfare of native-born workers are complex, differentiated, and not easy to measure. Some are widely diffused among individuals and across areas—the effects on prices of consumer goods and returns to capital; some are highly localized—wage rate effects—but diminish over time. Indeed, to the extent that immigrants are investors, migration being one form of investment, and augment their skills while in the United States, the overall and local impact on the economy of any particular immigrant cohort may change substantially over time. Information on the economic mobility of immigrants thus also sheds light on who benefits most and who the least by immigration. We assess the economic progress of foreign-born cohorts below, where we also compare the use of the welfare system by the foreign-born and the native-born.

Illegal Aliens and the Economy

The focus of the Immigration Reform and Control Act of 1986 was on illegal aliens, and a primary motivation was concern over the adverse effects of illegal immigrants on the earnings of low-skill U.S. citizens. While no existing data that directly identify illegal aliens are also representative of the entire illegal population, it is possible to learn something about the characteristics of illegal immigrants from census data based on a priori considerations of immigration behavior and information about the immigration preference system. Such reasoning suggests that illegal aliens are likely to have low levels of skills, to immigrate from areas proximate to the United States, to reside in the United States on a less permanent basis than legal immigrants (even if not discovered and deported), and to invest less in skills specifically rewarded in the United States.

As we have seen, in the 1970s and 1980s as a result of the preference system embodied in immigration law, fully established in 1978, most non-refugee legal immigrants are sponsored by U.S. citizens and resident aliens on the basis of family relationships. As a consequence, the characteristics of new (non-refugee) immigrants should be similar to those of prior immigrants. Similarities in schooling levels among siblings and assortative mating in the marriage market militate against sharp changes in schooling distributions or levels across entering cohorts of the foreign-born. Thus, the increase in the proportion of foreign-born adults with less than five years of schooling from the Western Hemisphere between 1970 and 1980, seen in Table 7.4, probably reflects an increase in the flows of illegal immigrants during that period.

We would expect that illegal immigrants with low levels of skills would migrate from areas relatively proximate to the United States in order to minimize the cost of multiple entries into the United States that might arise owing to the possibility of being apprehended and returned home. The possibility of deportation and the reduced cost of returning home voluntarily because of the proximity of the origin country also decreases the return to investing in English language skills, as we discuss in the next chapter.

Closer inspection of the characteristics of the foreign-born men with less than five years of schooling who entered the United States from the Western Hemisphere between 1975 and 1980 based on census data suggests that this group is likely to contain a large illegal population. Eighty percent are from Mexico, and 86 percent reported that they could not speak English at all or "not well." Moreover, 45 percent reside in California and 20 percent in Texas, states bordering Mexico. In contrast, only 28 percent of Western Hemisphere new entrants with over five years of schooling reside in California and 7 percent reside in Texas, and 29 percent of Eastern Hemisphere new entrants reside in California and 5 percent in Texas. The sharp rise in the stream of the new-entrant foreign-born residing in California between 1970 and 1980, seen in Table 7.5, is thus in large part due to the immigration of these low-skill and most likely illegal workers from Mexico.[2] Only 20 percent of the low-skill new-entrant foreign-born are farm workers, the next largest occupation being janitors and cleaners, at 10 percent. Thus the (initial) wage employment effect of the immigration of this group is not confined to rural labor markets.

If these inferences about the legal status of the low-skill, Western Hemisphere new entrants are correct, then attempts to curtail the flow of illegal migration would importantly decrease the immigration of low-skill workers. The primary beneficiaries would be those U.S. citizens and legal aliens who also have low skill levels. Because a large proportion of what appear to be illegal migrants are farm workers, both growers in California and Texas and consumers of the types of fruits and vegetables grown in those areas would be adversely affected by such restrictions. However, in

---

[2]Passel and Woodrow (1984), in their estimates of the size of the illegal population, consistent with our inferences, conclude that half of the undocumented population recorded in the census resided in California, most having arrived some time during the 1970s.

part because of the high costs imposed upon one industry, the new 1986 immigration law specifically provided a legalization program for undocumented farm workers. Of this group, over 1.3 million had applied for legalization as of May 1989.

Of course, illegal immigrants are also located in nonborder areas, but it is as difficult to measure the characteristics of this population, spread out over the nation, as it is to apprehend its members. More information on at least one portion of the illegal populations may be forthcoming based on those undocumented immigrants who had applied for legalization under the 1986 Immigration Reform and Control Act. But even this group (those workers who entered the United States prior to 1982 and who remained interested in becoming permanent resident aliens in the United States) may be highly unrepresentative of the population of illegal migrants in 1980 or any other year. Those who choose to legalize may be quite different from those who choose not to remain in the United States and those who choose to remain but not to legalize.

Immigrant Economic Status and Progress: Evidence from Aggregate Census Data

Changes in the Earnings of the Foreign-Born and Native-Born

The data from the 1960, 1970, and 1980 censuses provide detailed information on labor force participation, earnings, and income, by source, and hence enable many comparisons between native-born and foreign-born workers in terms of their economic status. Figure 7.1 depicts the average earnings of native-born and foreign-born males aged 20–44, separately by race, for 1960, 1970, and 1980. Because of changes in price levels over the period, we deflate the nominal earnings values by the consumer price index and express all earnings in terms of 1960 dollars. We will refer to these price-adjusted measures of earnings as "real" (1960) earnings, following common practice. Figure 7.1 contains three striking findings. First, for all race/nativity groups (within the prime-age class of males aged 20–44), real earnings were greater in 1970 than in 1960 and, for all groups except native-born blacks, were lower in 1980 than in 1970, albeit at levels higher than in 1960; these trends would appear to reflect the state of the economy, on the one hand, and the progress of blacks during the two decades, on the other hand. Second, controlling for race, there is great similarity between the earnings of the native-born and the foreign-born. Third, black earnings increased relative to white earnings. Looking more closely, foreign-born earnings are lower than native-born earnings for all race-year groups except

FIGURE 7.1
*Real Mean Earnings of Native-Born and Foreign-Born Men Aged 20–44,
by Race and Census Year: 1960–1980*

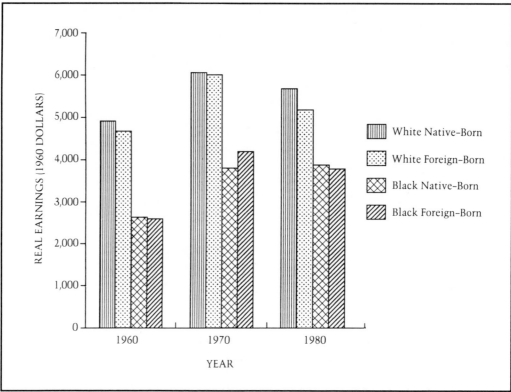

one: blacks in 1970. Within year the foreign-born earnings deficit appears to be greater among whites than among blacks, while within race the foreign-born earnings deficit is greater in 1980 than in 1970.

What do these figures mean? As noted above, the foreign-born population may differ importantly by entry year and by origin area. Moreover, the selective forces of immigration and emigration influence the change in the economic status of the foreign-born. Thus, the figures cannot reveal, for example, whether foreign-born additions to the 20–44 age pool (through immigration or through aging into the pool) between 1970 and 1980 had lower-than-average earnings or whether instead foreign-born losses from the pool (through emigration or through aging out of it) had higher-than-average earnings.

To assess the role of immigration selectivity in shaping differences across foreign-born entry cohort across the period 1960–1980, we examine the earnings of recent entrants in each of the three census years. As discussed in the Introduction, the censuses enable construction of recent-entrant cohorts for each of the census years in this period.[3] Figure 7.2 depicts the real average earnings of native-born and recent-entrant males aged 20–44, separately by race, for the three census years. These figures indicate that part of the relative decline in the average earnings of the total foreign-born population between 1970 and 1980 is due to a decline, again in real terms, in the earnings of new arrivals; recent entrants in the 20–44 age group in 1980, who represent 25 percent of all of the foreign-born in that age group in 1980, had lower real mean earnings than similarly aged recent entrants in 1970, who represent 18 percent of the foreign-born in that age group in 1970.

Comparing the recent entrants from Figure 7.2 with all the foreign-born in Figure 7.1 shows that in each of the census years the recent entrants have lower real average earnings than the whole of the foreign-born in the age group. That the foreign-born who have spent more time in the United States exhibit higher earnings than recent arrivals could be due to a persistent, historical decline in the "quality" of immigrants or to U.S. experience increasing the earnings of the foreign-born. To further disentangle differences in entry cohorts from the effects of the experience of a single cohort, we focus on the 1960 and 1970 recent-entrant cohorts, which, as discussed in the Introduction, can be "followed" for a decade. Both of these recent-entrant cohorts are observed twice at comparable durations, at on average 2.5 and 12.5 years after entry.

Figures 7.3 and 7.4 depict the decadal changes in the average real earnings of native-born and recent-entrant males aged 20–44, for whites and blacks, respectively. Both figures indicate that the real mean earnings of all age/nativity/race groups increased after ten years. Thus, the real mean earnings of both the 1960 and 1970 foreign-born recent-entrant cohorts increased during the decade subsequent to their admission. Earlier entrants have higher earnings than more recent entrants at the same point in time in part owing to increases in the earnings of an entry cohort over time, net of age effects. As noted above, however, it is not possible to know whether the cohort members at the second observation point constitute a random sample of the original cohort members. The observed decadal increases in the average earnings of both the 1960 and 1970 entry cohorts are consistent with several interpretations: (1) the average earnings of the original cohort

---

[3]The 1960 recent-entrant cohort consists of foreign-born persons who in 1960 report that they lived abroad five years earlier and who in 1970 report year of entry between 1955 and 1959. The 1970 recent-entrant cohort consists of foreign-born persons who in 1970 report entering between 1965 and 1970 and who in 1980 report entering between 1965 and 1969. The 1980 recent-entrant cohort consists of foreign-born persons who report entering between 1975 and 1980.

FIGURE 7.2

*Real Mean Earnings of Native-Born and New-Entrant Men Aged 20–44,
by Race and Census Year: 1960–1980*

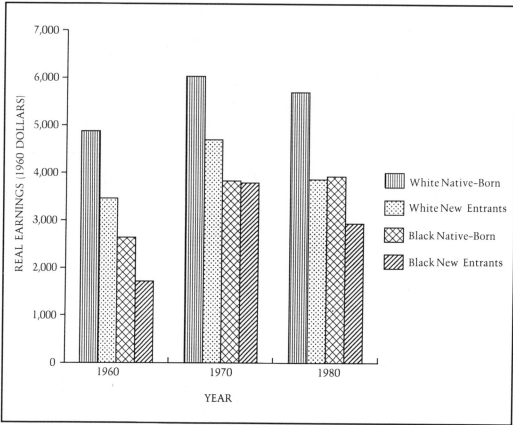

members increased; (2) low earners among the original cohort members emigrated and the earnings of the survivors increased less than it appears (or not at all); and (3) high earners among the original cohort members emigrated and the earnings of the survivors increased more than it appears.

Tables 7.6–7.9 express the earnings of recent entrants relative to those of the native-born, within five-year age groupings, for whites and blacks, respectively, at the two observation points—that is, at on average 2.5 ("at entry") and 12.5 years after entry. The figures indicate that, for all prime-age groups, the recent entrants in 1970 at entry were closer in earnings to their native-born counterparts than were the recent entrants in 1960 at entry. These differences were mild for whites but dramatic for blacks; while the white foreign-born/native-born earnings ratio increased from .73 to .78,

FIGURE 7.3
Cohort Growth in Real Earnings, by Race: 1960–1970,
Native-Born and 1960 New-Entrant Men Aged 20–44 in 1960

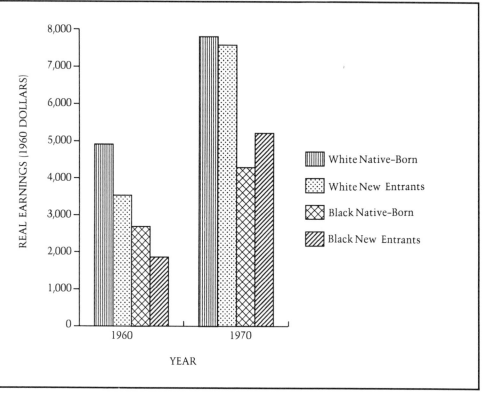

the black ratio increased from .63 to .99. In every five-year age grouping, recent-entrant blacks in 1970 had higher earnings relative to native-born blacks at entry than recent-entrant blacks in 1960; among whites the same is true for only two of the five five-year age groupings.

The progress of the two recent-entrant cohorts relative to that of the native-born cohorts also reveals important cohort and race differences. Among whites, the *relative* decadal progress was greater for the 1960 cohort than for the 1970 cohort. In the 1960–1970 period the 1960 white recent entrants aged 20–44 in 1960 attain average earnings levels that are within 4 percent of those of the white native-born in the same age group within 10–15 years of entry. The 1970 white recent-entrant cohort, while experiencing an average earnings growth greater than that of the native-born in the 1970–1980 decade, still have earnings in 1980 more than 10 percent less than do their white native-born counterparts. The parallel com-

FIGURE 7.4

Cohort Growth in Real Earnings, by Race: 1970–1980, Native-Born and 1970 New-Entrant Males Aged 20–44 in 1970

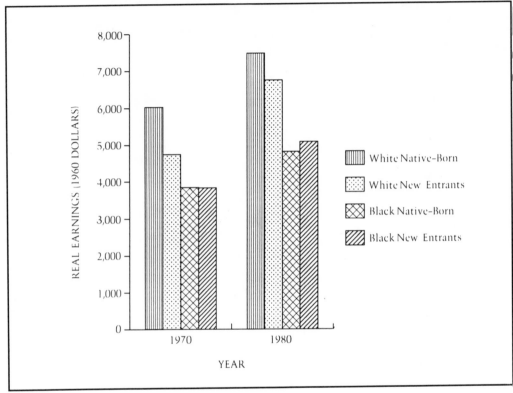

TABLE 7.6

Cohort Earnings for White Native-Born and 1970 New-Entrant Non-Farm Men, by Age: 1970 and 1980

Cohort Age in 1970	Native-Born		New Entrants		Ratio: New Entrants/ Native-Born	
	1970	1980	1970	1980	1970	1980
20–24	3,825	18,019	3,307	15,702	.865	.871
25–29	7,495	21,706	5,435	19,565	.725	.901
30–34	9,226	21,481	7,268	21,147	.788	.984
35–39	10,157	22,190	7,874	19,340	.775	.872
40–44	10,528	22,117	7,388	16,666	.702	.754
20–44	7,945	20,797	6,165	18,550	.776	.892

TABLE 7.7
Cohort Earnings for White Native-Born and 1960 New-Entrant Non-Farm Men,
by Age: 1960 and 1970

Cohort Age in 1960	Native-Born		New Entrants		Ratio: New Entrants/ Native-Born	
	1960	1970	1960	1970	1960	1970
20–24	2,630	9,339	2,070	9,050	.787	.969
25–29	4,243	10,224	3,133	10,115	.738	.989
30–34	5,018	10,495	4,061	10,341	.809	.985
35–39	5,523	10,682	4,082	10,200	.739	.955
40–44	5,513	9,952	4,008	8,681	.727	.872
20–44	4,601	10,151	3,365	9,795	.731	.965

TABLE 7.8
Cohort Earnings for Black Native-Born and 1970 New-Entrant Non-Farm Men,
by Age: 1970 and 1980

Cohort Age in 1970	Native-Born		New Entrants		Ratio: New Entrants/ Native-Born	
	1970	1980	1970	1980	1970	1980
20–24	3,258	12,153	3,170	16,022	0.973	1.318
25–29	4,952	11,027	3,856	13,487	0.773	0.962
30–34	5,632	11,029	5,316	14,676	0.944	1.048
35–39	5,760	14,919	5,937	14,152	1.031	0.949
40–44	5,916	12,788	7,555	11,637	1.277	0.9101
20–44	4,994	13,387	4,965	14,222	0.994	1.062

TABLE 7.9
Cohort Earnings for Black Native-Born and 1960 New-Entrant Non-Farm Men,
by Age: 1960 and 1970

Cohort Age in 1960	Native-Born		New Entrants		Ratio: New Entrants/ Native-Born	
	1960	1970	1960	1970	1960	1970
20–24	1,662	5,636	1,256	8,133	0.756	1.44
25–29	2,683	5,782	1,498	7,400	0.558	1.28
30–34	2,805	6,032	1,483	7,225	0.529	1.12
35–39	3,201	5,540	2,160	5,564	0.675	1.00
40–44	2,798	5,252	3,057	6,671	1.093	1.27
20–44	2,625	5,643	1,655	7,073	0.630	1.25

TABLE 7.10

Real Percent Decadal Growth Rates in Cohort Earnings
for White Native-Born and New-Entrant Non-Farm Men: 1960–1970 and 1970–1980

Cohort Age in Base Year	1960 New Entrants: 1960–1970			1970 New Entrants: 1970–1980		
	Native-Born	New Entrants	Ratio	Native-Born	New Entrants	Ratio
20–24	171	234	1.37	122	124	1.02
25–29	83.8	146	1.74	36.5	69.6	1.90
30–34	59.7	94.4	1.58	9.7	37.1	3.82
35–39	47.6	90.7	1.91	2.9	15.7	5.41
40–44	37.8	65.3	1.72	−1.0	6.3	—
20–44	68.4	122	1.78	23.3	41.8	1.79

parison is more difficult to make for blacks, since the 1970 cohort began with the high ratio of 0.99. While recent-entrant earnings for the 1970 cohort rise faster than for native-born blacks, with their average earnings exceeding those of native-born blacks by 6 percent in 1980, the figures show that progress for the 1960 cohort was dramatic, rising from an overall ratio of 0.63 at entry to 1.25 in 1970. Thus, unlike earnings for recent-entrant whites, the average earnings of recent-entrant blacks in both 1960 and 1970 overtake those of native-born blacks within 10–15 years of entry.

Within five-year age groups every age/cohort group of whites registered an increase in the recent-entrant foreign-born/native-born earnings ratio across the decade. While every age group among the 1960 black cohort also experienced an increase in the ratio, the same is not true for the 1970 black cohort; for the latter, the two oldest groups (35–39 and 40–44 years) show a decline in the earnings ratio.

Tables 7.10 and 7.11 display the real percent decadal growth rates in earnings, for whites and blacks, respectively. For all age/race/nativity groupings except two, real earnings increased across the decade. The two exceptions, both in the 1970 cohort and both aged 40–44 in 1970, are native-born whites, whose real earnings declined by 1 percent, and recent-entrant blacks, whose real earnings declined by 27 percent. Note that it is unlikely that the earnings of any black person who immigrated in 1970 actually fell by 27 percent; selective emigration is the likely reason; some higher-income black immigrants may have re-emigrated.

While the overall recent-entrant/native-born earnings growth ratio is the same for whites in the two historical periods, the age-specific growth ratios signal important activity by age, with the recent entrants aged 30–39 at the beginning of the decade making four to five times the progress of their native-born counterparts. Among blacks, recent entrants made dramatic progress relative to the native-born in the decade of the 1960s. That the relative progress of immigrants is considerably attenuated in the decade

TABLE 7.11
Real Percent Decadal Growth Rates in Cohort Earnings
for Black Native-Born and New-Entrant Non-Farm Men: 1960–1970 and 1970–1980

Cohort Age in Base Year	1960 New Entrants: 1960–1970			1970 New Entrants: 1970–1980		
	Native-Born	New Entrants	Ratio	Native-Born	New Entrants	Ratio
20–24	159	394	2.48	75.8	138	1.82
25–29	64.4	277	4.30	32.5	64.8	1.99
30–34	64.0	272	4.25	17.2	30.1	1.75
35–39	32.0	96.5	3.02	22.1	12.3	0.56
40–44	43.2	66.4	1.54	1.9	−27.4	—
20–44	64.0	226	3.53	26.3	35.0	1.33

of the 1970s is possibly the result of the impressive gains exhibited by the native-born and the emigration of the successful foreign-born.

Changes in the Distribution of Income Among the Foreign-Born and Native-Born

The average income of a group is just one of many summary statistics describing the distribution of the group's income. For policy purposes the mean of the earnings distribution may not be the only characteristic that matters. For example, the size of the subpopulation that is poor and how it fares, given that there are programs designed to augment the incomes of persons in the lowest-income strata, may be of particular interest. The economic impact of immigrants in terms of their use of governmental transfer funds may thus depend more on the distribution of their incomes than on the average of those incomes.

Table 7.12 reports the distribution of total income for foreign-born and native-born men aged 25–65 in 1970 and 1980, from the bottom fifth to the top fifth as ranked by income. In both years, the income distribution of the foreign-born is more unequal than that of the native-born, in that the bottom fifth of the foreign-born population has a lower share and the top fifth a higher share of total income than the relevant bottom and top fifths of the native-born population. The difference is more pronounced in 1980. Between 1970 and 1980 among the foreign-born there is a fall in the income share of the bottom fifth, from 4.2 to 2.7 percent, and an increase in the income share of the top fifth, from 44.8 to 47.8 percent, but a change of only 1 percentage point for the two shares in the native-born population.

To understand better the forces generating income inequality and its dynamics among the foreign-born it is useful to compare the changes between 1970 and 1980 in the distribution of incomes for the 1970 entry cohort and a similarly aged native-born cohort. To the extent that new

TABLE 7.12
Distribution of Income of Men Aged 25–65,
by Nativity in 1970 and 1980:
Percent Shares of Total Income, by Quintile

Quintile	1970		1980	
	Foreign-Born	Native-Born	Foreign-Born	Native-Born
Bottom	4.2	4.7	2.7	3.8
Second	11.7	12.8	9.9	12.0
Third	16.9	17.7	16.0	17.8
Fourth	22.4	22.8	23.7	23.7
Top	44.8	41.9	47.7	42.8

TABLE 7.13
Decadal Cohort Change in Income Distribution
for 1970 New-Entrant and Native-Born Men Aged 25–55 in 1970:
Percent Shares of Total Income, by Quintile

Quintile	1970 New Entrants		Native-Born	
	1970	1980	1970	1980
Bottom	2.7	4.1	5.5	3.7
Second	10.9	11.0	13.3	11.9
Third	17.2	16.2	17.9	17.5
Fourth	24.5	23.2	22.8	23.3
Top	44.7	45.5	40.5	43.6

entrants work part time (students) or that those immigrants who initially fare less well in the United States re-migrate, the income share of the bottom fifth of the foreign-born entry cohort may increase over time relative to that of the native-born. Table 7.13 reports the decadal changes in income shares by population quintile for the 1970 recent-entrant and native-born males aged 25–55 in 1970. The figures indicate that, indeed, the share of total income of the bottom fifth of this entry cohort population rose over the decade from 2.7 percent in 1970 to 4.1 percent in 1980. Over the same period, the share of the bottom fifth of the native-born population ranked by income actually declined and fell below that of the foreign-born.

To see how public programs contribute to the distribution of incomes, in Table 7.14 we report the decadal changes in income shares for the two populations netting out all public assistance monies (e.g., food stamps, AFDC). Excluding governmental transfer income does not substantially alter the income distribution of the 1965–1970 recent entrants in 1970, suggesting that most of this group did not receive such income "at entry"

258

TABLE 7.14
Decadal Cohort Change in Income Distribution
for 1970 New-Entrant and Native-Born Men Aged 25-55 in 1970:
Percent Shares of Total Income Net of Public Assistance, by Quintile

Quintile	1970 New Entrants		Native-Born	
	1970	1980	1970	1980
Bottom	2.6	3.5	4.1	2.8
Second	10.9	11.1	12.9	11.8
Third	17.2	16.3	17.9	17.7
Fourth	24.5	23.3	23.0	23.5
Top	44.8	45.8	42.2	44.2

(see below), but does significantly increase the shares of income earned by the bottom fifth of the 1970 recent entrants in 1980 and the bottom fifth of the native-born populations in both 1970 and 1980. With or without public transfers included, the income share of the bottom fifth of the recent-entrant foreign-born population in 1970 rose while that of the bottom fifth of the native-born population declined between 1970 and 1980. In Table 7.15, we see that the rise in the income share of the bottom fifth of the 1970 recent entrants from 1970 to 1980 occurs among all area-of-origin groups, with the greatest rise occurring among the bottom fifth of the 1970 recent entrants from Asia. Length of residence in the United States by the foreign-born thus appears to reduce the group's income inequality, through either selective emigration or a change in the returns to income-generating activities of those who remain. Transfer programs are not a major factor in the cohort change in the distribution of income among the foreign-born, however.

Changes in Welfare Program Participation Among the Native-Born and Foreign-Born

Figure 7.5 reports the percentage of the native-born and foreign-born populations aged 25–64, by area of origin and by sex, who received income from welfare or public assistance programs in 1980. The figures indicate that participation in such programs is slightly lower for the foreign-born than for the native-born population. The exceptions are men from Asia, perhaps reflecting the refugee status of a high proportion of that group (almost 25 percent are from Vietnam, Laos, and Cambodia), and women from the Western Hemisphere. Average public assistance incomes received by foreign-born men, however, are slightly higher than those for native-born men, as reported in Figures 7.6 and 7.7, with incomes for native- and

TABLE 7.15

Decadal Cohort Change in Income Distribution
for 1970 New-Entrant Foreign-Born Men Aged 25–55 in 1970, by Area of Origin:
Percent Shares of Total Income, by Quintile

Quintile	Western Hemisphere		Europe		Asia	
	1970	1980	1970	1980	1970	1980
Bottom	2.9	4.2	3.9	5.3	1.6	4.4
Second	11.5	12.0	12.6	12.3	8.9	10.2
Third	17.2	16.5	18.1	17.4	16.2	16.1
Fourth	23.5	23.2	24.4	23.2	25.7	23.3
Top	44.8	44.1	41.0	41.7	47.7	45.9

foreign-born women almost identical. These patterns of public assistance income by area of origin generally parallel those for program participation rates.

The patterns displayed in Figures 7.5–7.7 are somewhat misleading because a high proportion of the foreign-born in 1980 are recent entrants, many of whom are ineligible for public assistance, and many of whom do not therefore receive such incomes, as is consistent with Tables 7.13 and 7.14. A criterion of legal immigration is that a person not become a "public charge"; the legal immigration system is designed to screen out potential welfare recipients. Among the recent-entrant foreign-born who are not legal immigrants, moreover, many may be foreign-born students on scholarships and those nonstudents in illegal status may be reluctant to participate in governmental programs, even if eligible. Thus, the fact that participation in transfer programs is lower among the recent-entrant foreign-born than among similarly aged native-born, as seen in Figure 7.5, may merely reflect the presence of both illegal immigrants and legal non-immigrants in the foreign-born population.

In Figures 7.8 and 7.9 average public assistance income levels for 1970 recent entrants (in 1980 dollars) in 1970 and in 1980 are displayed by area of origin for both men and women. In 1970 for both sex groups, average public assistance income is lower at entry for the recent entrants from all areas than for the native-born, as expected. However, while average public assistance income fell for both native-born men and women over the decade, it increased for all of the 1970 recent-entrant groups with the exception of men from Asia. For women from Asia and Europe who entered between 1965 and 1970, the level of governmental transfer income is still less than that for their native-born counterparts in 1980; however, again for both men and women, the 1970 recent entrants from the Western Hemisphere received a greater average level of public assistance income than did the native-born by 1980. Indeed, the 1970 recent-entrant women from the

FIGURE 7.5
*Percentage of Persons Aged 25–64 Receiving Public Assistance Income,
by Sex, Nativity, and Area of Origin: 1980*

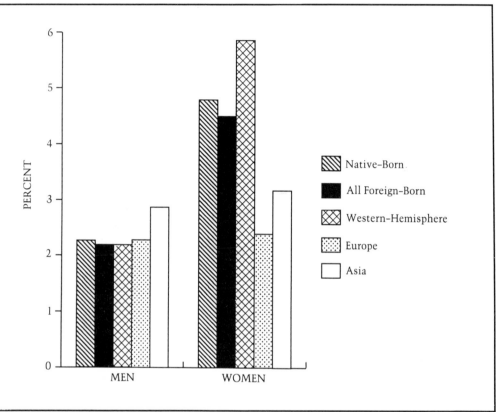

Western Hemisphere who have been in the United States between 10 and 15 years receive almost 62 percent more transfer income on average than do native-born women of the same age, while those women from Europe and Asia receive about 30 percent less transfer income. And recent-entrant men from the Western Hemisphere received 16 percent more transfer income than do native-born men, while those men from Europe and Asia received 17 and 31 percent less, respectively.

Homeownership

Owning a home is typically considered part of the American dream. A homeowner is also considered to be someone who has a stake in the gover-

261

FIGURE 7.6

Mean Public Assistance Income, Men Aged 25–64 in 1980, by Nativity

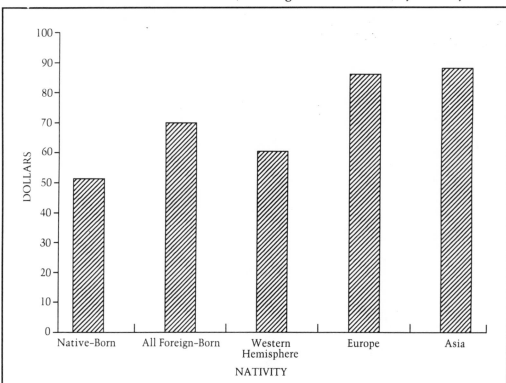

nance of the society; indeed, many of the Founding Fathers of the United States considered property ownership a prerequisite for the right to vote. Homeownership is thus one symbol of both the success of immigrants and their rootedness in the United States. Indeed, the variable has been considered of sufficient importance throughout the history of the United States that it is one of the few attributes about which there has been a question in each of the decennial censuses since 1890. We thus can examine the propensity of foreign-born entry cohorts to acquire their own homes while in the United States compared with the native-born based on the Public Use Microdata Samples of 1900, 1910, 1960, 1970 and 1980, all of which also supply date of entry information for the foreign-born.

Figures 7.10–7.12 display the percentage of households with native-born and foreign-born recent-entrant heads aged 25–34 who own homes in 1900, 1960, and 1970 within five years after entry and after another ten years of U.S. residence. In all of these census years, not surprisingly, home-

FIGURE 7.7
Mean Public Assistance Income, Women Aged 25–64 in 1980, by Nativity

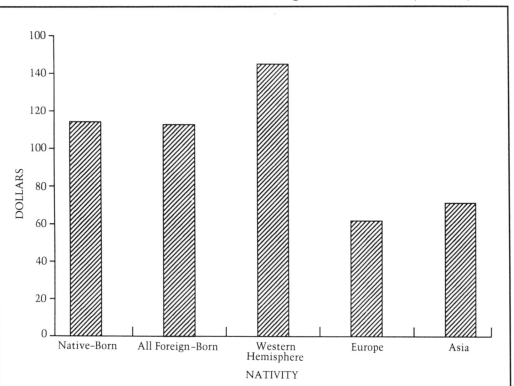

ownership rates are considerably less for the recent entrants within five years of their entry than for the native-born. Interestingly, while the percentage of the native-born household heads aged 25–34 owning homes has almost doubled between 1900 and 1970, from 30.7 to 55.2 percent, the ratio of the recent-entrant to native-born homeownership rates is the same in 1900 and 1970: 0.25. In 1960, however, the "at entry" discrepancy in ownership is less, the ratio being 0.38.

Ten years subsequent to the initial census year, rates of homeownership rise significantly more for the recent-entrant foreign-born than for the native-born of the same age in each of the three decades. The ratios of foreign- to native-born homeownership rates increase from 0.25 to 0.69 in the 1900–1910 period, from 0.38 to 0.88 in the 1960–1970 period, and from 0.25 to 0.83 in the 1970–1980 period. Although these figures indicate that immigrant cohorts take root relatively rapidly after entry, at least in terms of acquiring U.S. residential property, the relatively more rapid rise in

FIGURE 7.8
*Cohort Change in Mean Public Assistance Income 1970–1980,
for Native-Born and 1970 New-Entrant Men Aged 25–55 in 1970,
by Area of Origin*

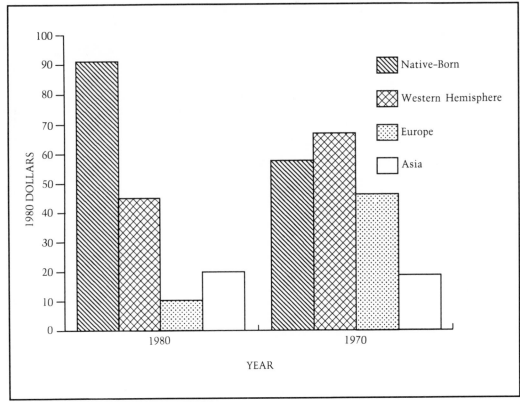

homeownership among the recent-entrant households does not necessarily mean that the foreign-born purchased homes at a more rapid pace over the ten-year interval than did the native-born. Those among the recent-entrant foreign-born not owning homes in the initial period in the United States are likely to have had higher emigration rates. A rise in rates of homeownership for a foreign-born entry cohort could be due solely to the emigration of those without property. Nevertheless, there appears to be convergence in homeownership across the foreign- and native-born populations.

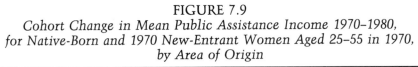

FIGURE 7.9
Cohort Change in Mean Public Assistance Income 1970–1980,
for Native-Born and 1970 New-Entrant Women Aged 25–55 in 1970,
by Area of Origin

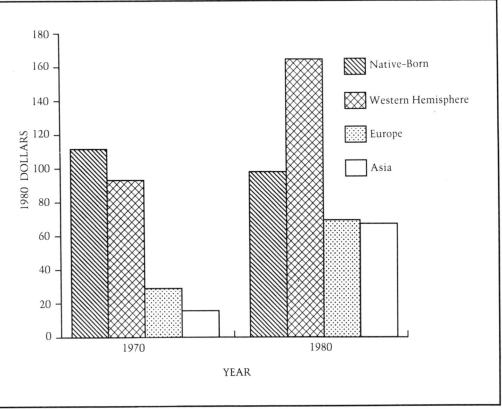

Self-Employment

Leaving one's own place of residence for a new and alien country entails great risks. It would not be surprising therefore to observe that a larger proportion of immigrants are "risk-takers" compared to the native-born. Initiating and managing one's own business enterprise is certainly a risky activity compared with seeking wage employment in most cases. On the other hand, employment discrimination against the foreign-born, language difficulties, and the constraint of illegal status may make self-employment preferable to wage or salary employment. Are the foreign-born more likely to be self-employed than the native-born? Figure 7.13 reports the percentage of black and white foreign- and native-born men aged 20–44

265

FIGURE 7.10
*Decadal Cohort Change in Percent Owning a Home
Among 1900 New-Entrant and Native-Born Household Heads
Aged 25–34 in 1900: 1900–1910*

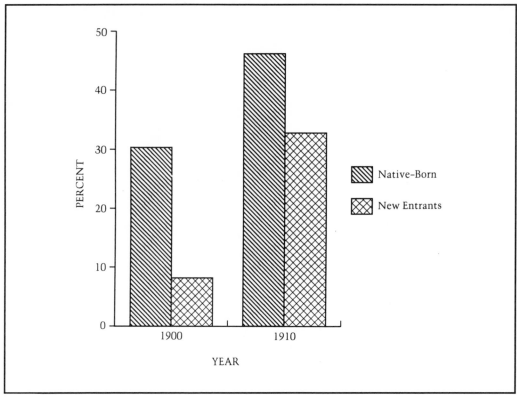

who report income from self-employment, excluding farming, in 1960, 1970, and 1980. In all three census years, within race groups, the foreign-born are slightly more likely to be receiving income from self-employment than are the native-born, although by 1980 this differential had almost completely disappeared. Again, however, this smaller differential could be due to there being a significantly larger proportion of new entrants among the foreign-born in 1980 because of the larger flow of immigrants in the 1970–1980 decade (25 percent in 1980 versus 18 percent in 1970). If the investments entailed in initiating a business require considerably more time than do investments in employee-related skills, then the composition of the foreign-born in terms of their length of residence in the United States may matter.

In Figure 7.14 the decadal changes in the proportion of men aged

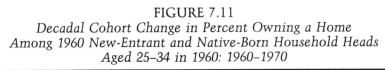

FIGURE 7.11
*Decadal Cohort Change in Percent Owning a Home
Among 1960 New-Entrant and Native-Born Household Heads
Aged 25–34 in 1960: 1960–1970*

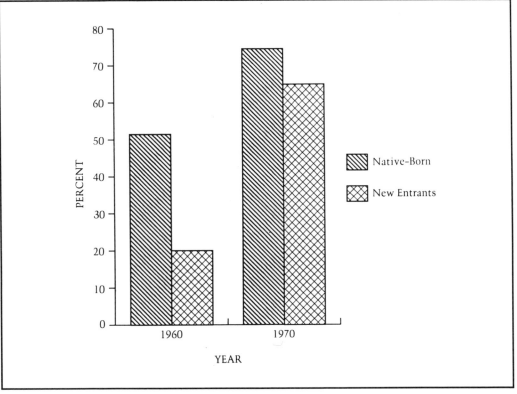

20–44 who are self-employed is displayed for 1960 and 1970 recent entrants and for comparably aged native-born cohorts. In both 1960–1970 and 1970–1980, the recent entrants, while initially having a lower proportion of self-employed workers than the native-born (3 percent versus 7–8 percent), overtake the native-born after ten years. The proportion of the foreign-born cohort who are self-employed rises to 13 percent (1970) or 14 percent (1980) compared with 11 percent (1970) or 13 percent (1980) for the native-born. This decadal growth path for the 1970 recent entrants in the incidence of self-employment is considerably steeper than that for earnings or homeownership. The recent entrants in both 1960 and 1970 did not catch up to the native-born after a decade in terms of either average earnings or homeownership, but they surpassed the native-born with respect to self-employment within ten years.

FIGURE 7.12
*Decadal Cohort Change in Percent Owning a Home
Among 1970 New-Entrant and Native-Born Household Heads
Aged 25–34 in 1970: 1970–1980*

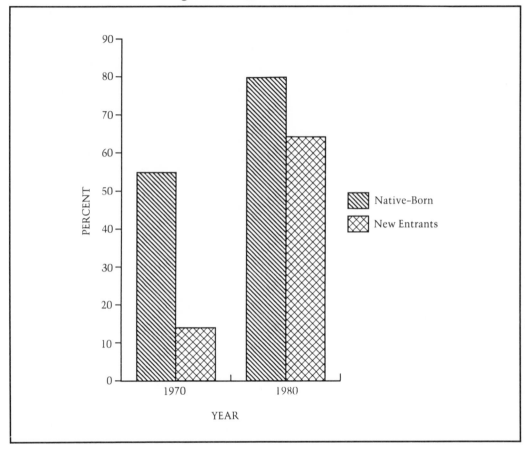

The incidence of self-employment among the foreign-born also appears to differ greatly across area-of-origin groups. Figure 7.15 presents the proportions of men aged 30–54 who are self-employed in 1980 by nativity and by area of origin. The foreign-born from Asia have the highest proportion of self-employed (17.1 percent); the incidence of self-employment among men from Asia exceeds that among the native-born by 40 percent. The foreign-born from Europe have the next highest proportion (15.9 percent), with the incidence considerably lower among foreign-born men from the Western Hemisphere (6.6 percent). These area-of-origin patterns of self-employment among the foreign-born are consistent with the hypothesis that

FIGURE 7.13
Percent Self-Employed in Own (Non-Farm) Business,
by Census Year and Race: Native-Born and Foreign-Born Men Aged 20–44

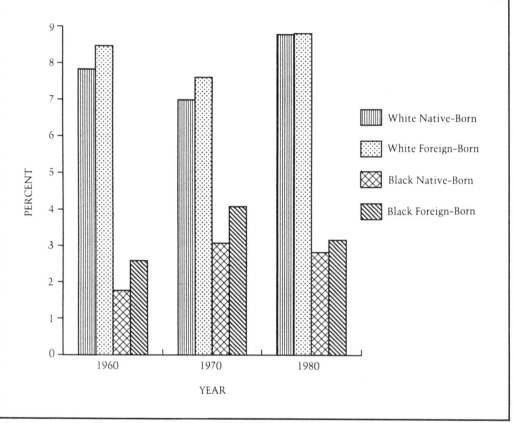

the distance of a migratory move screens out those potential immigrants averse to risk-taking, although self-employment may also signal employment discrimination. Note, however, that Asians also appear to experience the highest growth in earnings of all foreign-born groups, as indicated below.

Labor Force Participation

The effect of the presence of immigrants on the economy depends most basically on the decisions of immigrants to participate in the labor market. Figure 7.16 displays the labor force participation rates for native-

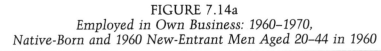

FIGURE 7.14a
Employed in Own Business: 1960–1970,
Native-Born and 1960 New-Entrant Men Aged 20–44 in 1960

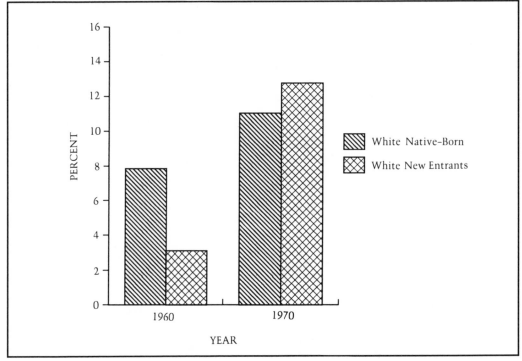

born, foreign-born, and recent-entrant men aged 20–44 in 1960, 1970, and 1980; Figure 7.17 displays the rates for women. Among the men, rates of participation in the labor force fell for all three groups between 1960 and 1980, particularly so for recent entrants. While labor force participation rates are approximately the same among the overall native- and foreign-born male populations in each of the years, those for recent entrants fell from 97 percent of the native-born rate in 1960 to 84 percent in 1980.

In contrast, rates among the women in the same age group rose for all nativity and entry groups between 1960 and 1980. Indeed, by 1980, the participation rate of native-born women in the 20–44 age group had risen to 75 percent of that of native-born men. The rise in participation rates for native-born women between 1960 and 1980 exceeded those for foreign-born women, in large part because of the almost stable trend in the labor force participation rates of recent-entrant women between 1970 and 1980. While in 1960 and 1970 the participation rates of recent-entrant women exceeded or were equal to those of native-born and all foreign-born women,

FIGURE 7.14b
Employed in Own Business: 1970–1980,
Native-Born and 1970 New-Entrant Men Aged 20–44 in 1970

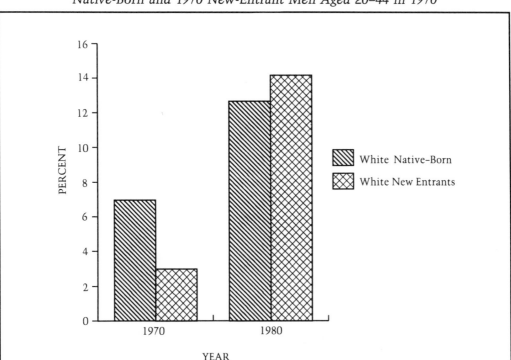

by 1980 their rates had fallen to 80 percent of those of both the native-born and foreign-born populations of women.

Tables 7.16 and 7.17 display male and female labor force participation rates, respectively, by nativity and for recent entrants within five-year age groups. These tables reveal that the widening of the differential between the labor force participation rates of recent entrants and those of the native-born that occurred between 1960 and 1980 took place mainly within the two youngest age groups. This trend mainly reflects differential growth rates in school attendance between the recent-entrant population and the native-born populations in those age groups. Figures 7.18 and 7.19 display the percentage of native-born and recent-entrant men and women in the 20–24 and 25–29 age groups who were attending school in 1960, 1970, and 1980. While school attendance among recent entrants fell between 1960 and 1970 and then rose between 1970 and 1980, in both age groups and for both sexes, with the exception of women aged 20–24 in 1970, a

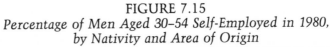

FIGURE 7.15
*Percentage of Men Aged 30–54 Self-Employed in 1980,
by Nativity and Area of Origin*

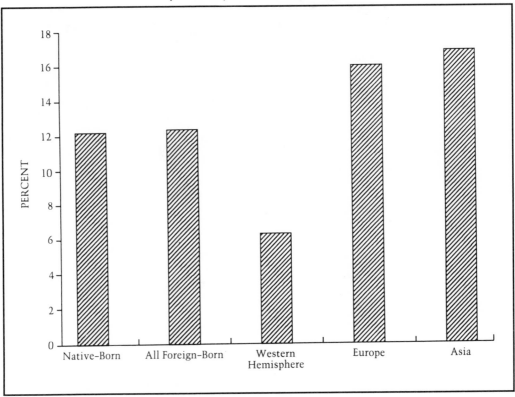

significantly higher percentage of recent entrants were attending school than were the native-born between 1970 and 1980. Among men, there is a particularly large increase in school attendance among the recent entrants aged 25–29 between 1970 and 1980 compared with that in the same age group among the native-born, and the gap between the school attendance of the recent entrants and the native-born in the 20–24 age group also widens between 1970 and 1980. Among recent entrants aged 25–29, school attendance rose from 17 percent in 1970 to almost 29 percent in 1980, while among the native-born attendance rates rose from 7 percent in 1970 to only 14 percent in 1980.

School attendance rates for recent-entrant women aged 20–24 and 25–29 exhibit the same steep rise between 1970 and 1980 as the rates for recent-entrant men aged 25–29. While 12 percent of recent-entrant women aged 20–24 were attending school in 1970 compared with 16 percent of

FIGURE 7.16
Percentage of Men Aged 20–44 in the Labor Force,
by Nativity: 1960–1980

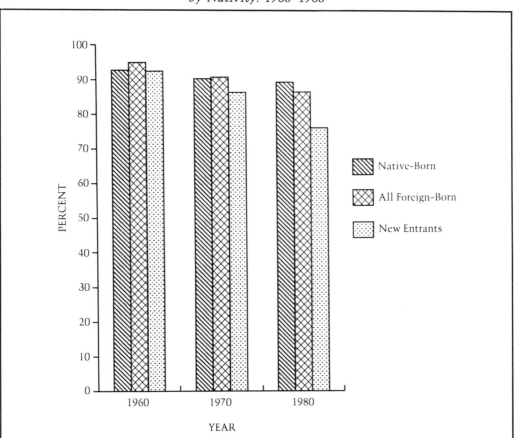

native-born women, 27 percent of them were attending school in 1980 compared with 21 percent of native-born women. School attendance rates rose from 3 to 14 percent between 1970 and 1980 for recent-entrant women aged 25–29, and from 3 to only 9 percent for native-born women.

The lower labor force rates exhibited by recent entrants compared with the native- and foreign-born populations in 1980 thus is accounted for by the higher school attendance rates of the former and is unlikely to persist as these populations age; as Figures 7.20 and 7.21 show, the labor force participation rates of both recent-entrant men and women aged 20–44 in 1970 surpassed that of their native-born counterparts a decade later. Again, in part this may be due to the emigration of those among the 1970 entry

FIGURE 7.17
Percentage of Women Aged 20–44 in the Labor Force,
by Nativity: 1960–1980

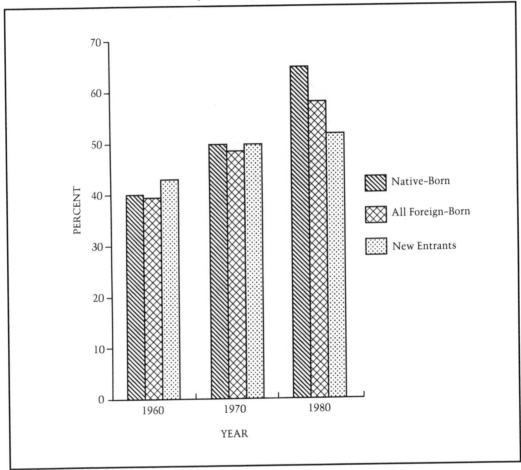

cohort who came to the United States solely to receive a higher education
or of those with a lower attachment to the labor force and is not necessarily
reflective of the life-cycle labor supply behavior of immigrants.

TABLE 7.16

Percentage of Men Aged 20–44 in the Labor Force, by Age and Nativity: 1960–1980

Age	1960			1970			1980		
	Native-Born	Foreign-Born	New Entrants	Native-Born	Foreign-Born	New Entrants	Native-Born	Foreign-Born	New Entrants
20–24	86.3	86.5	86.6	80.7	76.7	71.5	77.0	74.3	61.8
25–29	93.8	94.4	92.7	93.6	89.4	84.7	92.2	80.5	71.1
30–34	95.7	97.0	96.5	94.9	95.2	92.0	95.2	92.4	88.6
35–39	96.0	97.6	97.6	95.5	97.0	96.0	93.4	94.9	89.1
40–44	94.8	96.9	94.6	94.2	97.3	95.5	95.3	95.7	94.6
20–44	93.4	95.2	93.0	91.0	91.4	86.6	89.6	86.7	75.7

TABLE 7.17
Percentage of Women Aged 20–44 in the Labor Force, by Age and Nativity: 1960–1980

Age	1960			1970			1980		
	Native-Born	Foreign-Born	New Entrants	Native-Born	Foreign-Born	New Entrants	Native-Born	Foreign-Born	New Entrants
20–24	45.1	45.8	43.3	56.5	53.6	48.4	68.4	55.2	48.1
25–29	35.3	39.0	39.6	46.0	46.0	48.5	63.3	60.3	56.0
30–34	34.5	36.1	49.1	44.9	42.6	44.0	62.0	55.2	50.0
35–39	40.8	39.2	44.1	48.2	48.1	53.9	62.3	63.4	56.1
40–44	44.2	39.4	44.8	52.4	52.8	62.5	65.4	56.7	50.0
20–44	40.0	39.5	43.5	50.0	48.5	49.8	65.0	58.1	51.7

276

FIGURE 7.18
Percentage of Men Aged 20–29 Attending School, by Age Group,
Native-Born and New Entrants, 1960–1980

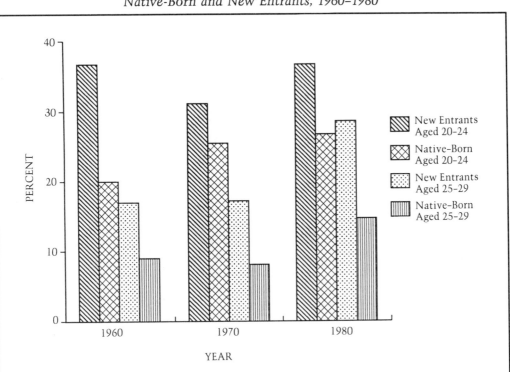

The Effects of U.S. Experience on the
Economic Status of Legal Immigrants:
Evidence from the 1971 Immigrant Cohort

The evidence from adjacent censuses on the decadal changes in the economic status of foreign-born entry cohorts suggests strongly that their economic well-being changes relatively rapidly as duration of residence in the United States lengthens. However, as noted, it is impossible to infer from such data how well any individual immigrant fares because (1) the composition of a foreign-born cohort changes over time owing to nonrandom emigration and (2) the census provides no information on the legal status of the foreign-born. Such heterogeneity of the foreign-born in the census data sets would be of little concern if legal status were unrelated to earnings potential or to the pace of assimilation. But direct participation in the U.S. labor market—what is usually meant by experience in the United

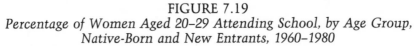

FIGURE 7.19
*Percentage of Women Aged 20–29 Attending School, by Age Group,
Native-Born and New Entrants, 1960–1980*

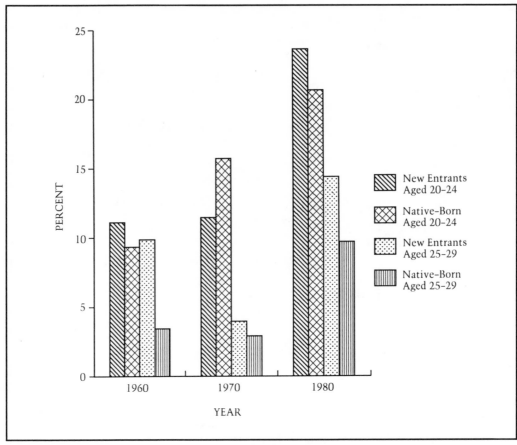

States—is *differentially* accessible to the foreign-born. While permanent
resident aliens may move about freely, maneuver for job-skills acquisition
and for employment, those non-immigrants who have work authorization
are tied to one employer as a condition of their visa and, of course, the
illegals must perform all job searches while officially out of sight.

Additionally, the question used in census data sets to ascertain length
of stay (or year of entry) does not elicit the date of entry into any status
recognized by statute. Thus, even if all foreign-born in a data set were
permanent resident aliens at the time of interview, we still would not know
their years of participation in the U.S. labor market *as permanent resident
aliens.* Many would have pre-immigration U.S. experience, some as legal

FIGURE 7.20
*1970–1980 Cohort Change in Percentage of Men in the Labor Force,
Native-Born and 1970 New Entrants Aged 20–44 in 1970*

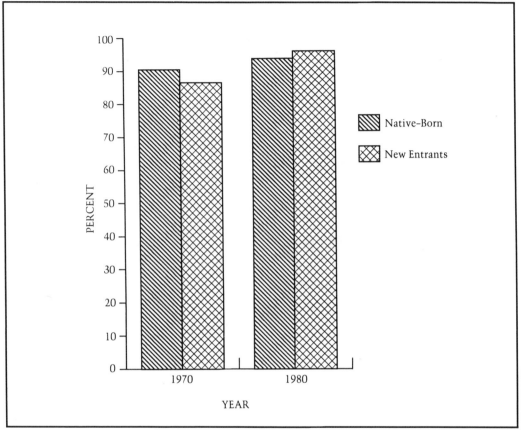

non-immigrants and others as illegals. Because of the constraints on the labor mobility of non-immigrants and illegals, such experience would be of quite a different character from post-immigration U.S. experience. Thus, returns to the two types of experience may differ significantly. Moreover, because the composition of the foreign-born population with respect to histories of legal status may differ substantially across country-of-origin groups, estimates of the differential economic mobility of various country-of-origin groups obtained from census-type data may be misleading.[4]

---

[4]There are (at least) two additional reasons why the year in which legal permanent residence was obtained is important. First, it may be associated with the entry cohort effects discussed above. Second, year of immigration determines date of eligibility to naturalize. Since

FIGURE 7.21

*1970–1980 Cohort Change in Percentage of Women in the Labor Force,
Native-Born and 1970 New Entrants Aged 20–44 in 1970*

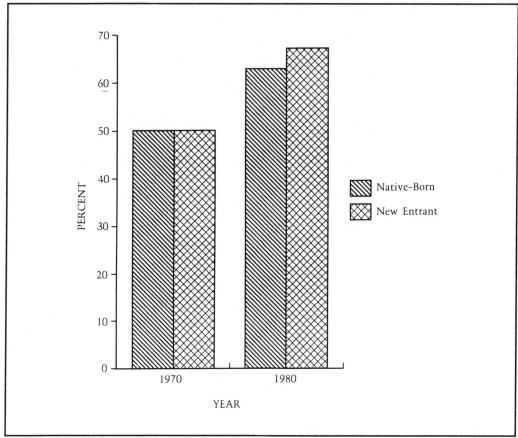

In this section we use the 1971 INS cohort sample of immigrants to estimate the effects of pre- and post-immigration experience in the United States on the economic status of legal immigrants and to disentangle, in part, the change in the economic status of an immigrant from the aggregate change in an immigrant cohort that occurs because of selective emigration. Of all data sets currently available, only the INS cohort sample identifies legal immigrants and provides information on the date of admission to permanent resident alien status; and of all the data sets with substantial

---

naturalization removes all bars to the exercise of all occupations (except those of President and Vice President of the United States), the decision to naturalize may be related to the occupational progress of immigrants eligible to naturalize.

numbers of foreign-born, only the INS cohort sample provides longitudinal information on individuals. Unfortunately, the INS data do not include information on earnings; hence, our analysis focuses on occupational status and on that component of economic progress attributable to change in occupation. To assess comparability of census data, we perform parallel analyses whenever possible based on a census sample.

The INS and Census Samples

Both samples were discussed in a preliminary way in Chapter 1. In this section we note their specific features pertinent to an analysis of economic status and progress.

The INS 1971 Immigrant Cohort Sample: The immigrant cohort sample used for this analysis—consisting of all males aged 21–65 at the time they were admitted to permanent resident status who are in the 1-in-100 random sample of recent immigrants in FY 1971—provides information based on the new immigrant record on age, date of admission to permanent residence, country of birth, whether or not the immigrant is adjusting status from a non-immigrant status (and, if so, the type of non-immigrant visa previously held as well as the date of admission to that non-immigrant status), and occupation. The new immigrant records have been linked with the INS naturalization files so that for those members of the cohort sample who naturalized between July 1971 and February 1981, inclusive, data include as well the date of naturalization and occupation at the time of naturalization.

Two features of this data set influence our choice of measurement and estimation strategies: (1) the data do not provide measures of schooling or wages; (2) while the data provide longitudinal information on naturalization for the entire cohort sample, they provide longitudinal information on other characteristics, such as occupation, only for the subset who naturalize, a nonrandom sample of the original immigrant cohort. Fortunately, we can use our estimates of the determinants of naturalization, which in this case is also the sample selection rule, in order to correct for sample selectivity bias in estimating the economic returns to experience and as well to assess the nature of the selectivity.

The INS sample provides exact information on post-immigration U.S. experience and less exact information on pre-immigration U.S. experience as a non-immigrant. Post-immigration experience is measured by the length of the period between the date of admission to permanent residence and the date of naturalization. Pre-immigration experience is measured by the length of the period between date of immigration and date of admission to prior non-immigrant status. In 1971, U.S. law did not permit status adjustment for natives of Western Hemisphere countries who were entering under "normal-flow" immigration procedures. Thus, the only natives of the Western Hemisphere adjusting status in the INS sample are Cubans "paroled" into the United States during the political upheavals of the early 1960s. Hence, our measure of pre-immigration U.S. experience ignores the pre-immigration U.S. experience of all other natives of the Western Hemisphere, experience not immediately prior to immigration, and experience in an illegal status.

Occupation in the new immigrant record represents (1) for labor-certified immigrants the occupation for which labor certification is granted and (2) for all other immigrants the occupational title they provide on their immigration documents. Thus, while the occupational title certainly denotes occupation at the start of permanent residence for the labor-certified immigrants and almost certainly denotes the same for status-adjustment immigrants, who together constitute over 45 percent of our sample, for the remainder of the immigrants it may denote occupation in the country of origin or the occupation aspired to in the United States. Occupation at the time of naturalization, however, may be regarded with the same confidence as reported occupation in all U.S. data sources, so that we can assess any biases in the use of the occupational titles provided by the immigration records. At both time periods, occupation is recorded by the three-digit code used in the 1970 U.S. Census.

In our empirical procedures (below) we correct for the possible biases that might arise from the omission of schooling in assessing the effects of experience on occupational status as well as from erroneous measurement of pre-immigration experience. Because schooling attainment is included in the census sample, we can also directly assess the sensitivity of results to the omission of this variable using these data.

The absence of wage information in the INS cohort sample means that we must rely on occupational attainment as a measure of economic status. The information on occupation lends itself easily to the construction of an ordinal measure of occupational attainment. Accordingly, we constructed a six-category ordinal index, termed "occupational rank." We constructed as well a cardinal measure, termed "occupation earnings," in which each occupation is represented by the log of the mean earnings of full-time, year-round male workers in that occupation group in the United States, based on the 53 occupation groups from the 1979 CPS (U.S. Bureau of the Census 1982, Table 58). To ensure that all observations are in constant dollars, all occupations were accorded their mean earnings in 1979.[5]

---

[5]We do not claim that our indices of occupation are indicators of earnings or wage rates. It may be that the differential in post- and pre-immigration returns is less strong for wage rates than for occupational status, to the extent that experience is rewarded within occupations.

Table 7.18 reports the means and standard deviations of the principal characteristics of the INS sample and the proportions in the six categories of the occupational-rank measure. The figures in Table 7.18 replicate what was seen in Chapter 2—that the decision to naturalize is not random. The occupational and country-of-origin distributions for the entry cohort and for the naturalized subset differ markedly. For example, while about 25 percent of the new immigrants report a professional or technical occupation, 40 percent of the new citizens do so; while 10 percent of the new immigrants are from Mexico, less than 1 percent of the naturalized citizens are of Mexican origin, reflecting the low naturalization rates of Mexican immigrants, as seen in Chapter 2.

The Census Sample: The census sample consists of a random sample drawn from among all foreign-born men aged 21–64 included in the 1980 census Public Use A sample who report that they came to the United States to stay between 1960 and 1980. For these men, the data include reported income from wage and salary earnings and from self-employment, as well as weeks and hours worked and occupational title. To establish comparability, we measured occupational attainment using the same cardinal and ordinal coding schemes constructed for the INS sample.

As noted above, the census provides no information on the immigration status of the foreign-born or the years in such status. Accordingly, we cannot construct from the census sample measures of pre-immigration (in the legal sense) and post-immigration U.S. experience; instead we construct, as in all prior studies, a single total U.S. experience measure.[6] This measure represents the length of the period between April 1980 and the midpoint of the response category to the question on year of immigration. Note that the census measure of total U.S. experience does not capture U.S. experience prior to the point the foreign-born person currently regards as the time he "came here to stay."[7]

Table 7.18 also reports the principal characteristics of the census sam-

---

Nevertheless, occupational mobility is a principal route to earnings change. The correlation between census earnings and our occupation index is .22; inclusion of the occupational earnings variable in an "actual" earnings equation increases explanatory power by 70 percent.

[6]This heterogeneous experience measure is sometimes measured by a set of dummy variables, following the census interval coding. Our results are not sensitive to how the census information is specified.

[7]As noted in the Introduction, an additional problem with the census data is that nativity, citizenship, and year of immigration are not accurately measured for certain subgroups. For example, an individual born in the United States (and hence a U.S. citizen by birth) whose mother's residence at the time of the birth was in a foreign country and who subsequently came to live in the United States would have difficulty providing a simultaneously truthful and coherent set of answers to the census questions. If such an individual provided the answer requested by the census questionnaire to the nativity question, he or she would appear to be foreign-born. It is believed that while many foreigners have historically chosen American hospitals for childbirth, their number is particularly large among natives of the two contiguous countries, Canada and Mexico.

TABLE 7.18

Sample Characteristics and Variables Used in the Analysis of Earnings and Occupational Attainment

	Samples					
	1971–1981 INS Immigration Cohort				1980 Census	
	At Immigration		At Naturalization			
Variable	Mean	S.D.	Mean	S.D.	Mean	S.D.
Occupation Ranking						
Professional, technical	.255	—	.408	—	.140	—
Managerial	.0026	—	.118	—	.0989	—
Sales, pre-college teachers, nurses	.193	—	.118	—	.146	—
Craftsmen, operators	.360	—	.228	—	.384	—
Services	.160	—	.0621	—	.113	—
Laborers, household workers	.0298	—	.0651	—	.118	—
Occupation Mean Earnings, Log	9.676	.325	9.961	.451	9.708	.375
Age, Years	33.9	10.0	38.3	7.77	35.3	10.6
Pre-immigration Time in U.S., Years	.841	1.79	1.32	2.09	—	—
Post-immigration Time in U.S., Years	—	—	6.41	1.65	—	—
Total Time in U.S., Years	.841	1.79	7.73	1.84	8.49	5.55
Origin Country/Region						
Cuba	.0582	.243	.0816	.274	.0632	.243
Mexico	.102	.303	.0087	.0932	.216	.412
Hispanic	.251	.434	.140	.347	.307	.462
Asian	.190	.393	.329	.470	.230	.421
Origin-Country Characteristics						
Distance to U.S.	3411	2502	—		—	
Per capita GNP in 1978	2207	2294	—		—	
Literacy rate in 1975, percent	77.8	22.3	—		—	
U.S. military base	.242	.429	—		—	
English an official language	.134	.340	—		—	
Voice of America broadcasts in native language	.835	.371	—		—	
Inflation rate 1970–78, percent	13.6	12.4	—		—	
Centrally planned economy	.0955	.294	—		—	
SINPO-rating of broadcast quality (0-5) from origin-country to U.S.	3.51	1.48	—		—	
Sample size	946		343		998	

ple. Comparison of the characteristics of the census and INS samples suggests that they are indeed drawn from two quite different populations. The two occupational distributions indicate that the foreign-born in the United States in 1980 with less than 20 years of "residence" in the United States were far less likely to be in a professional or technical occupation and far more likely to be in a laboring occupation than the legal permanent resident aliens entering in 1971 or the naturalized citizens from that immigrant cohort. With respect to origin country, the proportion of Mexicans among the foreign-born in the census sample is twice as great as the proportion of Mexicans in the immigrant sample. This may reflect overrepresentation of Mexicans among non-immigrants, illegal aliens, or those groups who are U.S. citizens by birth but who appear in the census as foreign-born.

Procedures for Estimating U.S. Experience Effects

To obtain a direct estimate of the effects of *pre-immigration U.S. experience*, the INS information obtained at the time of admission to permanent residence is used to estimate the determinants of occupational attainment. As discussed above, we use two measures of occupational attainment: occupation earnings and occupational rank. Accordingly, we estimate two versions of the occupational-attainment equation. In the occupation-earnings equation, the dependent variable is the log of the mean earnings for the occupation. The occupational-rank equation is specified as an ordered-response equation and estimated by ordered probit, that is, assigning a normal form to the distribution of the disturbance.[8]

To obtain estimates of the effects of *both pre- and post-immigration U.S. experience*, we estimate the occupational-attainment equation for the subset of the immigrant cohort who naturalize. Since the probability of naturalizing and reporting an occupational title (and hence of appearing in our sample at the second data point) may be related to unmeasured occupation-relevant characteristics of immigrants (ability, ambition, etc.), the resulting estimates obtained from this subsample may be biased. For example, those immigrants who tend to do well in terms of occupational attainment may also be more likely to naturalize. To correct for such selectivity bias, we use the two-step procedure developed by Heckman (1979), assuming that the unobservables in both the occupational-attainment and the sample-inclusion equations are jointly normally distributed. First, we estimate on

---

[8]If y is a continuous latent measure of occupational attainment, then we assume that an immigrant belongs to occupation category 1 if y falls below some threshold μ_1, to category 2 if $\mu_1 < y < \mu_2$, and so on. Maximum-likelihood procedures, under the assumption that the latent variable is distributed normally, yield consistent and efficient estimates of the βs and of the occupational-rank threshold parameters.

the full entry sample a probit equation for the probability of subsequent sample inclusion (i.e., the probability of both naturalizing and reporting an occupation). Second, we use the results of the probit naturalization equation to correct for the selection bias in the occupational-earnings equation by including as an explanatory variable the inverse of the Mills ratio predicted from the estimated probit.[9] The inclusion of the Mills-ratio variable not only corrects for the bias, due to selection, in the observed occupation-earnings equation, but its coefficient is a consistent estimate of the covariance between the unobserved components of the occupation-earnings and sample-inclusion equations. To the extent that persons who do not naturalize are qualitatively similar to persons who emigrate, we thus can detect the direction and importance of emigration selectivity in aggregate cohort measures of immigrant mobility.

The procedures just described yield consistent estimates under the assumption that any omitted variables are uncorrelated with the regressors. To test the specification, we also obtain estimates of the effects of post-immigration U.S. experience on the cardinal measure of occupational attainment using information on occupational status at both immigration and naturalization. Since immigrants choose when to naturalize, subject to residence requirements for naturalization, the observed length of the post-immigration U.S. experience is fixed by the immigrant and not by the investigator. It is thus possible that our measure of post-immigration U.S. experience is jointly determined with occupational attainment. If, however, unobserved factors jointly influencing occupational status and the timing of naturalization are time-invariant, then by regressing the *change* in occupational status on the *change* in length of residence all biases associated with unmeasured events and conditions (such as origin-country conditions, pre-immigration schooling attainment, and earnings potential) are eliminated.

We also estimate the returns to experience based on the sample of foreign-born from the 1980 census, using the comparable measures of occupational attainment. Comparison of the results obtained from the INS and census samples enables assessment of the extent to which coverage differences, the operation of the two types of experience in the United States, and selective emigration lead to distorted estimates of the effects of time in the United States when these estimates are obtained from census and CPS data.

As discussed, the specifications from the INS data distinguish between pre-immigration and post-immigration U.S. experience, while the census-based specifications include a total U.S. experience term. In all specifica-

---

[9]Note that applying a selectivity correction to an ordered-probit model would not yield consistent estimates. Hence, we obtain estimates only of the equation specified with a cardinal dependent variable.

tions, in conformity with prior studies, the immigrant's age is used in place of total labor force experience, which is not directly measured. To capture nonlinearities, quadratic terms are included for age, post-immigration U.S. experience, and total U.S. experience.

The INS data, which are longitudinal for the naturalized subsample, permit an assessment of the relative importance of the two forces of selectivity—that associated with immigration and that associated with emigration. The selectivity-"corrected" estimates of the occupational-attainment equation thus yield the determinants of immigrant occupational earnings solely as a function of immigration selectivity, that is, net of naturalization selectivity.

Separating out immigration from re-migration or naturalization selectivity effects using the selection-correction procedure requires that we have a plausible set of variables that influences the decision to stay and naturalize (sample inclusion), but that does not influence earnings directly or through the original decision to immigrate. Of all the country-specific variables used in the analysis of the determinants of naturalization in Chapter 3, only the *post*-immigration, origin-country inflation rate (1970–1978) and per capita GNP (1978) and the broadcast reception quality variables meet these criteria. The nonlinearities inherent in the probit specification also serve to identify the influence of selection associated with naturalization.

Because the criteria for admitting immigrants treated natives of the Eastern and Western hemispheres differently until 1978, all equations are estimated separately for the two hemispheres. Accordingly, the Western Hemisphere specifications exclude Voice of America broadcasts, since all countries in that hemisphere receive native-language Voice of America broadcasts, and the resident co-national population variables, which represent sources of U.S. visa entitlements primarily for the Eastern Hemisphere (until 1978). An unfortunate consequence of the decision to obtain within-hemisphere estimates is that the Western Hemisphere equations cannot be estimated from the INS sample, since there are not enough cases in the naturalized subsample to sustain a multivariate analysis.

The Returns to U.S. Experience

Emigration Selectivity and the Returns to U.S. Experience: Table 7.19 reports estimates of the occupational-attainment equations. The specifications estimated from the INS sample at different points in the U.S. experience of an immigrant and using different measures of occupational attainment yield remarkably similar results; the three specifications sharing the same dependent variable (occupation earnings) and estimated at two points in the U.S. experience of an immigrant, at entry and at naturalization, produce coefficients not only of the same sign (among statistically significant coefficients) but of roughly similar magnitude. The signs and levels of statistical significance of the coefficients estimated from the census sample are also not sensitive to the method of measuring occupational attainment. However, while the age effects estimated in the census sample are similar to those estimated from the INS sample, the two samples, as expected, yield rather different estimates of U.S. experience effects.

Column 1 reports estimates of the effect of residence in the United States as a non-immigrant, estimated from the INS sample at entry. The results indicate that each additional year of pre-immigration U.S. experience increases average occupational earnings by 3 percent. The coefficient is highly statistically significant, as it is in the ordered-probit equation.

The selectivity-corrected estimates of occupation earnings at naturalization (column 3) indicate that the returns to residence in the United States as a legal immigrant are nonlinear, increasing each year when experience is less than 6.3 years and thereafter decreasing, suggesting that the period of greatest learning about the U.S. labor market occurs immediately after achieving permanent residence. The estimated return from a year of post-immigration experience exceeds that from a year of pre-immigration U.S. experience for about the first five years after immigration. The estimate of the pre-immigration U.S. experience effect based on the naturalized-immigrant subsample, corrected for selectivity, is remarkably similar to that in the at-entry equation.[10]

The coefficient of the inverse Mills ratio, which yields an estimate of the covariation between the probability of sample inclusion and occupational attainment, is statistically significant and negative, indicating that those migrants with greater occupational attainment net of age and experience effects have a *lower* probability of naturalizing. The correlation between the error terms in the sample-inclusion and occupational-earnings equations, -0.61, is substantial. This result suggests that if those immigrants who tend to "take root" in the United States are negatively selected with respect to occupational attainment, net of experience and age effects, estimates from census data comparing aggregate foreign-born groups over time may understate true experience returns. The negative selectivity may simply reflect greater occupation-related benefits of naturalization among incumbents of relatively lower-earnings occupations than among those of higher-earnings occupations.

In column 4 of Table 7.19 we provide an estimate of the returns to post-immigration U.S. experience that is obtained by estimating how *differ-*

---

[10]Of course, our estimate of the returns to the pre-immigration U.S. experience *of immigrants* is not an estimate of the returns to the *non*-immigrant U.S. experience of all foreign-born in the United States or of all the foreign-born who might potentially migrate to the United States.

TABLE 7.19

Occupational Attainment and Time in the United States: Male Immigrants Aged 21–65, INS and 1980 Census Samples

| | 1971–1981 INS Sample | | | | 1980 Census Sample | |
| | At Immigration (1971) | | At Naturalization | Pooled | | |
Dependent variable = Estimation Procedure	Occupation Earnings OLS	Occupational Rank Ordered Probit	Occupation Earnings SC-OLS	Occupation Earnings Fixed effects	Occupation Earnings OLS	Occupational Rank Ordered Probit
Age	.0185 [a] (2.48)	.102 [b] (3.42)	.0552 [c] (2.42)	—	.0473 [a] (6.18)	.116 [b] (5.80)
Age Squared ($\times 10^{-3}$)	-.225 (2.38)	-1.39 (3.67)	-.584 (2.20)	-.126 [a] (0.47)	-.586 (6.06)	-1.44 (5.73)
Pre-immigration U.S. Experience	.0321 (5.53)	.165 (7.25)	.0379 (3.21)	—	—	—
Post-immigration U.S. Experience	—	—	.147 (2.27)	.114 (4.39)	—	—
Post-immigration Experience Squared	—	—	-.0116 (2.37)	-.0100 (3.91)	—	—
Total U.S. Experience	—	—	—	—	-.000654 (0.07)	.00880 (0.34)
Total U.S. Experience Squared ($\times 10^{-3}$)	—	—	—	—	.119 (0.25)	-.142 (0.11)
Constant	9.30 (67.58)	.0738 (0.13)	8.47 (18.09)	—	8.83 (61.97)	-.983 (2.60)

TABLE 7.19 (continued)

Dependent variable =	1971–1981 INS Sample				1980 Census Sample	
	At Immigration (1971)		At Naturalization	Pooled		
	Occupation Earnings OLS	Occupational Rank Ordered Probit	Occupation Earnings SC-OLS	Occupation Earnings Fixed effects	Occupation Earnings OLS	Occupational Rank Ordered Probit
Estimation Procedure						
λ	—	—	-.283 (4.60)	—	—	.458 (11.77)
$\mu(1)$	—	1.02 (11.91)	—	—	—	1.50 (27.65)
$\mu(2)$	—	2.08 (22.23)	—	—	—	1.95 (32.38)
$\mu(3)$	—	2.65 (27.24)	—	—	—	2.31 (35.32)
$\mu(4)$	—	2.66 (27.29)	—	—	—	—
F	13.64	—	—	32.16	10.06	—
χ^2	—	76.27	64.16	—	—	32.95
Sample Size	946	946	343	348	998	998

[a] t-ratios in parentheses.
[b] Asymptotic t-ratios in parentheses.
[c] Corrected t-ratios in parentheses.

290

ences over time in occupational statuses are influenced by differences in age and in experience. Such estimates are purged of biases that may arise from the omission of time-invariant variables (such as schooling). However, because the estimates reported in columns 1–3 do not separate the effects of time-invariant variables from the effects of time-varying variables, the age effects they yield incorporate both the biological aging effects and the effects of labor force experience accumulated prior to coming to the United States. The estimates based on over-time differences, however, separate these two types of variables, removing the effects of all time-invariant variables—including the origin-country labor force experience of the immigrants. Thus, the age element incorporated in the linear effect of post-immigration U.S. experience is the purely biological effect of aging which, if negative, may bias downward the obtained estimate. Since it is unlikely that the biological aging effect would be positive, the estimated effect may be regarded as a lower bound on the returns to post-immigration U.S. experience. Indeed, the estimate of the returns to post-immigration experience, based on the actual change over time in occupational status, is remarkably similar to that obtained from the selectivity-corrected at-naturalization estimates, the returns peaking at approximately 5.7 years after immigration and the estimated return from post-immigration experience exceeding that from pre-immigration U.S. experience for the first four years.

The results of the analysis of the cross-sectional census sample imply that the returns to total U.S. experience, which confound the experience of immigrants and non-immigrants—are of trivial magnitude and are not statistically significant, in contrast to those obtained from the 1971 cohort of immigrants.[11] The understatement of experience returns is consistent with negative selectivity associated with out-migration, suggested in the estimates in column 2, and with the confounding of differentially important immigrant and non-immigrant experience effects, evident in columns 1 and 3. It is also possible that the small experience effect obtained from the census cross-section may be due to the foreign-born of earlier "vintages" being of *lower* quality than more recently arrived (as of 1980) foreign-born. However, our comparisons of (actual) earnings within and across foreign-born cohorts from the 1970 and 1980 censuses in the first section of this chapter, which permit identification of such entry cohort effects, indicate a decline in the earnings of foreign-born entry cohorts between 1970 and 1980. Thus cohort differences cannot account for the census-sample underestimates of the returns to the U.S. experience of immigrants.

Origin-Country Differences in the Returns to U.S. Experience: Immigrants from different countries or regions of origin appear to differ in earn-

---

[11]These census-based results for experience are not changed in any significant way when education is included in the specification.

ings, in use of the welfare system, and in occupational attainment, as shown in Table 7.18, and in the decision to naturalize, as shown in Chapter 2. Moreover, as revealed in Table 7.18, the composition of the foreign-born by origin country differs across the immigrant and census samples. Of the models reported in Table 7.19, only the specification employing over-time differences in variables essentially controls for the operation of origin-country factors on the level of occupational attainment. None allows for differences in the returns to U.S. experience by country or region of origin. To ascertain if the different origin-country composition of the INS and census samples accounts for any of the differences in the average experience-returns estimates reported in Table 7.19 and to compare how the two samples depict country-of-origin occupational mobility differentials, we add to each occupational-attainment equation four country/region indicator variables corresponding to those groups usually defined in studies of the foreign-born in the United States as well as interactions between the experience terms and the country- or region-specific indicator variables.[12] The results, reported in Table 7.20, indicate that there are, indeed, substantial country- or region-specific differences in the effects of post-immigration U.S. experience and that these differences are understated by the census data.

The estimates of occupational attainment at immigration indicate that the returns to pre-immigration U.S. experience do not differ significantly by country or region of origin. The coefficients remain quite similar to the estimates reported in Table 7.19. On the other hand, there are important level differences at entry; for example, the column 1 estimates indicate that immigrants from Asian countries in the 1971 immigrant cohort are in occupations whose average earnings are almost 12 percent higher than those of non-Asian, non-Hispanic immigrants, while immigrants from Cuba and Mexico are in occupations with substantially lower average earnings than those of other Hispanic or non-Hispanic immigrants.

The specification of the selectivity-corrected at-naturalization equation includes a full set of dummy variables and interactions, but few of the coefficients attain statistical significance. However, the sets of country indicator variables and country/region interactions are jointly statistically significant at the 0.01 level of significance. The net effect of pre-immigration U.S. experience among Cubans appears to be negative (by about 3 percentage points) while that among Asian immigrants appears to be mildly positive.

The estimates based on the change in experience and occupational status over time indicate that the returns to post-immigration U.S. experi-

---

[12]The set of Hispanic countries includes all Western Hemisphere countries whose official or dominant language is Spanish.

TABLE 7.20

Occupational Attainment and Time in the United States: Male Immigrants Aged 21–65, by Country/Region of Origin

	1971–81 INS Cohort Sample				1980 Census Sample	
	At Immigration (1971)		At Naturalization	Pooled		
Dependent Variable =	Occupation Earnings	Occupational Rank Ordered Probit	Occupation Earnings	Occupation Earnings	Occupation Earnings	Occupational Rank Ordered Probit
Estimation Procedure	OLS		SC-OLS	Fixed Effects	OLS	
Age	.00897 (1.22)[a]	.0724 (2.36)[b]	.0512 (2.32)[c]	—	.0364 (5.14)[a]	.0892 (4.24)[b]
Age Squared (×10⁻³)	-.0872 (0.73)	-.903 (2.30)	-.528 (2.02)	-.178 (0.67)[a]	-.460 (5.15)	-1.19 (4.48)
Pre-immigration U.S. Experience	.0351 (3.79)	.188 (6.10)	.0768 (4.02)	—	—	—
Pre-immigration × Cuba	-.0235 (0.77)	-.0865 (0.86)	-.106 (1.89)	—	—	—
Pre-immigration × Asian	-.00766 (0.60)	-.0833 (1.28)	-.0668 (2.73)	—	—	—
Post-immigration U.S. Experience	—	—	.0340 (0.42)	.109 (4.22)	—	—
Post-immigration Experience Squared	—	—	-.00582 (2.00)	-.0104 (4.06)	—	—
Post-immigration × Cuba	—	—	.0208 (0.26)	-.0205 (0.82)	—	—
Post-immigration × Mexico	—	—	.0771 (0.63)	-.0748 (1.33)	—	—
Post-immigration × Hispanic	—	—	.0231 (0.35)	.0265 (1.60)	—	—
Post-immigration × Asian	—	—	.0215 (0.68)	.0290 (3.56)	—	—
Total U.S. Experience	—	—	—	—	-.00370 (0.34)	-.00391 (0.13)

TABLE 7.20 (continued)

Dependent Variable =	1971–81 INS Cohort Sample				1980 Census Sample	
	At Immigration (1971)		At Naturalization	Pooled		
	Occupation Earnings	Occupational Rank Ordered Probit	Occupation Earnings	Occupation Earnings	Occupation Earnings	Occupational Rank Ordered Probit
Estimation Procedure	OLS		SC-OLS	Fixed Effects	OLS	
Total U.S. Experience Squared	—	—	—	—	-.000186 (0.41)	-.000343 (0.24)
Total U.S. Experience × Cuba	—	—	—	—	.00668 (0.69)	.0598 (1.90)
Total Experience × Mexico	—	—	—	—	.00036 (0.05)	.00634 (0.26)
Total Experience × Hispanic	—	—	—	—	.00231 (0.32)	.0264 (1.21)
Total Experience × Asian	—	—	—	—	.0115 (2.06)	.0431 (2.48)
Cuba	-.170 (1.47)	-.899 (2.68)	-.399 (0.68)	—	-.0666 (0.52)	-.626 (1.51)
Mexico	-.205 (4.19)	-.935 (4.61)	-.898 (0.92)	-	-.296 (3.56)	-.886 (3.49)
Hispanic Country	.0207 (0.53)	.252 (1.84)	.183 (0.37)	—	.0561 (0.70)	.0518 (0.21)
Asian Country	.116 (3.81)	1.210 (7.10)	.154 (0.70)	—	.0166 (0.32)	.133 (0.83)
Intercept	9.45 (69.64)	.579 (1.00)	8.88 (17.96)	·	9.08 (66.60)	-.0771 (0.18)
λ	-	-	-.232 (3.27)	-	-	-
F/χ²	13.92	249.65	122.77	16.31	13.30	183.17

a t-ratios in parentheses.
b Asymptotic t-ratios in parentheses.
c Corrected t-ratios in parentheses.

ence are highest for immigrants from Asian countries, by almost 14 percent over those for all non-Hispanic immigrants, with the returns almost as high for immigrants from Hispanic countries. In contrast, returns for immigrants from Cuba are somewhat lower, by about 9 percent, while returns for those from Mexico are about 4 percent lower than for non-Hispanic, non-Asian immigrants.

The census-based estimates appear to understate the return to U.S. experience relative to that estimated from the immigration cohort sample even when origin-country compositional effects are accounted for. In contrast to the over-time estimates from the immigration sample, the census estimates indicate that non-Hispanic, non-Asian immigrants experienced no occupational advancement during the time they were in the United States, net of aging effects. The census estimates do replicate the higher occupational progress of Asian-country immigrants evident in the over-time estimates from the immigrant cohort sample but understate the Asian differential in experience returns by 60 percent. The ordered-probit estimates from both the census and the immigrant samples display lower occupational status "at entry" for Cubans. The cross-sample similarity in these latter results may be due to the relative homogeneity in legal status and the lack of ambiguity in dates of entry for this refugee group.

Why Country of Origin Matters

Both the census and INS data sets, which report the country of birth or last residence of the foreign-born, clearly indicate that the economic behavior and characteristics of the foreign-born in the United States differ across country- or area-of-origin groups. Such differences could exist for two principal reasons: (1) there is discrimination in the U.S. labor market that varies across country-of-origin groups, and/or (2) immigrants from different countries differ in their earnings capacities due to the *differentially* selective process of migration (and emigration) associated with the characteristics of the home country.

In this section we explore the extent to which migration-related processes can explain earnings and occupational attainment differences among "named" country-of-origin groups of the foreign-born in the United States. We utilize the basic framework set out in Chapter 1; that is, we focus on the fact that foreign-born persons resident in the United States at a point in time are a subset of persons from their home country who decided and were able to emigrate to the United States and who had not yet decided (or carried out the decision) to leave the United States after entry. Thus, the observed characteristics (earnings, age, etc.) of the U.S. foreign-born reflect two decisions: to immigrate to the United States and to remain in the

United States. To the extent that such decisions are based on a comparison of U.S. and home-country conditions, as these influence the relative well-being of the potential immigrant, the personal characteristics of foreign-born U.S. residents will be correlated with their origin-country characteristics.

Such an approach suggests a number of relationships between home-country characteristics and the earnings of a U.S. migrant. (1) For given migration costs and home-country characteristics, the higher the migrant's home-country income, the higher must be his or her expected U.S. income to make the move worthwhile. (2) For given home-country income, migrants from locations associated with high migration costs will have, on average, higher earnings in the United States than other immigrants, as only migrants who expect higher U.S. earnings will be willing to incur such costs. (3) For given home-country income and migration costs, migrants from more "attractive" countries will on average have (require) higher U.S. earnings than other immigrants.

Given that information is imperfect (costly), immigrants' expected and realized post-immigration U.S. incomes may diverge. Therefore, a migrant group from a country where little information about the United States is available is likely to have lower average realized earnings in the United States than a similar migrant group from a country where generally superior information is available. For the subset of immigrants whose U.S. incomes fall short of expectations, given unchanged home-country circumstances, a return home may be optimal. Such U.S. immigrants compare realized well-being in the United States with post-return well-being at home. These re-migration decisions reinforce immigration selectivity: only (expected) high-U.S.-income individuals immigrate from high-income and otherwise attractive origin countries and only those among them with high realized U.S. incomes remain in the United States. However, while high migration costs act as a barrier to immigrants with low expected U.S. incomes, such costs also make it less profitable for immigrants with relatively low realized incomes in the United States to return, given home-country earnings. The relationship between migration costs and the observed earnings of the foreign-born in the United States is thus ambiguous, although it is more likely to be positive the less imperfect is pre-immigration information about the United States.

To test the hypothesis that differences among the foreign-born by "named" countries of origin are fundamentally differences associated with (1) the opportunity costs of migration, (2) the direct costs of migrating, and (3) the quantity and quality of information available about the United States, we utilize our set of country-specific variables described in the Introduction.

Effects on Occupational Attainment

Can the observed differences in occupational attainment across country-of-origin groups be traced to differences in attributes of the origin countries as measured by these variables? Table 7.21 reports estimates of the determinants of the log of occupation earnings, for the Eastern Hemisphere subsets of the census and INS samples of prime-age males. Columns 1–3 report the census-based estimates from three specifications. In the first, country-of-origin influences are represented exclusively by variables that simply indicate the name of the foreign-born person's country of birth; in the second, the origin-country characteristic variables are added; and in the third, the indicator variables naming countries are excluded. Comparison of the estimates from the first and second specifications permits a test of the hypothesis that the set of coefficients associated with the names of origin countries are merely proxies for the operation of country-of-origin influences on migrant selectivity, because if the country characteristics we have measured capture these factors to a significant extent, their inclusion in the second specification should reduce or even eliminate earnings differences across "named" foreign-born groups.

The regressors included in all of the occupational-earnings equations to characterize personal attributes are the individual's age and its square. The INS-based specifications also include the three experience measures described and used above, while the census-based specifications include indicator variables indicating the individual's race and whether the person entered the United States between 1970 and 1974.

Comparison of specifications 1 and 2 indicates that inclusion of the set of country characteristics completely eliminates the influence of the variables naming countries. In the first specification, which excludes the country characteristics, the results suggest that individuals from Europe, the Philippines, and Japan are in occupations with significantly lower earnings than the other foreign-born from the Eastern Hemisphere, controlling for age and quinquennium of entry. However, all of these named-country differentials become statistically insignificant in the second specification which includes country-specific conditions. In contrast, the set of country-characteristic variables is statistically significant (F-test, 1 percent level).

All of the signs of the country-characteristic coefficients conform to the implications of our framework, although only three of eight are statistically significant at conventional levels. In particular, those migrants from high-GNP countries and from distant countries appear to be in high-earnings occupations, suggesting the importance of both opportunity and direct migration costs in migration decisions. Moreover, migrants from countries receiving Voice of America broadcasts appear to be in higher-earnings occupations, suggesting the possibility that such broadcasts provide useful infor-

TABLE 7.21
Determinants of Log of Occupation Earnings:
U.S. Foreign-Born Men from the Eastern Hemisphere, Census and INS Cohort Samples

Variable	Census Sample			INS Sample			
	(1)	(2)	(3)	OLS	SC-OLS	SC-OLS	SC-OLS
Age	.0653 (7.64)[a]	.0654 (7.67)	.0654 (7.70)	.0988 (3.51)[a]	.0973 (3.55)[b]	.108 (3.84)[b]	.105 (3.76)[b]
Age squared	-.000794 (7.53)	-.000788 (7.49)	-.000790 (7.54)	-.00114 (3.39)	-.00109 (3.30)	-.00123 (3.28)	-.00118 (3.37)
Pre-immigration Experience	—	—	—	.0358 (3.00)	.0325 (2.71)	.0326 (2.67)	.0354 (3.05)
Post-immigration Experience	—	—	—	.0476 (0.55)	.0418 (0.49)	.0418 (0.49)	.0805 (0.97)
Post-immigration Experience Squared	—	—	—	-.00340 (0.54)	-.00530 (0.86)	-.00522 (0.84)	-.00755 (1.24)
Immigrated 1970–1974	.00815 (0.32)	-.00166 (0.06)	.00474 (0.18)	—	—	—	—
Black	-.183 (2.57)	-.173 (1.77)	-.187 (2.55)	—	—	—	—
Europe	-1.83 (5.16)	-.0759 (1.12)		-.303 (4.85)	-.228 (2.73)	-.0778 (0.28)	—
Taiwan, Hong Kong	-.0227 (0.39)	.0224 (0.31)		-.0487 (0.37)	-.0495 (0.38)	.0116 (0.08)	—
India	.0289 (0.64)	.0130 (0.15)		.0817 (1.14)	.114 (1.54)	-.0582 (0.36)	—
Japan	-.105 (1.73)	-.0374 (0.38)		-.523 (2.17)	-.476 (2.02)	-.585 (1.74)	—
Philippines	-.217 (4.83)	-.166 (1.79)		-.106 (1.50)	-.134 (1.84)	-.202 (1.02)	—
GNP, 1970 ($\times 10^{-4}$)		.257 (2.24)	.244 (3.24)			.910 (1.53)	.426 (0.93)

TABLE 7.21 (continued)

	Census Sample			INS Sample			
Variable	(1)	(2)	(3)	OLS	SC-OLS	SC-OLS	SC-OLS
Literacy Rate	—	-.00169	-.00166	—	—	-.00177	-.00152
		(1.08)	(2.06)			(0.44)	(0.59)
Distance (×10⁻⁴)	—	.365	.325	—	—	.142	.0836
		(2.28)	(2.90)			(2.57)	(2.86)
English Language	—	.0294	.0570	—	—	.145	.194
		(0.63)	(1.30)			(0.82)	(1.67)
U.S. Military Base	—	-.0492	-.0457	—	—	.115	.120
		(1.12)	(1.26)			(0.66)	(1.15)
Centrally Planned	—	-.0660	-.0860	—	—	.147	.118
		(1.01)	(1.58)			(1.51)	(1.45)
VOA Broadcasts	—	.0825	.0491	—	—	-.0422	-.0507
		(2.08)	(1.27)			(0.19)	(0.35)
Foreign-born in the United States (×10⁻³)	—	-.220	-.271	—	—	-.337	-5.02
		(0.83)	(1.81)			(0.06)	(1.96)
Naturalized Citizens in the United States (×10⁻⁴)	—	1.10	.833	—	—	-.0835	.221
		(0.29)	(0.32)			(0.24)	(0.86)
Constant	8.71	8.57	8.45	8.16	8.25	7.21	7.30
	(52.8)	(37.3)	(41.3)	(14.0)	(14.4)	(8.61)	(9.36)
λ	—	—	—	—	-.148	-.101	-.139
					(1.31)	(0.24)	(0.88)
χ²	—	—	—	89.1	103.0	122.7	112.6
ρ²	—	—	—	—	.146	.0716	.128

a t-ratios are shown beneath regression coefficients.
b Selectivity-corrected t-ratios are shown beneath regression coefficients.

mation about the United States. Finally, there is marginal support for the hypothesis that migrants from less attractive centrally planned, authoritarian countries have lower occupational earnings.

As in the census data, the INS sample of immigrants from which we can estimate the determinants of earnings represents a self-selected subsample, in this case those among (also self-selected) immigrants who decided to become U.S. citizens within 11 years of becoming immigrants. However, for this sample, unlike for the census, we can estimate the determinants of the sample selection rule associated with naturalization, as in Table 7.20.

Columns 4–7 in Table 7.21 report estimates from four specifications of the log of occupational earnings at naturalization, for the INS Eastern Hemisphere sample of male legal immigrants. Columns 4 and 5 report ordinary-least-squares (OLS) and selectivity-corrected (SC-OLS) estimates of the restricted model in which all origin-country influences are represented only by indicator variables naming the country or area. The set of "named" variables is statistically significant, with those for Europe and Japan strongly statistically significant. There is not much difference between the estimates in the two specifications, suggesting that, as confirmed by the marginal significance of the inverse-Mills-ratio variable, and subject to the strength of the identifying instruments, emigration-naturalization selectivity does not strongly affect the earnings estimates for the Eastern Hemisphere (in part because of the relatively high naturalization rates of Asian immigrants, as seen in Chapter 2).

Column 3 reports estimates from the specification including both the country-name variables and the country-conditions variables. All of the coefficients of the variables representing country names lose their statistical significance when country characteristics are included except that for Japan, which remains negative and marginally significant. As in the census sample, the set of named country variables is not statistically significant in the full specification, while country characteristics as a whole are statistically significant. Also, as in the census sample, both per-capita GNP and distance are positively related to occupational earnings, with GNP only marginally statistically significant, however. Of the remaining country variables, only the presence of a U.S. military base approaches statistical significance; its coefficient is positive, consistent with the positive effects of information about the United States that may be associated with proximity to a major U.S. military installation.

When the equation is estimated without the (insignificant) indicator variables for named country of origin, the English-language variable and the number of natives among recent entrants to the United States achieve marginal statistical significance. The effect on occupation earnings of coming from a country where English is spoken is positive, as was found in the census samples, a finding consistent with such immigrants having superior pre-immigration information as well as the advantage in the U.S. labor market of English-language skills, as shown in Chapter 8.

Inclusion of all the origin-country characteristic variables leads to rejection of the hypothesis that the selectivity associated with naturalization significantly affects the parameter estimates for the Eastern Hemisphere immigrants, consistent with our findings that immigrants from the Eastern Hemisphere tend to have significantly higher naturalization rates *and* significantly lower emigration rates (Jasso and Rosenzweig 1982) than Western Hemisphere immigrants. The association between country of origin and occupational attainment thus appears to be mainly due to the selectivity associated with immigration decisions and the admission criteria of U.S. immigration law for the Eastern Hemisphere foreign-born.

Table 7.22 repeats the analyses of Table 7.21 for the Western Hemisphere foreign-born. Because, as noted, there are not enough cases in the Western Hemisphere INS naturalized subsample to sustain a hemisphere-specific multivariate analysis, Table 7.22 reports only the specifications based on the census sample. In the first specification of occupational earnings, which excludes country characteristics, the coefficients for Mexico, Canada, and Brazil are strongly statistically significant, and the coefficient for Cuba approaches significance as well, indicating that Canadian and Brazilian males are significantly more likely to be in occupations with higher average earnings than the left-out group (non-blacks from all the remaining Hispanic countries in the Western Hemisphere), while Mexicans are in occupations with lower average earnings than all the other Western Hemisphere groups.

Inclusion of the country characteristics eliminates the difference between foreign-born Brazilians, Canadians, and Hispanics and reduces the Mexico differential by 37 percent. However, the Cuba effect almost triples. Thus, migrants from Mexico appear to be in occupations with average earnings lower by 10 percent than all migrants, net of country characteristics, while migrants from Cuba are in occupations with average earnings higher by 15 percent than all Western Hemisphere migrants, even when country characteristics are taken into account.

The partial immutability of the negative Mexico occupational-attainment differential to the inclusion of country characteristics may reflect the operation of legal status, as a larger proportion of the Mexico-origin foreign-born than other groups may be in illegal status or may hold non-immigrant visas, as suggested by the differential in sample proportions for Mexicans in the immigrant and census samples in Table 7.22. The anomalous positive occupational attainment of Cubans may in part reflect their initial special status as refugees, which made them beneficiaries of resettlement programs not provided to other foreign-born migrants from the Western Hemisphere.

TABLE 7.22
Determinants of Log of Occupation Earnings:
U.S. Foreign-Born Men from the Western Hemisphere, Census Sample[a]

Variable	Log of Occupational Earnings		
	(1)	(2)	(3)
Age	.0231	.0220	.0220
	(3.73)	(3.58)	(3.51)
Age Squared	−.00320	−.000307	−.000286
	(3.91)	(3.78)	(3.46)
Immigrated	.00645	−.00945	.0195
1970–1974	(0.36)	(0.53)	(1.09)
Black	−.0152	−.00443	−.0164
	(0.45)	(0.10)	(0.41)
Mexico	−.169	−.106	—
	(7.76)	(2.01)	
Canada	−.307	.0264	—
	(6.48)	(0.10)	
Cuba	.0585	.153	—
	(1.47)	(1.94)	
Brazil	.157	.0191	—
	(2.10)	(0.22)	
GNP 1970 ($\times 10^{-4}$)	—	5.66	.452
		(1.20)	(3.71)
Literacy Rate	—	−.2549	1.04
($\times 10^{-3}$)		(0.17)	(1.33)
Distance ($\times 10^{-5}$)	—	.690	1.05
		(2.23)	(8.43)
English Language	—	.00995	.0896
		(0.14)	(1.48)
U.S. Military Base	—	−.0627	−.0120
		(1.34)	(0.30)
Constant	9.26	9.17	8.98
	(83.2)	(70.7)	(72.3)

[a]t-ratios are shown in parentheses beneath regression coefficients.

Effects on Wages

We turn now to examine the effects of origin-country conditions on the foreign-born person's actual wage in the United States, using the census sample which provides this information. Table 7.23 reports specifications of origin-country influences on the log (hourly) wage, for the Eastern Hemisphere subset. Column 3 estimates indicate that the named country of origin is not significantly associated with the wage. Thus, there is not much of an effect for the country characteristics to remove. Note, however, that the operation of the country characteristics in the third specification is qualitatively the same as in the results for the occupation-earnings equations, except for the effects of a centrally planned economy and the two compatriot-population variables. Of these, only the latter approach statistical significance. Thus, these results hint at differences between the process of climbing the occupational ladder and the process of increasing one's wage within an occupation.

Table 7.24 reports the estimates of the log (hourly) wage specifications in the Western Hemisphere subset of the census sample. The named country differentials in the first specification (excluding country characteristics) conform to the pattern displayed in the comparable occupation-earnings specification, with the negative Mexico and positive Canada wage effects again highly statistically significant. Here, however, inclusion of the country characteristics eliminates all country-specific differences; the set of named country wage coefficients loses statistical significance when differences in country characteristics are accounted for, although, as in the occupation-earnings specifications, the positive Cuba "effect" increases (but not to statistical significance). Observed hourly wage differences between the foreign-born Mexican population and other foreign-born populations, noted in almost all studies of immigrant or ethnic earnings determination, thus appear to be wholly explained by Mexico's unique combination of two important factors determining who immigrates to and remains in the United States—distance and per capita GNP. These factors appear to be positively and significantly correlated with the wage and occupational earnings of the foreign-born from both hemispheres. Of all countries, Mexico is, with Canada, the shortest distance from the United States, but, unlike Canada, has relatively low per capita income.

Summary

In this chapter we examined census data to assess the distribution of the effects of immigration across members of the native-born population and historical and recent changes in the economic status of the foreign-born relative to the native-born. We found that native-born consumers of fruits and vegetables, shoes and apparel, as well as of the services of tailors and jewelers, were likely to have benefited the most, and that low-skill native-born workers, particularly those located in the southwestern border areas of the United States, benefited the least. However, firm conclusions about the full consequences of immigration on earnings, relative prices, returns to and levels of investment could not be made on the basis of existing data or studies.

We reviewed the changes in the economic characteristics of the foreign-

TABLE 7.23
Determinants of Log Wage Rates:
U.S. Foreign-Born Men from the Eastern Hemisphere, Census Sample

Variable	Log of Hourly Wage		
	(1)	(2)	(3)
Age	.0994	.0982	.0969
	(5.83)	(5.78)	(5.74)
Age Squared	−.00116	−.00114	−.00113
	(5.47)	(5.40)	(5.37)
Immigrated	.176	.200	.200
1970–1974	(3.50)	(3.92)	(3.93)
Black	−.217	−.431	−.283
	(1.49)	(2.20)	(1.72)
Europe	−.00624	−.107	—
	(0.09)	(0.79)	
Taiwan, Hong Kong	−.0543	.0695	—
	(.047)	(0.48)	
India	.0962	.0142	—
	(1.08)	(0.08)	
Japan	.0899	.0433	—
	(0.75)	(0.33)	
Philippines	−.0432	.168	—
	(0.51)	(0.78)	
GNP. 1970 ($\times 10^{-4}$)	—	.942	.836
		(4.31)	(4.58)
Literacy Rate	—	−.00693	−.00509
		(2.25)	(2.90)
Distance ($\times 10^{-4}$)	—	.0388	.0257
		(1.84)	(1.17)
English Language	—	.0678	−.0517
		(0.73)	(0.67)
U.S. Military Base	—	−.0389	−.0109
		(0.48)	(0.15)
Centrally Planned	—	.0925	.0449
		(0.73)	(0.42)
VOA Broadcasts	—	.0278	.0578
		(0.31)	(0.74)
Foreign Born in the	—	.186	.416
United States		(0.36)	(1.49)
($\times 10^{-4}$)			
Naturalized Citizens	—	−2.30	−7.10
in the United		(0.31)	(1.36)
States ($\times 10^{-4}$)			
Constant	−.349	.165	−.340
	(1.06)	(0.36)	(0.87)

[a]t-ratios are shown in parentheses beneath regression coefficients.

TABLE 7.24
Determinants of Log Wage Rates:
U.S. Foreign-Born Men from the Western Hemisphere, Census Sample

Variable	Log of Hourly Wage		
	(1)	(2)	(3)
Age	.0296	.0274	.0276
	(1.95)	(1.83)	(1.84)
Age Squared	−.00352	−.000328	−.000330
	(1.76)	(1.65)	(1.62)
Immigrated	.153	.168	.174
1970–1974	(3.16)	(3.84)	(4.02)
Black	−.209	−.306	−.217
	(2.57)	(2.78)	(2.34)
Mexico	−.163	−.0635	—
	(3.05)	(0.48)	
Canada	−.6773	.0932	—
	(5.99)	(1.36)	
Cuba	.0209	.263	—
	(0.21)	(1.37)	
Brazil	.148	−.0832	—
	(0.71)	(0.35)	
GNP 1970 (×10⁻⁴)	—	2.58	.863
		(2.15)	(3.03)
Literacy Rate	—	−.551	4.13
(×10⁻⁴)		(0.16)	(2.19)
Distance (×10⁻⁵)	—	1.20	1.35
		(1.59)	(4.43)
English Language	—	.173	.212
		(0.99)	(1.50)
U.S. Military Base	—	−.00822	.00533
		(0.07)	(0.06)
Constant	−.800	.475	.238
	(2.95)	(1.50)	(0.80)

[a]Absolute values of *t*-ratios are shown in parentheses beneath regression coefficients.

born and native-born populations from 1960 to 1980, and the evolution of these characteristics for both the 1960s and 1970 new-entry cohorts of the foreign-born in the decade after their entry. The data suggest that (1) movements in the average earnings and labor force participation rates of the foreign- and native-born populations have followed similar patterns since 1960, with the average earnings of the foreign-born populations generally just slightly lower than those of the native-born for both blacks and whites; (2) 1980 recent entrants had lower real mean earnings than the 1970 recent entrants; (3) however, school attendance rates among 1980 recent entrants aged 20–29 were substantially higher than those of 1970 recent entrants in the same age group, and higher than those of the native-born; (4) the rise in the earnings of the 1960 and 1970 recent-entrant cohorts over the 1960–1970 and 1970–1980 decades exceeded the rise in the earnings of identically aged native-born cohorts in these periods; (5) despite the higher real growth rates in earnings experienced by both the 1960 and 1970 recent-entrant foreign-born, their average earnings did *not* catch up to those of the native-born in the white population within 10–15 years of entry; however, the earnings of both the 1960 and 1970 black recent-entrant cohorts surpassed those of their black native-born counterparts, within 10–15 years for the 1960 entry cohort and within both 0–5 and 10–15 years for the 1970 entry cohort.

We also found that income inequality has been higher among the foreign-born population than the native-born population and has increased more than that in the native-born population between 1960 and 1980. However, the income inequality of a foreign-born entry cohort appears to decline with time in the United States, such that in the 1970–1980 period the share of the income earned by the bottom fifth of the 1970 recent-entrant population exceeds that of the bottom fifth of the native-born population by 1980. Transfer income programs do not explain this change. On average, the foreign-born are less likely to participate in governmental income assistance programs, although average transfer income levels increase and participation rates in such programs appear to rise with length of stay in the United States. Only among the foreign-born from the Western Hemisphere, however, did use of such programs exceed that of the native-born.

Self-employment is more prevalent among the foreign-born than among the native-born on average. The incidence of self-employment among the 1960 and 1970 recent-entrant cohorts rose considerably faster within a decade than did that for the native-born over the same periods. Among the foreign-born, those from Asia and Europe are substantially more likely to receive income from self-employment than are those from the Western Hemisphere.

The comparison of entry cohorts of the foreign-born at different points in time does not permit a precise understanding of how well immigrants fare in the United States. This is principally because such data confound (1) differences in entry cohort "quality" and assimilation effects; (2) the progress of an individual over the life course with the compositional change of an aggregate cohort over time (emigration selectivity); and (3) legal immigrants and the larger set of foreign-born, which may include, differentially by origin country, legal non-immigrants and illegal aliens whose constraints in terms of economic activities may be quite different.

We attempted to obtain a clearer picture of assimilation by empirically investigating the occupational attainment of the two distinct yet overlapping groups: legal immigrants and the foreign-born. Because our INS legal-immigrant sample permits estimation of the effects on occupational attainment of two types of U.S. experience—experience before and after the achievement of permanent resident status—and of the selectivity associated with naturalization on the occupational attainment of permanent resident aliens, we were able to quantify some of the major sources of changes in the economic behavior of the foreign-born documented in census-type data. Our results suggest that because of the selective emigration of higher-occupation immigrants and the significantly lower returns to pre-immigration U.S. experience, the observed changes in the average occupational attainment of a foreign-born entry cohort may significantly understate the returns to the U.S. experience of *immigrants* and significantly understate the higher occupational upward mobility of both Asian and non-Cuban Hispanic immigrants relative to other immigrant groups.[13]

With respect to the well-documented empirical association between a foreign-born person's earnings in the United States and his or her country of origin, our results strongly suggest that the specific social, economic, geographic, and political features of origin countries, which importantly affect migration and re-migration decisions, underlie most of the observed differentials in the U.S. earnings of immigrants from different countries. These results thus imply that changes in the earnings of foreign-born persons in the United States may depend more on changes in U.S. immigration policy than on changes in the U.S. labor market.

---

[13]Our results must be interpreted with caution; in order to circumvent some of the shortcomings of our data bases we had to impose some additional structure and make some as yet unverifiable assumptions. These included the assumption that the error structure characterizing propensities to earn and to naturalize is bivariate normal, that measurement error is not serious for occupation reported at immigration for those who immigrate without labor certification, that time to naturalization is not significantly affected by time-varying influences on occupational success, and that selectivity biases from emigration and non-naturalization are similar. In studying how well immigrants do, there is no perfect substitute for a data set which tracks the foreign-born from first entry to last emigration or to the end of life, whichever comes sooner.

8

ENGLISH LANGUAGE PROFICIENCY
AND THE LOCATIONAL CHOICES
OF IMMIGRANTS

I N THE DECADE 1971–1980, over 25 percent of new legal immigrants were from countries whose official or dominant language is English.[1] In that same period, however, over 32 percent of legal immigrants originated in countries whose official or dominant language is Spanish.[2]

[1]Although the United States does not have an *official* language, English was the language of its birth and its development and is today the dominant native language of its population. For example, according to the U.S. Census of 1980, only 0.3 and 0.4 percent of the enumerated adult males and females, respectively, could not speak English. The set of foreign countries for which English is an official or dominant language is constructed, as discussed in the Introduction, from the *Atlas of United States Foreign Relations*, supplemented by the *Encyclopaedia Britannica*. The 25 percent figure is compiled from INS (1985, Table IMM 1.2) and includes (1) the United Kingdom, Ireland, and Canada; (2) India, Pakistan, the Philippines, and Hong Kong; (3) Australia and New Zealand; (4) all of the Caribbean countries except Cuba, the Dominican Republic, and Haiti; (5) Guyana; and (6) the U.S.-administered Pacific Islands. This figure may be an underestimate, as it does not include immigrants from those English-language countries which are not separately identified in the published INS tabulations. This latter set includes all the English-language countries of Africa, as well as other English-language countries around the world, such as Malta, Malaysia, Bangladesh, Brunei, Belize, and Suriname. On the other hand, the 25 percent figure includes immigrants from countries with more than one official or dominant language, such as Canada, India, and the Philippines.

[2]This figure, again compiled from INS (1985, Table IMM 1.2), includes immigrants from (1) Spain; (2) Mexico; (3) all of Central America; (4) Cuba and the Dominican Republic, from among the Caribbean countries; and (5) all of South America except Brazil and Guyana. It thus may be a slight overestimate, as it includes the non-Spanish-language countries of Belize (in Central America) and French Guiana and Suriname (in South America), which could not be identified separately in the published tabulations.

The dominance of the Spanish language among recent immigrants has led to fears that, at least in certain parts of the United States, English could be displaced by Spanish as the local language. This possibility has raised concerns about the appropriate methods of teaching English in schools and has led to suggestions that English language skills become a criterion for immigration.

The dominance of a single foreign language among new immigrants, however, is not new. In the late eighteenth and the nineteenth centuries, German was the dominant language among immigrants. Between 1891 and 1900, for example, only 18 percent of the new legal immigrants were from English-language countries, while approximately 14 percent were from Germany and another 16 percent were from what was then Austria-Hungary, whose official language was German, for a total of almost 30 percent. Figure 8.1 depicts the number of immigrants from German-language countries for 1891–1900, Spanish-language countries for 1971–1980, and English-language and other-language countries for both periods. The dominance of German over English appears stronger in the 1891–1900 decade than the dominance of Spanish over English in the 1971–1980 decade.

Of course, because a common language, like a common currency, facilitates exchange, the possibility of language bifurcation becomes more likely if the individuals whose native tongue is not English enter into transactions with each other rather than with individuals who speak English. The settlement patterns of the common-language groups, to the extent that proximity is related to the number of "own"-language transactions, thus may be an important factor in determining the potential for the viability of a second language in the United States. It follows that the process of English-language acquisition may be importantly linked to the choice of a residential location by immigrants.

The extent to which non-English languages persist as common tongues in the United States depends as well on the acquisition of English-language skills by the *children* of immigrants. Accordingly, attention must also be paid to the process by which they acquire English-language skills, in particular to the differential influence of the home and the community environments.

In this chapter we assess the prospects for the growth of non-English-speaking populations in the United States by examining the English-language skills and locational choices of the major foreign-language groups in the United States in both 1900 and 1980. Among the questions we examine are: How do the English-language proficiency and geographical concentration of the Spanish-speaking foreign-born in 1980 compare with those of the German-speaking foreign-born in 1900? Do the spatial concentrations of non-English language groups influence the propensity of such groups to acquire English-language skills? Is the process of attaining English-language

FIGURE 8.1
*Language of the Country of Origin:
New Immigrants in 1891–1900 and 1971–1980*

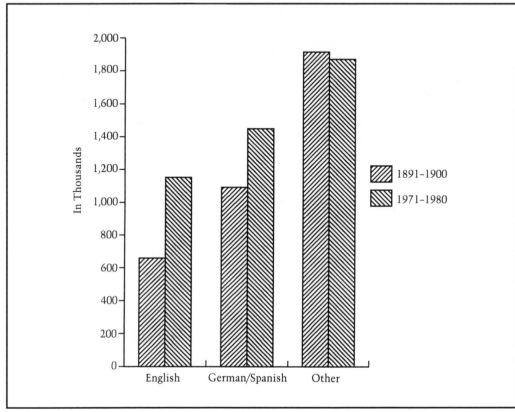

proficiency different in 1980 than in 1900? In particular, are the rewards to acquiring English language skills as high today as they were in the earlier period? Are the children of foreign-born parents more or less likely today to be proficient in English? Have the effects of the family environment on a child's English-language skills changed between 1900 and 1980?

First, we examine the English-language skills of current immigrants to the United States, the non-English native languages they bring with them, and the geographical concentration of Spanish-language immigrant groups, comparing these phenomena with their counterparts in 1900. Second, we investigate intensively the interrelationships among (1) the concentration of common-language groups across localities; (2) investments in English-language skills; and (3) the costs of and returns to English-language proficiency based on the censuses of 1900 and 1980, both of which provide information on English language proficiency. Third, we test for differences in the language and locational behavior of the two principal non-English-language groups of immigrants in 1900 and 1980 (German- and Spanish-speaking, respectively). Finally, we examine the determinants of the English-language proficiency of the children of immigrants with particular attention to the effects, in both 1900 and 1980, of the family and the community environment.

English-Language Skills in 1900 and 1980

The U.S. censuses of 1900 and 1980 enable direct examination of the English-language skills of the enumerated foreign-born population. As previously discussed, census data include other foreign-born besides legal immigrants but are restricted to those foreign-born who are in the United States at the time of the census. Table 8.1 compares the language-relevant characteristics of the 1980 and 1900 foreign-born populations aged 20–64.[3] As would be expected, the proportions who speak English are high. Among 1980 foreign-born, 25 percent of the men and 28 percent of the women speak only English at home. Another 30 percent of the men and 27 percent of the women speak English "very well" and a further 24 and 21 percent of men and women, respectively, speak it "well." If we assume that those who speak only English at home speak it at least "well," then almost 80 percent of the male and 76 percent of the female adult foreign-born speak English well.

A striking finding in Table 8.1 is that in 1900, when the proportion of the total population born outside the United States was over twice what it was in 1980,[4] a higher proportion of the adult foreign-born could not speak English, by a factor of almost two to one. The two dominant, non-English common-language groups represented a similar proportion of the total foreign-born population in 1900 and 1980: 29 percent of the foreign-born in 1900 came from German-language countries, and 29–32 percent of the foreign-born in 1980 came from Spanish-language countries. In both census years, the average age of the adult foreign-born populations and their aver-

---

[3]The information is based on the following questions. The 1900 census asks whether or not each person can speak English. In the 1980 census, question 13a asks, "Does this person speak a language other than English at home?" If the answer is yes, then two further questions are asked. Question 13b asks, "What is this language?" Question 13c asks, "How well does this person speak *English?*" and provides four response categories, "Very well," "Well," "Not well," and "Not at all."

[4]In 1900, the proportion foreign-born of the whole population was 13.61 percent (Series A73 and C228 in *Historical Statistics of the United States*). In 1980 the foreign-born constituted 6.22 percent of the population.

TABLE 8.1
Language Characteristics of Foreign-Born Populations
Aged 20–64, by Sex: Census Years 1980 and 1900

Characteristic	1980		1900	
	Men	Women	Men	Women
Percent from English-Language Countries	23.1	27.1	29.6	37.3
Percent from Dominant/Non-English Language Countries	31.6	29.1	29.3	29.4
Percent Speak Only English at Home	25.3	28.2	—	—
Percent Speak Other Language at Home	74.7	71.8	—	—
Percent Speak English Very Well	29.7	27.4	—	—
Percent Speak English Well	24.0	20.6	—	—
Percent Speak English Not Well	15.4	15.2	—	—
Percent Speak English Not at All	5.6	8.5	—	—
Percent Cannot Speak English	(5.6)	(8.5)	11.9	15.3
Mean Age	38.1	39.7	39.3	40.1
Mean Years in U.S.	14.7	16.3	18.7	19.9
Sample Size	2075	2295	2843	2178

NOTES:
1. The set of English-language countries includes countries for which English is an official or dominant language.
2. The prevalent common non-English language is German in 1900 and Spanish in 1980. The set of German-language countries includes Germany, Prussia, and Austria. The set of Spanish-language countries includes Spain, Mexico, all of Central America except Belize, only Cuba and the Dominican Republic from the Caribbean, and all of South America except Brazil, French Guiana Guyana, and Suriname.
3. The 1900 census asked for a binary response to the question, "Can this person speak English?" The 1980 census asked for a four-category response to a question on English-language skill that was asked only of persons who speak another language at home.

age duration in the United States are similar, so these factors do not account for the difference in English proficiency.

Notwithstanding the apparent linguistic dominance of German at the turn of the century and the fears then expressed about the German-speaking immigrants' unwillingness to relinquish their native language, or at least to add English to their linguistic repertoire, German did not displace English. On the other hand, some of the fears were not unfounded. Anecdotal evidence suggests that many children were raised not knowing a word of English.[5]

Table 8.2 provides a listing of the top ten origin countries of the foreign-born population aged 20–64 in 1900 and 1980, ranked by the proportion who could not speak English. In both periods, the listings are dominated for the most part by countries newly providing immigrants in those years—Southern and Eastern European immigrants in 1900 and Latin American immigrants in 1980. The foreign-born from such countries would therefore have spent fewer years in the United States on average than other foreign-born groups. Mexico, however, appears in the top three of countries whose emigrants in the United States cannot speak English in both the 1900 and 1980 census years, with the Mexican-origin foreign-born representing a much larger proportion of the total foreign-born population in 1980. Proximity to the United States may thus play a role in determining the returns to English-language investments, as it appears to do for naturalization (note the presence of French Canadians in the top-ten list for women in 1900).[6]

Table 8.3 reports the principal languages of the adult foreign-born who are unable to speak English in 1900 and 1980, by sex. There is a markedly more uniform distribution of languages across the non-English-speaking foreign-born in 1900. While German was the language of 19–29 percent of those unable to speak English in 1900, Spanish was the language of 75–79 percent of those unable to speak English in 1980.

Table 8.4 compares the characteristics in 1900 and 1980 of the foreign-born from German- and Spanish-language origin countries, respectively. While the proportions of the German-language foreign-born and Spanish-language foreign-born in the total foreign-born populations were approximately the same across the two census years, the Spanish-language foreign-born were almost 40 percent less likely to be able to speak any English in 1980 than the German-language foreign-born in 1900. As Table 8.4 suggests, however, this may be due in part to the higher proportion of recent entrants among the Spanish-language foreign-born: from 21 to 23 percent of the Spanish-language foreign-born had been in the United States less than five years in 1980 compared with less than 7 percent of the German-language foreign-born in 1900.

The most important difference between the two dominant non-English-language groups in 1900 and 1980 appears to be in the degree of geographical concentration of the two groups. Table 8.5 provides a listing of the top ten U.S. localities—urban areas with a population size of 25,000

---

[5]Consider, for example, the story of the Iowan Bill Zuber, who learned English in his first season as a professional baseball player (Yankees).

[6]French Canadians are not separately identified in the 1980 census.

TABLE 8.2

Top Ten Major Countries of Origin, by Percentage of Population
Unable to Speak English, Ages 20–64, by Sex: 1900 and 1980

	1900			1980	
Country	Percent Unable to Speak English	Percentage of Foreign-Born Population	Country	Percent Unable to Speak English	Percentage of Foreign-Born Population
			Men		
Japan	74.2	1.1	Guatemala	30.8	0.6
Mexico	70.4	1.0	Dominican Republic	26.7	1.4
China	49.1	2.0	Mexico	18.0	18.5
Poland-Austria	40.0	0.7	Portugal	13.3	1.4
Poland-Russia	34.0	1.8	Russia	10.0	1.0
Italy	37.0	5.6	El Salvador	7.1	0.7
Austria	36.5	3.7	Cuba	7.0	5.5
Finland	33.3	0.7	Taiwan	5.6	0.9
Hungary	33.3	1.8	Greece	5.1	1.9
Poland-Germany	30.3	1.2	Colombia	4.5	1.1
Foreign-Born population	12.0	100.0	Foreign-Born population	5.6	100.0
Total Population	1.7	—	Total Population	0.3	—
			Women		
Poland-Austria	84.6	0.6	Mexico	28.9	15.3
Mexico	83.3	0.8	Dominican Republic	22.6	1.4
Italy	62.3	3.5	Ecuador	22.2	0.8
Poland-Germany	47.8	1.1	Cuba	21.2	4.5
Austria	47.5	2.8	Portugal	20.0	1.1
Portugal	45.4	0.5	El Salvador	17.6	0.7
Bohemia	39.3	1.3	Hong Kong	15.4	0.6
Hungary	37.9	1.3	Greece	11.8	1.5
Netherlands	30.0	0.9	Russia	10.7	1.2
French Canada	27.8	3.6	China	10.5	2.5
Foreign-Born population	15.5	100.0	Foreign-Born population	8.5	100.0
Total Population	2.2	—	Total Population	0.4	—

or more in 1900 and county groups in 1980—ranked by the proportions of their total adult populations in 1900 and 1980 who were born in a German- or Spanish-language country. While the proportions in 1900 for the German-language foreign-born range from 5.6 to 11.5 percent in the top ten localities, the proportions of the Spanish-language foreign-born range from 22.8 percent (in Cameron County, Texas) to 69.4 percent (in Hialeah, Dade County, Florida). Moreover, while in 1900 eight states appear among the top ten localities ranked by common-language group concentration, inclusive of four in the Midwest, in 1980 only four states appear among the top ten, all but one of which is in the South or Southwest.

Table 8.5 also reports the top ten localities ranked by the proportion of

TABLE 8.3

Principal Languages of Foreign-Born Unable to Speak English, Ages 20–64, by Sex: 1900 and 1980

Men

Language of Country of Origin	1900			Language of Country of Origin	1980		
	Percentage of Population No English	Percentage of Foreign-Born Population	Percentage of Total Population		Percentage of Population No English	Percentage of Foreign-Born Population	Percentage of Total Population
German	19.8	2.4	0.3	Spanish	79.3	4.4	0.2
Italian	16.9	2.0	0.3	Portugese	3.5	0.2	—
Chinese	8.3	1.0	0.1	—	—	—	—
Japanese	6.8	0.8	0.1	—	—	—	—
French	4.7	0.6	0.1				

Women

Language of Country of Origin	1900			Language of Country of Origin	1980		
German	29.4	4.6	0.6	Spanish	75.0	6.4	0.3
Italian	14.4	2.2	0.3	Chinese	3.1	0.3	—
French	7.8	1.2	0.2	Portugese	2.6	0.2	—
Spanish	4.5	0.7	0.1	Italian	2.6	0.2	—
Japanese	2.1	0.3	—	—	—	—	—
Chinese	1.5	0.2	—	—	—	—	—

TABLE 8.4
Language Characteristics of Major Common Language Groups
in 1980 (Spanish) and 1900 (German):
Foreign-Born Aged 20–64

Characteristic	1980 (Spanish)		1900 (German)	
	Men	Women	Men	Women
Percent No English	13.8	21.2	8.1	15.9
Percent English Not Well	41.9	45.9	—	—
Mean Years in U.S.	14.7	16.3	20.7	20.0
Percent in U.S. Less Than 5 Years	22.7	20.8	6.8	6.3
Mean Age at Entry	23.4	23.8	20.2	19.1

the non-English-speaking populations in those localities. While the proportions are similar in the two census years—ranging from 26.5 percent (Milwaukee, Wisconsin) to 41.7 percent (Portland, Oregon) in the top ten 1900 communities and from 26.4 percent (Fresno, California) to 38.9 percent (Hidalgo County, Texas) in the top ten 1980 communities—only three states are represented in the top ten localities in 1980—Texas, California, New Mexico—while eight states are found among the top ten localities in 1900. Both the communities with high proportions of the dominant non-English common-language group and the communities with high concentrations of the foreign-born unable to speak English were geographically dispersed in 1900; both types of communities are predominantly in southern border or coastal states in 1980.

Investments in and Returns to English-Language Skills

English-Language Skills and Economic Status

That English-language proficiency and choice of residential location by immigrants are linked in an important way rests on the assumption that the frequency of transactions in the immigrant's own language differs across localities. To test this hypothesis, we employ census samples of Spanish-language origin-country foreign-born males aged 20–64 in 1980 and German-language origin-country foreign-born males aged 20–64 in 1900 to estimate the labor market returns to speaking English.[7] While the 1980

[7]The sample of Spanish-language foreign-born males is extracted from a 2.5 percent random sample of all households in the United States in 1980 and includes all foreign-born males from South America, excluding Brazil and French Guiana, from Central America excluding Belize, and from Spain. Of course, the sample excludes persons born in Puerto Rico, who

census provides information on earnings, occupation, and schooling attainment, the 1900 census provides information only on an immigrant's occupation and a "prestige" index based on occupational attainment. Accordingly, we estimate the determinants of the (log of) wages (hourly) from the 1980 sample and the determinants of the (log of) the occupational-prestige index from the 1900 sample. For comparability across censuses, we use the dichotomous indicator of English-language proficiency: whether or not the individual speaks English. We expect that those foreign-born men without the ability to speak English would earn significantly less or would have lower socioeconomic status than those who have acquired such a skill, but this differential should be smaller in local areas where there is a higher proportion of persons in the population speaking the same (non-English) language.

To define the local area we use, for 1980, the county group and, for 1900, urban areas with 25,000 or more persons, the smallest available identifiable geographical grouping in each census sample. For each of these areas, we obtained the proportion of the population born in countries where either Spanish (1980) or German (1900) was the predominant language. Table 8.5 provides the top ten areas ranked by these proportions for both census years.

Also included among the determinants of the log of the hourly wage for 1980 are the number of years since the person completed his schooling, as a proxy for labor market experience, and its square, schooling attainment, and years in the United States and its square. Because schooling attainment is not available for 1900, we cannot use this variable or compute years of post-school experience. Age and its square are employed instead of the experience variables. For comparability, a similar specification is also estimated from the 1980 sample.

Table 8.6 reports the least-squares estimates of the determinants of the log wage and log occupational-prestige index. The results across the census samples are similar: lack of English-language skill reduces significantly the hourly wage in 1980 and the index of occupational prestige in 1900. The male foreign-born in these language groups who cannot speak English have a 23 percent lower wage (1980) and a 36 percent lower index of occupational prestige (1900). In both years, however, the presence of greater numbers of persons in the local area who speak the immigrant's own language reduces the impact of English-language deficiency; the English-language skill coefficient and that for its interaction with own-language group concentration are individually and jointly statistically significant at the .01 level for

are considered native-born U.S. citizens and for whom there is no information on length of stay or time of entry in the 50 States. The sample of German-language foreign-born males is extracted from the 1-in-250 1900 Public Use Sample and includes all males born in Germany, Prussia, and Austria.

TABLE 8.5

Top Ten Locations, by Proportion of Population
Composed of Largest Foreign-Born Common Language Group
and by Proportion Unable to Speak English in 1900 (German) and 1980 (Spanish)

Percent Foreign-Born Common Language Group in Total Population			Percent Unable to Speak English in Foreign-Born Population		
			1900		
State	Locality[a]	Percent	State	Locality[b]	Percent
Michigan	Bay City	11.5	Oregon	Portland	41.7
Utah	Salt Lake City	9.1	Mass.	New Bedford	40.0
New Jersey	Bayonne	7.3	Michigan	Grand Rapids	35.7
Mass.	Fitchburg	7.0	New Jersey	Newark	34.4
Ohio	Canton	6.8	Ohio	Dayton	33.3
Iowa	Cedar Rapids	6.7	Mass.	Holyoke	33.3
New Jersey	Atlantic City	5.9	Hawaii	Honolulu	30.0
Iowa	Council Bluffs	5.9	Mass.	Fall River	29.4
Nebraska	South Omaha	5.9	Penn.	Allegeny	27.2
Conn.	New Britain	5.6	Wisconsin	Milwaukee	26.5
			1980		
State	Locality[a]	Percent	State	Locality	Percent
Florida	Hialeah City (Dade County)	69.4	Texas	Hidalgo	38.9
Florida	Miami (Dade)	51.7	Texas	Webb	29.9
Florida	Olympia Hts, Sweetwater	41.0	Texas	Cameron	29.3
Texas	Hidalgo	32.6	California	Oxnard	68.4
New Jersey	Lowell (Middlesex)	30.4	Texas	Valverde	28.0
Texas	El Paso	27.7	Texas	McAllen, Edinburgh (Hidalgo)	27.8
Texas	Webb, Zapata, Jim Hogg	25.7	California	Pinellas	27.1
California	Oxnard	23.5	New Mexico	Sierra, Socoro	27.1
Texas	Valverde	23.4	Texas	Harrison, Gregg	26.5
Texas	Cameron	22.8	California	Fresno	26.4

[a]For 1900, locations are urban areas with a population size of 25,000 or more. For 1980, locations are county groups as defined in the 1980 census.
[b]For 1900, locations with less than 6 foreign-born in the public use sample were excluded. States in the top 10 excluded by this criteria are Pennsylvania, Wisconsin, Illinois, and Oregon.

1980 and jointly statistically significant at the .05 level ($F(2, 765) = 5.67$) for 1900.

The point estimates indicate that in 1980 those Spanish-language for-

TABLE 8.6
Effects of Inability to Speak English on Economic Status of Men:
Major Language Groups in 1980 and 1900

	1980 Hispanic			1900 German	
	Log of Hourly Wage			Log of Occupational Prestige Index	
	(1)	(2)	(3)	(1)	(2)
Age	—	—	.0492	.0240	.0235
			(7.78)	(1.38)	(1.35)
Age Squared (×10⁻³)	—	—	-.549	-3.27	-3.17
			(6.88)	(1.55)	(1.53)
Experience	.0278	.0280	—	—	—
	(9.19)[a]	(9.25)			
Experience Squared (×10⁻³)	-.413	-.418	—	—	—
	(7.00)	(7.08)			
Years in U.S.	.0330	.0328	.0348	.0300	.0299
	(9.25)	(9.18)	(9.52)	(3.28)	(3.26)
Years in U.S. Squared (×10⁻³)	-.570	-.564	-.584	-.307	-.310
	(6.15)	(6.08)	(6.13)	(1.79)	(1.81)
Schooling Attainment	.0407	.0407	—	—	—
	(15.0)	(15.0)			
No English	-.098	-.163	-.297	-.363	-.436
	(3.09)	(3.89)	(7.18)	(3.19)	(3.32)
No English × Proportion of Local Population Speaking Same Language	—	.497	.466	—	7.14
		(2.37)	(2.19)		(1.09)
Proportion of Local Population Speaking Same Language	-.297	-.375	-.305	-3.48	-4.16
	(3.81)	(4.44)	(3.55)	(1.31)	(1.52)
Constant	.708	.718	.429	2.13	2.15
	(14.4)	(14.5)	(3.73)	(6.17)	(6.23)
R²	.116	.117	.088	.131	.132
F	96.3	85.0	70.7	16.4	14.5
Sample Size	5137	5137	5137	771	771

[a]Absolute values of t-ratio in parentheses.

eign-born men residing in a local area with substantial Spanish-language concentrations (concentrations of approximately 33 percent in the column 2 estimates and 64 percent in the column 3 estimates) suffer no penalty for not knowing English. (Table 8.5 indicates that Dade County in Florida has a concentration of Spanish-language persons at this level.) The results also suggest that the Spanish(German)-language foreign-born receive lower wages (prestige) net of the effects of their English proficiency when they reside in areas characterized by a greater prevalence of Spanish(German)-language persons. This suggests that Spanish(German)-language immigrants prefer (preferred), net of the incentives associated with the returns to English-language proficiency, to reside in areas with higher proportions of own-language residents since they are evidently willing to pay, in the form of lower wages, for this proximity to their common-language residents.[8]

Finally, the set of coefficients associated with years in the United States is jointly statistically significant in all specifications for both periods.[9] These results suggest that for the major language groups in 1900 and 1980, earnings growth associated with years in the United States is not due solely to the accumulation of English-language skills, which grow as time in the United States increases, as we shall see below.

Determinants of English-Language Skills

In this section we investigate the effects of age at entry in the United States and length of residency on English-language proficiency. By estimating these effects, we can also ascertain whether the propensity to learn English among the major common-language groups in 1900 and 1980 differs from that among the other foreign-born during those time periods, net of the effects of entry age and time in the United States.

As noted above, the measure of English-language skill provided by the 1900 census is dichotomous, while that provided by the 1980 census is ordered in five categories.[10] To analyze both sets of data in a unified framework, we assume that the true but unobserved (latent) English-language skill level is characterized by a normal distribution. We thus specify a maximum-likelihood binary-probit model for the 1900 data and a maximum-likelihood ordered-probit model for the 1980 data. Both procedures permit estimation of the relationship between English-language proficiency and the characteristics of the foreign-born, exploiting all of the available information.

[8]To assess the bias, if any, in the English-language proficiency coefficient arising from the omission of ability, we also selected a sample of *all* foreign-born males and estimated the wage equation using two-stage least squares. A variable indicating whether or not the immigrant was born in a country where English was an official/dominant language and that variable interacted with age at entry and years in the United States were used as identifying instruments. The results suggest that use of least squares, as in Table 8.6, results in an underestimate of the negative effect of lack of English-language skill on hourly earnings, by about 20 percent. This bias indicates again that the foreign-born choose locations not just to minimize the costs of deficiencies in English-language skills.

[9]Use of the five-category measure available in the 1980 census, instead of the dichotomy employed in Table 8.6, does not alter the effects of the U.S. residence variables on hourly earnings. Of course, the U.S. residence variables may also reflect immigrant cohort effects and the influence of selective re-migration.

[10]More precisely, the 1980 census provides a four-category ordinal measure of English-language skill, for only those persons who use another language at home. If we assume that individuals who speak only English at home speak it at least as well as those who report that they speak it *very well*, then the information in the 1980 census may be used to construct a five-category ordinal index.

TABLE 8.7

Maximum Likelihood Probit Estimates:
Determinants of Inability to Speak English, by Sex,
Foreign-Born Population Aged 20–64 in 1900

Characteristic	Men	Women
Age at Entry	.0689	.0397
	(3.93)[a]	(2.90)
Age at Entry Squared ($\times 10^{-3}$)	−.616	−.00872
	(2.07)	(0.04)
Years in U.S.	−.111	−.0762
	(10.67)	(7.25)
Years in U.S. Squared ($\times 10^{-3}$)	.183	.126
	(6.99)	(5.51)
English-Speaking Origin Country	−1.14	−1.54
	(7.69)	(10.36)
German-Speaking Origin Country	−4.27	−2.50
	(4.77)	(2.86)
Distance of Origin Country ($\times 10^{-3}$)	.110	.0778
	(4.58)	(2.31)
Constant	−1.56	−1.07
	(5.62)	(4.23)
−ln likelihood	691.5	655.7
Sample Size	2824	2167

[a]Asymptotic t-values in parentheses.

English-language proficiency will depend on the characteristics of both the individual and the origin country, which influence who immigrates. We examine the effects of the language of the home country, represented by two binary variables for whether or not English and German (1900) or Spanish (1980) are an official/dominant language, its distance, and, for the 1980 sample, its per-capita Gross National Product and literacy rate, as well as whether or not its economy is centrally planned.

Table 8.7 reports the estimates of the determinants of English-language proficiency among the foreign-born aged 20–64 in 1900, separately for men and women; Table 8.8 reports the corresponding estimates for 1980. The estimates from both census samples, describing populations separated by 80 years, are remarkably similar (rigorous tests of structural differences are postponed to the next section). All sets of estimates indicate that those foreign-born entering at older ages are less likely to have attained proficiency in English, given their length of stay, while, for given age at entry, those foreign-born with more years in the United States are significantly more proficient in English.

One striking difference across the 80-year period is that while the

TABLE 8.8

Maximum Likelihood Ordered Probit Estimates:
Determinants of English Language Difficulties, by Sex,
Foreign-Born Population Aged 20–64 in 1980

Characteristic	Men		Women	
	(1)	(2)	(3)	(4)
Age at Entry	.0352	.0653	.0456	.0383
	(4.39)[a]	(3.11)	(6.39)	(5.36)
Age at Entry Squared ($\times 10^{-3}$)	−1.165	−.0676	−.336	−.334
	(1.16)	(0.46)	(2.85)	(2.79)
Years in U.S.	−0.468	−0.504	−0.524	−.0591
	(6.02)	(6.43)	(6.75)	(7.52)
Years in U.S. Squared ($\times 10^{-3}$)	.603	.522	.797	.825
	(3.29)	(2.80)	(4.38)	(4.47)
English-Speaking Origin Country	−1.17	−1.01	−1.53	−1.39
	(17.3)	(14.8)	(22.1)	(20.0)
Spanish-Speaking Origin Country	.643	.764	.296	.260
	(6.02)	(7.18)	(3.35)	(2.89)
School Attainment	—	—	−1.00	−.0987
	—	(16.7)	—	(16.9)
Centrally Planned Origin Country	−.0747	.0627	−.112	.0119
	(0.88)	(0.73)	(1.23)	(0.13)
GNP (1978) in Origin Country ($\times 10^{-4}$)	−.666	−.405	−1.24	−1.04
	(4.52)	(2.77)	(9.75)	(8.21)
Distance of Origin Country ($\times 10^{-4}$)	.0712	.777	.0047	.286
	(0.49)	(5.11)	(0.04)	(2.58)
Literacy Rate in Origin Country ($\times 10^{-3}$)	−9.71	−2.38	1.75	.938
	(0.51)	(0.13)	(0.93)	(0.50)
Constant	1.11	2.13	1.30	2.78
	(4.94)	(9.36)	(6.34)	(12.9)
$\mu(1)$	1.18	1.25	1.18	1.24
	(27.0)	(27.8)	(28.0)	(28.5)
$\mu(2)$	2.12	2.30	2.04	2.19
	(38.7)	(40.0)	(40.2)	(41.1)
$\mu(3)$	3.14	3.47	2.92	3.19
	(43.3)	(44.0)	(46.2)	(47.0)
χ^2	1074.0	1322.4	1373.3	1610.6
Sample Size	1831	1831	2006	2006

[a]Asymptotic t-values in parentheses.

foreign-born from a German-language country in 1900 were more likely to be proficient in English than other foreign-born (other than those from English-language countries), in 1980 the foreign-born from a Spanish-language country are less likely than other foreign-born to be skilled in English. The average difference observed in Table 8.4 between the Spanish- and German-speaking foreign-born across census years is thus not entirely due to differences between the two groups in either average age at entry or years of residence in the United States.

The specifications reported in columns 2 and 4 of Table 8.8 include schooling attainment. The results with respect to age at entry or years in the United States are not substantially changed by the inclusion of the schooling variable. Those adult foreign-born with more schooling are, however, significantly more likely to be proficient in English.

We also tested whether for given duration in the United States and age at entry the female foreign-born were less likely to speak English well or at all than the male foreign-born, given that both in 1900 and 1980 women were less likely to participate in the labor market. Results (not shown) for both samples were consistent with this hypothesis, suggesting that the returns to English-language skills are higher in the labor market than in the nonmarket sector and that, again, the propensity of the foreign-born to invest in English-language skills depends on the returns to those skills.

The finding in Tables 8.7 and 8.8 that English-language proficiency increases with duration in the United States is subject to the alternative cohort interpretation—that successive entering cohorts were less likely to know English—and to the emigration-selectivity interpretation—that the tendency to emigrate is associated with inability to speak English. To directly examine the effect of time in the United States, but inclusive of emigration effects, we report in Table 8.9 the proportion who speak English, in 1900 and 1910, among those immigrants who report entering in the years 1895–1899 and who are aged 20–44 in 1900.[11] Because ability to speak English was not measured in the U.S. Census of 1970, no longitudinal cohort analysis is possible for more recent immigrants; such analysis must await the 1990 census. As shown in Table 8.9, for both men and women and in every five-year age group, the percentage who speak English increased across the decade. The increases were greater among men than among women for the group as a whole and for three of the five age groups; they ranged from 10.8 percentage points among women aged 40–44 to 36.9 percentage points among women aged 35–39. Although a higher proportion of women than men spoke English at entry—61 versus 55 percent—a decade later a higher proportion of men than women spoke English—79 versus 76 percent (Figure 8.2).

The results shown in Table 8.9 and Figure 8.2 rule out the strict cohort interpretation—that observed differences by duration in the United States solely reflect differences at entry—but are consistent with both an assimilationist interpretation and an emigration-selectivity interpretation. No doubt while some immigrants among those unable to speak English in 1900 learned to speak it by 1910, others among them emigrated. To the extent that men are more likely to emigrate than women, the higher percentage

---

[11]The 1910 census asked whether each person was "able to speak English," thus obtaining a dichotomous measure.

TABLE 8.9
1900–1910 Decadal Cohort Change in Percent Who Speak English,
Among 1895–1899 Entry Cohort, by Sex and Age

Age in 1900	Men		Women	
	1900	1910	1900	1910
20–24	63.8	85.1	64.7	80.6
25–29	57.2	85.1	68.1	76.5
30–34	52.2	71.0	52.6	73.8
35–39	46.2	62.0	35.1	72.0
40–44	44.2	75.6	52.2	63.0
20–44	55.3	79.4	60.7	76.4
Sample Size	546	636	417	441

SOURCE: U.S. Census of Population, Public Use Samples.

increases in knowledge of English observed among men lend credence to the emigration hypothesis. Thus, a prudent interpretation of Table 8.9 would note the possible operation of both mechanisms: learning English and leaving the United States (by those with lesser English-language skills).

English-Language Skills and Labor Force Participation

The finding that the female foreign-born are less likely to be proficient in English than the male foreign-born is, as noted, consistent with the hypothesis that market transactions have higher returns to English-language skills than do nonmarket transactions. If so, those who have less proficiency in English should be less likely to participate in the market sector. We can test this hypothesis directly by ascertaining if among the female foreign-born of labor force age, those with no English-language skills are less likely to be employed in the labor market or to be looking for work in that sector.

Since ability or other unmeasured variables may influence both the decision to work in the market sector and the decision to acquire English-language skills, we use an instrumental-variables procedure. Both the measure of language proficiency and the dependent variable, employment in the labor force, are dichotomous variables; hence we employ a two-stage probit model (Mallar 1977), treating each variable as an indicator of an underlying latent variable. The identifying variables, influencing English-language skill but not labor force participation net of English-language skill, are those describing the language of the immigrant's origin country and age at entry.

Table 8.10 reports the two-stage probit estimates for both 1980 and

FIGURE 8.2

*1900–1910 Decadal Cohort Change in Percent Who Speak English
Among Immigrants, Aged 20–44 Years in 1900, Who Entered in 1895–1899*

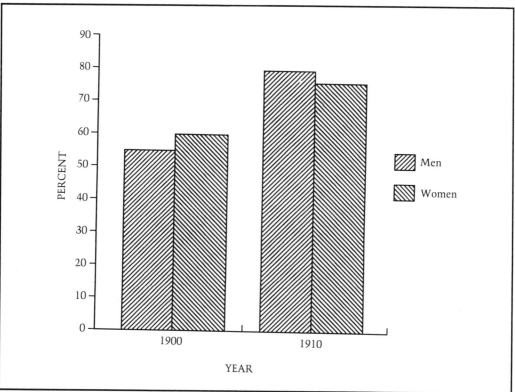

1900. Again, the results across censuses, taken 80 years apart, are similar—in both 1980 and 1900, foreign-born women, net of the effects of age and years in the United States, are significantly less likely to participate in the labor market if they cannot speak English.

Differences in Language and Locational Behavior in 1900 and 1980

The preceding empirical results provided support for two hypotheses. First, in terms of the frequency of transactions in an immigrant's own language, location does influence the returns to investments in English in both 1900 and 1980 for the major non-English common-language groups in those periods. Second, those foreign-born who spend less of their time in an

TABLE 8.10
Maximum Likelihood Two-Stage Probit Estimates:
Effects of Inability to Speak English on Labor Force Participation
Among Foreign-Born Women Aged 20–64 in 1900 and 1980

Characteristic	1980		1900
	(1)	(2)	
Age	.0878	.0897	−.0755
	(5.01)[a]	(5.01)	(3.95)
Age Squared	−.00104	−.00105	−.000878
	(4.96)	(4.98)	(3.69)
Years in U.S.	.00045	−.00438	−.0938
	(0.04)	(0.32)	(8.02)
Year in U.S. Squared	−.000326	−.000278	.00127
	(1.51)	(1.19)	(6.73)
No English[b]	−.209	−.255	−.399
	(4.74)	(2.67)	(6.63)
Hispanic (1980) or	−.0505	−.00628	−.316
German (1900)	(0.45)	(0.05)	(0.38)
Distance from Origin Country (×10⁻⁴)	—.297	−.278	.568
	(2.06)	(1.88)	(1.94)
GNP of Origin Country (×10⁻⁴)	−.386	−.387	—
	(3.17)	(3.18)	
Schooling Attainment	—	−.00815	—
		(0.54)	
Constant	−1.51	−1.51	.942
	(4.20)	(4.25)	(2.53)
−ln likelihood	1335.1	1334.9	983.1
Sample Size	2006	2006	2155

[a]Asymptotic t-ratios in parentheses.
[b]Endogenous variable.

environment where English-language skills reap returns—because they enter the United States at a later age or because of lower participation rates in the market sector within the United States—are less likely to augment their proficiency in English. These findings together suggest that the foreign-born with fewer English-language skills will prefer to locate in communities where there are higher proportions of persons speaking their language. However, there may be differences in the locational and language-investment behavior between the German-speaking foreign-born in 1900 and the Spanish-speaking foreign-born in 1980.

Table 8.11 presents the average percentage population shares of German-language (1900) and Spanish-language (1980) residents in the communities of residence of the German-language and Spanish-language foreign-born in 1900 and 1980, respectively, stratified by their ability to speak English and by sex. In both census periods, those less able (or unable) to speak English do reside in communities with a higher proportion of persons from countries with the same national language. However, the association in 1980 is stronger; indeed, the hypothesis that there is no association between English-language proficiency and location can be rejected only at the 1 percent level for the Spanish-language foreign-born in 1980. The relevant F-statistics are provided in the bottom row of Table 8.11.

Consideration of the returns to and costs of locational and language choices suggests why the locational clustering by language proficiency exhibited by the Spanish-language foreign-born in 1980 is stronger than that evident among the German-language population in 1900. As indicated in Table 8.5, the concentrations of the Spanish-language foreign-born among localities in 1980 are far greater than those for the German-language foreign-born in 1900. As a consequence, if we regard for the moment the locational distributions of the foreign-born as given, the returns to choosing a "concentrated" locality for a new, Spanish-language immigrant in 1980 were much higher than those for a German-language immigrant in 1900. If we assume, for additional simplicity, that local own-language concentration has the same effect on the returns to English-language proficiency in both 1900 and 1980, we see from Tables 8.5 and 8.6 that a German-language immigrant can reduce the impact of his English-language deficiency by at most 18.6 percent (by moving to Bay City, Michigan, where the proportion of German-speaking residents is 0.12); while the Spanish-language immigrant can almost completely eliminate the effects of lack of English-language proficiency (e.g., by locating in Dade County, Florida, where the proportion of Spanish-speaking residents lies in the range 0.52 to 0.69).

TABLE 8.11
Average Percentage of Population with Same Native Language
in Localities of German-Speaking (1900) and Spanish-Speaking (1980)
Foreign-Born Aged 20–64, by their English Language Ability

English Ability	1900[a]		1980	
	Men	Women	Men	Women
None	2.5	2.0	13.9	11.0
Not Well	—	—	14.8	10.4
Well	—	—	11.1	9.6
Very Well	—	—	11.2	9.9
Only English	2.1	1.7	5.6	7.0
Sample Size	413	344	664	546
F	1.50	1.38	4.53	4.40

[a]Localities with 25,000 or more.

Moreover, the communities in which concentrations are high in 1980 are also those communities located for the most part close to where the Spanish-language foreign-born enter the United States (Florida, Texas, California). Costs of moving to such communities are lower for the Spanish-language immigrants in 1980 than for the German-language immigrants in 1900, when such homogeneous language communities were substantially more dispersed.

There is another reason why Spanish-language immigrants would be less likely to invest in English and more likely to locate in concentrated communities. The proximity of the United States to the major sending countries of the Spanish-language foreign-born means that (1) costs of moving to the United States are relatively low, so that less "committed" immigrants are not screened out (*immigration selectivity*) and (2) costs of returning to the origin country are low (*emigration selectivity*). As a consequence, among immigrants with the same age at entry, those from Spanish-language (proximate) countries may expect to spend less time in the United States on average. They have fewer incentives therefore to make investments in English or to locate in communities far from ports of entry. The higher emigration and lower naturalization rates characterizing immigrants from countries located near the United States (Jasso and Rosenzweig 1982, 1986a) are consistent with these effects of proximity. Of course, the relative attractiveness of the origin country matters; for example, Cuban refugees may not expect (want) to return to Cuba and thus may be more willing to invest in English-language skills.

We can test whether those foreign-born who entered the United States at older ages, for given years in the United States, and who are from countries located closer to the United States are both less likely to have invested in English-language skills and more likely to reside in areas with own-language groups, by estimating the determinants of both language proficiency and location. By controlling for age at entry and time in the United States, we can thus also ascertain whether the propensity to learn English among the major common-language groups in 1900 and 1980 differs, net of the effects of entry age and time in the United States, and can test if there are differences in the language and locational behavior of the two common-language groups in 1900 and 1980.

Table 8.12 presents estimates of the determinants of (lack of) English-language proficiency and of location, the latter measured by the proportion of the local population with the same language as the sample person. Table 8.12 also reports the results of tests of the equality of coefficients based on a pooled sample of German-language and Spanish-language foreign-born males aged 20–64 in 1900 and 1980, respectively.[12] The estimates indicate that, first, individuals who enter the United States at a later age, for given years in the United States, are both less likely to be able to speak English and more likely to be located in communities where there are greater concentrations of own-language residents. Moreover, years in the United States reduce both the incidence of English-language deficiency *and* the likelihood of location in a concentrated community. Finally, among the foreign-born from Spanish-language countries, those from countries located nearer to the United States are both less likely to have acquired English-language skills and more likely to be located in communities with higher proportions of Spanish-language residents.[13]

The estimates in Table 8.12 also indicate that there are significant differences in the behavior of the two groups. In particular, the German-language foreign-born in 1900 were more likely to be able to speak English prior to coming to the United States and were less likely to locate in a more concentrated own-language community at entry (the intercept indicator for German-language is positive and statistically significant in the language equation and is negative and significant in the residence equation). More important, German-language foreign-born men were significantly more likely to achieve English-language proficiency as their residence in the United States lengthened than were Spanish-language foreign-born men in 1980.[14]

---

[12]To limit the size of the pooled sample and to have the 1900 and 1980 populations contribute approximately equal weights, a 10 percent random sample of the 1980 Spanish-language foreign-born males aged 20–64 from the 2.5 percent household sample extract was used.

[13]The results for English-skill acquisition are not sensitive to the use of only one English-skill category or the exclusion of schooling attainment (for comparability). In Appendix Table 8.A maximum-likelihood ordered-probit and binary-probit estimates of the determinants of English-language deficiencies among Spanish-language foreign-born males aged 20–64 from the 1980 2.5 percent household sample are presented. While the ordered-probit estimates make use of the five categories of skill levels available in the 1980 census survey, the binary probit uses the dichotomous indicator for not speaking English at all. Nonetheless, both the ordered- and binary-probit estimates yield similar results. All coefficients except that for Cuba are robust to the inclusion of schooling attainment, which appears to also contribute significantly to English-skill acquisition. Moreover, the distance coefficient is not sensitive to the inclusion of other variables characterizing the Spanish-language countries, such as per capita GNP and literacy rates.

[14]In the standard language classifications, modern English, German, and Low German belong to the West group of the Germanic branch of the Indo-European languages, along with (modern) Dutch, Flemish, Frisian, Afrikaans, and Yiddish. Spanish, in contrast, belongs to the Romance group of the Italic branch. Future research might investigate the role of native language in determining the ease with which English is learned. Interesting avenues are immediately suggested. For example, those Sephardic Jews who spent time in the Netherlands before migrating to the United States might be expected to learn English more easily than those Sephardic Jews who instead lived in Arab countries before migrating to the United States.

English-Language Proficiency
Among the Children of Immigrants:
Parental and Community Influences

In this section we assess how the characteristics of foreign-born parents, particularly their deficiencies in English, influence the English-language proficiency of their children. We also assess whether the association between the English-language skills of parents and those of their children changed between 1900 and 1980.

Table 8.13 reports the characteristics of the children and parents in sampled *households* in which the mother is aged 20–44 and foreign-born,

TABLE 8.12
Tests of Equality of Coefficients:
Determinants of Inability to Speak English
and to Reside in Locality with Same Language Group
Among Major Language Group Male Foreign-Born
Aged 20–64 in 1980 (Spanish) and 1900 (German)

Characteristic/ Estimation Procedure	No English		Proportion Same Language in Locality($\times 10^{-2}$)	
	Maximum Likelihood Probit	Maximum Likelihood Probit	Maximum Likelihood Tobit	Maximum Likelihood Tobit
Age at Entry	.0356	.0331	.0433	.0855
	(6.81)[a]	(4.82)	(1.76)	(3.21)
Years in U.S.	−.0454	−.0302	−0.226	−.0461
	(6.98)	(3.42)	(0.64)	(0.96)
Distance From Origin Country ($\times 10^{-3}$)	−.274	−2.79	−.755	−.757
	(3.20)	(3.24)	(2.08)	(2.08)
German (1900)	.829	1.02	−9.66	−7.92
	(2.56)	(2.14)	(6.79)	(2.97)
Age at Entry × German	—	.00630	—	—.0974
		(0.60)		(1.40)
Years in U.S. × German	—	−.0307	—	.0261
		(2.33)		(0.35)
Cuban	−.751	−.765	18.5	18.2
	(3.40)	(3.39)	(25.7)	(25.4)
Constant	−1.32	−1.39	8.24	7.58
	(7.72)	(6.40)	(7.84)	(6.42)
−ln likelihood	409.6	406.3	568.4	570.3
Sample Size	1495	1495	1495	1495
χ^2	—	6.6	—	3.8

[a]Asymptotic *t*-ratios in parentheses.

taken from the 1900 and 1980 census Public Use Samples.[15] These statistics indicate that while a much higher proportion of the children of foreign-born mothers were born outside the United States in 1980 than in 1900 (29 versus 10 percent), a higher proportion of the children were unable to speak English in 1900 than in 1980 (6 versus 3 percent).

Table 8.14 presents estimates of the determinants of the proportion of children who are unable to speak English in households in which the wife is foreign-born. The estimation procedure used, maximum-likelihood two-limit probit, takes into account the fact that the dependent variable—the proportion of children in the household unable to speak English or to speak English well—must lie between zero (no children unable to speak English) and one (all children unable to speak English), with concentrations at both of those bounds. Column 1 reports estimates from the 1900 household sample; columns 2–5 present estimates from the 1980 household sample, two specifications for each of two measures of children's average English-language skill. The first three independent variables listed in Table 8.14 control for differences in the age composition and nativity of children across households. The remaining variables characterize the English-language proficiency of the parents and whether or not the mother is German-language (1900) or Spanish-language (1980), and measure household

TABLE 8.13

Characteristics of Children Present in Households of Married, Spouse-Present Foreign-Born Women Aged 20–44: 1900 and 1980

Characteristic	1900	1980
Mean Age	12.0	8.97
Mean Maximum Age	16.6	11.0
Percent Foreign-Born	9.53	29.1
Percent No English	5.95	2.61
Percent Speak English Not Well	n.a.	8.15
Percent Mother No English Ability	13.8	8.23
Percent Mother Speaks English Not Well	n.a.	25.8
Percent Father No English Ability	5.95	4.45
Percent Father Speaks English Not Well	n.a.	18.2
Percent Mother German-Speaking (1900), Spanish-Speaking (1980)	35.4	31.5
Percent Father U.S. Born	15.6	35.1
Average Number of Children in Household	3.96	2.36

[15]The 1980 sample is based on a 10 percent random sample of all married, foreign-born, spouse-present women aged 20–44 in the 2.5 percent household extract. The 1900 sample is based on households with married, spouse-present foreign-born women aged 20–44 in the 1900 Public Use Sample.

TABLE 8.14

Maximum Likelihood Two-Limit Probit Estimates:
Determinants of English Language Ability of Children Present in Households
of Married, Spouse-Present Foreign-Born Women
Aged 20–64 in 1900 and 1980

	1900	1980			
Characteristic	No English	No English	No English	English Not Well	English Not Well
Mean Age of Children	−.0632 (3.61)[a]	−.0587 (1.26)	−.0630 (1.37)	−.0204 (0.78)	−.0185 (0.70)
Maximum Age of Children	−.0422 (1.76)	−.0840 (.04)	−.0813 (1.02)	−.0838 (2.42)	−.0843 (2.42)
Proportion Children Foreign-Born	.123 (0.46)	.837 (3.22)	.846 3.07)	.778 (5.09)	.774 (5.02)
Mother No English	.963 (6.38)	.631 (2.06)	.589 (1.88)	—	—
Mother Bad English	—	—	—	.674 (4.12)	.692 (4.21)
Father No English	.471 (2.61)	.824 (2.84)	.821 (2.81)	—	
Father Bad English	—	—	—	.854 (5.33)	.861 (5.35)
Mother German-Speaking (1900), Spanish-speaking (1980)	.0580 (0.44)	.591 (2.32)	.544 (1.98)	.150 (0.89)	.163 (0.94)
Proportion Local Population German-Speaking (1900) or Spanish-Speaking (1980) × German (1900), Spanish (1980)	−.141 (1.29)	1.24 (1.14)	1.28 (1.18)	1.35 (2.14)	1.35 (2.14)
Husband's Occupational Prestige (1900), Earnings (1980)	−.00957 (2.49)	−.252 (2.52)	−.234 (2.15)	−.0521 (1.01)	−.0572 (1.10)
Wife's Schooling	—	—	−.0158 (0.66)	—	.0071 (0.46)
Intercept	−.611 (3.19)	−1.91 (4.16)	−1.70 (3.35)	−1.72 (7.72)	−1.82 (5.85)

[a]Asymptotic t-ratio in parentheses.

resources—the occupational-prestige score of the husband for the 1900 sample and husband's earnings for the 1980 sample.

The results from both samples indicate that the household environment matters for the accumulation of English-language skills among children. In households where parents are deficient in their English-language skills, their children are also significantly more likely to be deficient, for given resources (and maternal schooling). In households with more resources, however, for given parental English-language skills, children are significantly less likely to be unable to speak English. The estimates also suggest that in 1900 children in households with German-speaking mothers were no more likely than children of other foreign-born mothers to be proficient in English; in 1980, however, the children of Spanish-speaking foreign-born mothers, given parental schooling, earnings, and English-language skills, were significantly less likely to be able to speak English than were the children of other foreign-born mothers.

These results thus suggest that the differential language-investment behavior exhibited by the adult Spanish-language foreign-born is transmitted to their children in three ways. First, because adult Spanish-language foreign-born men and women are less likely to be proficient in English than other foreign-born, their children will be less likely to be able to speak English, for given resources. Second, for given household resources and skills, investments in English-language skills among children are also evidently lower, most likely for the same reasons that the adult Spanish-language foreign-born invest less in acquiring English-language skills for themselves than do other foreign-born groups, as elaborated above. Finally, the lower English-language proficiency of the Spanish-language foreign-born compared with other foreign-born means that they will have lower family resources (earnings), thereby diminishing the likelihood of their children attaining English-language proficiency.

The effects of parental characteristics and resources on children's acquisition of English-language proficiency are mediated importantly by children's schooling and by the community environment. It has been hypothesized that the encouragement of English-language proficiency is less strong in contemporary schooling systems than it was in prior decades. If so, we would expect that the household and community environment would be more influential today in determining children's English-language skills than in the past. To test these hypotheses, we pooled the households containing German-language mothers in 1900 with those of Spanish-language mothers from the 1980 sample and reestimated the equations determining English-language proficiency among children, omitting the measures of household resources and parental schooling (which are not comparable across the censuses) but including the measure of own-language concentration in the local area in which each household resides.

The estimates from the pooled sample are reported in Table 8.15. They provide some support for the hypothesis that where there is a greater proportion of persons speaking the same (non-English) language in the local community, children speaking that language are less likely to be proficient in English, given parental English-language skill; the community environment also matters, although the coefficient is not highly significant statistically. The results also indicate that, net of the parents' ability to speak English, children of German-speaking, foreign-born parents in 1900 were less likely to be proficient in English than were children in households with

TABLE 8.15

Maximum Likelihood Two-Limit Probit Estimates:
Determinants of Children's Inability to Speak English
in German-Speaking (1900) and Spanish-Speaking (1980) Households

Characteristic	(1)	(2)	(3)
Mean Age of Children	−.184	−.178	−.182
	(2.82)[a]	(2.59)	(2.81)
Maximum Age of Children	.0579	.0539	.0567
	(1.27)	(1.13)	(1.25)
Proportion Children Born Abroad	.536	.560	.532
	(1.82)	(1.87)	(1.80)
Mother No English	.935	.722	.936
	(4.14)	(1.92)	(4.18)
Father No English	.427	.639	.449
	(1.54)	(1.70)	(1.63)
Proportion Local Population from	1.15	1.20	1.24
Own Country	(1.14)	(1.18)	(1.21)
Sample household from 1900	.482	.524	.595
(German)	(2.09)	(1.94)	(2.34)
Mother No English × 1900 Sample	—	.435	—
		(1.01)	
Father No English × 1900 Sample	—	−.473	—
		(0.86)	
Proportion Local Population from		−9.49	−9.90
Own Country × 1900 Sample		(1.05)	(1.07)
Constant	−1.57	−1.53	−1.58
	(5.00)	(4.64)	(5.02)
−ln likelihood	287.6	286.3	286.9
Number of Pooled Households	971	971	971
Number of 1900 Households	553	553	553
χ^2		2.60	1.4

[a]Asymptotic t-ratios in parentheses.

foreign-born Spanish-language mothers in 1980. Table 8.14 suggests that this differential could be due to differences in total resources between households in 1900 and 1980, but we cannot test this proposition rigorously. The estimates indicate that in households in which the mother is unable to speak English the children are twice as likely not to have learned English; when neither parent is able to speak English the children are three times as likely not to have learned to speak English.

In columns 2 and 3 of Table 8.15 we report tests of whether the influence on children's English-language proficiency of parents' inability to speak English or of the community concentration of potential own-language transactions is different in 1900 and 1980. The chi-square statistics associated with the likelihood-ratio test indicate that we cannot reject the hypothesis that parents' English-language skills and the community influence children's English-language proficiency in a similar way in both 1900 and 1980. Indeed, the results suggest that despite the higher incidence of English-language-skill deficiencies among the Hispanic households in 1980 than among the Germanic households in 1900 (21 versus 13 percent for the mothers; 11 versus 5 percent for fathers), the incidence of English-language deficiencies among children is almost identical in 1900 and 1980 for the modal non-English-language foreign-born: 5.4 percent in 1980 (Spanish) versus 5.0 percent in 1900 (German).

Of course, the child's own time in the United States matters as well. In particular, native-born children, with one or two foreign-born parents, are exposed from earliest years to the English language. Even in localities with high concentrations of non-English-speaking persons and even when neither parent speaks English, English reaches the young child via television, movies, and billboards. The young child hears English, even in non-English environments, in the conversations of doctors, teachers, and passers-by. It is striking that even in the years before television and movies, the overwhelming majority of the native-born children of foreign-born parents learned English: in 1910—the most recent census year for which microdata are available on both ability to speak English and parental nativity—94.4 percent of all native-born children aged 10–19 with at least one foreign-born parent spoke English; in the subgroup of children one of whose parents reported German as his/her mother tongue, 98.3 percent spoke English.[16]

Summary

In this chapter we used census data from 1900 and 1980 to compare the behavior of the major common-language groups of the foreign-born with respect to their English-language investment behavior and locational choices. We found that in both 1980 and 1900, when a far larger proportion of the U.S. population was foreign-born and did not speak English, higher economic rewards were associated with knowledge of English, and rewards to English-language proficiency and location were linked such that costs of lack of English-language proficiency were smaller in areas with greater concentration of persons speaking the same non-English native lan-

---

[16]Information on both ability to speak English and parental nativity was collected, for the last time, in the U.S. censuses of 1920 and 1930 (Shryock and Siegel 1975, pp. 21–22). Public Use Microdata Samples from these censuses are not available at this time.

guage. In part as a consequence, those foreign-born in 1900 and 1980 who expected to spend less time in the United States were less likely to acquire English-language skills and to move to locations with lower proportions of individuals speaking the same language. We also found that in both time periods the English-language proficiency of the children of immigrants appeared to be influenced in similar ways by the English-language skills of their parents, by their household resources, and by the community environment.

The similarity in the qualitative language-investment and location behavior of the foreign-born and in the structure of language and locational incentives within the United States in both 1900 and 1980 does not imply that there are no important differences between the time periods. Indeed, the spatial concentrations of persons speaking a common non-English language in 1980 are of far greater magnitude than they were in 1900. Our results suggest that this differential in residential patterns is due to the significantly closer proximity to the United States of the origin countries of the 1980 Spanish-language foreign-born, with such immigrants thus having lower incentives to invest in skills specific to the U.S. environment and for whom domestic U.S. distances represent a greater proportion of the total distance associated with immigration.

Regardless of the reasons for the present (1980) spatial concentrations (in border areas) of Spanish-language foreign-born, our results indicate that future Spanish-language immigrants will be more likely to reside in such communities and will be less likely to invest in English. Moreover, the Spanish-language foreign-born in 1980 are significantly less likely than German-language immigrants in 1900 to acquire English-language proficiency as their residence in the United States increases.

Since our findings suggest that the spatial clustering of the foreign-born from Spanish-language countries is not likely to change absent interventions that reduce spatial differentials in English-skill returns, the survival or growth of an alternative non-English-language population in the United States will depend on (1) the future number of Spanish-language immigrants, (2) their fertility, and (3) the acquisition of English-language skills by the children of these immigrants. With respect to the latter, our results suggest that the children of the Spanish-language foreign-born are no less likely to attain English-language proficiency, as of 1980, than the children of the German-language foreign-born in 1900. Moreover, the degree to which parental English-language deficiencies are transmitted to children, a function in large part of the school system, appears no stronger in 1980 than in 1900. Our results also suggest, however, that household resources, as well as parental English-language skills, matter in the acquisition of English-language proficiency by children. The progress of immigrants in the

APPENDIX TABLE 8.A
Maximum Likelihood Ordered Probit and Probit Estimates:
Determinants of English Deficiencies and Lack of English Ability
Among Foreign-Born Hispanic Men Aged 20–64

Estimation Procedure	Maximum Likelihood Ordered Probit		Maximum Likelihood Probit (No English)	
Variable	(1)	(2)	(1)	(2)
Age at Entry	.0509	.0340	.0351	.0112
	(10.5)[a]	(6.96)	(3.88)	(1.13)
Age at Entry Squared	−.0311	−.0144	−.00484	.0183
(×10⁻²)	(3.80)	(1.80)	(0.33)	(1.15)
Years in U.S.	−.0545	−.0568	−.0861	−.0971
	(11.2)	(11.4)	(10.9)	(11.5)
Years in U.S. Squared	.0830	.0796	.175	.188
(×10⁻²)	(6.61)	(6.17)	(8.12)	(8.09)
Schooling Attainment	—	−.116	—	−.122
		(34.3)		(19.1)
Distance (×10⁻³)	−.277	−.141	−.342	−.163
	(21.3)	(10.1)	(11.4)	(5.17)
Cuba	−.457	−.0544	−.438	.0346
	(9.30)	(1.04)	(5.53)	(0.39)
μ(1)	1.29	1.39	—	—
	(43.7)	(45.3)		
μ(2)	2.15	2.35	—	—
	(66.8)	(70.4)		
μ(3)	3.16	3.49	—	—
	(88.8)	(93.5)		
Constant	1.65	3.07	−1.12	.177
	(20.3)	(33.7)	(7.91)	(1.07)
−ln likelihood	7290.1	6794.5	1995.2	1733.6
Sample Size	5427	5427	5427	5427

[a] Asymptotic t-ratio in parentheses.

labor market and/or their access to income-transfer programs thus will importantly influence the persistence of an alternative common language in the United States.

9

FINDING REFUGE IN THE UNITED STATES

THE CLASSICAL view of immigration is that prospective migrants compare their own future well-being in the home country with that in another country, both forecasts conditioned by the information available to them. Subject to the laws on exit and entry, migrants make their choices to enter a particular country and, to improve their chances for success, pursue a particular route to immigration. Thus, a potential migrant may "shop" for a new country, much like a prospective tourist. Moreover, if dissatisfaction with the home country is strong, the migrant may apply for visas to several countries, subsequently going to whichever of the potential host countries grants the visa first.

Political and economic turmoil, however, may interfere with the classical processes, producing migrants who must flee at once, migrants whose way of life or, indeed, whose very lives are in danger. Before 1921—that is, before there were restrictions on the number of persons who could enter the United States—the migrant's reasons for coming to the United States were purely personal. Whether an émigré merely opposed a particular regime or was instead on a regime's execution list, whether an émigré wished to avoid military service or life as a peasant or death by starvation—those were private matters. From the perspective of the United States, all such diverse motivations blended to produce "immigrants."

The advent of numerical restrictions on immigration changed that. If immigration was to become a scarce good, then should not some rule favor applicants whose lives were in danger? The history of twentieth-century immigration policy in the United States is in large part a chronicle of discussions of such a rule, of legislation enacted and legislation not enacted, of refuge provided and refuge denied.

If refuge denied may be said to characterize events from 1921 through the end of World War II, then refuge provided may be said to characterize post–World War II U.S. immigration policy. The Presidential Directive of 22 December 1945 and special legislation beginning with the Displaced Persons Act of 1948 and culminating in the Refugee Act of 1980 (supplemented by the Cuban/Haitian Entrants Act of 1986) have made possible the settlement in the United States of large numbers of what have come to be called "refugees." Table 9.1 lists all the pertinent legislation, together with the total number of persons granted immigrant visas under the provisions of each piece of legislation (and of the Presidential Directive of 1945), through FY 1988. The total of immigrant visas granted under all the special refugee admissions programs from 1945 to the end of September 1988 is 2,323,612 (INS 1988, Table 37). This number, of course, reflects the continuing immigration restrictions. Consider, for example, that in the first decade of this century alone, over 8 million persons immigrated to the United States.[1]

Current U.S. law (Refugee Act of 1980) defines a "refugee" as

> any person who is outside any country of such person's nationality or, in the case of a person having no nationality, is outside any country in which such person last habitually resided, and who is unable or unwilling to return to, and is unable or unwilling to avail himself or herself of the protection of, that country because of persecution or a well-founded fear of persecution on account of race, religion, nationality, membership in a particular social group, or political opinion. . . .

To this basic definition are added several stipulations. First, in special circumstances the President may assign refugee status to persons residing in their country of nationality (or of habitual residence). Second, a person who satisfies the definition of "refugee" but who is inside the United States or at a U.S. port of entry is defined as an "asylee." Third, a person who otherwise appears inadmissible to the United States may be allowed to enter under emergency or humanitarian conditions and is designated a "parolee."

Under U.S. law, the refugee/asylee/parolee categories are temporary, transitional categories. A parolee must depart when the conditions supporting the parole cease to exist—or, if eligible, change to another visa category.

---

[1]Even if the figures in the official data series (U.S. Bureau of the Census 1975, Series C89-119; INS 1988, Tables 1 and 2) are reduced by the number of persons known to have previously entered the United States (Hutchinson 1958), the total number of new immigrants still exceeds 8 million.

TABLE 9.1
Refugees and Asylees Granted U.S. Permanent Residence: 1945–1988, by Enabling Administrative/Legislative Action and Principal Origin Countries to 1985

Administrative/Legislative Action	Total Number	Country of Birth	Number
Presidential Directive of 22 December 1945	40,324	Germany Poland	16,071 11,660
Displaced Persons Act of 25 June 1948	409,696	Poland Germany Latvia USSR Lithuania Yugoslavia	135,302 62,123 36,006 35,747 24,698 33,367
Orphan Act of 29 July 1953	466	Japan Austria	287 75
Refugee Relief Act of 7 August 1953	189,025	Italy Germany Yugoslavia Greece	57,026 20,922 17,425 16,922
Refugee-Escapee Act of 11 September 1957	29,462	Hungary Korea Yugoslavia	5,172 3,793 3,002
Hungarian Refugee Act of 25 July 1958	30,752	Hungary	29,905
Azores and Netherlands Refugee Act of 2 September 1958	22,213	Indonesia Netherlands Portugal	12,133 5,033 4,811
Refugee Relatives Act of 22 September 1959	1,820	Italy	953
Fair Share Refugee Act of 14 July 1960	19,799	Yugoslavia Romania	6,443 4,438
Refugee Conditional Entrants Act of 3 October 1965	142,103	Yugoslavia USSR China/Taiwan	22,973 20,159 15,047
Cuban Refugee Act of 2 November 1966	483,028	Cuba Spain	403,034 6,774
Indochinese Refugee Act of 28 October 1977	174,988	Vietnam Laos Cambodia	141,038 21,246 8,569
Refugee Parolee Act of 5 October 1978	138,495	Vietnam Laos U.S.S.R. Cambodia	51,666 35,293 24,966 7,893
Refugee Act of 17 March 1980	607,805	Vietnam Laos Cambodia U.S.S.R.	161,147 61,493 59,926 18,619
Cuban/Haitian Entrants Act of 6 November 1986	33,636	Haiti Cuba	—

NOTES and SOURCES: The figures for the total number of refugees represent the total number of immigrant visas granted from enactment of the legislation through the end of Fiscal Year 1988 (Table 37, INS *1988 Statistical Yearbook*). The figures for the principal countries represent, for all legislation through the Refugee Conditional Entrants Act of 1965, the totals through the end of Fiscal Year 1978 (Table 1, *Review of U.S. Refugee Resettlement Programs and Policies*, U.S. Congressional Research Service, 1980). The per-country totals for the remaining legislation represent the totals through FY 1985 and are compiled from INS *Statistical Yearbooks* (Table 6E for 1978 and 1979, Table 11 for 1980 and 1981, and Table REF 4.2 for 1982-1985); country-and-legislation-specific figures for 1986–1988 are not available in published sources.

Individuals admitted to the United States as refugees or asylees are eligible to become permanent resident aliens after a specified period of residency (e.g., under the Refugee Act of 1980, a period of one year). However, the time spent as a refugee or asylee may differ between the two categories, as asylees, unlike refugees, are subject to a numerical limitation of 5,000 adjustments to permanent residence per year (Refugee Act of 1980; INS 1988).

While refugees and asylees are not required to adjust to permanent resident status (INS 1986, p. xxi), the INS believes that 95 percent of refugees do adjust (U.S. General Accounting Office 1988b, pp. 5, 26, 113); and asylee adjustments have reached the 5,000 ceiling in each of the last five fiscal years (1984–1988). Thus, persons who at first are (legally and officially) refugees or asylees (and thus appear in the administrative records and published reports of the INS) subsequently become "immigrants" (and thus appear in the INS records and reports).

There is no easy correspondence between, on the one hand, the statutorily recognized status of "refugee" and its kindred legal statuses, "asylee" and "parolee," and, on the other hand, the social, economic, and behavioral conditions associated with the idea of "refugee." For example, two similar persons, both under execution orders, both escaping, may subsequently find themselves in the United States, one of them a "refugee" and the other an "immediate relative" (such as the father of a U.S. citizen who as a student had married an American and subsequently naturalized).

The two largest groups of foreign-born persons who in the vernacular of the 1980s are called "refugees" consist of persons from Cuba and from the three countries of Indochina. Many of them entered the United States in "refugee" status or in a "refugee"-like status, such as that of "parolee"; others entered with immigrant visas. The number of refugees in these groups may be calculated in several different ways: for example, by counting only persons born in the particular country or only persons admitted under a particular piece of legislation. As noted above, restricting attention to "refugee" visas may be deceptive, as persons who are behaviorally refugees may enter under the normal immigration provisions. Thus, the exact number of "refugees" in a particular group depends on the way in which the group is defined.

Table 9.2 summarizes the number of Cubans and Indochinese admitted to permanent resident status, calculated by defining the groups in three different ways (subject to data availability). The narrowest definition includes persons who were born in the specified country and who became permanent residents under provisions governing persons in refugee and refugee-like status. Under this definition, 486,426 Cubans became permanent residents between 1961 and 1988. During that same period, 111,436

TABLE 9.2
Number of Cuban and Indochinese Persons
Granted Permanent Residence in the United States: 1951–1988

Cohort	1951–1960	1961–1970	1971–1980	1981–1988	1961–1988
A. Cuban					
Refugees and asylees	6	131,557	251,514	103,355	486,426
Cuba last residence	78,948	208,536	264,863	125,619	599,018
Born in Cuba	26,885[a]	256,769	276,788	138,566	672,123
B. Cambodian					
Refugees and asylees	0	0	7,739	103,697	111,436
Cambodia last residence	na	na	na	na	
Born in Cambodia	na	na	8,426	105,316	113,742
C. Laotian					
Refugees and asylees	0	0	21,690	121,108	142,798
Laos last residence	na	na	na	na	
Born in Laos	na	na	22,566	122,744	145,310
D. Vietnamese					
Refugees and asylees	2	7	150,266	282,033	432,306
Vietnam last residence	335	4,340	172,820	252,853	430,013
Born in Vietnam	na	4,478[b]	179,681	314,888	499,047

NOTES and SOURCES: The figures for refugees and asylees represent persons born in the specified country and granted permanent residence under refugee/asylee provisions of U.S. immigration law (INS *1988 Statistical Yearbook*, Table 38). The figures for country of last residence (INS *1988 Statistical Yearbook*, Table 2) and for country of birth (compiled from INS *Annual Report*, 1958–1960 (Table 6), 1971 and 1977 (Table 14); INS *Statistical Yearbook*, 1980 (Table 13) and 1988 (Table 3)) represent persons admitted to permanent resident status under *all* provisions of U.S. immigration law.

[a]1958–1960. Earlier years not available.
[b]1962–1970. 1961 not available.

Cambodians, 142,798 Laotians, and 432,306 Vietnamese also became permanent residents in virtue of their refugee status.

Two broader definitions are used to define the groups in Table 9.2, one including all persons *residing* in the specified country and the other including all persons *born* in the country—regardless of the provisions of U.S. immigration law under which they attained U.S. permanent resident status. These definitions include persons who might be considered "refugees" in a social or behavioral sense but who were admitted to permanent resident status on an occupational visa or a kinship visa. Of course, the size of a group defined to include entrants under all immigration-law provisions would be greater than that restricted to refugee-status entrants. Moreover, the number of persons *born* in a country would be larger than the number last residing in it, as refugees may, upon fleeing, initially settle in countries not their first choice as a permanent destination.

As shown in Table 9.2, the number of persons born in each of the four countries and subsequently admitted to U.S. permanent residence indeed exceeds the corresponding number admitted with a refugee visa or residing in the given country prior to admission. For example, the number of persons born in Cuba and admitted to permanent residence between 1961 and 1988 is 672,123, compared with 486,426 admitted during the same period holding a refugee visa.

The difference in the group size according to the various definitions is itself interesting. For example, the proportion admitted to permanent residence under non-refugee provisions between 1961 and 1988, for given country of birth, is substantially greater among Cuban and Vietnamese refugees (28 and 13 percent, respectively) than among Cambodians and Laotians (2.0 and 1.7 percent, respectively). This difference across refugee groups represents the first hint that there may be important differences between them in contacts and involvement with the United States.

By the broader country-of-birth definition, the number of Cuban refugees in the United States who had been admitted to permanent residence by late 1988 exceeds 670,000 (depicted in Figure 9.1). The corresponding number for Vietnamese refugees is almost 500,000, while those for Laotians and Cambodians hover near 145,000 and 114,000, respectively. However, these numbers do not reflect recent refugee arrivals who had not yet adjusted to permanent resident status (for which they are eligible within one year).[2] As well, future growth is possible in both the Cuban and the Indochinese refugee populations.[3]

In this chapter we examine the four largest refugee groups—Cubans, Vietnamese, Cambodians, and Laotians. We look at their patterns of naturalization, schooling, employment, and geographic residence. We compare these patterns across refugee group, across entry cohorts within refugee group, and with those of non-refugee immigrants.

[2]For example, in FY 1988 the INS approved 22,120 applications of Vietnamese persons for refugee status; during that same period the arrival of 17,626 Vietnamese refugees was recorded (INS 1988, Tables 24 and 26). (Note, however, that the latter figure is obtained from a system which records all entries of persons with non-immigrant status and, therefore, may overstate the number of new refugee arrivals; see INS 1988, p. xxvii and Table 26.) For estimates of the time series of Indochinese refugee *arrivals*, see Gordon (1985).

[3]Three indicators of future growth are the number of refugee cases awaiting processing by the INS abroad, the number of asylum cases awaiting INS processing in the United States, and the number of visa applicants registered at U.S. consular offices abroad. For example, the number of applications for asylum filed by Cubans and pending at the end of FY 1988 was 13,873 (INS 1988). The number of Cubans eligible for and awaiting normal-flow immigrant visas, as of January 1989, was 17,982, while that for Vietnam was 121,884, of whom 90,997 were registered in the fifth-preference (siblings) category (U.S. Department of State). In contrast, the number of visa applicants under the normal immigration provisions from Cambodia and Laos were 3,520 and 1,544, respectively. This difference may reflect, in part, agreements between the United States and particular countries, such as the Orderly Departure Program with Vietnam.

FIGURE 9.1
*Persons Born in Cuba and Indochina Who Were Admitted
to Permanent Residence Under Both Refugee and Immigrant Provisions
of U.S. Law: 1961–1988*

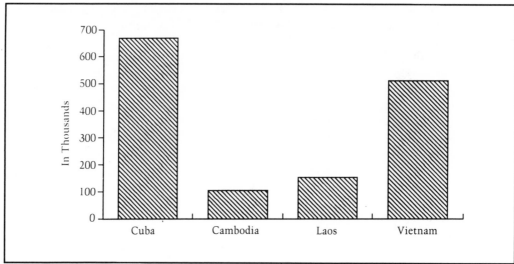

Of course, a full assessment of the adjustment of refugees to the United States would require investigation of the circumstances of their uprooting, of the forces that led them to seek refuge in the United States and the forces that led the United States to provide it. "Why them?" "Why us?" "Why not Angolans or Palestinians?" "Why not Brazil or Belgium?" Thus, these fundamental questions of selection in the study of migration phenomena are also relevant to refugees. As we have stressed, everything that happens after migration—the decision to remain in the United States, the decision to seek naturalization, the decision to learn English, the extent and pace of integration into the U.S. society and economy—is conditioned in a fundamental way by these dual selection processes.

Background of U.S. Involvement with Cuba and Indochina

The United States has a distinctive history of national and personal involvement with each of the four nations of special interest in this chapter: Cuba, Cambodia, Laos, and Vietnam. These bilateral relationships have importantly shaped the two events—refuge sought and refuge provided—that produced the refugee populations to be studied.

We examine Cuba first. The most obvious tie between Cuba and the United States is their proximity, Cuba lying about 90 miles south of the Straits of Florida. Another tie is at the nation-state level: the United States tried unsuccessfully many times to purchase Cuba from Spain; later assisted in Cuba's war of independence (1895–1898), twice occupying the new republic (1899–1901 and 1906–1909); and has held since 1901 a major naval base at Guantánamo Bay. Meanwhile, the peoples of the two countries forged many relationships, so that among Cubans there was, certainly at the time of the war of independence, substantial sentiment favoring annexation to the United States. Affinities in artistic and literary endeavors and in religion provide personal ties between the United States and Cuba. Americans knew several Cubas and several Havanas—the Cuba of Alicia Alonso, Hemingway's Havana. The majority of Cubans were Roman Catholics, as was a quarter of the U.S. population.[4]

Thus, the United States seemed a natural destination for opponents both of the Batista regime in Cuba and subsequently of the Castro regime. In the two years between New Year's Day of 1959, when Castro took power, and the end of diplomatic relations between Cuba and the United States on 3 January 1961, the socialist and Communist inclinations of the new Cuban rulers became increasingly clear. Persons who did not wish to live in such a regime left or attempted to do so. Moreover, the Castro regime had disavowed Cuba's military pact with the United States and also seized U.S. financial and land holdings. It was natural for the United States to welcome exiles from such a regime.

In Indochina, though substantial Western contact dates to the Portuguese presence in the sixteenth century, U.S. involvement became large and visible only in 1954 when, following the Geneva Conference and the ensuing partition of Vietnam, the U.S. Navy assisted in the evacuation of the approximately 1 million refugees from the north to the south of Vietnam. The refugees were predominantly Roman Catholic and many of them French-educated. Their story was told in three bestselling books, which for one cohort of Americans forged the determination to prevent the South from "falling" to the Communists.[5] It is not difficult to understand the ties between the anti-Communist Catholics of South Vietnam and the Americans who came to know them and champion their cause. Thus, the U.S.–Vietnam relation dates to 1954 and, though the military ingredient would overshadow all the others, includes as an important ingredient an affinity based on Roman Catholic principles as well as on Gallic elements.

[4]For a detailed look at the U.S.-Cuba relation in the period 1898–1902, see Healy (1963). For a more general history, see Thomas (1971).

[5]The U.S. medical missionary Dr. Thomas A. Dooley, whose own story is retold on the grounds of the University of Notre Dame, told the Indochinese story in *Deliver Us from Evil* (1956), *The Edge of Tomorrow* (1958), and *The Night They Burned the Mountain* (1960).

In contrast, U.S. ties to the peoples of Laos and Cambodia appear to have been rooted in military activities.[6] There do not appear to be artistic or religious affinities on the scale of those linking Cubans and Vietnamese to the United States.

It is reasonable to speculate that at the collapse of the U.S. stand in Vietnam in 1975, two kinds of groups would try to leave. The first would include persons with direct ties to the United States, persons involved in the U.S. military effort either directly or indirectly; these might be the immediate target of retaliation. The second group would include persons who did not wish to live in a Communist regime, with its attendant centrally planned economy and infringements on personal freedom. The United States would be a natural destination for the first group and an appealing one for the second. For its part, the United States would feel an obligation to protect its allies in the military effort and as well a certain moral pleasure at the resistance to the new way of life.

If this brief sketch faithfully represents the origin-country experiences of U.S. refugees, then it suggests the possibility of substantial differences across the refugee groups in the extent and pace of their adjustment to a life in the United States. We would expect Cubans and Vietnamese—who had a longer and richer history of involvement with the United States—to more rapidly adjust than Cambodians and Laotians. Moreover, persons with a background in complex market economies—as characterized the urban sectors of Cuba and Vietnam—would more quickly become integrated into the U.S. economy than persons with less of such experience.

Crosscutting such intercountry differences is a phenomenon noticed by virtually all students of migration processes, usually called a "wave" effect. It is widely believed that the timing of departure from the origin country reflects both the urgency of the situation and the affinity to the host country. Thus, a person on an execution list would leave sooner than a person who (merely) thought that life in the sugar fields would be unbearable. Similarly, an avid reader of U.S. magazines and books or an afficionado of U.S. sports or arts would leave sooner than an otherwise comparable person with less developed tastes for things American. To the extent that these aspects and attitudes influence the refugee's subsequent behavior, we would expect a wave effect to be manifested in both naturalization and employment patterns.

Among Cuban refugees, we can discern an initial wave which can be bounded approximately by the date on which the revolutionary forces led by Fidel Castro proclaimed victory, New Year's Day 1959, and October 1962, when daily flights from Havana were discontinued. While sub-

[6]We do not ignore Dr. Dooley's medical involvement or other similar small-scale involvements.

sequently there were refugees fleeing Cuba by boat as well as others entering the United States after third-country sojourns, a second large wave did not begin until September 1965, when Cuba again permitted flights to Miami. Those flights ended in 1973, ending the second wave. A third wave dates to 1980.

With respect to the Indochinese refugees, there is a clear first wave, beginning with the fall of Saigon and of Phnom Penh in 1975. These refugees were evacuated by the United States beginning in April 1975 and were all in the United States by the end of December of that year. A second large wave began in 1978, when persons fleeing Cambodia, Laos, and Vietnam were accepted under enabling legislation enacted in 1977 and 1978 (see Table 9.1).

According to the wave hypothesis, the first wave would include persons with the most to lose under the new regime, that is, persons whose lives were in danger as well as persons whose way of life would be substantially worsened under a Communist regime. Persons whose lives were in danger would include domestic political opponents as well as partisans of the United States. As for the rest, to the extent that a Communist regime can be characterized by infringements on religious and other freedoms and by a policy of equalizing incomes so that the differential returns to skills are reduced or eliminated, it would be likely that persons with the highest skills and persons closely associated with religion, with the press, or with artistic production would have the most to lose. Adult first-wave refugees would therefore display higher schooling and skill levels than their second-wave counterparts.

Cuban and Indochinese Refugee Wave Cohorts

Data for the analyses in this chapter are drawn from two sources extensively used in previous chapters—the INS FY 1971 Immigrant Cohort Sample and the U.S. Census Public Use Microdata Samples of 1970 and 1980—and from one additional source—the INS Alien Address Report Program (AARP) 1979 Indochina-Born Sample. The INS AARP Indochina-Born Sample consists of all persons born in Indochina who reported their addresses in January 1979 to the INS under the AARP, matched to the naturalization records for the FYs 1979–1985. The appendix to this chapter describes more fully the Indochina data set and discusses the comparability of the several refugee data sources; the Alien Address Report was discussed in Chapter 3.

Our goal was to construct, for each of the four nationality groups, cohorts approximating the substantively meaningful entry waves. As described in the appendix to this chapter, the available data made possible the identification of three Cuban cohorts: (1) first-wave Cuban cohort (entered 1960–1964), based on census data; (2) second-wave Cuban cohort (entered 1965–1970), based on census data; (3) combined first- and second-wave Cuban cohort (entered before July 1971 and were admitted to permanent residence between July 1970 and June 1971), based on the INS FY 1971 Immigrant Cohort Sample. For the Indochinese, three wave cohorts were constructed: (1) 1975 entry cohort (entered during CY 1975), based on the INS AARP 1979 Indochina-Born Sample; (2) 1978 entry cohort (entered during CY 1978), based on the INS AARP 1979 Indochina-Born Sample; and (3) combined wave cohort (entered before 1 April 1980), based on census data.

The Naturalization of Refugees

As discussed in Chapter 2, naturalization is one of the most important immigrant behaviors. It signals both a relatively higher degree of commitment to the United States and a relatively higher degree of "success" in the United States. Naturalization entails both benefits and costs. It confers the right to vote, the right to enter any occupation except those of President and Vice President of the United States, and the right to sponsor the immigration of kin. But it is not a free good. For all aliens except those few entitled to dual nationality, naturalization entails renunciation of the former country. Moreover, since naturalization requires knowledge of English (except, as noted in Chapter 2, for aliens who are over age 50 and who have been permanent resident aliens for at least 20 years), it requires that the immigrant, if not already a speaker of English, invest the not inconsequential resources needed to learn a new language.

As discussed in Chapter 2, three main factors are thought to influence the decision to seek naturalization. The first is occupational advancement; it would be expected that the greater an immigrant's attachment to the labor force the greater the propensity to naturalize. The second is immigration-sponsorship benefits; refugees with family members (of the requisite kind, under U.S. immigration law) still in the origin country would be more likely to seek naturalization. The third is the transfer of peculiar nation-state loyalties to the United States. For the refugee, it entails the twin conclusions that in one's lifetime the origin country will not revert to a friendlier regime and that the United States will be a congenial permanent home.

What would we expect to find a priori for refugees? With respect to the immigration-sponsorship benefits of naturalization, the patterns would reflect not only the presence of relatives in the origin country but also the opportunities for "normal-flow" immigration, including the origin country's emigration policies as well as the existence of special bilateral agreements enabling immigration to the United States. Such bilateral agreements have a complicated life span; for example, the chronicle of U.S.-Cuba immigration agreements includes approaches and retreats by both parties. And while the United States, through the Orderly Departure Program, has arrangements with Vietnam for the immigration of Vietnamese nationals to the United States, there are no comparable arrangements with Cambodia and Laos. Thus, other things being the same, we would expect that the propensity to naturalize would be greater among refugees from high-fertility countries—as there would potentially be more siblings wishing to be sponsored into the United States—and greater among refugees from countries having (or expected to have) bilateral immigration agreements with the United States. Available data suggest that Laos had a higher total fertility rate than Cambodia or Vietnam and that Cuba had the lowest total fertility rate. Accordingly, on this count we would expect Cuban refugees to show the lowest naturalization rates and Laotians the highest. On the other hand, recent history suggests that while emigration from Vietnam and Cuba is possible, prospects for emigration from Cambodia and Laos are dim, and thus on this count we would expect Cambodians and Laotians to have lower naturalization rates than Cubans and Vietnamese.[7]

With respect to occupational advancement, it is a commonplace to expect that, because of the operation of this factor, men would have higher naturalization rates than women. But additional predictions are possible. Consider that the main kinds of jobs requiring citizenship are jobs in the U.S. government and that the U.S. government has extensive activities requiring fluency in the Spanish language. Jobs with the Voice of America, say, or with the Agency for International Development would be more likely to require Spanish fluency than fluency in Khmer, Lao, or even French. Accordingly, we would expect that the occupational-advancement factor would be stronger for Cubans than for the other refugee groups.

Knowledge of English, required for naturalization, would be more likely among Cubans and Vietnamese than among Laotians and Cambodians, owing to the long history of extensive contacts between these groups and the United States.

Combining these factors, we would expect that Cubans and Vietnamese would have the highest naturalization rates, that men would have higher rates than women, and that, within the country-specific cohorts, the earlier immigrants would have higher naturalization rates, for given length of stay in the United States.

Table 9.3 reports the percent naturalized within ten years after entry across all the INS-based cohorts—that is, including FY 1971 Cubans and

---

[7]For discussion of emigration from the Indochinese countries, see Gordon (1985).

TABLE 9.3

Percent Naturalized Within Ten Years After Entry:
FY 1971 Cuban and Asian Immigrants
and 1975 Indochinese Entry Cohorts,
Aged 21–65 at Admission to Permanent Resident Status

Cohort	Men	Women
A. FY 1971 Immigrant Cohort		
Born in Asia	68.6	61.4
Born in Europe	30.0	24.3
Born in Cuba	58.2	40.9
Holding Cuban refugee visa	59.1	41.0
Born in Western Hemisphere, excluding Cuba	15.4	16.4
Born in Western Hemisphere, excluding Cuba, Canada, Mexico	24.6	25.1
B. CY 1975 Indochinese Entry Cohort		
Born in Cambodia	48.3	35.4
Born in Laos	51.5	47.8
Born in Vietnam	54.8	49.1

SOURCES: U.S. INS FY 1971 Immigrant Cohort Sample; U.S. INS AARP 1979 Indochina-Born Sample.

Asian, European, and Western Hemisphere immigrants, as well as the 1975 Indochinese refugee cohorts.[8] Figure 9.2 depicts the percentage naturalized for the four refugee groups. As expected, among the Indochinese refugees, the Vietnamese have the highest naturalization rates after a decade in the United States—55 and 49 percent, respectively, for men and women. Laotians have the next highest rates, and Cambodians the lowest—the latter with 48 and 35 percent, respectively.

The FY 1971 Cubans, whether looked at as immigrants or as refugees, have naturalization rates of almost 60 percent among the men—higher than any of the Indochinese cohorts. Cuban women, however, have rates around 41 percent, which are lower than the rates among Laotian and Vietnamese women.

[8]For all the groups shown in panel A of Table 9.3, except the row for persons holding a Cuban refugee visa, the time to naturalization is calculated as the time between date of admission to permanent residence and date of naturalization (both coded to the nearest month). For the FY 1971 refugee-visa Cubans—and consistent with U.S. law on the residency requirements for the naturalization of Cuban refugees—the time to naturalization is calculated as the time between date of admission to permanent residence and date of naturalization *plus* up to 2.5 years of pre-immigration time in the United States. Similarly, for the 1975 Indochinese cohorts, the time to naturalization is calculated as the time between date of entry and date of naturalization—since U.S. law permitted them to count all time in the country toward the residency requirement for naturalization.

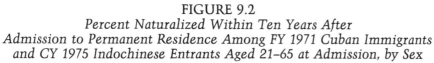

FIGURE 9.2
*Percent Naturalized Within Ten Years After
Admission to Permanent Residence Among FY 1971 Cuban Immigrants
and CY 1975 Indochinese Entrants Aged 21–65 at Admission, by Sex*

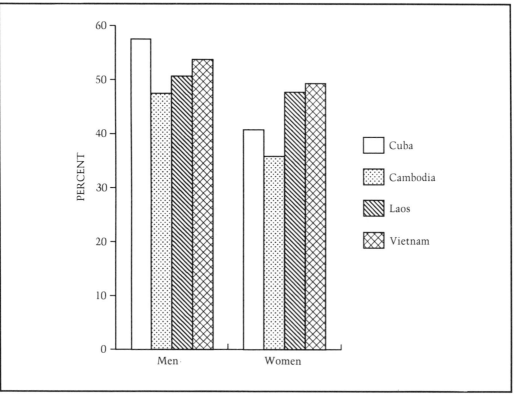

How do the naturalization rates of refugees compare with those of non-refugee immigrants? As shown in Table 9.3 and as depicted in Figure 9.3, Europeans and non-Cuban natives of the Western Hemisphere have relatively low naturalization rates—30 percent for European men and 25 percent for men from Western Hemisphere countries, excluding Canada and Mexico, whose rates are even lower. In contrast, as shown in Figure 9.4, Asian immigrants have naturalization rates—69 and 61 percent, for men and women, respectively—higher than any other group of immigrants or refugees. Thus, while FY 1971 Cubans have naturalization rates higher than all other Western Hemisphere groups, 1975-wave Indochinese have naturalization rates higher than those for FY 1971 Europeans but lower than those for FY 1971 Asian immigrants.

Table 9.3 also shows that, as expected, in every refugee group men

FIGURE 9.3
*Percent Naturalized Within Ten Years After
Admission to Permanent Residence Among FY 1971 Immigrants
Aged 21–65 at Admission, from Cuba,
Other Countries of the Western Hemisphere, and Europe, by Sex*

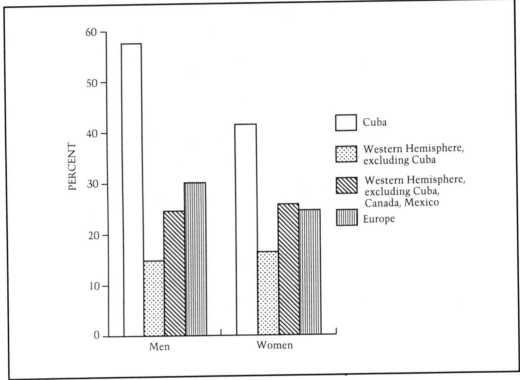

have higher naturalization rates than women, presumably reflecting differential labor force attachment. Another way to assess the sex differential in naturalization is by comparing the male/female ratio in percentage naturalized. These ratios, depicted in Figure 9.5, indicate that among the refugee groups Laos has the narrowest sex differential, followed closely by Vietnam, and that Cuba and Cambodia have the greatest differential. Figure 9.5 also shows that non-refugee immigrants from the Western Hemisphere are the only group in which the female percentage naturalized exceeds the male percentage naturalized.

The INS-based Asian refugee data and the FY 1971 immigrant data permit a more detailed look at the timing of naturalization across refugee waves and between refugee and immigrant groups. Tables 9.4–9.9 report—separately for the 1975 and 1978 Indochinese wave cohorts, as well as for

FIGURE 9.4
*Percent Naturalized Within Ten Years After Admission
to Permanent Residence Among CY 1975 Indochinese Entrants
and FY 1971 Asian and European Immigrants
Aged 21–65 at Admission, by Sex*

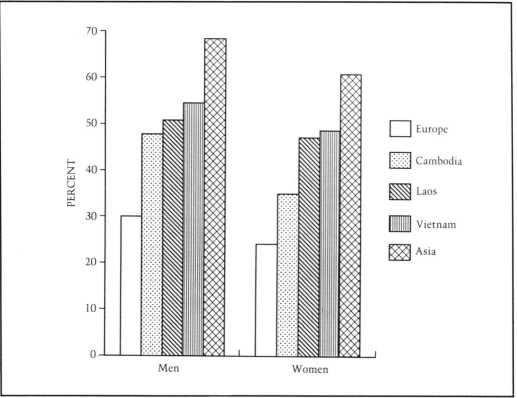

the FY 1971 immigrants and Cuban refugees, and for men and women—
the proportion naturalized in each of the first six years after admission. The
information in the table is restricted to the first six years, as data for the
1978 Indochinese waves are not yet available for the seventh and subsequent years.[9]

The results for both Cambodians and Laotians conform to the wave
hypothesis: the naturalization rate is substantially higher among the 1975
wave than among the 1978 wave. For example, among Cambodian men,
the total naturalized by the end of the seventh year since admission is 23.1

[9]For the convenience of the reader, Tables 9.4–9.9 also report the comparable figures for
non-refugee groups.

FIGURE 9.5
*Female/Male Ratio in Percent Naturalized
Among FY 1971 Immigrants and CY 1975 Indochinese Entrants,
by Country or Region of Birth*

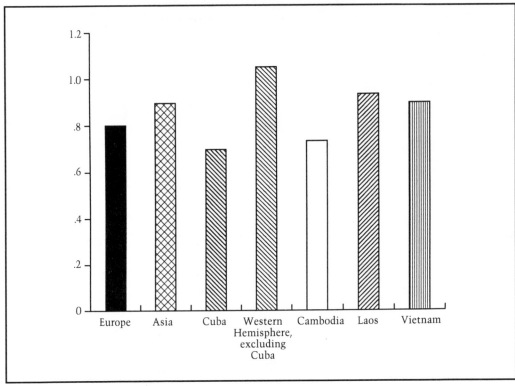

percent in the 1975 wave and 11.7 percent—or less than half—in the 1978 wave. Among Vietnamese, however, there is no evidence of a wave effect on naturalization behavior.

To examine the wave effect among Cubans, we report in Table 9.10 the percentage naturalized among the two census-based Cuban wave cohorts, as measured in the U.S. censuses of 1970 and 1980. The figures for 1970 are difficult to interpret, because not all cohort members were yet eligible to naturalize. By 1980, however, all the members of the two wave cohorts would have been eligible to naturalize for several years. Moreover, if most naturalizations occur soon after eligibility, then the 1980 figures would reflect near-complete proportions naturalized.[10] If so, then the census data

---

[10]Both INS published tabulations and analysis of the FY 1971 immigrant cohort sample

TABLE 9.4

Percent Naturalized in FY 1979–1985 Among Cambodian Refugees
(Aged 21–65 at Entry) Who Reported Their Addresses in January 1979,
by Duration of Residence in the United States and by Sex

Years Since Admission	1975 Entry Cohort		1978 Entry Cohort	
	Men	Women	Men	Women
One	—	—	0.3	—
Two	—	—	0.0	1.0
Three	—	—	0.6	1.0
Four	.1	.4	0.0	0.0
Five	9.3	5.5	5.4	1.0
Six	13.7	10.2	5.4	5.0
Total Naturalized (FY 1979–1985)	48.3	35.4	12.7	8.5
Cohort size	971	560	354	199

SOURCE: U.S. INS AARP 1979 Indochina-Born Sample.

NOTES: Each cohort consists of all persons who reported their addresses in January 1979, under the Alien Address Report Program, whose identifier, birth year, and year of entry had readable codes, and whose age at entry was 21 to 65.

show a strong wave effect among Cuban refugees. The first-wave cohort—those who entered between 1960 and 1964—had naturalization rates of 70 percent by 1980 compared with 42 and 38 percent, respectively, for men and women, among the second-wave cohort. Figure 9.6 displays the wave differential among Cuban refugees.

Since the FY 1971 Cuban cohort includes Cuban refugees from both waves, we expected the FY 1971 Cuban cohort to display a proportion naturalized that would be at an intermediate point between those of the two census-based wave cohorts. That is clearly the case among men. For them, the proportion naturalized in the FY 1971 group—approximately 60 percent—is between the 42 and 71 percent figures observed in the census-based cohorts. The corresponding figures for women, however, are puzzling. First, the FY 1971 figure of 40 percent is much closer to the second-wave census figure of 38 percent than to the first-wave figure of 70 percent. Second, while the INS data suggest important sex differences in the naturalization of Cubans, the census data show only trivial sex differences. These discrepancies could be due to a peculiarity of the group of Cuban refugees who adjusted to permanent resident status in FY 1971 or they could be due to reporting errors in the census.

suggest that the peak year for naturalization occurs at six years after admission to permanent resident status.

TABLE 9.5

Percent Naturalized in FY 1979–1985 Among Laotian Refugees
(Aged 21–65 at Entry) Who Reported Their Addresses in January 1979,
by Duration of Residence in the United States and by Sex

	1975 Entry Cohort		1978 Entry Cohort	
Years Since Admission	Men	Women	Men	Women
One	—	—	0.0	0.0
Two	—	—	0.1	0.0
Three	—	0.6	0.1	0.2
Four	1.5	0.6	0.1	0.1
Five	8.2	8.1	3.1	2.5
Six	13.4	11.2	6.3	3.4
Total Naturalized (FY 1979–1985)	51.5	47.8	11.2	7.1
Cohort size	194	161	1,360	1,253

SOURCE: U.S. INS AARP 1979 Indochina-Born Sample.

NOTES: Each cohort consists of all persons who reported their addresses in January 1979, under the Alien Address Report Program, whose identifier, birth year, and year of entry had readable codes, and whose age at entry was 21 to 65.

The findings on naturalization thus reveal the expected intergroup and cross-sex differences—Cubans and Vietnamese naturalizing at much higher rates than Cambodians and Laotians, and men at generally higher rates than women—as well as evidence of a strong wave effect among Cubans, Cambodians, and Laotians, but, interestingly, no wave effect among Vietnamese.[11]

Residential Patterns of Refugees

Where do refugees settle? The process of choosing a place to live may differ across refugee and non-refugee groups. The refugee's initial residential location may be as much the choice of the host country or sponsoring agency as that of the refugee; moreover, the precipitous nature of flight may inhibit or interrupt the process of gathering information and weighing the alternatives. After initial settlement, however, and depending on the nature and duration of the links to the governmental or sponsoring agency, the

[11]It is perhaps somewhat early to speculate. But if the Vietnamese fail to display a wave effect, it is possible that of the two conceptually distinct types of refugees discussed above, the United States evacuated only the group that had cooperated in the military effort, thus relegating to the second wave individuals equally strongly motivated to life in the United States.

TABLE 9.6
Percent Naturalized in FY 1979–1985 Among Vietnamese Refugees
(Aged 21–65 at Entry) Who Reported Their Addresses in January 1979,
by Duration of Residence in the United States and by Sex

Years Since Admission	1975 Entry Cohort		1978 Entry Cohort	
	Men	Women	Men	Women
One	—	—	—	0.1
Two	—	—	0.7	1.0
Three	0.0	0.2	1.3	1.4
Four	0.2	0.7	1.3	1.1
Five	8.2	8.2	7.0	6.8
Six	13.8	12.4	13.4	14.0
Total Naturalized (FY 1979–1985)	54.8	49.1	27.5	27.9
Cohort size	21,755	18,191	3,622	2,736

SOURCE: U.S. INS AARP 1979 Indochina-Born Sample.

NOTES: Each cohort consists of all persons who reported their addresses in January 1979, under the Alien Address Report Program, whose identifier, birth year, and year of entry had readable codes, and whose age at entry was 21 to 65.

TABLE 9.7
Percent Naturalized in FY 1971–1981 Among FY 1971 Immigrants
Born in Asia and Europe (Aged 21–65 at Entry),
by Duration of Residence in the United States and by Sex

Years Since Admission	Born in Asia		Born in Europe	
	Men	Women	Men	Women
Zero	0.3	0.5	0.0	0.0
One	0.6	0.5	0.0	0.0
Two	0.0	0.5	0.3	0.0
Three	3.8	6.6	1.3	2.0
Four	1.7	3.0	1.3	2.8
Five	25.9	18.3	7.3	5.1
Six	18.9	16.0	9.8	8.8
Total Naturalized (FY 1971–1981)	68.6	61.4	30.0	24.3
Cohort sample size	344	394	317	354

SOURCE: U.S. INS FY 1971 Immigrant Cohort Sample.

TABLE 9.8
Percent Naturalized in FY 1971–1981
Among FY 1971 Cuban Immigrants (Aged 21–65 at Entry),
by Duration of Residence in the United States and by Sex

	Born in Cuba		Holding Cuban Refugee Visa	
Years Since Admission	Men	Women	Men	Women
One	7.3	1.5	0.0	0.0
Two	9.1	7.6	0.0	0.0
Three	10.9	9.1	0.0	0.0
Four	3.6	3.0	12.2	6.6
Five	9.1	6.1	14.3	3.3
Six	14.6	6.1	6.1	13.1
Total Naturalized (FY 1971–1981)	58.2	40.9	59.2	41.0
Cohort sample size	55	66	49	61

SOURCE: U.S. INS FY 1971 Immigrant Cohort Sample.

NOTE: The time since admission in the "Holding Cuban Refugee Visa" column is calculated according to the residency requirements for the naturalization of Cuban refugees: up to 2.5 years of pre-immigration time in the United States is added to the time between admission to permanent resident status and date of naturalization.

refugee has both the time to search for a more permanent location and the freedom to move. In this section we examine the residential patterns of Cuban and Indochinese refugees at two points in time: first, at a time close to entry and, second, at naturalization, among the INS-based cohorts, and a decade later, among the census-based cohorts.

We look first at the residential location of Cubans. Given the proximity of Cuba to Florida and Florida's long history as an important Spanish colony, as the home of Cuban and other Spanish-speaking immigrants, and as the favored sojourn and vacation spot of Cubans, it is not surprising that in the early days of 1959 Miami would be the initial destination of Cuban refugees. Indeed, partly in response to requests for assistance urgently made by Florida and Dade County in the face of the sudden and large population growth, the U.S. government in 1961 instituted a policy which included assistance to refugees wishing to relocate away from Miami.

Table 9.11 reports the top five states of residence of the two census-based Cuban wave cohorts, each observed in 1970 and in 1980. At the first observation, the first-wave cohort had already been in the United States between five and ten years and may have already moved subsequent to initial settlement; the second-wave cohort, having been in the United States less than five years, is more likely to reflect initial residence. At the second

TABLE 9.9

Percent Naturalized in FY 1971–1981 Among FY 1971 Immigrants
Born in the Western Hemisphere (Aged 21–65 at Entry),
by Duration of Residence in the United States and by Sex

	Born in Countries of the Western Hemisphere			
	Excluding Cuba		Excluding Cuba, Canada, Mexico	
Years Since Admission	Men	Women	Men	Women
One	0.0	0.0	0.0	0.0
Two	0.0	0.0	0.0	0.0
Three	0.7	0.6	1.1	0.5
Four	0.0	0.3	0.0	0.5
Five	2.3	1.7	3.4	2.4
Six	3.3	1.7	5.7	2.9
Total Naturalized (FY 1971–1981)	15.4	16.4	24.6	25.1
Cohort sample size	305	347	175	207

SOURCE: U.S. INS FY 1971 Immigrant Cohort Sample.

TABLE 9.10

Decadal Cohort Change in Percent Naturalized:
Cuban Entry Cohorts (Aged 25–45 in 1970), by Sex

	Men		Women	
Cohort	1970	1980	1970	1980
Entered 1960–1964	39.8	71.3	28.4	70.1
Entered 1965–1970	10.1	41.8	10.2	37.8

SOURCE: U.S. Census of Population, Public Use Samples.

observation, in 1980, both cohorts had had ample time to decide where they would like to live and to move there, so that these patterns would more accurately reflect the refugees' long-term decisions.

Table 9.11 and Figure 9.7 reveal a striking fact: that among both wave cohorts and in the face of considerable incentives to relocate away from Florida, the proportion of Cubans residing in Florida grew in the decade between 1970 and 1980. The proportion of the first-wave cohort residing in Florida increased from 47 to 60 percent during the decade, while that of the second-wave cohort increased from 43 to 64 percent. Every other state among the top five lost Cubans to Florida (except for the trivial gain, from 10.1 to 10.5 percent, in first-wave Cubans registered by New Jersey).

FIGURE 9.6
1970–1980 Decadal Cohort Change in Percent Naturalized
Among First-Wave (Entered 1960–1964) and Second-Wave (Entered 1965–1969)
Cuban Refugees Aged 25–45 in 1970, by Sex

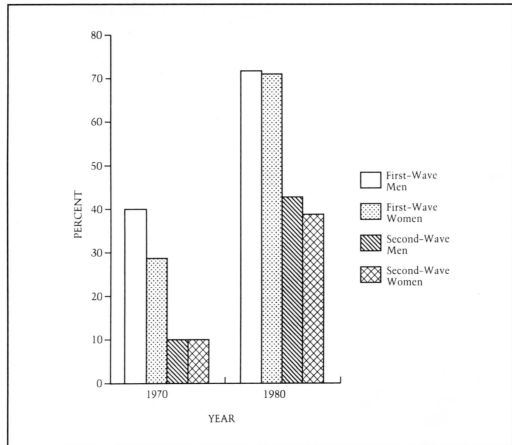

Second-wave Cubans are somewhat more likely to live in Florida than first-wave Cubans (64 versus 60 percent), more likely to live in New Jersey (15 versus 10 percent) and considerably less likely to live in New York (6 versus 16 percent), but these differences pale in comparison to the high propensity displayed by both wave cohorts to reside in Florida.

At the evacuation in 1975 of the first-wave Indochinese refugees, U.S. policy encouraged wide dispersal to all 50 states.[12] The interplay of this

[12]Valuable exposition of the Indochinese settlement and resettlement programs is found in Baker and North (1984), Forbes (1984), and Gordon (1985).

TABLE 9.11
Decadal Cohort Change in the Residence of Cuban Refugees
(Aged 25–45 in 1970) in 1970 and 1980:
Percent Residing in Top Five States

State	Entered 1960–1964		Entered 1965–1970	
	1970	1980	1970	1980
California	9.0	6.3	10.2	7.1
Florida	47.2	59.5	42.6	64.4
Illinois	4.6	2.0	4.2	1.4
New Jersey	10.1	10.5	19.6	15.3
New York	16.4	15.8	13.7	5.7
Total in Top Five	87.3	94.1	90.3	93.9

SOURCE: U.S. Census of Population, Public Use Samples.

policy with the resources available locally and through sponsoring agencies yielded an initial settlement consisting of small subsets of the 1975-wave Indochinese refugees distributed in communities around the country, with each state except Alaska hosting at least 100 refugees, and produced as well settlement of over 20 percent of the refugees in California.

The 1975-wave refugees, however, moved quickly. As described by Baker and North (1984) and Gordon (1985), if initial settlement had not been in the place of their choice—for Vietnamese, an urban place in a temperate zone and with an Asian-origin contingent—the 1975-wave refugees moved.

When the second wave of Indochinese refugees began to arrive, U.S. policy was somewhat different. Now it emphasized placement near relatives or compatriots. And thus the initial settlement of second-wave Indochinese would reflect the decisions of first-wave Indochinese. To the extent that second-wave Indochinese, if given the time to search and the freedom to move, would have reached the same decision as the first-wave Indochinese, we would expect less relocating among the second wave than among the first wave. On the other hand, second-wave Indochinese without ties to first-wave refugees would repeat the cycle of initial settlement, search, and relocation.

Tables 9.12–9.14 report the top five states of residence of the 12 nationality/gender/wave-specific INS-based Indochinese cohorts, observed in January 1979 and, for the naturalized subset, at naturalization. Because much first-wave relocation would already have occurred by 1979, geographic mobility would be less for the first-wave cohorts than for the second-wave cohorts, other things being the same. However, as just noted, second-wave cohorts placed near already relocated first-wave compatriots

FIGURE 9.7
*1970–1980 Decadal Cohort Change in State of Residence
Among First-Wave and Second-Wave Cuban Refugees
Aged 25–45 in 1970*

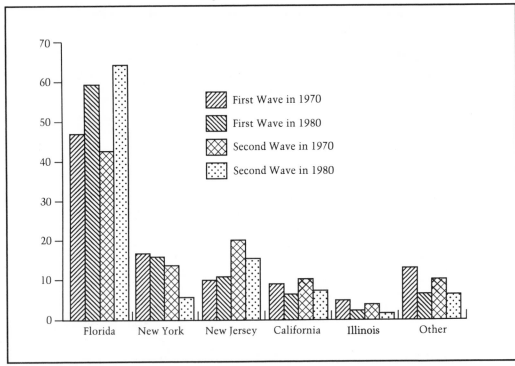

would also be less likely to move. Of course, caution must be exercised in drawing inferences, as the naturalized subsets of each cohort may not be representative of the entry cohort; moreover, while groups whose naturalized subsets are small are included in the table for the convenience of the reader, their residential patterns are not discussed.

Tables 9.12–9.14 indicate very small amounts of residential mobility among Indochinese refugees, suggesting that, as expected, the first-wave cohorts had already moved by January 1979 and the second-wave cohorts were initially placed in more desirable locations. The mobility patterns reveal a preference for California, especially among first-wave Cambodian men and Vietnamese of both waves and sexes.

The Vietnamese cohorts display an interesting pattern. First, the increases in the proportion in California between 1979 and naturalization are larger for the first-wave cohorts than for the second-wave cohorts, suggesting that not all relocation of first-wave refugees had been completed by

TABLE 9.12
Percent Residing in Top Five States:
Cambodian Refugees (Aged 21–65 at Entry) in 1979
and at Naturalization, by Entry Cohort and Sex

	Men		Women	
State	1979	At Naturalization	1979	At Naturalization
A. 1975 Entry Cohort				
California	32.5	33.9	35.5	31.8
Maryland	—	5.5	—	6.1
New York	—	—	—	5.6
Oregon	8.9	6.2	9.7	7.6
Texas	8.1	7.9	7.5	10.1
Virginia	6.4	—	6.1	—
Washington	6.0	6.2	7.0	—
Total in Top Five	61.9	59.7	65.9	61.1
Number	970	469	557	198
B. 1978 Entry Cohort				
California	24.1	22.2	25.8	11.8
Colorado	7.2	15.6	8.1	—
New York	—	—	—	11.8
Oregon	—	6.7	6.1	17.6
Pennsylvania	—	6.7	—	—
Rhode Island	6.6	—	—	—
Texas	12.4	—	13.1	—
Washington	10.9	11.1	11.1	17.6[a]
Total in Top Five	61.2	62.2	64.1	58.8
Number	348	45	198	17

SOURCE: U.S. INS AARP 1979 Indochina-Born Sample.
[a]Top four.

early 1979. Second, the proportion residing in California in early 1979 is larger for the second-wave cohort than for the first-wave cohort, suggesting the possibility of growth in attentiveness to refugee wishes or, alternatively, of initial settlement anticipatory of first-wave compatriots' relocation. Third, the proportion residing in California at naturalization, in all four wave/sex cohorts, is in the relatively small range of 37 to 40 percent, and the proportions in other states (at naturalization) are also remarkably similar—suggesting a convergence of both waves to a single residential pattern, dominated by the preference for California.

Laotian refugees of both waves and sexes also exhibit, though less strongly than the Vietnamese, a trend toward convergence. In this case, the

TABLE 9.13
Percent Residing in Top Five States:
Laotian Refugees (Aged 21–65 at Entry) in 1979
and at Naturalization, by Entry Cohort and Sex

State	Men		Women	
	1979	At Naturalization	1979	At Naturalization
A. 1975 Entry Cohort				
California	16.0	17.0	18.1	19.5
Hawaii	—	—	5.0	6.5
Illinois	8.8	9.0	—	7.8
Iowa	16.0	13.0	12.5	6.5
Minnesota	—	6.0	—	—
Pennsylvania	—	—	5.0	—
Texas	5.2	—	6.9	7.8
Virginia	9.8	7.0	8.8	6.5
Total in Top Five	55.7	52.0	56.3[a]	54.5[a]
Number	194	100	160	77
B. 1978 Entry Cohort				
California	22.9	21.6	20.9	16.9
Hawaii	—	—	—	7.9
Illinois	6.3	—	6.2	—
Iowa	—	—	—	7.9
Minnesota	5.7	6.5	5.5	—
New York	—	5.9	—	11.2
Oregon	—	5.9	—	—
Pennsylvania	6.1	—	7.7	—
Texas	7.9	11.8	6.9	12.4
Wisconsin	—	9.2	—	9.0
Total in Top Five	48.9	60.8[a]	47.2	65.2[a]
Number	1,351	153	1,244	89

SOURCE: U.S. INS AARP 1979 Indochina-Born Sample.
[a]Top six.

resultant pattern differs markedly from the Vietnamese pattern in that the proportion residing in California—hovering near 20 percent—is approximately half that of Vietnamese.

The Cambodian refugees, in contrast, show the possibility of strong differences in the residential patterns of the two waves. The numbers in the subsets are not sufficiently large to warrant drawing inferences. Nonetheless, it would appear that the preference for California is stronger in first-wave than in second-wave refugees, by about 10 percentage points. Gordon (1985) notes that the second-wave Cambodians were less likely than the

TABLE 9.14
Percent Residing in Top Five States:
Vietnamese Refugees (Aged 21–65 at Entry) in 1979
and at Naturalization, by Entry Cohort and Sex

	Men		Women	
State	1979	At Naturalization	1979	At Naturalization
A. 1975 Entry Cohort				
California	32.0	37.5	34.4	38.1
Louisiana	4.5	—	4.0	—
Pennsylvania	5.5	5.3	4.3	4.7
Texas	10.6	9.5	10.1	8.8
Virginia	4.0	3.1	4.8	3.7
Washington	—	3.7	—	4.0
Total in Top Five	56.6	59.1	57.7	59.2
Number	21,582	11,904	18,064	8,913
B. 1978 Entry Cohort				
California	35.5	36.6	38.1	40.1
Illinois	4.3	—	—	—
New York	—	—	—	4.0
Oregon	—	3.5	—	—
Pennsylvania	5.1	5.1	4.7	4.0
Texas	10.3	10.4	10.0	11.3
Virginia	—	—	3.5	—
Washington	3.9	4.4	3.4	3.8
Total in Top Five	59.1	60.0	59.6	63.2
Number	3,590	995	2,717	758

SOURCE: U.S. INS AARP 1979 Indochina-Born Sample.

other Indochinese to have first-wave relatives; thus, their initial settlement would not replicate the relocation patterns of first-wave Cambodians. Tables 9.12–9.14, however, also hint that second-wave Cambodians do not move to California, as the Vietnamese do.

The results on residential patterns thus indicate that Cuban refugees of both waves favor Florida, that Vietnamese refugees of both waves favor California, and that cross-wave differences in residential location are strong only for Cambodians. Figure 9.8 depicts the top three states of residence for Cuban and Indochinese refugees; there is no overlap. However, while the Cuban predilection for Florida is distinctive, the Vietnamese preference for California is characteristic as well of other recent immigrants.

FIGURE 9.8
Residence of Two Major Refugee Populations in 1980,
Top Three States: Indochinese and Cubans

Cubans
Indochinese

Levels of Schooling Attained by Refugees

The levels of schooling at entry of adult refugees are likely to reflect the circumstances of the uprooting. We would expect Cuban refugees to be relatively well schooled because, other things being the same, political opponents of the Castro regime would tend to come from the wealthier educated classes and because the negative effect of the upheaval in the system of economic rewards would be stronger among those who had invested heavily in education.

The situation is less clear among the Indochinese refugees. Of course, those whose way of life was threatened would attempt to flee, and this group would include the well educated. However, the Indochinese refugee group includes a second kind of refugee: namely, those who cooperated in the U.S. military effort and whose lives consequently would be in danger under the new regime. Cooperation in the U.S. military effort did not entail any particular level of schooling. Indeed, many partisans of the United

TABLE 9.15
Average Years of Schooling Completed:
Recent Major Refugee and Immigrant Cohorts Aged 25–65, by Sex

Cohort	Men	Women
Cuban, Entered 1960–1964 (in 1970)	11.6	10.9
Cuban, Entered 1965–1970 (in 1970)	9.2	8.6
Non-Cuban, Entered 1960–1964 (in 1970)	10.6	9.7
Non-Cuban, Entered 1965–1970 (in 1970)	11.4	10.1
Cambodian, Entered 1975–1980 (in 1980)	7.5	7.0
Laotian, Entered 1975–1980 (in 1980)	8.5	5.7
Vietnamese, Entered 1975–1980 (in 1980)	11.9	10.2
Non-Indochinese, Entered 1975–1980 (in 1980)	12.0	11.0

SOURCE: U.S. Census of Population, Public Use Samples.

States were relatively unschooled rural villagers. As discussed above, this second kind of refugee is probably more heavily represented among the Laotian and Cambodian refugees than among the Vietnamese refugees.

Thus, *a priori* we would expect to observe higher levels of schooling among Cubans and Vietnamese than among the other two refugee groups. Among Cubans, the only group for which we can observe schooling for two waves—since the INS data do not contain information on schooling—we would expect to find evidence of the wave effect, the first wave being, on average, more highly educated than the second wave.

Table 9.15 reports the average years of schooling completed among Cubans of both waves and non-Cuban foreign-born persons (entering in the same periods as the two Cuban waves) as measured in the 1970 census and among Cambodian, Laotian, Vietnamese, and non-Indochinese recent entrants in 1980, all in the 25–65 age group. Figure 9.9 displays the levels of schooling for the four refugee groups. The first-wave Cubans and the Vietnamese have remarkably similar schooling levels—11.6 and 11.9 years for Cuban and Vietnamese men, respectively, and 10.9 and 10.2 years for Cuban and Vietnamese women.

As expected, the two Cuban waves display different schooling levels. The average schooling of first-wave Cubans is more than two years greater than that of second-wave Cubans, among both men and women. In fact, as shown in Figure 9.10, while first-wave Cubans had more schooling than non-Cuban foreign-born of the same age entering at the same time, the second-wave Cubans had less schooling than their non-Cuban counterparts.

Among the Indochinese (shown in Figures 9.8 and 9.10), the Vietnamese had, as expected, the most schooling. Among men, the Vietnamese average of 11.9 years was almost as high as that of non-Indochinese for-

FIGURE 9.9
*Average Years of Schooling Completed
Among First- and Second-Wave Cubans Observed in 1970
and Indochinese Observed in 1980, by Sex*

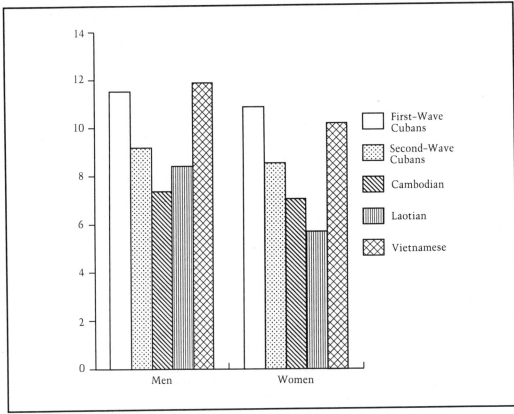

eign-born (12.0 years); among women, the average schooling level of 10.2 years for Vietnamese is close to the 11.0 years for non-Indochinese.

The average schooling of Laotians and Cambodians was substantially less than that of all other groups identified in Table 9.15. While Laotian men had more schooling than Cambodian men—8.5 versus 7.5 years—the opposite was true for women, Cambodians registering an average of 7.0 years and Laotians of 5.7 years.

The data on schooling thus conform to the wave hypothesis—for Cubans—revealing the higher educational attainment of the first-wave Cubans. The data also show that, as expected, the Vietnamese have higher schooling levels than the other Indochinese groups and, most interestingly because the census-based Vietnamese cohort is a mixture of two waves, that

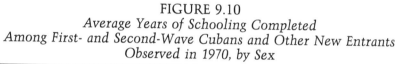

FIGURE 9.10
*Average Years of Schooling Completed
Among First- and Second-Wave Cubans and Other New Entrants
Observed in 1970, by Sex*

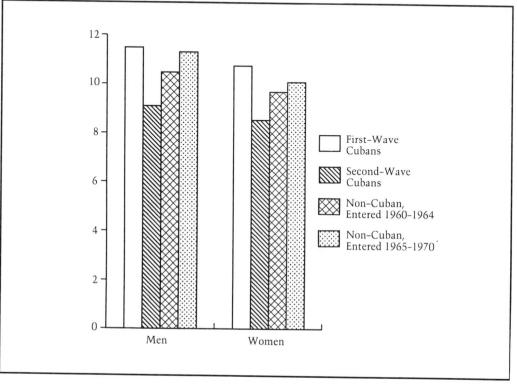

the Vietnamese schooling attainment is almost as high as that of the first-wave Cubans.

Occupational Attainment and Mobility

It is widely believed that the U.S. employment careers of refugees, like those of most migrants, begin at a point somewhat lower than their skills would dictate, as they may be unfamiliar with the U.S. labor market and not fluent in English. In this section we examine the occupational attainment of refugees, first, at a point close to the time of entry and, second, at naturalization for the INS cohorts and ten years later for the census cohorts.

For comparability, occupation in all the data sets is classified according

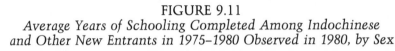

FIGURE 9.11
*Average Years of Schooling Completed Among Indochinese
and Other New Entrants in 1975–1980 Observed in 1980, by Sex*

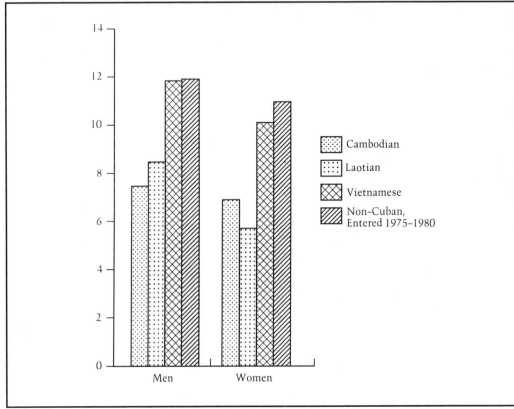

to the system used by the INS. This scheme consists of 25 occupation
groups—a subset of the 1980 census occupational classification system—
supplemented by four categories for persons without an occupation. Appendix Table 9.A lists the INS occupation groups, together with the corresponding census numerical codes.

Complete information on occupation is available for all census-based
cohorts and, for the FY 1971 immigrant cohort sample, at two points in
time: at admission to permanent residence and at naturalization. The INS-
based Indochinese refugee cohort data sets contain information on occupation at naturalization, for all naturalized cohort members, and in January
1979 (when the address reports were completed) for a 10 percent subset of
the AARP Indochinese respondents.

We begin by examining occupation at a point close to the time of entry into the United States. Using census data we can look at the cohorts who entered during the five years preceding the census—that is, at second-wave Cubans in 1970 and mixed-wave Indochinese in 1980, together with comparable non-refugee recent entrants. Table 9.16 reports the top five major occupation groups of recent-entrant men aged 25–65 at the time of each of the two censuses. The similarity in the rankings of second-wave Cubans and mixed-wave Vietnamese is striking. The top three occupation groups for both of these cohorts are the same: "operators, fabricators, laborers," "precision production," and "service." The Cuban and Vietnamese rankings diverge in the fourth and fifth places. The "administrative support" category is fourth for Cubans and fifth for Vietnamese. The "technologists and technicians" category is fourth for Vietnamese, and the "executive, administrative, managerial" category is fifth for Cubans. Thus, these data suggest that the more highly skilled among second-wave Cubans in 1970 gravitated to the "executive" category while their counterparts among the mixed-wave Vietnamese in 1980 tended to the "technologists" category. Of course, these observations are ten years apart, suggesting the possibility that these findings reflect a secular trend toward technical occupations; however, such a shift is not visible among the non-refugee recent-entrant cohorts.

We turn to comparisons within the same period. Over a third of the second-wave Cubans in 1970 were in the "operators" group compared with a fifth of the non-Cubans. While fewer second-wave Cubans than non-Cubans were in the "executive" group, more were in the "administrative support" group. Equal proportions of second-wave Cubans and non-Cubans were employed in "service" occupations. These results are consistent with the lower schooling attainment of second-wave Cubans, compared with non-Cubans, shown in Table 9.15.

The mixed-wave Vietnamese in 1980 had proportions similar to those of non-Indochinese in the "operators" and "service" groups. The Vietnamese proportion in the "executive" group was less than half that of the non-Indochinese, while the proportion in the "technologists" group was over three times as large as that of the non-Indochinese.

The mixed-wave Laotian refugees in 1980 differed from their Vietnamese counterparts in that 26 percent were employed in "service" occupations, as opposed to 13 percent of the Vietnamese (and non-Indochinese), and in their heavy representation in "farming, forestry, fishing" occupations—11 percent of the Laotians versus 2 percent of the Vietnamese (and 6 percent of the non-Indochinese recent entrants). Again, these differences are consistent with the lower schooling attainment of Laotian refugees compared with both Vietnamese refugees and non-Indochinese recent entrants, shown in Table 9.15.

Thus, except for the heavy representation of mixed-wave Vietnamese

TABLE 9.16
Percent in Top Five Major Occupation Groups:
Male Recent-Entrant Refugees Aged 21 to 65,
in Comparison with Other Male Recent Entrants: 1970 and 1980

Occupation Group	1970 Census		1980 Census		
	Cuban	Non-Cuban	Laotian	Vietnamese	Non-Indochinese
Executive, Administrative, Managerial	5.8	7.3	(5.7)	(5.6)	10.3
Technologists and Technicians, Except Health	(2.4)	5.5	(5.7)	11.8	3.8
Administrative Support	10.2	6.1	(0.0)	8.7	5.8
Service	11.9	11.3	25.7	12.8	13.1
Farming, Forestry, Fishing	(0.9)	3.0	11.4	(2.0)	5.7
Precision Production, Craft, Repair	25.7	21.6	20.0	18.5	14.6
Operators, Fabricators, Laborers	34.8	20.2	25.7	23.6	23.8
Total in Top Five	88.3	—	82.9[a]	75.4	—
Employed as Percentage of Cohort	96.5	95.4	76.1	87.0	90.1

SOURCE: U.S. Census of Population, Public Use Samples.

NOTE: This table highlights the top five occupation groups of the Cuban, Laotian, and Vietnamese groups. Occupation rates are included for all occupation groups thus identified; for refugee groups, occupation rates which are not in the top five are enclosed in parentheses.

[a]Top four.

in technical occupations and that of second-wave Cubans in operator-type occupations, both these groups were similar to their non-refugee counterparts. Mixed-wave Laotians, on the other hand, were considerably more likely to be in service occupations and in farming or fishing.[13]

While the INS-based Indochinese cohort data contain too few observations on occupation in January 1979 (except for the occupation of Vietnamese, as will be seen below), they do provide ample information on occupational attainment for the subset who naturalized between 1979 and 1985. Although the naturalized subsets are a self-selected group and cannot be regarded as representative of the original cohorts a decade later, never-

[13]This may reflect the presence of highland-Lao peoples. For discussion of estimates concerning the proportion highland in the Laotian waves, see Gordon (1985).

theless they can be used to assess the wave effect on occupational attainment, within national-origin groups. Tables 9.17–9.19 report the top five major occupation groups for all the naturalized Indochinese wave cohorts, separately for men and women.

Among men in all three Indochinese nationality groups, the proportions in "executive" and "technical" occupations are substantially higher for the first wave than for the second wave. For example, among Cambodian and Vietnamese men, the proportion in "executive" occupations in the 1975 wave is approximately twice that in the 1978 wave; among Laotian men, it is 16 times as large. Tables 9.17–9.19 also show that the proportion in "service" occupations is greater in the 1978 wave among Laotian and Vietnamese men, again supporting the wave hypothesis for these naturalized groups.

The situation appears somewhat different among women. The number of 1978-wave Cambodian women and of Laotian women who naturalized and reported an occupation is too small to permit drawing inferences. Ac-

TABLE 9.17
Percent in Top Five Major Occupation Groups:
Naturalized Cambodian Refugees
Aged 21–55 at Entry, by Entry Cohort and Sex

Occupation Group	1975 Entry Cohort		1978 Entry Cohort	
	Men	Women	Men	Women
Executive, Administrative, Managerial	9.6	10.6	5.4	(0.0)
Technologists and Technicians, Except Health	14.5	(4.6)	5.4	7.1
Administrative Support	11.3	24.5	5.4	21.4
Service	15.9	9.3	13.5	28.6
Precision Production, Craft, Repair	18.1	19.2	13.5	7.1
Operators, Fabricators, Laborers	15.9	20.5	43.2	35.7
Total in Top Five	75.7	84.1	86.5[a]	100.0
Number Employed	415	151	37	14
Employed as Percentage of Naturalized	89.4	77.0	84.1	82.4

SOURCE: U.S. INS AARP 1979 Indochina-Born Sample.

NOTE: Figures in parentheses represent the percent employed in an occupation which is not in the top five for that group.

[a]Top six.

TABLE 9.18
Percent in Top Five Major Occupation Groups:
Naturalized Laotian Refugees
Aged 21–55 at Entry, by Entry Cohort and Sex

Occupation Group	1975 Entry Cohort		1978 Entry Cohort	
	Men	Women	Men	Women
Executive, Administrative, Managerial	12.9	(0.0)	(0.8)	(1.4)
Social, Recreational, Religious	(2.2)	9.6	5.3	2.8
Technologists and Technicians, Except Health	8.6	(1.9)	(3.0)	(0.0)
Administrative Support	9.7	17.3	9.1	11.3
Service	14.0	28.8	18.2	25.4
Precision Production, Craft, Repair	(6.5)	7.7	19.7	16.9
Operators, Fabricators, Laborers	29.0	23.1	32.6	35.2
Total in Top Five	74.2	86.5	84.8	91.5
Number Employed	93	52	132	71
Employed as Percentage of Naturalized	93.9	67.5	86.3	81.6

SOURCE: U.S. INS AARP 1979 Indochina-Born Sample.

NOTE: Figures in parentheses represent the percent employed in an occupation which is not in the top five for that group.

cordingly, while the information is reported in Tables 9.17–9.19 for the interested reader, we confine our discussion to the Vietnamese wave cohorts. Among Vietnamese women, the figures do not show evidence of a strong wave effect. The proportion in the "executive" group declines across waves, but the proportion in the "technical" group increases across waves. Moreover, virtually the same proportion of the naturalized subsets in both waves is employed—slightly over 70 percent.

A more pointed assessment of progress is possible by comparing the top five occupations of the same prime-age cohort at two points in time. Table 9.20 reports the top five occupation groups for the men in the two census-based Cuban wave cohorts (aged 25–45 in 1970) and in the INS-based 1975-wave Vietnamese cohort (aged 21–55 in 1975).[14]

---

[14]Note that while the Cuban wave cohorts are constructed from census data and hence may contain different individuals, the Vietnamese cohort is a microdata panel consisting of all

TABLE 9.19
Percent in Top Five Major Occupation Groups:
Naturalized Vietnamese Refugees
Aged 21–55 at Entry, by Entry Cohort and Sex

Occupation Group	1975 Entry Cohort		1978 Entry Cohort	
	Men	Women	Men	Women
Executive, Administrative, Managerial	(7.6)	6.9	(3.5)	(4.6)
Technologists and Technicians, Except Health	15.9	(6.3)	12.9	8.0
Administrative Support	8.3	23.7	8.7	23.9
Service	8.4	14.5	16.7	19.9
Precision Production, Craft, Repair	19.2	15.7	16.5	12.1
Operators, Fabricators, Laborers	18.4	17.6	18.6	16.3
Total in Top Five	70.2	78.4	73.4	80.3
Number Employed	10,418	6,343	824	527
Employed as Percentage of Naturalized	89.7	72.1	85.7	70.5

SOURCE: U.S. INS AARP 1979 Indochina-Born Sample.

NOTE: Figures in parentheses represent percent employed in occupations which are not in the top five for that group.

While both Cuban wave cohorts show a decline in persons employed as operators, they differ dramatically in other ways. The first-wave cohort had, by 1970, 14.5 percent employed as executives, a figure which grew to 20.9 percent a decade later; the corresponding figures among the second-wave cohort are 6.1 percent in 1970 and 8.7 percent a decade later. Similarly, while the proportion employed in "administrative support" occupations grew for the earlier cohort, from 8.5 percent to 11.8 percent, the figure declined for the second cohort, from 11.2 percent to 4.7 percent; and while the percentage employed in "service" occupations declined for the first-wave Cuban cohort, it increased for the later Cuban cohort. These figures suggest a substantial wave effect in the occupational attainment of prime-age Cuban refugees.

With respect to the 1975-wave Vietnamese, the substantial decline in employment in the "service," "precision production," and "operators" cat-

individuals whose occupation was coded in January 1979 and who also report an occupation at naturalization.

TABLE 9.20
Occupational Mobility Among Male Refugee Cohorts: Percent in Major Occupations

| | Cuban | | | | Vietnamese | |
| | Entered 1960–1964 | | Entered 1965–1970 | | Entered 1975 | |
Occupation	1970	1980	1970	1980	1979	At Natural-ization
Executive, Administrative, and Managerial	14.5	20.9	6.1	8.7	(2.1)	(5.3)
Technologists, and Technicians, Except Health	(4.1)	(2.0)	(1.4)	(1.3)	9.6	19.1
Sales	9.8	11.8	(4.4)	4.7	(6.4)	(4.3)
Administrative Support	(8.5)	11.8	11.2	4.7	9.6	9.6
Service	9.8	(9.2)	8.8	14.8	19.1	12.8
Precision Production, Craft and Repair	21.8	17.6	25.8	30.2	18.1	14.9
Operators, Fabricators, and Laborers	21.1	11.8	36.4	27.5	19.1	14.9

SOURCES: U.S. Census of Population, Public Use Samples; U.S. INS AARP 1979 Indochina-Born Sample.

NOTES: Figures in parentheses represent percent employed in occupations which are not in the top five for that group. The two Cuban cohorts are aged 25 to 45 in 1970. The Vietnamese cohort is aged 21 to 55 in 1975.

egories and the concomitant doubling in the "technologists" category is striking.[15]

If progress can be gauged by mobility into "executive" and "technologists" occupations and out of "service" occupations, then first-wave Cuban and first-wave Vietnamese refugees appear to have made more progress than second-wave Cubans. Thus, not only do first-wave Cubans and first-wave Vietnamese enter with higher schooling attainment than second-wave Cubans, but they also show a higher degree of upward occupational mobility.[16]

Summary

Refugees may be thought of as persons whose way of life in their country of origin suddenly crumbles and whose very lives may be threat-

[15]Unfortunately, the data do not permit examination of occupational mobility in a panel of 1978-wave Vietnamese, as occupation in 1979 was coded for only five of the 995 men (aged 21–65 at admission in 1978) who naturalized by 1985.

[16]Note, however, that these results compare all the Cubans with only the naturalized subset of Vietnamese refugees.

ened. In the face of such political and social turmoil, quick flight becomes the course of choice. Where refugees go—and how they adjust to their new life—depends in part on the history of involvement between the country of origin and potential destination countries, including social and cultural affinities predating the political events that produced the refugees. Moreover, those refugees who have the most to lose if they remain in their home country or who have the strongest ties to the host country are likely to be the first to leave and, consequently, to more readily take up their new life.

Since World War II, the United States has granted over 2.3 million permanent-residence visas under special refugee programs; other persons who behaviorally might resemble refugees have gained permanent-residence visas under regular immigrant provisions. Of the 2.3 million official refugees who were granted permanent visas by September 1988, the most recent large groups were 486,426 Cubans and 686,540 Indochinese; during that same period, the number of additional immigrants from Cuba and Indochina were 185,697 and 71,559, respectively, not counting further numbers of arrivals who had not yet achieved permanent residence.

How are these newest refugees doing? Although a full answer will take many decades and must consider as well the children of refugees, the evidence currently available suggests that there are important differences both between and within the four refugee groups. Common across the four groups is what appears to be a "wave" effect; first-wave refugees appear to have higher levels of schooling and higher rates of occupational advancement and, in most cases, higher naturalization rates for equal numbers of years in the United States. Country-level affinities also appear to play a large role in explaining differences across groups in the process of adjustment to the United States. The richer the history of involvement between the United States and the country of origin, the stronger is the likelihood of a refugee becoming a naturalized U.S. citizen and the greater the occupational advancement. Thus, first-wave refugees from Cuba and Vietnam appear to be better educated and to have advanced occupationally and attained citizenship faster than both second-wave refugees from those countries and first- and second-wave refugees from Cambodia and Laos.

Appendix

The INS Indochinese Refugee Cohorts of 1975 and 1978

The parent INS Indochinese data set consists of all persons who reported their addresses in January 1979 under the now-defunct AARP and who declared their country of nationality to be Cambodia, Laos, or Vietnam.[17] The total number of AARP respondents was 157,150. As with the FY 1971 immigrant cohort sample, our goal was to observe these persons over time, matching their records to the naturalization records maintained by the INS in fiscal-year files. Because matching is based on the individual's A-number (the chief identifying variable) and the A-number is missing from 11 percent of the records, the usable Indochinese AARP data set was reduced to 139,495.

Our goal was to construct entry cohorts approximating the two identifiable waves of Indochinese refugees. The first wave is clearly defined by entry in CY 1975. The second large wave began in CY 1978. Because the AARP data include date of entry, it was possible to construct two wave cohorts by date of entry, one representing the 1975 wave and the other the start of the 1978 wave. For each entry cohort we distinguish by sex and nationality, so that there are 12 wave/nationality/sex-specific cohorts.

Because we focus on naturalization and employment behavior, we restricted the cohorts to persons aged approximately 21–65 at entry. Thus, the 1975 wave cohort includes persons born between 1910 and 1954, while the 1978 cohort includes those born between 1913 and 1957.

By definition, all the persons in the Indochinese AARP data set are aliens. The ideal cohorts would include all persons who entered in the specified year; that is, the cohorts should not yet have been reduced by naturalization. The normal residency requirement for naturalization is five years after admission to permanent resident status; this period is shortened, however, for spouses of U.S. citizens and for certain other aliens such as adopted children of U.S. citizens and persons who served honorably in the U.S. armed forces in specified theaters of war. We can be confident that the 1978 wave cohort is virtually intact—that is, that in the nine months of 1978 before October (the start of FY 1979) few, if any, persons would have naturalized. We can also be reasonably confident that the 1975 wave cohort is close to intact, for statutory "refugees" were not even allowed to adjust to permanent resident status until 1978.[18]

As with the FY 1971 immigrant cohort sample, the Indochinese AARP data records were matched to the naturalization records, in this case for FYs

---

[17]As discussed in Chapter 3, the United States required the annual registration of aliens from 1951 to 1981, in accordance with the provisions first of the Internal Security Act of 1950 and subsequently of the Immigration and Nationality Act of 1952. This registration program was conducted in January of each year as a mail-in self-report on an official INS form-questionnaire available in post offices around the country. The address-registration requirement was abolished by the INS Efficiency Act of 1981.

[18]The number of Vietnamese persons who entered in 1975 and who naturalized before January 1979 was 428 by October 1978 and 858 by October 1979 (INS 1975–1979, Table 44)—a small number. Moreover, some of these persons may have been adopted children and thus excluded from our cohorts for reasons of age.

1979–1985 (i.e., for the period from October 1978 to September 1985). Theoretically, the record-match procedure yields an exact and complete naturalization history for the entry cohort. However, the INS has noted that the FY 1984 naturalization files—recorded at 197,023—are incomplete, the recorded number representing approximately 90 percent of the total; and we have no way of knowing how the AARP matched data may be affected by the missing naturalization records.[19]

Data Comparability

As discussed, the INS 1979 AARP data set enables construction of 12 wave-specific Indochinese refugee cohorts. Patterns observed can be compared among these cohorts and also with patterns observed among Cuban refugees and non-refugee immigrant populations. The FY 1971 immigrant cohort sample yields cohorts of non-refugee immigrants as well as one cohort of Cuban refugees, those who became permanent resident aliens in FY 1971.

Data from the U.S. censuses of 1970 and 1980 enable construction of further cohorts. First, persons who entered between 1960 and 1964 and those who entered between 1965 and 1970 can be identified in both the 1970 and 1980 censuses.[20] Since the first Cuban wave spans the 1960–1964 period and the second is thought to date from September 1965, the census data enable construction of cohorts approximating the first two Cuban-refugee waves. Accordingly, census data can be used to assess the wave effect among Cubans. Second, 1980 census data can be used to construct a recent-entrant cohort of Indochinese persons—those who report entering since 1 January 1975.

How comparable are these various cohorts? In the absence of emigration, the foreign-born populations covered by the census and by the INS should be approximately the same. To the extent that fewer refugees than immigrants emigrate, the problems associated with emigration selectivity in census data would be minimal for refugee subsets.

Moreover, census-INS coverage differences attributable to respondent

---

[19]Nearly 23,000 cases are missing. These include 50 percent of the Chicago District's 14,000 cases, 67 percent of the Houston District's 4,500 cases, and 48 percent of the San Francisco District's 27,000 (INS 1986).

[20]As previously discussed, both the 1970 and 1980 census questions on period of entry include as a response category the interval "1960–1964." The 1980 census includes the category "1965–1969," while the 1970 census, taken on 1 April 1970, has the category "since 1965."

behavior would be at a minimum for the AARP data, for, like the census, the AARP utilized a self-report questionnaire.[21]

Of course, even barring emigration, systematic differences between INS and census data could still arise in two ways, as discussed in the Introduction. First, given that the census does not ascertain legal status, the exact correspondence between individuals of differing immigration-law statuses included in the census and their counterparts in INS data files would remain unknown. Second, because of that same lack of information on legal status in the census, the correspondence between INS admission-to-status cohorts and census-based entry cohorts would remain ambiguous.

Both these sources of ambiguity, however, are at a minimum in the case of refugees, and especially of Indochinese refugees, enumerated in the 1980 census. First, with respect to legal status, all refugees would be eligible for permanent resident status soon after entry. Thus, except for small numbers of Cuban and Indochinese non-immigrants—say, representatives of international organizations—all Cubans and Indochinese in the census would eventually become permanent resident aliens.

Second, with respect to date of entry, virtually all Indochinese in the United States in April 1980 had entered the United States beginning in 1975. Thus, in the 1980 census they had no choice but to report entering since 1975—regardless of any difference between date of entry and date of admission to permanent residence. How Cubans reported their date of entry in the census is a somewhat more difficult question. If they reported date of arrival in the United States, then the census-based wave cohorts correspond reasonably well to the actual waves. The INS FY 1971 Cuban cohort data, on the other hand, would contain individuals from both waves, as the exact date of adjustment to permanent resident status is a matter of personal choice.

Accordingly, we treat the INS Indochinese cohorts and the census Cuban cohorts as wave cohorts. Moreover, we expect that the 1980 census Indochinese cohort will contain a combination of both Indochinese wave cohorts and that the FY 1971 Cuban cohort will contain a combination of both Cuban wave cohorts.

---

[21]Data collection for the U.S. Census used a mail-out–mail-back procedure for approximately 60 percent of the population in 1970 and 90 percent in 1980 (Shryock and Siegel 1975; U.S. Bureau of the Census 1983).

APPENDIX TABLE 9.A
INS Occupational Classification, with INS Abbreviation and
Corresponding Occupation Codes from 1980 U.S. Census Classification

INS Major Occupation Group	INS Abbreviation	1980 Census Code
Executive, Administrative, and Managerial Occupations	EXC	003 - 037
Architects	ARC	043
Engineers, Surveyors, and Mapping Scientists	ENG	044 - 063
Mathematical and Computer Scientists	MCS	064 - 068
Natural Scientists	NSC	069 - 083
Physicians	DOC	084
Other Health Diagnosing Occupations	HLD	084 - 089
Registered Nurses	NUR	095
Other Health Assessment and Treating Occupations	HLT	096 - 106
Teachers, Postsecondary	TCU	113 - 154
Teachers, Except Postsecondary	TCO	155 - 159
Counselors, Educational and Vocational	COU	163
Librarians, Archivists, and Curators	LIB	164 - 165
Social Scientists and Urban Planners	SSC	166 - 173
Social, Recreation, and Religious Workers	SWK	174 - 177
Lawyers and Judges	LAW	178 - 179
Writers, Artists, Entertainers, and Athletes	ART	183 - 199
Health Technologists and Technicians	TNH	203 - 208
Technologists and Technicians, Except Health	TNO	213 - 235
Sales Occupations	SLS	243 - 285
Administrative Support Occupations, Including Clerical	ASP	303 - 389
Service Occupations	SER	403 - 469
Farming, Forestry, and Fishing Occupations	FFF	473 - 499
Precision Production, Craft, and Repair Occupations	PCR	503 - 699
Operators, Fabricators, and Laborers	LAB	703 - 889
Housewife/Househusband	HOU	
Unemployed or Retired	UNR	
Students and/or Children Under Age 16	STC	
Occupation Not Reported	NOT	

NOTE: The INS occupation coding scheme is based on the 1980 census system.

10

THE IMMIGRANT'S LEGACY: INVESTING IN THE NEXT GENERATION

I N CHAPTER 6 we examined how the characteristics and behavior of immigrants influence the size and composition of future immigrant flows through the family-reunification immigration multiplier; immigrants "reproduce" through the mechanisms created by immigration laws. Yet, even if all immigration were to cease, immigrants already in the United States would affect the future size and composition of the U.S. population through *natural* increase. The long-term effects of immigration depend, however, not only on the number of offspring of immigrants but on how these offspring differ, if at all, from those of the native-born. The children of the foreign-born are thus an important component of the legacy of immigrants.

It is widely believed that the fertility of foreign-born persons in the United States is substantially higher than that of native-born U.S. citizens. The origins of such beliefs are not difficult to understand. The total fertility rate—the average number of children a woman would have by the end of her childbearing years, assuming that age-specific birth rates are constant over time—was approximately 3.7 children in countries of the world outside the United States in the mid 1980s and 1.8 children in the United States.[1] Thus, if immigrant fertility behavior were not importantly affected

---

[1]The U.S. total fertility rate of 1.8 refers to all U.S. women, native-born and foreign-born (1988 World Population Data Sheet, released in April 1988).

by conditions in the United States and immigrants were randomly selected from the world's population, their fertility would be expected to be more than double that of U.S. citizens.

Of course, immigrants are not randomly (self-) selected. As we have shown, immigration is selective by country; that is, the origin-country composition of the U.S. foreign-born does not correspond to the distribution of the world's population across countries. What would be the total fertility rate of the U.S. foreign-born if the only selection mechanism operating were that by country? If we weight the 1985 country-specific total fertility rates using the origin-country distribution of the female foreign-born aged 20–64 in the United States in 1980, then the average total fertility rate of the U.S. foreign-born would be 2.85 children. Thus, if each foreign-born woman were randomly selected from *within* her country of origin and if her fertility behavior in the United States perfectly reflected that of the residents of her origin country, then the family size of actual immigrants in the United States would still be expected to be one child (55 percent) greater than that of U.S. citizens, although approximately one child less than average completed family size in the rest of the world.

Immigration is not likely to be unselective with respect to fertility, however, for two reasons. First, long-distance traveling by households is likely to be impeded by large numbers of (young) children; costs of migration rise with family size. Second, and perhaps more important, immigrants tend to be individuals who are more willing and able to undertake investments, to incur costs for the benefits of deferred returns. Thus, they may defer childbearing or reduce their number of children in order to devote more of their time and other resources to establishing their new life in the new country. Becoming American—acquiring new skills, learning English, starting a business—requires considerable investment. Moreover, such "investing" individuals may also be more concerned with building up their children's human capital. If so, they will not necessarily want large families. Resource constraints make it impossible to have large numbers of children, invest in migration, and devote substantial resources to each child. Given these essential trade-offs between family size, migration, and investments in children, as well as the importance of fertility and human capital investment in determining the legacy of immigrants, we examine in this chapter both immigrant fertility and the schooling received by the children of the foreign-born, one important measure of investments in children.

The available data suggest that since the early part of the twentieth century until the most recent period, the completed family size of the foreign-born has been less than that of the native-born. Between 1970 and 1980, however, there was a substantial increase in the population of immigrants coming from higher-fertility origin countries, and this shift is reflected in the higher age-specific fertility rates of the new-entrant foreign-born women. In particular, rates are higher among foreign-born women from Western Hemisphere countries who entered the United States between 1975 and 1980 than among comparably aged native-born and foreign-born women. Because our results also suggest that immigrants tend to bear children at higher rates than the native-born once in the United States, it is likely that the completed family size of the Western Hemisphere foreign-born will also exceed those of the native-born in the future.

The native-born children of the foreign-born appear to receive more schooling than do the native-born children of the native-born. This is reflected in the literacy rates and schooling levels of those groups from 1900 to 1979. The 1980 census indicates that enrollment rates for children of the foreign-born are similar to those for the native-born; however, once account is taken of the lower family incomes of the foreign-born parents, immigrant families appear to invest more in the schooling of their children than do their native-born counterparts. Mirroring the differentials in fertility among the foreign-born, school enrollment rates for children with parents from Western Hemisphere countries are significantly lower than rates for other immigrant groups. Children of parents from Asian countries exhibit the highest rates of school enrollment. All foreign-born groups, particularly European and Asian immigrants, appear to utilize parochial schools at substantially higher rates than do the native-born. Taxpayers thus support the costs of schooling for the foreign-born less than they do the costs for the native-born.

Fertility of the Foreign-Born and the Native-Born

The Public Use Samples of the U.S. Census of Population provide information on the number of children ever born for each woman over age 15. Table 10.1 reports the average number of children ever born to women aged 40–64 (i.e., completed family size), as of 1900, 1910, 1960, 1970, and 1980, for the total U.S. population of women, as well as separately for three groups—foreign-born women, U.S. native-born women with foreign-born parents (first generation), and U.S. native-born women with native-born parents (second and higher generation). In 1900 and in 1910 the completed family size of foreign-born women was higher than that of native-born women, and in 1900 the completed fertility of the first generation was slightly higher than that of the remainder of the native-born population, but lower than that of the foreign-born. However, in 1960, 1970, and 1980, foreign-born completed fertility was lower than native-born completed fertility (Figure 10.1). And in 1960 and 1970, when the nativity of parents was identified in the census, the fertility of the native-born children

TABLE 10.1
Average Number of Children Ever Born: Women Aged 40–64,
by Census Year and Nativity

| | | Native-Born | | |
Year	Foreign-Born	Foreign-Born Parents	Native-Born Parents	All
1900	5.63	5.03	4.98	4.98
1910	5.49	4.52	4.75	4.69
1960	2.28	2.26	2.42	2.33
1970	2.20	2.26	2.64	2.54
1980	2.75	n.a.	n.a.	2.84

SOURCE: U.S. Census of Population, Public Use Samples.

of immigrants was lower than that of the native-born children of native-born parents (Figure 10.2).

The fertility of women aged 40–64 does not reflect the fertility of the most recent immigrants to the United States, since very few of those women are over age 40. Do the data suggest that the patterns of completed fertility (Table 10.1) for the 1960–1980 period will persist for the younger, more recent immigrants? Table 10.2 presents hypothetical total fertility rates by immigrant entry cohort, calculated by weighting the 1985 origin-country total fertility rates with the actual origin-country composition of the six entry cohorts identified in the 1980 census. This table shows the effects on total fertility rates due solely to changes in the origin-country composition of the entry cohorts over time—if the fertility behavior of the immigrants were to correspond perfectly to that of their origin-country counterparts. The figures indicate that there was only a slight rise in the proportion of the foreign-born coming from high-fertility countries between 1950 and 1969, but in the decade of the 1970s, the average total fertility rate of the sending countries was almost 30 percent higher than the average for the sending countries in the prior two decades. Immigrants who entered the United States during the 1970s (and remained in the United States) thus were from substantially higher-fertility origin countries than the immigrants who entered prior to 1970 and who had remained in the United States as of 1980.

Very few of the foreign-born entering the United States in the 1975–1980 period had completed their fertility by 1980. Table 10.3 reports the total number of children ever born by five-year age groups for native-born women and recent-entrant foreign-born women aged 20–39 from the 1960, 1970, and 1980 censuses. For all age groups in 1960 and 1970, the recent-entrant foreign-born women exhibit substantially lower cumulative fertility than do native-born U.S. women. For two of the four age groups in

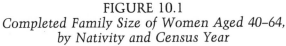

FIGURE 10.1
Completed Family Size of Women Aged 40–64,
by Nativity and Census Year

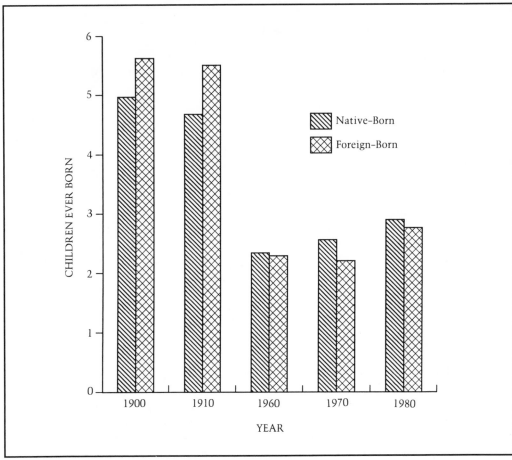

1980 (the youngest and oldest), however, the recent entrants exhibit higher fertility than their native-born counterparts. This is due mainly to the decline in the age-specific fertility of U.S. native-born women between 1970 and 1980. However, the effects of changes in origin-country composition do appear to be somewhat reflected in the actual fertility of the more recent cohorts of the foreign-born, as in two age groups the fertility of the 1975–1980 entry cohort of women exceeds that of women entering between 1965 and 1970.

Table 10.4 reports children ever born per ever-married woman. Again, recent entrants had lower marital fertility rates than the native-born in

FIGURE 10.2
Completed Family Size of Women Aged 40–64,
by Nativity, Generational Status, and Census Year

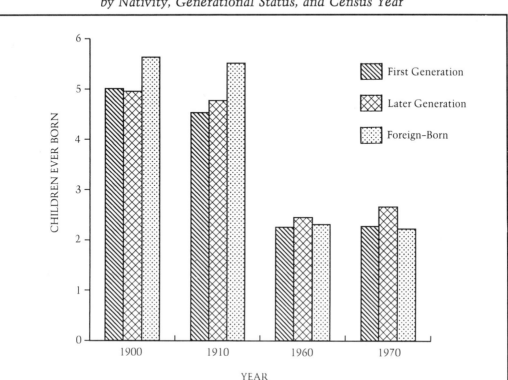

1960 and 1970, but in 1980, for three of the four age groups, the rates of the recent-entrant women exceeded those of the native-born (and exceeded those of the 1970 recent entrants in two age groups). Differences in the proportions of women married across age and entry cohorts and by nativity, displayed in Table 10.5, thus do not appear to account for much of the difference in fertility rates. However, it is interesting to note that in 1960 and 1970 a lower proportion of recent-entrant women than native-born women were ever-married, especially for the 25–29 age group, while differences in the proportions ever-married between the native-born and recent-entrant foreign-born women are almost nonexistent in 1980, mainly because of the decline in the proportions marrying for the native-born in the 20–29 age groups (greater postponement of marriage) between 1970 and 1980.

How important is the origin-country composition of the foreign-born

TABLE 10.2

Hypothetical Total Fertility Rates of U.S. Population Groups in 1980,
Based on the Total Fertility Rates of Origin Countries

Group	Total Fertility Rate
A. Observed Rate	
World, excluding the United States	3.70
United States	1.80
B. Hypothetical Rate for Foreign-Born Women in U.S. in 1980	
All	2.85
Entered 1975–1980	3.42
Entered 1970–1974	3.41
Entered 1965–1970	2.95
Entered 1960–1964	2.68
Entered 1950–1959	2.29
Entered Before 1950	2.06

SOURCES: U.S. Census of Population, Public Use Samples; 1988 World Population Data Sheet, Population Reference Bureau, April 1988.

NOTE: The hypothetical total fertility rates for foreign-born U.S. women are calculated by assigning to each woman the total fertility rate of her country of origin.

TABLE 10.3

Average Number of Children Ever Born, by Age and Census Year:
Native-Born and Recent-Entrant Women

	1960		1970		1980	
Age	Native-Born	Recent Entrants	Native-Born	Recent Entrants	Native-Born	Recent Entrants
20–24	1.02	0.78	0.69	0.61	0.46	0.66
25–29	1.99	0.88	1.72	1.12	1.06	1.02
30–34	2.45	1.51	2.51	1.73	1.76	1.49
35–39	2.54	1.10	2.92	2.18	2.31	2.90

SOURCE: U.S. Census of Population, Public Use Samples.

in accounting for their aggregate fertility behavior? Table 10.6 provides the number of children ever born to recent-entrant women and the percentage ever-married in 1980 by age and by three major areas of origin (accounting for 93 percent of all recent entrants). The table suggests that origin matters. The recent-entrant foreign-born women from the Western Hemisphere exhibit significantly higher fertility (at least initially) than the U.S. native-born and higher than their counterparts from Asia and Europe. Thus, if all of the recent entrants in 1980 were from Europe and Asia, fertility rates would be no higher for the recent entrants than for the native-born.

TABLE 10.4

Average Number of Children Ever Born per Ever-Married Woman,
by Age and Census Year: Native-Born and Recent-Entrant Women

	1960		1970		1980	
Age	Native-Born	Recent Entrants	Native-Born	Recent Entrants	Native-Born	Recent Entrants
20–24	1.42	1.09	1.05	0.97	0.88	1.23
25–29	2.22	1.21	1.94	1.35	1.33	1.34
30–34	2.62	1.76	2.70	1.94	1.92	1.64
35–39	2.69	2.34	3.09	2.46	2.46	3.05

SOURCE: U.S. Census of Population, Public Use Samples.

TABLE 10.5

Percent Ever Married, by Age and Census Year:
Native-Born and Recent-Entrant Women

	1960		1970		1980	
Age	Native-Born	Recent Entrants	Native-Born	Recent Entrants	Native-Born	Recent Entrants
20–24	72.4	72.2	65.9	62.7	52.1	53.5
25–29	89.8	72.5	88.8	82.9	80.1	76.1
30–34	93.5	86.0	93.1	89.1	91.7	90.8
35–39	94.4	89.8	94.6	88.9	94.1	95.1

SOURCE: U.S. Census of Population, Public Use Samples.

TABLE 10.6

Average Number of Children Ever Born (CEB) and Percent Ever Married (PEM),
by Age and Region of Birth: Recent-Entrant Women Aged 20–39 in 1980

	Native-Born		Foreign-Born Recent Entrants					
			Western Hemisphere		Europe		Asia	
Age	CEB	PEM	CEB	PEM	CEB	PEM	CEB	PEM
20–24	0.46	52.1	0.68	56.5	0.53	64.6	0.43	53.0
25–29	1.06	80.1	1.35	76.3	0.91	84.6	0.86	80.6
30–34	1.76	91.7	2.10	85.6	1.21	94.0	1.50	86.9
35–39	2.31	94.1	2.98	86.4	1.78	95.9	2.48	92.4

SOURCE: U.S. Census of Population, Public Use Samples.

To investigate more rigorously whether the fertility rates of the origin countries are reflected in the fertility behavior in the United States of the foreign-born, and to assess the effects of other origin-country characteristics on the fertility of immigrants, we performed a regression analysis of the number of children ever born, based on a sample of foreign-born women aged 20–64 in 1980. The regressors are the woman's age and her age at entry, her origin-country 1985 total fertility rate, per capita GNP, and literacy rate, the distance between her origin country and the United States, and dummy variables indicating whether the origin country had a centrally planned economy and whether English was one of its official languages. Column 1 of Table 10.7 reports the regression results from a specification including only the age variables and a binary variable indicating whether the woman entered the United States between 1970 and 1980. The significance level of the coefficient estimate for this variable dictates rejection of the hypothesis that there is no difference between the fertility of the foreign-born women who entered in the 1970s and that of the women who entered in prior decades; the magnitude of the coefficient indicates that among foreign-born women of the same age and age at entry, those who entered between 1970 and 1980 on average had 0.2 (10 percent) more children. This is a substantially smaller differential than would have been predicted on the basis of the shift in the origin-country composition of immigrants, as suggested in Table 10.2.

The origin-country total fertility rate is added to the specification in column 2. This variable alone increases the explanatory power of the regression by almost one third. The hypothesis that women from countries with a higher-than-average total fertility rate exhibit higher fertility in the United States cannot be rejected. Moreover, inclusion of the origin-country fertility rate reduces to insignificance the difference across entry cohorts; the shift in the extent to which higher-fertility countries are represented among the foreign-born entering the United States after 1970 does account for the slightly higher fertility of that cohort.

In column 3 the other origin-country characteristics are added to the specification. This additional set of variables increases the explanatory power of the regression by 7 percent, so that 21 percent of the variation in fertility across the foreign-born women is now explained by the set of regressors. The magnitude of the influence of the origin-country fertility rate is, however, diminished by 32 percent, although the variable still contributes significantly to predicting the U.S. fertility rates of the foreign-born, now net of origin-country income, literacy, and proximity to the United States. The estimated negative coefficient on distance is highly significant and is consistent with two distinct hypotheses: (1) that distance deters large-family migrants and (2) that migrants who are more willing to incur the higher costs of migration tend to want fewer children. The other estimates suggest that U.S. foreign-born women from countries with higher per capita incomes, that have centrally planned economies, and where En-

TABLE 10.7
Determinants of Children Ever Born Among Foreign-Born Women
Aged 20–64 in 1980

Variable/Specification	(1)	(2)	(3)	(4)
Country-of-Origin Characteristics				
Total fertility rate	—	.273	.185	.190
		(8.73)	(3.50)	(3.61)
GNP per capita, 1978	—	—	−.314	−.309
(×10⁻⁴)			(1.61)	(1.59)
Literacy rate, 1975	—	—	−.881	−.583
(×10⁻³)			(0.27)	(0.26)
Centrally planned economy	—	—	−.398	−.403
			(2.96)	(3.00)
Distance (× 10⁻³)	—	—	−.0702	−.0689
			(4.71)	(4.64)
English an	—	—	−.176	−.171
official language			(1.85)	(1.80)
Woman's Characteristics				
Age	.319	.319	.315	.307
	(13.1)	(12.9)	(12.4)	(12.9)
Age squared (×10⁻²)	−.326	−.317	−.312	−.305
	(11.6)	(11.2)	(10.6)	(10.7)
Age at entry	−.0314	−.0407	−.0354	−.0317
	(3.17)	(3.84)	(3.27)	(3.12)
Age at entry squared	.793	.872	.791	.794
(×10⁻²)	(4.62)	(4.84)	(4.28)	(4.30)
Entered 1970–1980	.208	.0789	.0266	—
	(1.71)	(0.64)	(0.98)	
Constant	−4.80	−5.22	−4.81	−4.63
	(10.2)	(11.3)	(7.69)	(7.75)
R^2	.169	.200	.214	.214
F	93.1	88.6	49.4	54.2
Sample Size	2295	2295	2295	2295

NOTE: Absolute values of *t*-ratios appear in parentheses under estimates.

glish is an official language also tend to bear fewer children than do otherwise similar foreign-born women.

Post-Immigration Fertility

Differences in cumulative fertility among recent-entrant foreign-born
women and between them and native-born women reflect mainly the operation of immigrant selectivity and the migration process, as very little of the

recent-entrant fertility experience occurs during the period of residence in the United States (on average, recent-entrant women have been in the United States less than 2.5 years at the time of the census). Such differences at entry may or may not persist depending on how immigrants adjust to their new environment. By observing the changes in the fertility of the foreign-born once they are in the United States, more information can be obtained about the relative importance of selection factors and of immigrant adjustment. How well the differential fertility rates of the younger recent immigrants predict their ultimate family size can also be assessed.

A number of hypotheses about the U.S. fertility experience of the foreign-born can be examined by following U.S. immigrants over time. (1) If the process of migration merely interrupts or postpones childbearing among younger women, then we would expect that post-immigration fertility rates would be higher for the foreign-born than for the native-born, whatever the differentials in cumulative fertility at entry, as foreign-born women attempt to make up for migration-related impediments to childbearing. (2) If, however, selection factors are most important and if the United States mainly attracts persons interested in intensive human-capital investments, then lower cumulative fertility rates observed at entry, compared with the native-born, will persist through the childbearing years. (3) If the foreign-born respond to U.S. conditions in a way similar to the native-born, whatever the cumulative fertility of the foreign-born at entry, it will converge with that of the native-born as their stay lengthens. The extent of convergence and/or adjustment to the interruption in childbearing caused by migration will, of course, depend on the number of childbearing years remaining after entry.

As we have noted, no longitudinal data sets exist that contain a sufficient number of (representative) foreign-born to permit reliable inferences about immigrant adjustment over time. The date-of-entry information in the adjacent 1970 and 1980 censuses allows, however, entry-cohort comparisons over time. But, as we have shown, the "survivors" of an entry cohort of the foreign-born are only a subset of the initial cohort because of emigration. Thus, differences in fertility observed over time for aggregate entry cohorts are also influenced by emigration selectivity. To the extent that higher fertility deters migration in general, higher fertility also makes emigration more costly. If so, the average cumulative fertility rates may increase for an entry cohort across census years relative to those of the native-born, simply because of selective, fertility-related emigration.

One way to test whether selective emigration is contaminating inferences about the fertility adjustment of the foreign-born obtained by using the entry-cohort comparison method is to examine how the fertility of a cohort would change if all immigrants had the same fertility as that of their origin-country residents. Any change in fertility across census dates for a cohort would then solely reflect changes in the country-of-origin composi-

TABLE 10.8

1970–1980 Decadal Cohort Change in Origin-Country Composition,
as Indicated by the Hypothetical Origin-Country-Based Total Fertility Rates:
1970 Recent-Entrant Women Aged 20–39 in 1970, by Age Group and Region of Birth

| Age in 1970 | All 1970 Recent Entrants | | Origin Area | | | | | |
| | | | Western Hemisphere | | Europe | | Asia | |
	1970	1980	1970	1980	1970	1980	1970	1980
20–24	2.91	3.08	3.52	3.60	1.70	1.69	3.28	3.51
25–29	2.77	2.91	3.39	3.29	1.66	1.68	3.27	3.56
30–34	2.87	2.91	3.58	3.28	1.69	1.70	3.26	3.44
35–39	2.88	2.62	3.62	2.92	1.70	1.72	3.29	3.05
20–39	2.85	2.92	3.50	3.33	1.68	1.70	3.27	3.46

SOURCE: U.S. Census of Population, Public Use Samples; 1988 World Population Data Sheet, Population Reference Bureau, April 1988.

NOTE: The hypothetical total fertility rates for foreign-born U.S. women are calculated by assigning to each woman the total fertility rate of her country of origin.

tion of the cohort due to emigration. Selectivity would imply that emigrants from the United States would more likely come from low-fertility origin countries. Thus, the hypothetical average origin-country fertility rate of an entry cohort should rise over time if this form of selectivity is important.

In Table 10.8 we report the hypothetical average total fertility rates, broken down by age group and area of origin, implied by the origin-country composition of the 1965–1970 entry cohort aged 20–39 in 1970 as observed in the 1970 and 1980 censuses. The figures do suggest an overall drift upward in the average total fertility rates of the cohort over the ten-year period due solely to the change in country composition, particularly for the largest group of women—those aged 20–24 at entry in 1970. However, there are important differences across areas of origin: the average recent-entrant woman in 1970 from the Western Hemisphere remaining in the United States in 1980 tended to be from a lower-fertility country relative to the typical cohort member residing in the United States in 1970. Selective emigration by the 1970 recent-entrant women from those countries more proximate to the United States thus tends to lower fertility over the 1970–1980 decade, while selective emigration appears to raise fertility for the 1965–1970 immigrants from Asian countries, with little change for the comparable cohort of foreign-born women from Europe.

The results in Table 10.8 suggest the possibility that emigration selectivity may affect inferences about the fertility experience of the foreign-born drawn from aggregate intercensal cohort comparisons, particularly about changes across country-of-origin groups. Since individual selectivity,

TABLE 10.9

1970–1980 Decadal Cohort Change in Average Number of Children Ever Born:
Native-Born and 1970 Recent-Entrant Women, by Age in 1970 and Region of Birth

| Age in 1970 | Native-Born | | Foreign-Born | | | | | |
| | | | Western Hemisphere | | Europe | | Asia | |
	1970	1980	1970	1980	1970	1980	1970	1980
20–24	0.69	1.76	0.70	2.24	0.63	1.84	0.47	1.78
25–29	1.72	2.31	1.28	2.14	1.07	2.03	0.91	1.87
30–34	2.51	2.78	2.36	2.64	1.49	1.93	1.45	1.90
35–39	2.92	2.92	2.80	2.77	2.02	2.22	1.55	2.38

SOURCE: U.S. Census of Population, Public Use Samples.

TABLE 10.10

1970–1980 Decadal Cohort Change in Ratios of Children Ever Born:
1970 Recent-Entrant Foreign-Born to Native-Born Women,
by Age in 1970 and Region of Birth

| Age in 1970 | All 1970 Recent Entrants | | Origin Area | | | | | |
| | | | Western Hemisphere | | Europe | | Asia | |
	1970	1980	1970	1980	1970	1980	1970	1980
15–19	1.17	1.19	1.07	1.33	1.20	1.09	0.13	0.71
20–24	0.88	1.16	1.01	1.27	0.91	1.05	0.68	1.01
25–29	0.65	0.88	0.74	0.93	0.62	0.88	0.52	0.81
30–34	0.69	0.82	0.94	0.95	0.59	0.69	0.57	0.68
35–39	0.75	0.83	0.96	0.95	0.69	0.76	0.53	0.82

SOURCE: U.S. Census of Population, Public Use Samples.

as opposed to cross-origin-country selectivity, cannot be measured, the results of Table 10.8 clearly understate the magnitude of the problem. With this caution in mind, in Table 10.9 we report the actual cumulative fertility at two points in time for the 1970 recent-entrant women and for native-born women, and in Table 10.10 we report the ratios of foreign-born to native-born fertility across the two census years.

If we ignore emigration selectivity, the figures indicate that foreign-born women entering the United States in 1965–1970 added to family size at a significantly higher rate than did native-born women over the 1970–1980 decade. The ratios of foreign-born to native-born fertility rise for almost every age group in every origin area. The one exception is for the entry group aged 35–39 from the Western Hemisphere for whom the ratio declines slightly over the decade. However, Table 10.8 suggests that this anomaly may be due to emigration selectivity, since this group experienced

TABLE 10.11
1970–1980 Decadal Cohort Change in Ratios of Percent Ever-Married:
1970 Recent-Entrant Foreign-Born to Native-Born Women,
by Age in 1970 and Region of Birth

Age in 1970	All 1970 Recent Entrants		Origin Area					
			Western Hemisphere		Europe		Asia	
	1970	1980	1970	1980	1970	1980	1970	1980
15–19	1.44	1.01	1.23	1.03	2.03	1.09	0.46	0.96
20–24	1.00	1.01	0.94	1.00	1.14	1.04	0.86	1.04
25–29	0.95	1.00	0.92	0.96	1.00	1.04	0.91	1.02
30–34	0.97	0.98	0.93	0.97	0.97	0.99	1.00	1.03
35–39	0.92	0.96	0.84	0.91	1.00	0.98	0.90	1.03

SOURCE: U.S. Census of Population, Public Use Samples.

the greatest downward shift in hypothetical expected fertility as a result of the change in its origin-country composition associated with emigration.

Differences in the percent ever-married in 1970 between the recent-entrant foreign-born women and native-born women, displayed in Table 10.11, were not nearly as large as the differences in cumulative fertility, and they converged over the subsequent decade. The higher birth rates observed between 1970 and 1980 among the 1970 recent-entrant foreign-born thus were due principally to their higher rates of marital fertility.

The more rapid accumulation of births after entry by foreign-born women in the 1965–1970 entry cohort and their low cumulative birth rates at entry compared with the native-born is consistent with the hypothesis that migration deters (negatively selects) women who have already had relatively large numbers of children prior to migration, but does not necessarily select out all women who intend ultimately to have large families. Table 10.10 suggests that among those immigrants of childbearing age who are young (under age 25) at entry, fertility is merely deferred. Indeed, the figures in Table 10.10 reject the convergence hypothesis; the cumulative fertility of the younger (aged 15–24) recent entrants surpasses that of the native-born after ten years, whether or not fertility was already higher at entry.

Among foreign-born women aged 30–34 in 1980 who had been in the United States approximately 12.5 years, the average number of children ever born exceeds that for native-born women of the same age by 27 percent for Western Hemisphere women, by 5 percent for European women, and by 1 percent for Asian women (Table 10.10). For the foreign-born women aged 25–29 at entry, however, cumulative fertility never catches up to that of similarly aged native-born women. And this age group of women represents 34 percent of all recent-entrant women in 1970, 60 percent of women in their childbearing years.

The upward adjustment in fertility rates after entry exhibited by all the foreign-born women relative to the native-born suggests that the higher average fertility rates of the recent-entrant foreign-born women observed in 1980 compared with immigrant women who entered in 1960 and 1970 will likely be reflected as well in their ultimate completed family size. In particular, the experience of the 1970 recent entrants over the 1970–1980 decade suggests that the higher initial fertility exhibited by the 1980 younger (aged 20–24) Western Hemisphere recent-entrant women compared with the other recent-entrant groups, displayed in Table 10.3, may understate differentials in the cumulative fertility of this cohort observed in 1990.

Schooling Rates of the Children of Immigrants

The lower fertility of the foreign-born relative to the native-born may simply reflect the lower level of resources available to immigrants as a consequence of their lower incomes and levels of schooling, at least initially. If so, it would not be surprising to find that they also have allocated fewer resources to their children. However, if immigration selects investors, then the lower fertility of the foreign-born may reflect differences in the way in which immigrants and the U.S. native-born choose to allocate resources for the future, as embodied in their children.

The U.S. censuses of 1900, 1910, 1960, and 1970 provide information on the nativity of parents. It is thus possible to compare the adult native-born offspring of the foreign-born (i.e., the first generation born in the United States) and the adult native-born children of the native-born (the later generations) with respect to outcomes of parental investment measured in those censuses—literacy in 1900 and 1910 and completed schooling and earnings in 1960 and 1970. Table 10.12 reports the percentage who can read and write a language, by nativity, generational status, and sex, among persons aged 25–59 in 1900 and 1910. A significant finding is that for both sexes and both census years native-born persons with at least one foreign-born parent have higher literacy (reading and writing) rates than either the foreign-born or the later-generation native-born. The literacy rates for the first generation hover at about 98 percent. In contrast, in 1900 all other groups have literacy rates under 90 percent, and in 1910 the highest rate attained is only 93.8 for the ability to read among later-generation males.

Tables 10.13 and 10.14 report, for men and women, respectively, aged 25–59, average years of schooling and average earnings (for those employed in the labor market), by nativity, generational status, and age in 1960 and

TABLE 10.12
Percent Able to Read and Write a Language,
by Sex, Age, and Generational Status: 1900 and 1910

	Reads			Writes		
	Foreign-Born	Native-Born		Foreign-Born	Native-Born	
Sex		First	Later		First	Later
A. In 1900						
Males	89.6	98.8	89.8	88.7	98.3	88.0
Females	87.7	98.4	86.7	85.8	98.0	84.1
B. In 1910						
Males	88.8	98.3	93.8	87.7	98.0	92.7
Females	87.4	98.2	93.1	85.5	97.7	91.7

SOURCE: U.S. Census of Population, Public Use Samples.

NOTE: If either parent is foreign-born, the person is classified as first generation if he/she is native-born.

1970. In both 1960 and 1970, for women and men and for every age group, the results exhibit a clear pattern: native-born children with at least one foreign-born parent attained higher schooling levels and higher earnings than did the native-born children of native-born parents. And this occurred despite the fact that foreign-born men had lower levels of schooling and, for the 25–49 age group, lower earnings than did either native-born group.

The average schooling differential between the first generation and later generations of native-born men was one half of a year in 1960, declining to one third of a year in 1970, while the average schooling level of foreign-born men was 1.5 (1960) to 0.9 years (1970) lower than that of the native-born male children of the foreign-born. The average (nominal) incomes of first-generation men exceeded those of native-born men of later generations by 16 percent in both 1960 and 1970 and exceeded those of foreign-born men by 10 percent in 1960 and 14 percent in 1970. Differences across generations in levels of schooling were smaller for women than for men; in 1960 the schooling advantage for first- over later-generation native-born women was 0.1 years in 1960 and 0.2 years in 1970. The earnings of employed native-born women of the first generation, however, were 15 and 11 percent higher than those of higher generations in 1960 and 1970, respectively.

The years of schooling completed by the adult children of foreign-born parents in the censuses of 1960 and 1970 reflect the resources allocated by the foreign-born who entered the United States, on average, more than 40 years prior to the date of the census. Thus, the numbers in Tables 10.13 and 10.14 do not necessarily reflect trends in the school investment behavior of

TABLE 10.13
Average Years of Schooling and Nominal Earnings of Men,
by Age and Generational Status: 1960 and 1970

	Schooling			Earnings		
	Foreign-Born	Native-Born		Foreign-Born	Native-Born	
Age Group		First	Later		First	Later
A. In 1960						
25–29	12.35	14.16	13.33	3392	4615	4022
30–34	12.69	13.69	12.96	4817	5611	4856
35–39	12.47	13.68	12.85	4756	6260	5420
40–44	11.94	12.88	12.33	5409	6326	5574
45–49	11.36	12.37	11.72	5953	6116	5241
50–54	10.82	12.01	11.32	5533	5793	4905
55-59	9.99	11.39	10.87	5213	5463	4685
25–59	11.31	12.87	12.33	5300	5880	4964
B. In 1970						
25–29	13.67	14.70	14.36	7125	8162	7143
30–34	13.72	14.94	13.95	8278	8330	10433
35–39	12.59	14.62	13.66	8734	9456	11523
40–44	13.02	13.90	13.38	9585	9677	11618
45–49	12.44	13.57	13.01	9928	10012	10954
50–54	12.35	13.15	12.51	9827	9528	10886
55–59	11.90	12.56	11.92	9721	9882	8764
25–59	12.78	13.68	13.38	9151	10690	8934

SOURCE: U.S. Census of Population, Public Use Samples.

NOTES: Average earnings are calculated for persons earning income. 1960 and 1970 earnings are not comparable because of inflation.

recent immigrants. In Table 10.15, therefore, we present the school-attendance rates of young children by the nativity of the parents and by type of school (public versus private or parochial) in 1960 and 1970. These figures for school attendance parallel those for schooling attainment: for every age group and in both census years except one (ages 10–14 in 1970) children with at least one foreign-born parent had higher school-attendance rates than did children whose parents are both native-born.[2]

In all age groups native-born children with a foreign-born parent were also much more likely to attend a private/parochial school than were the children of native-born parents. In 1960 (1970) in the approximate pre-college age range 5–19, 20.4 (16.2) percent of the native-born children of

[2]In the single exception, the magnitude of the differential is trivial; children aged 10–14 in 1970 with both parents native-born had a school-attendance rate .005 higher than that for comparable children with at least one parent foreign-born.

TABLE 10.14
Average Years of Schooling and Nominal Earnings of Women,
by Age and Generational Status: 1960 and 1970

	Schooling			Earnings		
	Foreign-Born	Native-Born		Foreign-Born	Native-Born	
Age Group		First	Later		First	Later
A. In 1960						
25–29	12.03	13.56	13.22	2068	2340	1984
30–34	12.27	13.41	13.02	2343	2386	1983
35–39	11.93	13.06	12.84	2173	2405	2038
40–44	11.80	12.69	12.53	2399	2485	2160
45–49	10.81	12.20	12.13	2263	2572	2241
50–54	10.05	11.88	10.84	2627	2608	2401
55–59	9.36	11.39	11.26	2431	2816	2227
25–59	10.88	12.57	12.51	2365	2520	2133
B. In 1970						
25–29	13.52	14.69	14.08	3280	4448	3494
30–34	12.53	13.98	13.70	3461	3962	3343
35–39	12.56	13.81	13.35	3986	3832	3290
40–44	12.06	13.48	13.23	3299	3919	3598
45–49	12.25	13.24	13.02	4039	4092	3975
50–54	11.64	12.82	12.70	3751	4025	3859
55–59	11.00	12.29	12.27	3924	4255	3857
25–59	12.22	13.26	13.27	3681	4070	3616

SOURCE: U.S. Census of Population, Public Use Samples.

NOTES: Average earnings are calculated for persons earning income. 1960 and 1970 earnings are not comparable because of inflation.

the foreign-born attended a private/parochial school while only 11.8 (10.8) of the children of native-born parents did so. Among the subset of children aged 5–19 *who attended school*, over 21 percent of the children of foreign-born parents attended a private/parochial school in 1960 (and in 1970, 16.5 percent); the comparable rates for children of the native-born were 11.6 percent in 1960 and 10.8 percent in 1970. Thus, a significantly smaller share of the schooling of the children of immigrants was directly financed by U.S. taxpayers in 1960 and 1970, despite the higher schooling rates of immigrants' children.

If we divide the non-public school category into its private and parochial components, we find that most of the non-public schooling is church-sponsored (parochial); thus, it is not necessarily true that foreign-born parents financed by themselves a greater share of their schooling investment than did native-born parents. Figures 10.3 and 10.4 display the school-

TABLE 10.15
Public and Non-Public School Attendance Rates of Native-Born,
by Age Group and by Nativity of Parents: 1960 and 1970

Age Group of Child	Foreign-Born Mother or Father				Native-Born Mother and Father			
	Public	Non-Public	Total	Non-Pub/Total	Public	Non-Public	Total	Non-Pub/Total
A. In 1960								
5–9	.679	.191	.870	.220	.707	.122	.829	.147
10–14	.739	.236	.975	.242	.848	.124	.972	.128
15–19	.560	.164	.724	.227	.600	.094	.695	.136
20–24	.116	.072	.187	.385	.094	.048	.143	.338
25–29	.043	.039	.082	.476	.039	.018	.057	.311
B. In 1970								
5–9	.735	.160	.895	.179	.762	.109	.871	.125
10–14	.791	.175	.966	.181	.861	.110	.971	.113
15–19	.663	.155	.818	.189	.679	.101	.780	.129
20–24	.166	.094	.260	.362	.136	.074	.210	.352
25–29	.048	.053	.091	.580	.052	.021	.072	.285

SOURCE: U.S. Census of Population, Public Use Samples.

NOTE: The non-public category includes both private and parochial schools.

attendance rates of two groups of native-born children aged 5–17 in 1970: those with two native-born parents and those with at least one foreign-born parent. As shown, the striking difference between the two groups is in their rates of *parochial* school attendance.

It is interesting to explore further two aspects of the preference of immigrant parents for parochial schooling—whether this propensity is conditioned by the parents' region of origin and by the nativity configuration of the parents. Table 10.16 reports the school-attendance rates separately for children with two foreign-born parents, for children with a foreign-born mother only or a foreign-born father only, and for the aggregate of children with *only* one foreign-born parent. These figures indicate that the propensity for parochial schooling is greater when both parents are foreign-born. However, the children of this group also have lower school-attendance rates than those with only one foreign-born parent. Indeed, children of mixed-nativity parents have higher school-attendance rates than children of two native-born parents.

To examine the operation of region of origin, we report in Table 10.17 the school-attendance rates among children of the three types of foreign-parent configurations, separately for persons from the Western Hemisphere, Europe, and Asia. These figures reveal that the propensity for parochial schooling is almost startlingly high among European immigrant couples (19.0 percent of their children are in parochial school) and substan-

FIGURE 10.3a
School Attendance of Native-Born Children
Aged 5–17 of Foreign-Born Parents: 1970

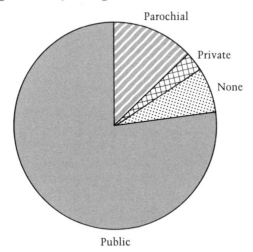

FIGURE 10.3b
School Attendance of Native-Born Children
Aged 5–17 of Native-Born Parents: 1970

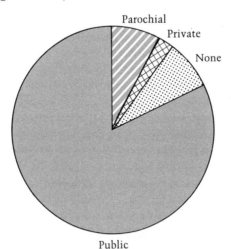

tially high among Asian immigrant couples (15.5 percent of their children are in parochial school). Among the mixed-nativity couples, Western Hemisphere and Asian immigrant women appear to favor parochial schooling more than their male counterparts; but the opposite is true for European

FIGURE 10.4a
*Type of School Attended by Native-Born Children
Aged 5–17 of Foreign-Born Parents: 1970*

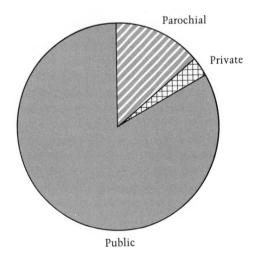

Parochial

Private

Public

FIGURE 10.4b
*Type of School Attended by Native-Born Children
Aged 5–17 of Native-Born Parents: 1970*

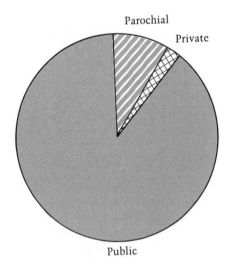

Parochial

Private

Public

immigrants, among whom 16.3 percent of the children of a European father are in parochial school. Table 10.17 also shows that the phenomenon of lower school-attendance rates among children with two foreign-born par-

TABLE 10.16

School Attendance Rates of Native-Born Children Aged 5–17,
by Nativity of Parents and School Type, 1970

Nativity of Parents	Type of School			
	Public	Parochial	Private	None
Both Parents Foreign-Born	70.9	15.2	3.2	10.7
One Parent Only Foreign-Born	79.5	12.4	2.6	5.5
Mother only foreign-born	80.2	11.8	2.9	5.2
Father only foreign-born	78.6	13.1	2.3	5.9
One or Both Parents Foreign-Born	77.0	13.2	2.8	7.0
Both Parents Native-Born	81.7	8.2	2.1	8.0

SOURCE: U.S. Census of Population, Public Use Samples.

ents is confined to parents from the Western Hemisphere and from Europe, the proportions not in school registering 10.4 and 11.7 percent, respectively. The proportion not in school of the children of Asian immigrant couples is remarkably low (1.4 percent), less than a quarter of that among children with two native-born parents (8.0 percent).

The 1980 census does not provide information on the birthplace of parents, so it is not possible to examine the schooling or earnings of the adult native-born by generational status as for 1960 and 1970. We can, however, look at the schooling of the foreign-born who entered the United States as children, as an indicator of the schooling decisions made by recent immigrant parents. Table 10.18 reports the proportions of native-born and foreign-born men and women aged 20–24 attending school, by years in the United States and by area of origin in both 1970 and 1980.

The 1970 figures (panels A and B of Table 10.18) comparing the school-attendance rates of the foreign-born children of foreign-born parents with those of the native-born are similar to the 1970 differentials in schooling between the native-born children of foreign-born parents and those of native-born parents shown in Tables 10.13–10.15. For all durations in the United States (except, among females, those who entered 15–19 years earlier), the foreign-born children of foreign-born parents who entered the United States as children had school-attendance rates greater than or equal to those of native-born children. Although a small proportion of the native-born had foreign-born parents, so that the differential understates slightly the effects on schooling of having foreign-born parents, the average rate of attendance for the foreign-born men aged 20–24 in 1970 who entered as

TABLE 10.17

School Attendance Rates of Native-Born Children Aged 5–17,
by Nativity of Parents, Origin Area of Foreign-Born Parents,
and School Type, 1970

Nativity of Parents	Type of School			
	Public	Parochial	Private	None
A. Western Hemisphere				
Both parents foreign-born	76.7	11.1	1.7	10.4
Mother only foreign-born	78.2	13.7	1.9	6.2
Father only foreign-born	81.5	10.4	2.0	6.2
B. Europe				
Both parents foreign-born	64.4	19.0	4.9	11.7
Mother only foreign-born	81.9	10.2	3.4	4.5
Father only foreign-born	75.1	16.3	3.1	5.4
C. Asia				
Both parents foreign-born	83.1	15.5	0.0	1.4
Mother only foreign-born	82.7	11.1	2.5	3.7
Father only foreign-born	82.5	9.5	0.0	7.9

SOURCE: U.S. Census of Population, Public Use Samples.

children was 25 percent higher than that for native-born men in that age group. Among women, however, the 1970 differential was only 1 percent.

In 1980 (panels C and D of Table 10.18) the schooling rates of the foreign-born aged 20–24 who entered as children were significantly higher than those of the comparably aged native-born for both sexes—by 20 percent for men and by 14 percent for women—despite the rise by 31 percent between 1960 and 1970 in the school-attendance rates of native-born women aged 20–24 (rates for males rose by only 5 percent).

Table 10.18 also reveals considerable heterogeneity in schooling rates across the foreign-born by area of origin. It is particularly interesting to note that the ranking of school-attendance rates for men across the three principal areas of origin is exactly the opposite of the ranking for cumulative fertility shown in Table 10.6. Thus, families are largest and school-attendance rates of young men entering as children are the lowest among the foreign-born from Western Hemisphere countries, while average family size is the lowest and average male school-attendance rates are the highest

TABLE 10.18
Percentage of Persons Aged 20–24 Attending School,
by Sex, Nativity, Years in the United States, and Census Year

Years in U.S.	Native-Born	Foreign-Born			
		All	Western Hemisphere	Europe	Asia
A. Males in 1970					
n.a.	25.4	—	—	—	—
0– 4	—	31.3	19.3	21.6	57.4
5– 9	—	31.2	27.4	31.1	46.2
10–14	—	33.1	26.0	33.3	51.6
15–19	—	28.2	14.9	28.5	63.6
B. Females in 1970					
n.a.	15.7	—	—	—	—
0– 4	—	15.8	10.0	6.5	22.8
5– 9	—	15.7	14.6	10.8	31.7
10–14	—	18.5	13.1	17.0	21.9
15–19	—	14.6	18.9	14.6	50.0
C. Males in 1980					
n.a.	26.6	—	—	—	—
0– 4	—	36.6	19.3	30.6	56.6
5– 9	—	31.7	14.6	31.7	48.0
10–14	—	33.1	28.4	32.9	63.6
15–19	—	32.4	29.9	29.2	55.3
D. Females in 1980					
n.a.	20.6	—	—	—	—
0– 4	—	23.6	16.2	19.6	35.9
5– 9	—	23.2	19.3	13.3	47.4
10–14	—	31.6	28.8	26.9	55.6
15–19	—	27.2	32.2	19.7	26.7

SOURCE: U.S. Census of Population, Public Use Samples.

among the foreign-born from Asia, with the European foreign-born in the middle for both variables. Among the foreign-born women aged 20–24, however, attendance rates for Western Hemisphere women exceed those for European women.

Another way to identify the children of foreign-born parents from the 1980 census data, in the absence of direct information on parental nativity, is by using information on children residing in households with their parents. Household members who are the children of foreign-born household heads and/or of heads married to foreign-born women can be compared with those who are the children of native-born household heads married to native-born women. One advantage of creating a sample of children based on household membership and kinship information is that both the nativity and socioeconomic characteristics of parents can be discerned. A problem, however, is that children not living with their parents are excluded; and there is no rigorous way of knowing how non-resident children differ systematically from resident children and, most important, how the residency of children is associated with parental characteristics.

We selected a random sample of 1,931 married, spouse-present foreign-born women from the 1980 census Public Use A sample and obtained for each woman information on the age distribution and school-attendance rates of her children. We also drew a random sample of 1,085 married native-born women, each still married to her first husband, who is also native-born, and assembled the same information on children. Table 10.19 provides descriptive statistics for these two samples. The average proportion of children in school is higher in the sample of native-born parents than in the sample of foreign-born mothers; however, the average age of children is higher in the native-born parent sample and both the mother's schooling attainment and the father's earnings (in 1979) are also higher among the native-born. Despite these differences, children of foreign-born mothers were 40 percent more likely to attend a private or parochial school.

To assess whether there is a difference by the nativity of the mother in the likelihood that a child residing with his or her parents attends school and to assess the effects of parental socioeconomic characteristics, we combined the two samples and estimated the effect of the mother's nativity on the proportion of children attending school, net of the effects of the age distribution of children, as characterized by the mean, minimum, and maximum age of the children, and net of the effects of mother's schooling attainment and husband's earnings. We also examined the effects of these variables on the likelihood of a child attending a non-public school.

Table 10.20 reports the coefficient estimates, obtained using maximum-likelihood probit. In the first column for each dependent variable, parental socioeconomic variables are excluded in order to obtain the gross differential in the schooling of children across mothers of different nativity. Net of the effects of differences in the age distribution of the children, there is no statistically significant difference in the probability that a resident child attends school according to whether or not the child's mother is foreign-born. While children of foreign-born mothers are no less likely to attend school, however, they are 40 percent more likely to attend a private/parochial school, and this difference is statistically significant.

In the second column, the mother's schooling attainment and the father's earnings are added to the specification. These estimates suggest that if households with a foreign-born mother were characterized by the same maternal schooling and earnings as households in which both parents are

TABLE 10.19
Characteristics of Households with Children,
by Nativity of Mother: 1980

Characteristic	Native-Born		Foreign-Born	
	Mean	Standard Deviation	Mean	Standard Deviation
Proportion Children in School	.709	.378	.683	.391
Proportion Children in Non-Public School	.107	.265	.145	.309
Average Age of Children	9.44	5.46	8.97	5.63
Minimum Age of Children	7.35	5.27	6.74	5.25
Maximum Age of Children	11.39	6.29	11.05	6.71
Schooling Attainment of Mother	12.35	2.29	10.89	4.23
Earnings of Father	17315	12380	16993	12531
Age at Entry of Foreign-Born Mother	—	—	22.81	9.61
Sample Size	1085		1931	

SOURCE: U.S. Census of Population, Public Use Samples.

native-born, children in households with a foreign-born mother would be almost 6 percent more likely to attend school. Moreover, net of the resources available to parents, children in households with a foreign-born mother are 48 percent more likely to attend a private/parochial school. Thus, among households with comparable total resources, those with a foreign-born mother invest more resources in schooling than do those with native-born parents.

The results in Tables 10.12–10.20 are consistent with the hypothesis that immigrants are investors. The data suggest that persons who are able and willing to invest in making a new life for themselves through migration tend also to invest in their children's future, at least through schooling. In Table 10.21 we look at how the origin-country characteristics of the foreign-born influence the differentials among the foreign-born on the schooling of their children. We include as regressors the same set of origin-country characteristics as we did in our analysis of fertility differentials among foreign-born women in Table 10.7, but we employ the sample of married, foreign-born women with children residing at home and also include as regressors the variables describing the children's age distribution.

In column 1 of Table 10.21 the results are a mirror image of the

TABLE 10.20

Determinants of School Attendance for Children Residing in Households
with Married, Spouse-Present, Foreign-Born
or Native-Born Mothers in 1980:
Maximum Likelihood, Two-Limit Probit Estimates

Variable	Proportion of Children Attending School		Proportion of Children in Non-Public School	
	(1)	(2)	(1)	(2)
Foreign-Born Mother	.0160	.0586	.398	.484
	(0.38)	(1.39)	(4.10)	(4.96)
Schooling Attainment	—	.0254	—	.0775
of Mother		(4.34)		(5.64)
Husband's Income ($\times 10^{-5}$)	—	.934	—	1.76
		(5.10)		(4.93)
Mean Age of Children in	.116	.116	−.120	−.0999
Household	(2.34)	(2.32)	(0.96)	(0.75)
Minimum Age of Children	.0624	.0568	.0662	.0469
in Household	(2.52)	(2.28)	(1.06)	(0.72)
Maximum Age of Children	−.0482	−0.429	.0603	.0624
in Household	(1.86)	(1.63)	(0.91)	(0.89)
Constant	.100	−.401	−1.78	−3.11
	(2.22)	(4.51)	(10.7)	(10.51)
χ^2	202.0	195.0	2536.0	2446.0
Sample Size	2972	2972	2972	2972

NOTE: Asymptotic t-ratios appear in parentheses beneath parameter estimates.

fertility estimates of Table 10.7, except for the effect of the total fertility
rate in the country of origin. In particular, the estimates of Tables 10.7 and
10.21 suggest that immigrants who travel over greater distances and who
come from countries with a higher level of per capita income, and thus who
bear greater costs associated with migration, raise smaller families but invest more in the schooling of their children. Moreover, women who enter
relatively late in their life cycle—who are more likely to be married and to
have had children prior to immigration—are characterized by larger family
size (Table 10.7) but higher rates of schooling investment.

In column 2 of Table 10.21 the mother's schooling attainment and her
husband's earnings are added to the set of regressors. These variables influence positively the rates of school attendance of children. The effects of
country-of-origin characteristics are reduced, suggesting that the foreign-
born who traverse greater distances to enter the United States and who
leave higher-income countries are themselves likely to have greater schooling levels and resources; but this only partly explains why, among all foreign-born, their children receive more schooling.

TABLE 10.21
Determinants of the Proportion Attending School in 1980
Among Children Residing in Households
with a Married, Spouse-Present, Foreign-Born Mother:
Maximum Likelihood, Two-Limit Probit Estimates

Variable/Specification	(1)	(2)
Origin-Country Characteristics		
Total fertility rate	.0494	.0493
	(1.42)	(1.42)
GNP per capita $(\times 10^{-4})$	.613	.445
	(3.68)	(2.62)
Literacy rate $(\times 10^{-2})$	.144	.189
	(0.68)	(0.90)
Centrally planned economy	.184	.168
	(1.89)	(1.72)
Distance $(\times 10^{-4})$	.337	.153
	(1.60)	(0.70)
English an	.129	.0683
official language	(1.80)	(0.91)
Parental Characteristics		
Mother's age at entry	.123	.118
	(8.44)	(8.17)
Age at entry squared $(\times 10^{-2})$	−.260	−.248
	(10.2)	(9.89)
Mother's schooling	—	.0217
		(2.93)
Husband's earnings $(\times 10^{-5})$	—	.710
		(2.45)
Characteristics of Children		
Mean age	.0936	.105
	(1.77)	(1.98)
Minimum age	.0976	.0896
	(3.55)	(3.24)
Maximum age	−.0112	−.0148
	(0.41)	(0.54)
Constant	−2.20	−2.39
	(6.19)	(6.74)
χ^2	632.6	654.2
Sample Size	1388	1388

NOTE: Asymptotic t-ratios appear in parentheses beneath parameter estimates.

Summary

Children are the chief legacy of immigrants. Thus, any examination of the achievements and contributions of immigrants must take account of the achievements and contributions of their children. The available evidence supports the view that immigrants have smaller families and school their children at higher rates than do native-born parents. The completed fertility of foreign-born women enumerated in the censuses of 1960, 1970, and 1980 is lower than that for their native-born counterparts. However, between 1970 and 1980 there was a substantial increase in the proportion of immigrants from high-fertility countries, and age-specific fertility rates of new immigrants in 1980 were slightly higher than those of the native-born and the new-entrant foreign-born of earlier years.

With respect to the human-capital investments in children, as indicated in the censuses of 1900, 1910, 1960, and 1970, which provide information on parentage, the native-born adult children of foreign-born parents have higher literacy rates (1900 and 1910) and higher levels of schooling and achieve higher earnings (1960 and 1970) than the native-born children of native-born parents. Examination of school enrollment rates in 1980, moreover, reveals that, at all ages, children with at least one foreign-born parent are more likely to be enrolled in school and far more likely to be enrolled in a private or parochial school than children with two native-born parents, particularly so if the parents are from Asian countries. We also found that both between origin-country groups of the foreign-born and across native-born and foreign-born parents, school enrollment rates and fertility rates tended to be inversely associated, with immigrants from countries located farther from the United States having both smaller families and greater rates of school enrollment for their children.

11

THE IMMIGRANTS OF THE 1980s:
ASSESSING THE 1965–1980 REFORMS

SINCE the 1920s the criteria by which foreign-born persons may qualify for a U.S. legal immigrant visa have undergone a number of important changes, as outlined in Chapters 1 and 9. The last major alterations in this set of criteria were embodied in 1965 and 1976 legislation, which established the immigrant selection system that, with only minor changes, has been in effect since 1978. Although the 1980 census provides information on only a few of the foreign-born admitted under these latest immigration laws, our analysis of census data and of INS data pertaining to immigrants in the 1980s provides a basis for examining current U.S. immigration policies. In this final chapter, we briefly assess U.S. immigration policies in the light of our findings and the trends in immigration from 1978 to 1988. In particular, we examine immigration laws in terms of their success in meeting some of the objectives of current U.S. immigration policy.

Since the 1920s, when the United States first instituted restrictions on the number of immigrants, U.S. immigration law has rested on two cardinal principles. First, in the tradition of its first 150 years, the United States permits the unlimited admission to permanent residence of certain categories of immigrants. Second, all other prospective immigrants are subject to numerical limitations on the total number of immigrants. The criteria for classifying visa applicants into each of the two categories as well as for selection of the numerically limited immigrants reflect five major goals—

facilitating the unification of families, inclusive of protecting the freedom of U.S. citizens to marry whomever they choose; meeting domestic labor market needs; providing refuge for persons fleeing persecution or disaster; maintaining moderate and stable levels of immigration; and achieving a balance in the country composition of the U.S. foreign-born.

The precise categories of persons qualifying for a numerically unrestricted immigrant visa have changed over the years, as have restrictions on the number of immigrants from particular countries of origin and the criteria for priority in the numerically limited class, as discussed in Chapters 1 and 9. For example, while the number of wives of U.S. citizens has never been restricted, that of husbands of U.S. citizens was not fully unrestricted until 1952; parents of U.S. citizens were accorded second preference under the 1952 Act, but under the 1965 amendments were moved to the numerically unlimited class. The Immigration Act of 1924 placed ministers and university professors in the numerically unrestricted class, but the 1952 Act retained only the ministers. Natives of the Western Hemisphere were in the numerically unrestricted class until 1968 and were not subject to either country-specific limitations or the preference-category system until 1977.

In this chapter we first consider the question of who benefits most directly from current U.S. immigration laws. We then examine the quantitative restrictions embodied in the 1965 and 1976 legislation in terms of how successful they have been in (1) controlling the number of persons who immigrate each year and (2) achieving a balance in the country composition of the U.S. foreign-born population without reliance on discriminatory quotas. Finally, we look at the current preference-category system. Although the available data provide no conclusive evidence on such questions as whether an emphasis on family reunification produces less successful cohorts of immigrants than an emphasis on skills, the data do show that the kinship emphasis produces large backlogs of persons entitled to an immigrant visa "sometime in the future."

The Direct Beneficiaries of Immigration

In the eleven-year period from FY 1978 to FY 1988, a total of 6,303,084 persons were admitted to permanent residence under the immigrant selection system established by the 1965 and 1976 Acts of Congress (and altered in only minor ways since then) and the adjustment-to-immigrant-status provisions of the Refugee Act of 1980.[1] These 6.3 million individuals were the principal beneficiaries of U.S. immigration law, per-

[1]As noted earlier, FY 1978 represents the first full year that admissions to permanent residence in both hemispheres were subject to the preference-category system.

sons who chose (and were permitted by U.S. law) to immigrate to the United States presumably because they believed that they would have a better life in the United States than in their native country (or any other country permitting their immigration).

However, as we have stressed, almost all immigrants admitted since 1978—principally excepting the small special-immigrant class and persons adjusting from refugee or asylee status—have required, in order to be admitted, the sponsorship of a U.S. citizen or permanent resident alien. Therefore, complete enumeration of the direct beneficiaries of U.S. immigration law requires that we add to the immigrants their sponsors—the relatives, spouses, or employers of immigrants—who chose to participate in the immigrant admission process presumably because their life, too, would thereby be made better. Table 11.1 reports the number of immigrants admitted to permanent resident status in FYs 1978–1988 under provisions requiring sponsorship—as immediate relatives, in the four kinship-based preference categories, and in the two occupation-based preference categories—together with the number of sponsors, by sponsor's citizenship status.[2] As shown, over 4.8 million persons became immigrants under the immediate-relative and preference-category provisions in the 11-year period. Their immigration required the action of 3.46 million sponsors, of whom at least 2.4 million were citizens of the United States. Thus, the direct beneficiaries of U.S. immigration law—immigrants and their sponsors—numbered almost 10 million in the 11-year period 1978–1988.

However, the calculation of the direct beneficiaries who are not themselves immigrants is inexact. On the one hand, the number of sponsoring individuals may be smaller than the number of immigrant principals, given that a single individual may sponsor several principals—spouse, parents, siblings, etc. On the other hand, the number of direct beneficiaries corresponding to one principal may exceed one—as, for example, in the case of a married couple adopting an orphan.

In a broad sense it could be said that all the citizen sponsors of immigrants are themselves either immigrants or the descendants of immigrants, but it would be useful to learn what proportion are native-born and what proportion are immigrants who naturalized. The only concrete pieces of information currently available pertain to the FY 1985 numerically unlimited immediate relatives; these are the GAO (1988a) finding that 64 percent of the sponsors were native-born U.S. citizens and our estimates, based on the GAO data and discussed in Chapter 6, that 80 percent of the sponsors of spouses were native-born while 96 percent of the sponsors of

---

[2]The number of sponsors is approximated by the number of immigrant principals in each category. This measure may be a slight overestimate for the third-preference category, which may include persons of such renown that no sponsor is required.

TABLE 11.1

Counting the Direct Beneficiaries of U.S. Immigration Law:
Sponsored Immigrants and Their Sponsors in FYs 1978–1988

Class of Admission	Immigrants	Direct Beneficiaries		
		Sponsors		
		Citizens	Residents	Either
A. Numerically Unlimited Immediate Relatives				
Spouses	1,201,242	1,201,242	NA	NA
Parents	405,079	405,079	NA	NA
Children	351,143	351,143	NA	NA
B. Numerically Limited Close Relatives and Their Spouses and Children				
First preference	84,971	70,860	NA	NA
Second preference	1,182,821	NA	803,061	NA
Fourth preference	190,748	55,777	NA	NA
Fifth preference	859,572	342,481	NA	NA
C. Numerically Limited Workers and Their Spouses and Children				
Third preference	246,659	NA	NA	108,229
Sixth preference	278,778	NA	NA	126,268
Total	4,801,013	2,426,582	803,061	234,497

SOURCES: U.S. INS *1982 Statistical Yearbook*, Table IMM 1.5; U.S. INS *1988 Statistical Yearbook*, Table 4.

NOTES: The number of sponsors is estimated by the number of principals awarded immigrant visas in each class of admission. The number of sponsors is thus correct for all classes of admission except third-preference, for which it may be a slight overestimate (given that a few third-preference principals of exceptional renown do not require a sponsor). The immediate-relative children category includes adoptees. The sponsor of a third-preference or sixth-preference immigrant may be a person (citizen or resident) or an institution. The table omits those classes of admission which do not require an immigrant-visa sponsor (such as American Indians born in Canada, investors, and refugees).

parents were naturalized (Chapter 6). If we apply these proportions to the immediate relatives for the entire 11-year period, then over 1.25 million U.S. citizen sponsors were native-born and of these almost 1 million sponsored spouses.

As noted, over 2.4 million of the 10 million direct beneficiaries were U.S. citizens at the time of the immigration event. This number is likely to grow with the passage of time. For example, many of the 0.8 million sponsors of second-preference immigrants will have naturalized subsequent to sponsorship, and many of the 6.3 million new immigrants also will naturalize. Indeed, if they naturalize at the same rates as did persons who became immigrants in the 1970s, then over 2 million will have naturalized within

10 years of entry. Thus, ignoring third- and sixth-preference sponsors, whose citizenship is unknown, between 1978 and 1988 almost 4.6 million U.S. citizens (new and native-born) and an additional 5 million foreign-born residents were direct beneficiaries of the current immigration laws. This is a relatively large constituency.

The benefits of U.S. immigration laws also accrue to native-born U.S. citizens who do not sponsor immigrants—those who consume the products made or services provided by, who learn from, or employ immigrants. But some native-born citizens bear the costs of immigration—those who directly compete with them in the labor market or who have their neighborhoods transformed rapidly, for example. As discussed in Chapter 7, the indirect beneficiaries and the benefits and costs of immigration are more difficult to describe and quantify. Based on census information on the composition of the labor force by industry and by skill, it would appear that U.S. consumers of fruits and vegetables and of shoes and apparel as well as of the services of tailors and jewelers were likely to have benefited the most. Low-skill native-born workers, particularly those located in the southwestern border areas of the United States, benefited the least. However, available studies do not provide evidence of substantial effects of immigration on native-born workers' earnings or of the consequences of immigration on relative price levels or on returns to and levels of investment in the United States.

Shaping the Flow of Immigrants

Controlling the Number of Immigrants

Whatever is the optimal number of immigrants that should be admitted on an annual basis to the United States—if there is such a number—large increases in the foreign-born population occurring in a short period of time may entail important short-run costs, particularly if such increases are not anticipated. Some restraints on the number of immigrants admitted per year might therefore be desirable.

Although there have been restrictions on the number of immigrant visas allocated to certain types of immigrants since the 1920s, the United States has never placed an overall limit on the annual number of immigrants. Certain categories of immigrants have always been exempted from numerical restrictions. The basic strategy of U.S. law—that of classifying prospective immigrants into two groups, the one subject to numerical limitations, the other not—would appear to be incompatible with an absolute ceiling on immigration. In particular, an absolute ceiling would conflict with two of the major principles used to define the numerically exempt group—allowing U.S. citizens to marry whomever they want from whatever country and providing a refuge for persons fleeing persecution—for the numbers of such marriages and of refugees cannot be known in advance.

For example, between 1979 and 1980 the number of immigrants increased by over 70,000 (15 percent), due principally to increases in refugee/asylee adjustments and in immediate relatives. The major component of the increase in refugee/asylee adjustments was the admission to permanent residence of 46,058 persons entitled by the Refugee Parolee Act of 1978 (see Chapter 9); this group included refugees from the three Indochinese countries (33,731), the Soviet Union (8,368), and Cuba (5,841).[3] The increase in immediate relatives reflected an increase in the number of marriages by U.S. citizens to the foreign-born by over 10,000 and increases in sponsored parents and children by almost 2,000 and 3,000, respectively.[4]

What are the sources of the annual fluctuation in admissions to permanent residence? Figure 11.1 shows the number admitted in each of four major groups in the period FY 1978–1988. The groups are defined as follows: The preference-category group consists of the six preference categories plus the nonpreference category. The second group includes the three categories of numerically exempt immediate relatives, namely, the spouses, parents, and minor children of adult U.S. citizens. The refugees/asylees group contains not only all refugee/asylee adjustments but also the seventh-preference immigrants for the years 1978–1981. The fourth group includes all other immigrants; it thus reflects the special-immigrant class, suspension-of-deportation cases, and a variety of judicial and legislative classes, such as the Silva Program and Registry Date Provision classes.[5]

As depicted in Figure 11.1, the group containing preference-category immigrants represents the normal flow of numerically limited immigrants under current law. As would be expected, the number is under the ceiling (270,000 since 1981) and, given that worldwide demand exceeds the supply of visas, relatively stable. In contrast, the immediate-relative group (over 61 percent of whom were spouses) displays a strong upward trend, the number increasing from 125,819 in FY 1978 to a high of 223,468 in FY 1986, and hovering about 220,000 since then. Twice in the 11-year period, the year-to-year increases exceeded 20,000, between 1981 and 1982 and again between 1984 and 1985; between 1985 and 1986 the 20,000 mark was missed by just 900. Indeed, if the leveling off in the last three years is

[3]The numbers of persons admitted to permanent residence in 1980 under provisions of the Refugee Parolee Act of 1978, classified by origin country, are reported in U.S. INS *1980 Statistical Yearbook*, Table 11.

[4]Classification of immigrants by class of admission is found in U.S. INS *1982 Statistical Yearbook*, Table IMM 1.5.

[5]The numbers are compiled from the U.S. INS *1982 Statistical Yearbook*, Table IMM 1.5, and the *1988 Statistical Yearbook*, Table 4.

FIGURE 11.1
*Persons Admitted to Permanent Resident Status,
by Class of Admission: FYs 1978–1988*

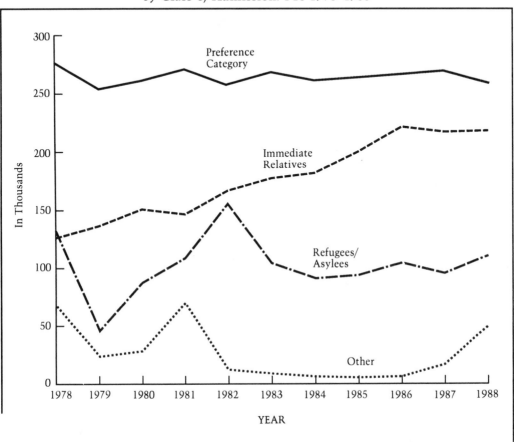

temporary, the immediate-relative group could soon overtake the preference-category group; three more annual increases of 20,000 would produce a flow of 280,000, larger than the numerically limited flow.

The refugees/asylees group exhibits the largest fluctuations—with peaks of over 132,000 in FY 1978 and over 156,000 in FY 1982—but has leveled off at about 100,000 since 1983. Of course, refugee/asylee adjustments reflect not only changes in world conditions (with a lag) but also the decision to adjust status and the timing of that decision, the latter also influenced by administrative factors (processing delays or accelerations). Finally, the plot for the residual group indicates a moderately high initial four-year period—corresponding to the Silva Program in FY 1978–1981 and including two peaks whose Silva Program components number 55,411 and 58,382[6]—followed by the expected low number in the years 1982–1986, followed by an increase to a peak of 50,000 in FY 1988. The last increase reflects legislation permitting the legalization of 40,101 illegal immigrants who had lived in the United States since 1972.[7]

The impact of immigration depends not only on the size of the inflow of immigrants but also on the outflow. The growth in the size of the foreign-born population depends on net, not gross, immigration. The emigration of U.S. immigrants is also not subject to any numerical restrictions under U.S. law. Yet emigration appears to be substantial and, as will be discussed below, selective. We have estimated (Chapter 3) that in the period 1960 to 1979 the average annual ratio of immigrants leaving the United States to immigrants admitted could have been as high as 41 percent. In the absence of direct information on emigration, however, estimates of emigration propensities and emigration rates must be cautiously interpreted.

Placing an overall numerical ceiling on the number of immigrant visas issued per year would not achieve full control of the size of the net additions to the foreign-born population, not only because of the contribution of uncontrolled emigration but also because of the entry of migrants who illegally circumvent the restrictions of U.S. law. It is clear that between 1970 and 1980 the foreign-born population in the United States increased, by up to 3 million persons, via illegal immigration, although the exact amount of the increase and its origin-country composition are not precisely known. It is not yet clear whether the 1986 IRCA restrictions on the employment of illegal aliens are or will be effective in reducing the flows of illegal immigrants. As long as the number of foreign-born persons who wish to immigrate exceeds the number of immigrants permitted, however, there will be a potential for illegal migration.

The desire to immigrate to the United States appears to remain quite high. As of January 1989, 2,328,479 persons were in the State Department's registry of active qualified visa applicants. It is interesting to recall

[6]Starting in 1968, when a numerical limitation was placed on the immigration of persons born in the Western Hemisphere, Cuban refugees adjusting to permanent resident status under the provisions of the Cuban Refugee Act of 1966 were counted against the Western Hemisphere ceiling. Judicial decisions declared this practice illegal, ordering (1) that Cuban refugee adjustments be exempt from the numerical limitation retroactive to 1968 and (2) the "recapture" of 144,999 visas used in Cuban adjustment cases and the allocation thereof to natives of the Western Hemisphere in the queue for numerically limited visas. Persons receiving these visas are known as Silva Program immigrants, from the title of the court case, *Silva v. Levi*. Subsequent legislation exempts refugees adjusting to permanent residence from the numerical limitations on immigration.

[7]As discussed in the introductory chapter, the United States, through Section 249 of the Immigration and Nationality Act, permits admission to permanent resident alien status for illegal aliens who have lived in the United States for a long period of time; the Immigration Reform and Control Act of 1986 changed the requisite date of inception of U.S. residence from 30 June 1948 to 1 January 1972.

that in October 1978 when Congress voted to establish the Select Commission on Immigration and Refugee Policy, one of the factors widely regarded as indicating the need for reform was the size of the visa backlogs—719,379 as of 1 January 1978 (see also U.S. Select Commission 1980a, p. 1), or less than a third of the 1989 backlog.

Indeed, the increase in annual immigration pales beside the increase in the backlogs, as shown in Figure 11.2. When viewed against the backlogs, the trend in annual immigration appears almost flat. If linear trends are fitted to immigration and to the visa backlogs, the estimated annual increase in immigration is 8,022 persons, while the estimated annual increase in the backlogs is 152,643 persons—19 times as large. Figure 11.2 suggests that current U.S. immigration law has resulted in a reasonably stable (despite the fluctuations in marriages and refugees discussed above) and only mildly increasing annual flow of immigrants, its chief drawback being that it also produces a dramatically increasing group of prospective immigrants with a claim on U.S. residence "sometime in the future." To the extent that such persons may indulge in anticipatory U.S. residence—not unlike cohabitation among the betrothed—they contribute to the size of the illegally resident population.

There is another way to gauge the success of current law in controlling the number of immigrants, and that is to compare current immigration levels with those prior to numerical restriction. The highest levels of immigration occurred in the decade 1901–1910, when the annual average was 879,539. In contrast, the annual average for the 1978–1988 period was 573,008—two-thirds of the earlier flow, despite the increase in the world's population.

Controlling the Origin-Country Composition of Immigrants

Rapid changes in the origin-country composition of the U.S. foreign-born were an important impetus to the enactment in the 1920s of the notorious national-origins quota system of immigrant selection. The 1965 and 1976 immigration acts, which established equal per-country ceilings on numerically limited immigration, attempted to avoid the racial and ethnic discrimination embodied in earlier immigration laws and at the same time attempted to maintain a balance in the origin-country composition of immigrants. Although "balance" is an amorphous concept, it would appear that what U.S. lawmakers had in mind was neither to replicate in the immigrant flow the U.S. ancestral composition (as in the national-origins quota system) nor to replicate the world's composition or even that subset of the world's population seeking a life in the United States, but rather

FIGURE 11.2
*Persons Admitted to Permanent Resident Status
and Qualified Visa Applicants Registered with the State Department:
FYs 1978–1988*

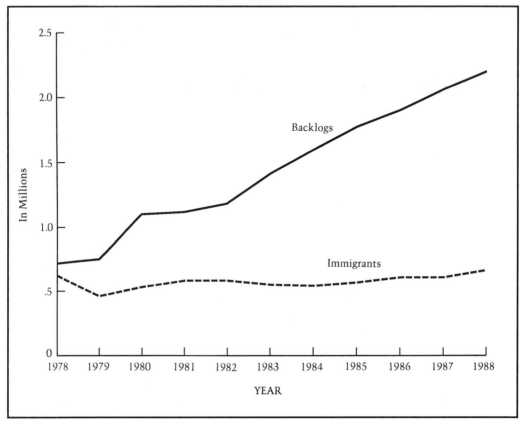

something departing not too greatly from a uniform distribution—roughly similar numbers from each origin country. Of course, country ceilings are but one factor in the process that shapes the country composition of immigrants; other important factors which may become obstacles to "balance" are cross-country differences in the desire to immigrate to the United States, in the likelihood of sponsorship by U.S. citizens for numerically exempt immigration, and in the propensity to emigrate from the United States.

The tripling in the number of Asia-born immigrants between the decades 1961–1970 and 1971–1980, from 439,857 to 1,423,125 (excluding Indochina-born immigrants), was the more-or-less anticipated result of the abolition of the racial quotas that had excluded Asian immigrants prior to

1965.[8] During the same period, however, the number of Europe-born immigrants dropped by over 35 percent, from 1,239,323 to 801,320—a less anticipated result. Thus, instead of merely achieving parity with the Europe-born contingent, the Asia-born contingent grew to a figure 1.75 times as large as the Europe-born in the 1971–1980 decade. Moreover, in the 11-year period 1978–1988, immigrants born in just one country, Mexico, outnumbered immigrants born in all of Europe, 770,153 to 716,502, and the number of immigrants from just two Asian countries, the Philippines (495,313) and Korea (363,205), exceeded that from Europe by 20 percent.[9]

As noted above, discrepancies between the per-country ceilings and the actual number of immigrants from a country arise because of the existence of categories of immigrants exempt from numerical restriction, particularly, but not exclusively, immigrants who qualify by marrying U.S. citizens. Indeed, as seen in Chapter 4, changes in the composition of immigrants by visa category over time appear consistent with the hypothesis that marriages to U.S. citizens by the foreign-born increase when numerical restrictions are instituted or become restrictive.

The uneven distribution across countries of origin among numerically exempt immigrants appears to be related to both the proximity of the citizens of those countries to U.S. citizens and to the attractiveness of those countries relative to the United States.[10] In particular, as discussed in Chapters 4 and 6, the presence of a U.S. military base is directly associated with a large flow of immigrants to the United States who qualify by dint of marriage to a U.S. citizen. It is no surprise, therefore, that a large number of immigrants from the Philippines and Korea are "marital" immigrants and include more females than males, as opposed to immigrants from, say, India or Pakistan. That military agreements beget marital alliances is also seen in Europe, where the most prominent immigrant-sending countries are West Germany and the United Kingdom. West Germany provides an especially dramatic example—in FY 1988 two-thirds of all immigrants were spouses of U.S. citizens and 72 percent of all immigrants were female. Almost half of the immigrants from Mexico (excluding the new 1972 registry provision immigrants) are also spouses of U.S. citizens, but because the country is proximate to the entire U.S. population, not just to a subpopula-

---

[8]The number for FY 1961–1970 includes all persons born in Asia except, for the years 1962–1970, those born in Vietnam (U.S. INS *1961 Annual Report,* Table 9, and *1971 Annual Report,* Table 14). The number for FY 1971–1980 is compiled from U.S. INS *1980 Statistical Yearbook,* Table 13, and excludes immigrants born in all three Indochinese countries.

[9]These numbers are compiled from U.S. INS *1988 Statistical Yearbook,* Table 3.

[10]The numbers of immigrants cross-classified by class of admission and country of birth, discussed in this section, are from U.S. INS *1988 Statistical Yearbook,* Table 7. The numbers cross-classified by country of birth and sex are from U.S. INS *1988 Statistical Yearbook,* Table 12.

tion that is mostly male, the marital immigrants from Mexico appear to be almost evenly divided between men and women.

That the relative attractiveness of the origin countries matters in determining the magnitude of immigrant flows also is evident—far fewer Canadian (4,473) than Mexican (30,755) citizens marry U.S. citizens, although both countries are contiguous to the United States; and far fewer citizens from the United Kingdom (5,499) and West Germany (4,426) marry U.S. citizens compared to citizens from the Philippines (13,079), although each country has a substantial U.S. military population.

The lack of numerical restrictions on marital migration and the different circumstances of sending countries are not the only reasons why per-country ceilings have not been very effective in controlling the country composition of U.S. immigrants. For example, a large proportion of immigrants from the Philippines are parents of U.S. citizens and a relatively large proportion of Korean immigrants are orphaned children adopted by U.S. citizens. These categories of immigrants are also numerically unrestricted, reflecting the policy objective of reuniting or preserving families.

Notwithstanding the large variation in the size of origin-country groups of immigrants, the per-country limits appear to have reduced somewhat the amount by which some countries are disproportionately represented among immigrant flows. This is especially evident in the fact that the country composition of the visa backlogs is less uniform than the country composition of immigrants. For example, the number of visa applicants in the queue from Mexico and the Philippines in 1989 was 403,523 and 422,357, respectively—or 17.3 and 18.1 percent of the total. In contrast, Mexico- and Philippines-born immigrants in FY 1988 constituted 13.0 and 9.8 percent, respectively, of the sum of the numerically limited and the immediate-relative immigrants. Of course, the entire FY 1988 cohort included the newly legalized 1972 registry provision immigrants (most of them Mexicans), so that the corresponding proportions increased for Mexico, to almost 15 percent, and decreased for the Philippines, to almost 8 percent.

The imbalance in the origin-country composition of recent immigrants is not as large as in the past. Immigrants from Italy, for example, exceeded 200,000 per year in the years 1903, 1905–1907, 1910, 1913, 1914, and 1921 (U.S. Bureau of the Census 1975); the annual average in the 1901–1910 decade was 204,588. In contrast, the largest country flow in the 1978–1988 period was 101,268—from Mexico in 1981 (including approximately 50,000 Silva Program cases)—and Mexico's annual average was 70,014, or just over one-third that of Italy in the earlier period.

The origin-country composition of the foreign-born also depends on the variation in the propensities to emigrate from the United States. Emigration rates appear to differ substantially across immigrant groups categorized by country of origin. In particular, immigrants from countries more proximate to the United States or from countries in Europe appear to have higher emigration rates and those from Asian countries the lowest. The policy of unrestricted emigration and the differential proximity and attractiveness of sending countries thus have contributed to the relatively large increase in Asian-origin individuals among the foreign-born in the United States. For example, the proportion of new permanent resident aliens from Asia increased from 35 percent in 1971–1980 to 45 percent in 1981–1988.[11] But if Asian immigrants exhibit the same low emigration propensities in the 1980s that they did in the 1970s, then net immigration from Asian countries may be rising even faster than gross immigration. This is speculative, however, as knowledge about emigration from the United States and its behavior over time is highly imperfect.

Why should U.S. immigration law be attentive at all to origin country? Does the country of origin of immigrants matter? As long as the costs (distance) of and gains (relative attractiveness) from migration influence who (among those who are eligible) chooses to come to the United States, U.S. immigrants from different countries will differ from each other, even if culturally homogenous. Origin-country characteristics operate just as selectively as explicit immigration criteria. In particular, and everything else the same, those foreign-born who find it easiest (least costly) to migrate will migrate when there is least to gain, and those foreign-born from poor countries will still reap high rewards from migration to the United States even if they fare less well than average U.S. residents or other immigrants.

We have found that the characteristics of origin countries—in particular their distance from the United States and their level of income per capita—do influence importantly who among those born in origin countries choose to immigrate. Country attributes thus are strongly correlated with the behavior and characteristics of immigrants in the United States. For example, the foreign-born who emigrate from countries located farther from the United States and from countries with higher levels of income do tend to have higher levels of skills, earn higher incomes, have lower levels of fertility, and are less likely to use public welfare services in the United States compared to immigrants from other countries. Immigrants from such countries are also more likely to remain in the United States after entry and are more likely to naturalize.

A potentially important consequence of the origin-country composition of immigrants that is not directly related to immigration selectivity is competition between English and other languages in the United States, as discussed in Chapter 8. In the decade 1971–1980, almost a third of legal

---

[11]These proportions are calculated from the figures in U.S. INS *1988 Statistical Yearbook,* Table 2.

immigrants originated in countries whose official or dominant language is Spanish. The importance of a single foreign language among new immigrants appears similar to that characterizing immigration at the end of the nineteenth century, when German was the language of approximately 30 percent of immigrants and a larger proportion of the U.S. foreign-born could not speak English. We have found that in both 1900 and 1980, however, there were significant economic rewards to acquiring English skills. Moreover, the influence of parental English abilities, household resources, and community characteristics on the English-language proficiency of the children of immigrants was similar. However, Spanish-language immigrants are far more likely to be clustered in communities with high proportions of other Spanish-speaking foreign-born, where the economic incentives for acquiring English skills are reduced. Such immigrants are significantly less likely to acquire English-language proficiency as their residence in the United States lengthens and the data suggest that future Spanish-language immigrants will be more likely to reside in such communities.

Although the evidence suggests that the children of Spanish-speaking immigrants are no less likely to acquire English language skills compared to children of German-speaking parents in 1900, the spatial concentration of the Spanish-speaking foreign-born is a modern phenomenon. The persistence and growth of an alternative common language in the United States, however, can presumably be influenced by school policies and, as our results suggest, by domestic policies facilitating the economic success of immigrants, which importantly influences the English abilities of the children of immigrants.

The country-of-origin composition of immigrants clearly matters for the growth of an alternative non-English language in the United States. However, immigration criteria attentive to language skills are a far more direct instrument for addressing this potential problem. Indeed, to the extent that it is the skills—language and labor market—of immigrants that are of concern, skill-based eligibility criteria may be preferred to direct numerical restrictions based on place of birth or last residence.

Criteria for the Selection of Immigrants: Family Reunification and Labor Market Skills

Since numerical limits were first placed on legal immigration, the principal form of rationing the numerically limited visas has been a preference system whereby visa applicants are granted priority on the basis of two criteria: the kinship of the foreign-born applicant to a U.S. citizen or permanent resident alien and the labor market skill of the applicant. In the 1952

Act, the first-preference category (in a system of four preference categories plus nonpreference) was solely skill-based (but including the spouses and children of skilled aliens) and was alloted half of each nation's quota. The 1965 amendments, however, reversed the priorities, creating two occupation-based preference categories for professionals and other needed workers and assigning them third and sixth preference, respectively, in a new system of seven categories (which in 1980 was reduced to six categories), plus nonpreference. Each of the two occupation-based categories can use up to 10 percent of the numerically limited visas. Thus, the current preference system, which has covered the Eastern Hemisphere since 1965 and the Western Hemisphere since 1976, has favored immigrants with family ties to U.S. citizens or legal immigrants. Indeed, under current law, fewer than 4 percent of all immigrants are screened according to labor market criteria.

While the current preference system clearly gives priority to the principle of reuniting families in allocating numerically limited visas, such a system is not necessarily inconsistent with a concern for the success of the immigrant in the United States. First, since such immigrants must be sponsored by a family member in the United States (parent, sibling, or adult child), the new immigrant is provided a "caseworker" and possibly a private "support network," at least initially. Indeed, as described in Chapter 5, we have found that foreign-born heads of households who have been in the United States less than five years are significantly more likely to co-reside with both their adult siblings and/or their parents than are native-born heads of households. Co-residence with elder parents, moreover, persists over time, although it does not for siblings. Second, if the characteristics of family members are similar, then given that priority in sponsorship is provided to naturalized immigrants, who presumably have had some success in the United States, the family preference system will select new immigrants who are also likely to succeed.

A major problem with allocating visas according to kinship is that it is inconsistent with controlling the number of eligible visa applicants, as Figure 11.2 shows. The system leads to immigration chaining in which each new immigrant begets, through kinship and marriage, a new set of foreign-born eligible for visas. The "multiplier," relating an immigrant to all those he or she sponsors as a result of family-based visa entitlements, is in principle infinite in size. However, for almost all family categories of immigration, the sponsor must be a U.S. citizen. And less than half of immigrants ever naturalize, as discussed in Chapter 2, although immigration sponsorship evidently represents a significant incentive for an immigrant to obtain citizenship.

We have estimated that in the first decade of permanent residence an immigrant principal not himself or herself sponsored by a family member sponsors on average approximately 0.7 new immigrants; incorporating the second sponsored generation (sponsored by the first sponsored generation) increases this number to between 1.1 and 1.3. Thus, an important implication of the immigration multiplier that is embodied in the kinship-priority system is that an increase in the number of visas to be allocated to immigrants based on skill criteria will increase the number of family-based immigrants by the same amount within 20 years. It is difficult to simultaneously maintain control over the magnitude of immigrant flows, enlarge the number of immigrants selected by skill criteria, and preserve family reunification entitlements. The visa backlogs provide the most dramatic indicator of the conflict between the numerical limitations on immigration and the principle of family-based entitlements (especially the sibling entitlement). For example, of the 121,884 Vietnamese persons in the visa queue in 1989, almost three-fourths were in the fifth-preference category.

There are not sufficient data to enable comparison of the economic success of immigrants admitted via kinship to those (few) immigrants who were selected on the basis of their labor market skills. The cohorts of the foreign-born who entered in 1975–1980, most of whom entered by family criteria, did have lower average earnings compared to the cohorts entering between 1955 and 1960 and between 1965 and 1970, when kinship was a less important criterion for immigrant selection. But this in part can be explained by an increase in unsponsored illegal immigrants. The Eastern Hemisphere foreign-born who entered the United States in 1965–1970 (fully under the kinship priority system) experienced a higher growth in earnings than similarly aged native-born U.S. citizens in the 1970s and no less a decadal rate of growth in earnings relative to that of the native-born than did the foreign-born who entered the United States under the skill-based priority system, in the 1955–1960 period.

Ultimately, it is not clear that the immigrant selection criteria embodied in immigration law importantly affect a basic attribute of immigrants—their above-average willingness to invest in themselves (via migration) and in their children. As discussed in Chapter 10, immigrants appear to have fewer children, to have them late, and to invest heavily in them. Census data for 1900, 1960, and 1970 indicate that the native-born adult children of the foreign-born (who had been admitted in years when very different immigration system were in place) had higher literacy rates, schooling attainment, and earnings than the similarly aged children of the U.S. native-born. And in 1980, the native-born children of the U.S. foreign-born exhibited higher schooling rates than did the children of the native-born.

Hardly a week passes that the popular press does not carry a story that touches one of the themes or questions that we have discussed in this book.

Perhaps it is a story of fact: that a remarkable number of high-school vale-dictorians are immigrants or the children of immigrants; that the new governor of a Mexican state was born in the United States; that the latest slang term in China for an American sweetheart is "airplane tickets"; that a person who has been residing in the United States for many years is about to be deported. Perhaps it is a story of policies, of arguments and counter-arguments: whether to reduce the U.S. military presence abroad; whether to alter the rules for the selection of refugees; whether to place in detention illegal entrants who claim they are fleeing persecution; whether to create a new category of independent immigrants selected on the basis of their skills.

Many of the empirical questions pertaining to immigration to the United States cannot be answered very well. Indeed, the existing data base is inadequate relative to the importance of a policy that directly and indirectly affects so many residents of the United States. Because of this we have proposed a variety of ways to collect new data and to report existing data—from such minor measures as publishing the annual number of persons who immigrate as the spouses of U.S. citizens separately by sex, to more costly measures such as building a file providing information on the sponsors of immigrants and initiating a large-scale longitudinal study of immigrants and non-immigrants entering in different years. With such information we may learn precisely how many immigrants, from which countries, become naturalized citizens and sponsor new immigrants; just how well do immigrants do, and how long it takes; and precisely how many immigrants never learn English. While information from the 1990 census will be useful for assessing the impact of current U.S. immigration policies, the need for new kinds of data, if some of the important and interesting questions are to be answered, cannot be overemphasized.

To the extent that questions of fact underlie questions of policy, a fuller and richer view of the facts will make it possible to formulate policies that are more precisely tailored to objectives. For now, it would appear that current policies represent a particular balancing of objectives. Permitting the numerically unrestricted immigration of immediate relatives simultaneously achieves the goal of unification of immediate families of U.S. citizens and honors the tradition of the country's first 150 years. Although it leaves the total number of immigrants unchecked, the size of immigration flows has been remarkably stable. However, the family-reunification emphasis in selection criteria makes immigration difficult or impossible for many foreign-born persons who might greatly benefit themselves and the United States but who do not possess the requisite U.S. relatives. The worldwide and country ceilings on the numerically restricted immigrants both contribute to a stable and moderate annual immigration level and temper the potential unevenness in the origin-country composition of immigrants—effects especially visible in comparison to the visa backlogs and to immigration prior to the 1920s. However, the origin-country composition of immigrants continues to be dominated by a few countries.

Finally, the current immigrant-selection system produces illegal immigrants. However, so long as more persons wish to immigrate than the United States is officially prepared to accept—an extraordinary acknowledgment of the primordial attractiveness of the political and economic freedoms that characterize this country—there will be illegal immigrants. Indeed, there may be no better testimonial to the relative attractiveness of the United States than the fact that numerous persons prefer life as an illegal alien in the United States to life as a citizen in another country.

As for the specific criteria by which the United States selects its immigrants, it may be that their effect is far outweighed by that of the chief characteristic of immigrants—their above-average willingness to invest in themselves and in their children. The long-run contributions and effects of immigration may be more influenced by the choices made by the foreign-born than by the selection criteria embodied in U.S. immigration laws.

Bibliography

Amemiya, Takeshi 1981. "Qualitative Response Models: A Survey." *Journal of Economic Literature* 19:1483–1536.

Bailar, Barbara A. 1985. "Comment." *Journal of the American Statistical Association* 80:109–114.

Baker, Reginald P., and David S. North 1984. *The 1975 Refugees: Their First Five Years in America.* Washington, DC: New TransCentury Foundation.

Bean, Frank D.; Allan C. King; and Jeffrey S. Passel 1983. "The Number of Illegal Migrants of Mexican Origin in the United States: Sex Ratio-based Estimates for 1980." *Demography* 20:99–110.

Belkin, Lisa 1986. "The Mail Order Marriage Business." *New York Times Sunday Magazine.* May 11, 1986.

Borjas, George J. 1985. "Assimilation, Changes in Cohort Quality, and the Earnings of Immigrants." *Journal of Labor Economics* 3:463–489.

Chiswick, Barry R. 1978. "The Effect of Americanization on the Earnings of Foreign-Born Men." *Journal of Political Economy* 86:897–921.

Citro, Constance F., and Michael L. Cohen 1985. *The Bicentennial Census: New Directions for Methodology in 1990.* Washington, DC: National Academy Press.

Dooley, Thomas A. 1956. *Deliver Us From Evil.* New York: Farrar, Straus and Cudahy.

——— 1958. *The Edge of Tomorrow.* New York: Farrar, Straus and Cudahy.

——— 1960. *The Night They Burned the Mountain.* New York: Farrar, Straus and Cudahy.

Fergany, Nader 1987. "Towards a Conceptual Framework for the Study of Contemporary International Migration." Paper presented at the IUSSP Workshop on International Migration Systems and Networks, Center for Migration Studies, New York.

Forbes, Susan S. 1984. "Residency Patterns and Secondary Migration of Refugees." Paper presented at the Refugee Policy Forum, Wingspread Conference Center, Racine, Wisconsin, February 6–8.

Fuchs, Lawrence H. 1983. "From Select Commission to Simpson-Mazzoli: The Making of America's New Immigration Law." In Wayne A. Cornelius and Ricardo Anzaldua Montoya, eds. *America's New Immigration Law: Origins, Rationales, and Potential Consequences.* San Diego: Center for U.S.–Mexican Studies.

Garcia y Griego, Manuel 1980. *El Volumen de la Migracion de Mexicanos no Documentados a los Estados Unidos (Nuevas Hipotesis).* Mexico City: Secretaria del Trabajo y Prevision Social, Centro Nacional de Informacion y Estadisticas del Trabajo.

Goering, John M. 1988. "The Immigration Multiplier: Fact or Fiction?" Paper presented at the annual meeting of the Population Association of America, New Orleans, Louisiana, April 1988.

Golini, Antonio 1987. "Population Movements: Typology and Data Collection, Trends, Policies." Paper presented at the European Population Conference, Finland.

429

Gordon, Charles, and Harry Rosenfield 1981. *Immigration Law and Practice.* 8 vols. New York: Matthew Bender.

Gordon, Linda W. 1985. "Southeast Asian Refugee Migration to the United States." Revised version of paper presented at the Conference on Asia-Pacific Immigration to the United States, East-West Population Center, Honolulu, Hawaii, September 1984.

Greenwood, Michael J., and John M. McDowell 1986. "The Factor Market Consequences of U.S. Immigration." *Journal of Economic Literature* 24:1738–1772.

——— 1988. "The Labor Market Consequences of U.S. Immigration: A Survey." Mimeographed. October 1988.

Harper, Elizabeth 1975. *Immigration Laws of the United States,* 3rd ed. Indianapolis: Bobbs-Merrill.

Healy, David F. 1963. *The United States in Cuba, 1898-1902: Generals, Politicians, and the Search for Policy.* Madison, Wisconsin: University of Wisconsin Press.

Heckman, James J. 1979. "Sample Bias as a Specification Error." *Econometrica* 47:153–162.

Heer, David M. 1979. "What is the Annual Net Flow of Undocumented Mexican Immigrants to the United States?" *Demography* 16:417–423.

Hill, Kenneth 1985a. "Indirect Approaches to Assessing Stocks and Flows of Migrants." In Daniel B. Levine, Kenneth Hill, and Robert Warren, eds. *Immigration Statistics: A Story of Neglect.* Washington, DC: National Academy Press.

——— 1985b. "Illegal Aliens: An Assessment." In Daniel B. Levine, Kenneth Hill, and Robert Warren, eds. *Immigration Statistics: A Story of Neglect.* Washington, DC: National Academy Press.

Hirschman, Charles O. 1978. "Prior U.S. Residence Among Mexican Immigrants." *Social Forces* 56:1179–1202.

Hobcraft, John; Jane Menken; and Samuel Preston 1982. "Age, Period and Cohort Effects in Demography: A Review." *Population Index* 48:4–43.

Huberich, C. H. 1947. *The Political and Legislative History of Liberia.* 2 vols. Foreword by Roscoe Pound. New York: Central Book Company.

Hutchinson, Edward P. 1958. "Notes on Immigration Statistics of the United States." *American Statistical Association Journal* 53:963–1025.

——— 1981. *Legislative History of American Immigration Policy, 1798-1965.* Philadelphia: University of Pennsylvania Press.

Jasso, Guillermina, and Mark R. Rosenzweig 1982. "Estimating the Emigration Rates of Legal Immigrants Using Administrative and Survey Data: The 1971 Cohort of Immigrants to the United States." *Demography* 19:279–290.

——— 1986a. "Family Reunification and the Immigration Multiplier: U.S. Immigration Law, Origin-Country Conditions, and the Reproduction of Immigrants." *Demography* 23:291–311.

——— 1986b. "What's in a Name? Country-of-Origin Influences on the Earnings of Immigrants in the United States." *Research in Human Capital and Development: Migration, Human Capital and Development* 4:75–106.

——— 1987. "Using National Recording Systems for the Measurement and Analysis of Immigration to the United States." *International Migration Review* 21:1212–1244.

——— 1988. "How Well Do U.S. Immigrants Do? Vintage Effects, Emigration Selectivity, and Occupational Mobility." *Research in Population Economics* 6:229–253.

——— 1989. "Sponsors, Sponsorship Rates, and the Immigration Multiplier." *International Migration Review* 23:856–888.

——— 1990. "Self Selection and the Earnings of Immigrants: Comment." *American Economic Review* 80:298–304.

Johnston, J. 1984. *Econometric Methods*, 3rd ed. New York: McGraw-Hill.

Judge, George G.; W.E. Griffiths; R. Carter Hill; Helmut Lütkepohl; and Tsoung-Chao Lee 1985. *The Theory and Practice of Econometrics*, 2nd ed. New York: Wiley.

Keely, Charles B. 1971. "Effects of the Immigration Act of 1965 on Selected Population Characteristics of Immigrants to the United States." *Demography* 8:157–169.

——— 1975. "Effects of U.S. Immigration Law on Manpower Characteristics of Immigrants." *Demography* 12:179–192.

——— 1982. "Illegal Migration." *Scientific American* 246:41–47.

Keely, Charles B.; Monica Boyd; Donald F. Heisel; and William Seltzer 1979. "Immigration Statistics: Problems and Recommendations." In *Current Issues in Population Statistics: Reports Prepared by the Subcommittees of the Committee on Population Statistics*. Washington, DC: Population Association of America.

Keely, Charles B., and Ellen Percy Kraly 1978. "Recent Net Alien Immigration to the United States: Its Impact on Population Growth and Native Fertility." *Demography* 15:267–283.

Kraly, Ellen Percy 1977. "U.S. Immigration Statistics: 1950 to 1975." Paper presented at the Roundtable on U.S. Immigration Statistics, U.S. Immigration and Naturalization Service Central Office, Washington, DC.

——— 1982. "Emigration from the United States Among the Elderly." Presented at the annual meeting of the Population Association of America, San Diego.

Kritz, Mary M. 1987. "International Migration Policies: Conceptual Problems." Paper presented at the IUSSP Workshop on International Migration Data, Ottawa.

Lancaster, C., and Frederick J. Scheuren 1978. "Counting the Uncountable Illegals: Some Initial Statistical Speculations Employing Capture–Recapture Techniques." *1977 Proceedings of the Social Statistics Section* Part 1, Washington, DC: American Statistical Association: 530–535.

Levine, Daniel B.; Kenneth Hill; and Robert Warren, eds. 1985. *Immigration Statistics: A Story of Neglect*. Washington, DC: National Academy Press.

McKelvey, Richard D., and William Zavoina 1975. "A Statistical Model for the Analysis of Ordinal Level Dependent Variables." *Journal of Mathematical Sociology* 4:103–120.

Maddala, G.S. 1983. *Limited-Dependent and Qualitative Variables in Econometrics*. Cambridge: Cambridge University Press.

Mallar, C.D. 1977. "The Estimation of Simultaneous Probability Models." *Econometrica* 45:1717–1722.

North, David S. 1978. *Seven Years Later: The Experiences of the 1970 Cohort of Immigrants in the U.S. Labor Market*. Washington, DC: Linton and Company.

Passel, Jeffrey S.; C.D. Cowan; and K.M. Wolter 1983. "Coverage of the 1980 Census." Paper presented at the annual meeting of the Population Association of America, Pittsburgh.

Passel, Jeffrey S., and Jennifer M. Peck 1979. "Estimating Emigration from the United States—A Review of Data and Methods." Paper presented at the annual meeting of the Population Association of America, Philadelphia.

Passel, Jeffrey S., and J. Gregory Robinson 1984. "Revised Estimates of Coverage of the Population in the 1980 Census Based on Demographic Analysis: A Report on Work in Progress." In *Proceedings of the Social Statistics Section of the American Statistical Association*. Washington, DC: American Statistical Association.

Passel, Jeffrey S.; Jacob S. Siegel; and J. Gregory Robinson 1982. "Coverage of the National Population in the 1980 Census, by Age, Sex, and Race: Preliminary Estimates by Demographic Analysis." *Current Population Reports*, Special Studies P-23, no. 115. Washington, DC: U.S. Government Printing Office.

Passel, Jeffrey S., and Karen A. Woodrow 1984. "Geographic Distribution of Undocumented Immigrants: Estimates of Undocumented Aliens Counted in the 1980 Census by State." *International Migration Review* 18:642–671.

——— 1987. "Change in the Undocumented Alien Population in the United States, 1979–1983." *International Migration Review* 21:1304–1323.

Portes, Alejandro 1983. "Of Borders and States: A Skeptical Note on the Legislative Control of Immigration." In Wayne A. Cornelius and Ricardo Anzaldua Montoya, eds. *America's New Immigration Law: Origins, Rationales, and Potential Consequences*. San Diego: Center for U.S.–Mexican Studies.

Portes, Alejandro, and Robert L. Bach 1980. "Immigrant Earnings: Cuban and Mexican Immigrants in the United States." *International Migration Review* 14:315–341.

Reimers, Cordelia W. 1983. "Labor Market Discrimination against Hispanic and Black Men." *Review of Economics and Statistics* 65:570–579.

Review of International Broadcasting Various issues.

Shryock, Henry S.; Jacob S. Siegel; and Associates 1975. *The Methods and Materials of Demography*, 3rd printing (rev.). Washington, DC: U.S. Government Printing Office.

Siegel, Jacob S. 1974. "Estimates of the Coverage of the Population by Sex, Race, and Age in the 1970 Census." *Demography* 11:1–23.

——— 1978. "Collection and Analysis of Immigration Data at the Census Bureau." Prepared statement submitted at hearings before the Select Committee on Population, 95th Cong., 2nd sess. In *Immigration to the United States*. Washington, DC: U.S. Government Printing Office.

Siegel, Jacob S.; Jeffrey S. Passel; and J. Gregory Robinson 1980. "Preliminary Review of Existing Studies of the Number of Illegal Residents in the United States." Report to the U.S. Select Commission on Immigration and Refugee Policy. (Reprinted in U.S. Select Commission 1981b.)

Thomas, Hugh 1971. *Cuba: The Pursuit of Freedom*. New York: Harper & Row.

Tomasi, Lydio F., and Charles B. Keely 1975 *Whom Have We Welcomed? The Adequacy and Quality of United States Immigration Data for Policy Analysis and Evaluation*. New York: Center for Migration Studies.

United Nations Various years. *United Nations Demographic Yearbook.* New York: United Nations.

U.S. Bureau of the Census 1975. *Historical Statistics of the United States: Colonial Times to 1970.* Washington, DC: U.S. Government Printing Office.

—— 1981. "Money Income of Persons and Families in the United States: 1979." *Current Population Reports,* series P-60, no. 129. Washington, DC: U.S. Government Printing Office.

U.S. Congress, Senate Subcommittee on Immigration and Refugee Affairs, Committee on the Judiciary 1987. *Legal Immigration to the United States: A Demographic Analysis of Fifth Preference Visa Admissions.* Washington, DC: U.S. Government Printing Office.

U.S. Congressional Research Service 1979. *U.S. Immigration Law and Policy, 1952–1979.* Washington, DC: U.S. Government Printing Office.

—— 1980. *History of the Immigration and Naturalization Service.* 1980. Washington, DC: U.S. Government Printing Office.

—— 1988. *U.S. Immigration Law and Policy; 1952–1987.* Washington, DC: U.S. Government Printing Office.

U.S. Department of Labor 1989. *The Effects of Immigration on the U.S. Economy and Labor Market.* Immigration Policy and Research Report no. 1, Bureau of International Labor Affairs. Washington, DC: U.S. Government Printing Office.

U.S. Department of State 1983. *Atlas of United States Foreign Relations.* Written by Harry F. Young. Washington, DC: U.S. Government Printing Office.

—— 1980–1989. *Annual Report of the Visa Office.* Washington, DC: U.S. Government Printing Office.

U.S. General Accounting Office 1988a. *Immigration: The Future Flow of Legal Immigration to the United States.* Washington, DC: U.S. Government Printing Office.

—— 1988b. *Immigration: Data Not Sufficient for Proposed Legislation.* Washington, DC: U.S. Government Printing Office.

U.S. Immigration and Naturalization Service 1943–1978. *Annual Report.* Washington, DC: U.S. Government Printing Office.

—— 1979–1985. *Statistical Yearbook.* Washington, DC: U.S. Government Printing Office.

—— 1983. *United States Immigration Laws: General Information.* Washington, DC: U.S. Government Printing Office.

U.S. Select Commission on Immigration and Refugee Policy 1980a. *Semiannual Report to Congress.* Issued March 1980. Washington, DC: U.S. Government Printing Office.

—— 1980b. *Second Semiannual Report to Congress.* Issued October 1980. Washington, DC: U.S. Government Printing Office.

—— 1980c. "Selecting Independent Immigrants to the United States: Alternative Systems." Working Paper issued 7 May 1980.

—— 1981a. *U.S. Immigration Policy and the National Interest: Final Report and Recommendations of the Select Commission on Immigration and Refugee Policy to the Congress and President of the United States.* Issued 1 March 1981. Washington, DC: U.S. Government Printing Office.

────── 1981b. *U.S. Immigration Policy and the National Interest: Staff Report of the Select Commission on Immigration and Refugee Policy.* Issued 30 April 1981. Washington, DC: U.S. Government Printing Office.

Warren, Robert 1979. "Alien Emigration from the United States, 1963–1974." Paper presented at the annual meeting of the Population Association of America, Philadelphia.

Warren, Robert, and Ellen Percy Kraly 1985. *The Elusive Exodus: Emigration from the United States.* Population Reference Bureau Occasional Paper no. 8. Washington, DC: Population Reference Bureau.

Warren, Robert, and Jeffrey S. Passel 1987. "A Count of the Uncountable: Estimates of Undocumented Aliens Counted in the 1980 United States Census." *Demography* 24:375–393.

Warren, Robert, and Jennifer Marks Peck 1980. "Foreign-Born Emigration from the United States, 1960–1970." *Demography* 17:71–84.

Weissbrodt, David 1984. *Immigration Law and Procedure: In a Nutshell.* St. Paul: West.

Winship, Christopher, and Robert D. Mare 1984. "Regression Models with Ordinal Variables." *American Sociological Review* 49:512–525.

Woodrow, Karen A. 1988. "Measuring Net Immigration to the United States: The Emigrant Population and Recent Emigration Flows." Paper presented at the annual meeting of the Population Association of America, New Orleans, April.

Woodrow, Karen A.; Jeffrey S. Passel; and Robert Warren 1987. "Preliminary Estimates of Undocumented Immigration to the United States, 1980–1986: Analysis of the June 1986 Current Population Survey." *Proceedings of the Social Statistics Section of the American Statistical Association*, San Francisco.

World Bank 1984. *World Tables*, vols. 1 and 2, 3rd ed. Baltimore: Johns Hopkins University Press.

World Radio TV Handbook Various years. New York: Billboard Publications.

Zlotnik, Hania 1987a. "The Concept of International Migration and the Identification of Migrant Types." Paper presented at the IUSSP Workshop on International Migration Systems and Networks. Center for Migration Studies, New York.

────── 1987b. "The Concept of International Migration As Reflected in Data Collection Systems." *International Migration Review* 21:925–946.

Zolberg, Aristide 1983. "The Political Economy of Immigration." In Wayne A. Cornelius and Ricardo Anzaldua Montoya, eds. *America's New Immigration Law: Origins, Rationales, and Potential Consequences.* San Diego: Center for U.S.–Mexican Studies.

Name Index

Subject Index

Boldface numbers refer to figures and tables.

O

P